Gunboat Command

Gunboat Command

The Life of 'Hitch'
Lieutenant Commander Robert Hichens,
DSO*, DSC** RNVR
1909 – 1943

Antony Hichens

Pen & Sword
MARITIME

First published in Great Britain in 2007 by
Pen & Sword Military
an imprint of
Pen & Sword Books Ltd
47 Church Street
Barnsley
South Yorkshire
S70 2AS

Typeset in Palatino Linotype, Garamond and Bernhard Modern by
Lamorna Publishing Services

Printed and bound in England by Biddles Ltd.

For a complete list of Pen & Sword titles please contact
PEN & SWORD BOOKS LIMITED
47 Church Street, Barnsley, South Yorkshire, S70 2AS, England
E-mail: enquiries@pen-and-sword.co.uk
Website: www.pen-and-sword.co.uk

This book is dedicated to the Officers and Men of Coastal Forces 1939 – 1945.

Contents

Acknowledgements

It is most unlikely that I would ever have written this book without the help and encouragement of my fellow trustees of Coastal Forces Heritage Trust. They asked me to join them because I was my father's son and they then supported my amateur efforts at writing naval biography. The web of contacts with ex-Coastal Forces personnel through CFHT has been invaluable.

In order to write this book I have had to learn a great deal about the history of Coastal Forces from 1939 to 1943. Without the help of Geoffrey Hudson, the acknowledged expert on Coastal Forces' boats, and Len Reynolds, the author of the most complete history of Coastal Forces, most especially *MTBs and MGBs at War in Home Waters*, this book would have been so full of errors as to become a laughing stock to the veterans who served during that period. They have been kind enough to supply me with an immense amount of data concerning Coastal Forces in general and the Sixth and Eighth MGB Flotillas in particular. The third source of vital information was Captain Trevor Robotham RN, who took off my back the task of searching Admiralty records via the Naval Historical Branch in Portsmouth. He is the Director of the Coastal Forces Heritage Trust but that research was no part of his duties as Director. Although I had some personal knowledge of my father's pre war life, my elder brother, Robert Hichens, had far more and from his home in Cornwall was able to dig up a great deal that neither of us previously knew.

I have been in correspondence with a large number of men who served in Coastal Forces, some of them in the Sixth or Eighth MGB Flotillas. I would particularly like to thank Sydney Dobson, sometime Able Seaman in the Eighth Flotilla, Roland Clarke sometime gunner in the Sixth Flotilla, Roland Clarke sometime gunner in the Sixth MGB Flotilla, John Motherwell, sometime Sub-Lieutenant, RCNVR, Charlie Mercer, sometime Oerlikon gunner in *MGB 21*, Cameron Gough, sometime Lieutenant RNVR who commanded *MGB 81* later in the war, James Shadbolt, sometime Lieutenant RNVR and a member of the Eighth Flotilla as a Midshipman and the late Lieutenant Commander Tom Ladner, RCNVR who commanded *MGB 75*. I was also greatly helped by Captain Michael Fulford Dobson RN, who served in fast patrol boats in the 1950's and provided valuable criticism of the book as a whole.

I have quoted from a number of sources but most particularly Peter Dickens' *Night Action* by courtesy of his widow, Mrs Mary Dickens, Major General Strictland's private diaries courtesy of his son, Ben Strictland, Judy Middleton's monograph of *King Alfred*, Peter Scott's *Battle of the Narrow Seas* and Gordon Holman's *The Little Ships*. Len Reynolds was also kind enough to let me quote from his book *Gunboat 658*, as did Roland Clarke from his book of recollections *Perlethorpe to Portsmouth*. I thank them all.

The maps were drawn and redrawn by Jane Michaelis as I found more and more places the reader needed to identify. She was both efficient and patient.

If the book is still full of typographical inaccuracies it is not the fault of either Geoffrey Hudson nor Hugh Robinson who both read it and corrected a multitude of errors. It reflects my own lack of attention to detail which I am now too old to curb.

I should also like to thank my long serving and long suffering secretary, Mrs Sheelagh Pigou, who produced multiple drafts with only the most occasional complaint, and Heather Holden-Brown, daughter of a distinguished Coastal Forces commander, who helped me through the publishing jungle but refused to take a fee for it.

Now I have written a book I realize how many unsung heroes there are behind every publication, though I suspect that in my case I owe more to the help of others than is normal.

Prologue

Why has this book been written more than sixty years after the events narrated? It is the story of a very unusual reserve officer in the Royal Navy who, between joining Coastal Forces to command his first boat in December 1940 and being killed in action in April 1943, came to dominate the evolution of motor gunboats into an effective fighting force, thus making a significant contribution to maintaining control of the Channel and the North Sea.

Its importance lies in recalling how, after the fall of France in June 1940, Britain had to struggle to maintain control of her coastal waters due to her failure to plan for fighting an enemy close enough to home to threaten her ability to move merchant shipping around our coasts. The German Navy had prepared for that moment by developing weapons suitable for that purpose, principally magnetic mines and the *Schnellboote* or German fast patrol boat, known to the British as the E-boat.

The Navy, beset on all sides, finding itself fighting Germany and Italy, and by December 1941 Japan as well, stretched to breaking point to convoy supplies of food and war material across the Atlantic, had serious problems in providing enough warships to transport vital supplies of coal and other essential materials down the east coast from Scotland and the Tyne to London and through the Channel. It had never planned that it would need to do so other than through defending itself against U-boats that had wreaked so much havoc towards the end of the First World War. The Navy had planned for the threat of the mining of its coastal waterways by German aircraft and U-boats, but had made no plans for fighting a swarm of E-boats, based in the Dutch, Belgian and French ports only a few hours away from the British coastal routes which they could mine and where they could attack convoys with torpedoes.

To meet this threat the Royal Navy commissioned a handful of small, lightly armed motor gunboats, designed originally as MTBs for the French, Dutch and other navies, but requisitioned and quickly converted to fight E-boats. It then built new MGBs from designs which currently existed, fast enough to find and fight the E-boat, yet small and cheap enough to be risked close to enemy air bases from which German aircraft could sink any warship found in daylight hours in the Narrow Seas. From its entirely inadequate force of destroyers, ships could only be earmarked for the protection of coastal convoys in small numbers, and they were thus an imperfect defence against E-boats, fighting always in darkness and moving so swiftly that they presented the most difficult of targets for a destroyer's guns in the days before radar controlled gunnery.

The man who became the dominant tactical thinker in motor gunboats, who was the first to challenge the E-boats successfully, and who ultimately led the way to the development of the far better armed and more robust second generation MGBs, was my father, Robert Hichens. Before the war a Cornish country solicitor, dinghy sailor and amateur motor racing enthusiast, by the time he was killed in April 1943 he had been awarded the Distinguished Service Order and bar, the Distinguished Service Cross and two bars and had been three times Mentioned in Dispatches. Posthumously, but unsuccessfully, he was recommended for the Victoria Cross.

Max Hastings, in his book *Warrior*, explains why the dedication and effectiveness of a small number of soldiers, sailors and airmen makes a crucial difference to the success or failure of armies, navies and air forces employing hundreds of thousands, even millions, of men who do broadly what is asked of them but no more. The handful of those who see it differently, whose sense of duty takes them regularly into exceptional danger, are the leavening that can alter the fighting efficiency of the great mass to a remarkable degree. Robert Hichens was one such and I believe his story is worth telling.

Anyone who reads the history of Coastal Forces will see the names of half a dozen officers with a comparable fighting record, highly decorated, whose lives would make interesting reading to those who wish to discern why some men excel in the stress and danger of war at sea; but history has a way of casting its light on one individual amongst many. There is no doubt that Robert Hichens' name is the name best remembered from Coastal Forces' struggle in the Channel and North Sea against the German Navy between 1940 and 1945.

A fellow Cornishman, himself a decorated naval reservist, Lord St Levan of St Michael's Mount, said to me recently 'Your father has become the patron saint of the RNVR.' There was an irony in his tone, perhaps a gentle rebuke to me in case I made too much of my father's achievements. Yet he acknowledged the fundamental truth that it is Robert Hichens' name that has emerged from the process of creating history as the archetypal Coastal Forces commanding officer. His name appears in every historical work about Coastal Forces in the Second World War. His portrait, painted posthumously by his friend and contemporary Coastal Forces commanding officer Peter Scott, hangs in the Naval Club above the RNVR Roll of Honour. The handsomely bound Roll of Honour beneath the portrait contains the names of over 6,000 officers and men who lost their lives while serving in the RNVR in the Second World War. The story of 'Hitch', as he became universally known in the Navy of his time, is their story and I believe that they would be content that it should be written as representative of their joint achievement.

Preface to

We Fought Them in Gunboats

One man who had every opportunity of observing Robert Hichens was David James, who served under him in command of motor gunboats in both the Sixth and Eighth MGB Flotillas, until he was taken prisoner-of-war after his boat was destroyed in February 1943. He was later an author himself and a Member of Parliament. In 1956 he edited a new edition of *We Fought Them in Gunboats*, the unfinished book which Robert Hichens wrote about his time in motor gunboats. His preface to that edition is quoted here:

> Robert Hichens was a remarkable man. Before the war he was a solicitor in Falmouth and had reached the first flight both as a dinghy sailor and as a racing motorist, but it was the war itself which revealed his true quality. In two brief years he played the major role in turning MGBs into an efficient weapon; indeed, without his persistence it is highly likely that they would have been scrapped as worthless, to the advantage of the E-boats and further crippling losses to our merchant tonnage.
>
> His secret lay in the unique combination of all the qualities necessary to his task – courage, powers of physical endurance and mental capacity. Many are fortunate enough to combine two of these qualities; a great leader in war must possess all three.
>
> Of his courage it is unnecessary to speak; all his flotilla have imprinted in their memory a clear-cut photograph of 'Hitch' standing on the whale-back canopy, his arm linked round the mast, his hair ruffled by the breeze as the bewildering colours of tracer bullets flashed by. The passage where he refers to the racing driver killed at Le Mans shows that this courage was not borne of any lack of imagination.

It took immense physical powers to be able to lead a unit at sea for long nights at a stretch and to do the administrative work of the flotilla by day. Officers ten years his junior, like myself, were extended to the utmost commanding their own boats, which went out in rotation so that we never had many nights in sequence and we had only to refuel and ammunition when we got in. Yet he took every unit to sea as Senior Officer and dealt with interminable staff conferences and rushed visits to the Admiralty, without showing any signs of fatigue. The focal power of concentration he brought to bear on the problem of destroying the enemy is well revealed in his writing – again all the creative thought was his.

The book was drafted during the last six months of his life and was probably three-quarters complete the day he died. It is a turbulent manuscript with the action passages pouring from his pen like molten lead, searing hot and without so much as a comma of subsequent correction. The passages describing technical difficulties and developments are less clear, with many pencilled alterations revealing the strength of his feelings. There is no doubt that he regarded this as his last testament as he frequently told me he was certain he would not survive.

Throughout the book there is a vein of criticism of the Service we were all so proud to belong to. This arose in part from the marked rigidity of mind which made it very hard for many in authority to see the use of weapons to their hand or even consider suggestions from below; though it is but fair to say that, at our level and at that time, it was hard to appreciate the appalling production and supply difficulties when it came to having the weapons we required. To us weeks, even days, meant frustration and loss of life, but you cannot tool the factories and switch production in such a short period of time.

It was an extraordinary experience for one so close to him to read the original manuscript after thirteen years and relive those days again. I wondered whether my feelings towards Hitch at the time were merely schoolboy hero worship. When I had finished I realised they were not, for here in truth stood a man.

David James

1956

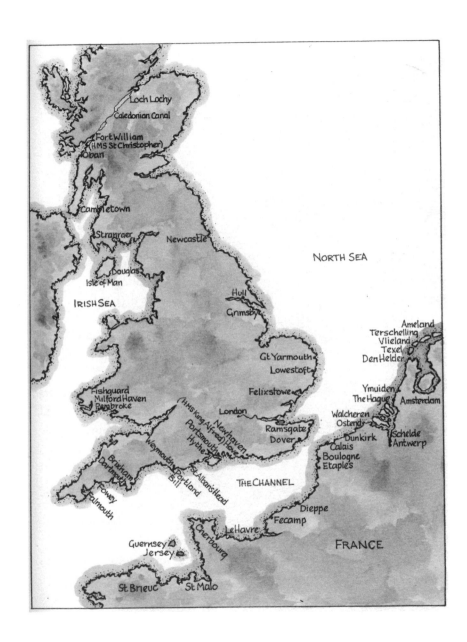

BRITISH COASTAL WATERS IN WHICH ROBERT HICHENS SERVED 1939–43

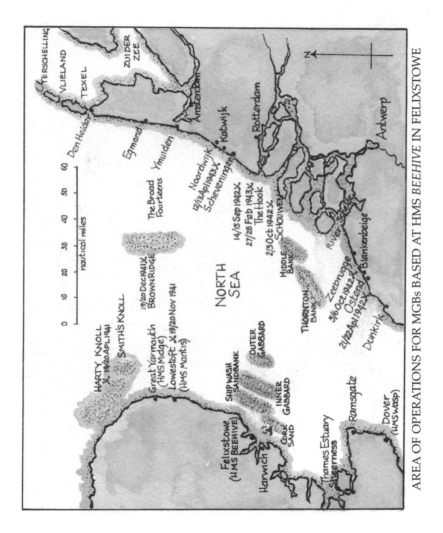

AREA OF OPERATIONS FOR MGBs BASED AT HMS *BEEHIVE* IN FELIXSTOWE

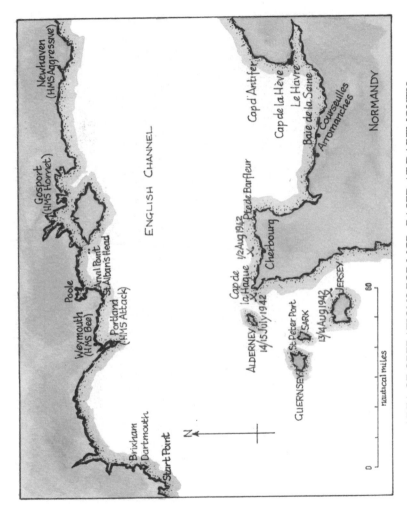

AREA OF OPERATIONS FOR MGBs BASED AT DARTMOUTH

Chapter One

Cornish Roots

Robert Hichens, Robert as I shall call him until he became universally known as 'Hitch' in Coastal Forces, saw himself as a Cornishman with his roots in that seafaring county. He was proud of that and it was one of the reasons why it was to the Navy that he went when the Second World War started. The Hichens' family records show that they were prosperous citizens of St Ives in Cornwall at least as early as the first quarter of the seventeenth century, and probably for 100 years or more before that. They claimed descent from Hichens of Saltash, a Tudor landed family, and displayed the same coat of arms, but whether they were a cadet branch, or simply adopted the arms without licence, is uncertain. They supplied St Ives with portreeves, the sea port equivalent of mayors, over a number of generations between the early seventeenth and the late eighteenth centuries. They had a ropewalk as the principal family business and other commercial interests, including pilchard fishing. They were sturdy, solid, minor gentry, no longer landed if they ever had been, but educated, with capital behind them, playing their part in provincial government.

As with so many families, one man can be picked out as having changed the family's fortunes and its way of life. He was also called Robert Hichens and was born in 1782 and, at the precocious age of seventeen, went off to London to make his fortune. He founded the firm of Hichens, Harrison & Sons, stockbrokers, in 1803, only one year after the foundation of the London Stock Exchange. Stockbroking was not regarded as an altogether reputable profession in those days. Some would say it still isn't, but it was certainly not in the same class as the Army, the Navy, the Church and the

1

Law in the early nineteenth century. However, it was capable of making a man's fortune and Robert Hichens made his as a stockbroker. He was Chairman of the London Stock Exchange between 1838 and 1842 and a leading figure in City circles over nearly half a century. He died in 1865 'possessed of a significant fortune'. A fine portrait survives of him showing a sensitive and intelligent face, and he appears to have had a reputation, perhaps unusual for a stockbroker of that time, as a cultivated gentleman with high ethical standards and a charitable disposition. His were genes worth inheriting.

Robert Hichens the stockbroker had two sons which concern us. Neither chose to go into the prosperous stockbroking firm founded by their father, where they might well have added to their family's fortune and perhaps, who knows, led a more eventful life than that usual amongst the rural clergy. Instead they chose to be clergymen, a far more respectable calling which their father's fortune made affordable. Frederick, born in 1836, became a Canon of Canterbury and his brother, Thomas, became Rector of Guilsborough in Northamptonshire. Nothing very remarkable is known of Canon Fred Hichens' life other than the belief on the part of his eldest son, another Robert Hichens, and a prominent Edwardian novelist, that he dissipated the family fortune to a marked degree. This was due more to inattention to business than to riotous living. He in turn had three sons. Robert the novelist, the author of works that are still remembered but seldom read today, such as *The Green Carnation, Bella Donna* and *The Garden of Allah*, went on to some fame and fortune. The youngest brother was my grandfather, Peverell Hichens. He went up to Oxford, to Magdalen College, in 1888 where he got a First in Physiology and became a distinguished consulting physician, settling in Northamptonshire where he was one of the consultants at the Northamptonshire General Hospital.

It is not clear why Peverell Hichens decided to go to Northamptonshire but it was probably related to the fact that his Uncle Thomas had a living there. It was probably through his uncle that he met his wife, Constance Downes, whose grandfather, the Reverend John Downes, was a brother clergyman of Thomas Hichens. Peverell and Constance married in 1906 and their first child, Loveday Hichens, was born in 1907. Robert was born in March 1909.

Descended from an ancient Shropshire family, John Downes's father made some money in the late eighteenth century and John was educated at Christ College, Cambridge, where he was a natural scientist of some note and the contemporary and friend of Charles Darwin. Their tutor, one Professor Henslow, according to family history asked John to join the *Beagle* as its scientist but, as he was going into Holy Orders, he declined the post and the choice fell upon Charles Darwin who went in his place and on to immortal fame. John went to Northamptonshire in 1834 and, continuing his interest in plants, collected an herbarium for his part of the county which is still on show in the County Museum. His eldest son, Leonard went into the Army and became a colonel in the Artillery and was the father of Constance who married Peverell Hichens.

Peverell and Constance lived in Northampton and brought up their family there until the start of the First World War. Great wars tend to stir the pot and many unexpected consequences flow. No doubt Peverell and Constance would have lived to a ripe old age in Northamptonshire, possibly retiring to Cornwall given the sentimental link with that county. What happened instead was that Peverell, who had been a pre-war territorial in the Royal Army Medical Corps, went out to France and his family went to live at St Mawes in Cornwall in 1915. He went as major to the Western Front where he commanded a succession of Casualty Clearing Stations, and was then promoted to lieutenant colonel and commanded a base hospital in Calais until the end of the war. In 1919 he was demobilized and returned to Northamptonshire.

Meanwhile Constance had taken a house in St Mawes and here Loveday and Robert lived until the end of the war. It must have seemed an idyllic existence. Both children immediately took to the water. A Major Tuke took them under his wing and taught them the disciplines of sailing. Constance purchased for them a small lug sail dinghy called the *Arethusa* which they sailed all over Carrick Roads and out beyond St Anthony's Point. Who was the captain and who was the crew? Feminists will snort at such a question and a surviving photograph of the two children, Loveday much the taller and older looking with her seniority of two years, does suggest that it should have been she rather than he, and yet? The leggy little boy in a Guernsey standing beside his older sister looks very determined and in the early twentieth century the assumption that a man should be in charge was a great deal more pronounced than it is today. Certainly I was always told as a boy that the *Arethusa* was Daddy's boat, not Aunt Loveday's, and that she crewed for him, or indeed left him to sail *Arethusa* by himself. Was this his first command? I think it was. It certainly gave him his first taste of the sea which he never lost and which to so great a degree influenced his choice of career and war service.

In due course Constance looked round for a more permanent home in Cornwall with a view eventually to retiring where her husband's family had come from and where her children were so obviously happy. In 1929 Peverell and Constance purchased the long lease of a house on the edge of the village of Flushing, looking across the Penryn Creek to Falmouth, and the family was to move there at the time of Peverell's death in 1930, calling it 'Bodrennick', 'house on the cliff' in Cornish. It still serves as the Hichens' family home. I was born there and my elder brother, Bob, lives there still.

Robert went off to prep school near Northampton when the family returned in 1919. It must have been for Robert a disagreeable change of life style to leave St Mawes and the *Arethusa* to return to an inland county and a boys' boarding school. He went on to his public school, Marlborough, in 1921.

In 1922 Peverell retired at the age of fifty-two from his work as a consulting physician at the Northampton General due to 'a mysterious illness' which struck him down. It now seems probable that the illness was encephalitis lethargica, a distressing and mortal brain disease. Peverell, as a distinguished doctor, must have known pretty well what was coming to him and he took decisive steps. The family moved to Guernsey, where there were no death duties, and he bought Havelet House, just outside St Peter Port on the sea, where they lived until his death in the spring of 1930.

This had the great virtue from Robert's point of view of taking him back to the sea, so that throughout his years at Marlborough and Oxford he could return to Guernsey to fulfil his passion for sailing. A second *Arethusa* was commissioned and was sailed around the rock-strewn and strongly tidal waters of Guernsey, thus consolidating the sound base laid down in St Mawes of familiarity with the sea. Perhaps the best photograph ever taken of Robert shows him sitting on the quayside opposite Havelet House with his back to the water, dressed in the oldest and most deplorable of trousers and a guernsey, looking tough and manly. It says more than any words can do about the development of the schoolboy

4

and the undergraduate into a tough, confident young seaman.

The last pre-Oxford event of which I have a record is Loveday's wedding in 1927 during Robert's last year at Marlborough. She married a man on home leave from Burma, Leonard Fletcher. The wedding was held in Cornwall, at Treriefe, the house of Constance's sister, Dorothy Le Grice, which lies just beyond Penzance. A photograph survives with a self conscious, good-looking young Robert in his morning coat. The bride is in a then fashionable short white wedding dress, surrounded by Hichens, Downes and Le Grice family members. It is the last photograph of Robert before man's estate.

Peverell died in March 1930, having been reduced in mental capacity by his dreadful illness, so that my mother, who only knew him at this time, always struggled to understand the huge love that Robert had for his father. Obituaries at the time recall him as a much respected physician in Northamptonshire and an even more successful RAMC officer in France. He was noted for his love of music, including his own playing of the piano, and a general interest in artistic matters which included the buying of pictures, some of which I still have because I share his taste for marine artists.

Peverell's ashes were brought down from London to Cornwall and buried at Mylor Church, one of the prettiest in the county, overlooking the sea. Constance had just moved into Bodrennick, hence the choice of Mylor Church, less than a mile away. His father's early death must have affected Robert profoundly. He was now the man of the family. Constance became ill. Loveday was in Burma. On Robert's shoulders descended responsibility for managing the family's affairs. It hastened the early maturity which is so clearly visible at each stage of the thirteen years of life left to him.

Robert went up to Magdalen College, Oxford in October 1927 at the age of eighteen to read law. Magdalen was the obvious choice of college given that his father and an uncle had been there. Magdalen had an enormous influence on Robert and it is worth describing the college of his time and thus the influences that were brought to bear upon him.

Sir David Kelly, later a distinguished British ambassador, went up to Magdalen in 1910 and in his memoirs describes the college in some detail as it was just before the First World War. The change from then to seventeen years later was, as far as one can see, modest. The Magdalen of 1910 had 150 undergraduates, all men. Magdalen had been radically changed by one of its greatest presidents, Sir Herbert Warren, who became head of house, at Magdalen called the President, in 1885 and remained in post until his death in 1928, a year after Robert came up. Warren is often remembered as a snob whose main claim to fame was turning Magdalen into one of the socially elite Oxford colleges and dominant on the river, but that is a superficial view of a very great President who cared deeply for the undergraduates in his charge. Whether he had a passion for rowing, or simply saw it as a means of furthering the prestige of his college, I do not know, but shortly after his appointment he began the practice, which continued until his death, of getting some of the best oarsmen from Eton each year to provide the core of the Magdalen boat. No doubt he also looked for talent elsewhere, but Eton supplied him with some outstanding oarsmen. The Magdalen Boat Club competed in the Olympics of 1908 and 1912, winning the coxless fours in the former year and the eights in the latter, an achievement that no college could conceivably match today.

Kelly, in defence of a man he clearly hero-worshipped, told the story of his own experience with Warren. Kelly had been at school at Uppingham and was not from an influential family, but he wished to enter the Foreign Office. In those days the Foreign Office was very largely manned by men who had been to the most prestigious public schools and had family connections who could introduce them at a senior level. Lacking these advantages, Kelly sought Warren's help. He promptly, no doubt because he saw exceptional qualities in Kelly, obtained the support of half a dozen distinguished old Magdalen men in the diplomatic service and Kelly got his job. This was not an isolated incident.

He remembered the dons, as the fellows of a college are commonly called, as extremely relaxed about whether men went to lectures or not so long as they filled a reasonable amount of their time with reading their discipline. It was not required that you sat for an honours degree. The requisites for remaining in *statu pupulari* were little more than attending Chapel and dining in Hall a set minimum number of times a term. You were also supposed to attend breakfast but the Junior Dean, standing at the foot of the staircase up to Magdalen's hall, would obligingly accept your name as you passed by in your dressing gown on your way to your morning bath.

Most men lunched in their rooms, served by their scout, a college servant, and dined in Hall two or three evenings a week. After dinner men would drop into the room at the foot of the stairs leading up to the Junior Common Room to have a drink under the auspices of Gunstone, always known as Gunner, the Junior Common Room steward, who had an endless flow of anecdotes about old members of the college, frequently of a salacious kind. Others would spend their evenings visiting each other's rooms to drink and talk. In an age when opinions of a liberal or radical nature were not necessarily popular in upper middle class circles, the young men could talk about anything they pleased, with no taboos, whether it was art, music, literature, religion or politics, and would perhaps never be able to do so again with the same intensity and freedom.

Women played almost no part in their lives. It was not done to pursue female undergraduates from the few women's colleges. The young men had entered a monastic world, following on the heels of the all-male British public school, and accepted it as such with good grace. These were the years they had set aside for talking, playing and learning in a man's world.

When Robert went up to Magdalen in 1927 he found himself allocated rooms in St Swithun's, a part of the college beside the porter's lodge overlooking the High. Douglas Dodds-Parker, a Wykehamist and experienced oarsman, had been allocated rooms above him and the two young men became firm friends. Douglas described to me a world remarkably similar to that that David Kelly observed. There was the same requirement to breakfast in Hall. It was not a requirement to dine but you had to pay for it whether you dined or not and the charge of 1s. 4d, perhaps £9 today, was enough to make most men dine most evenings in College. Before going into Hall it was usual to have a drink in what by then was known as Gyne's room. Gyne was the successor to Gunstone and, in turn, his successor was Bond who presided in my day. They dispensed sherry before dinner and port afterwards, and their room formed a club within the college for about 100 years. An introduction to Gyne's room was necessary before one dared enter the sacrosanct door.

Compton Mackenzie, in his novel *Sinister Street,* captured the essential attraction of this informal club, writing of Gunstone's era just after the Boer war in about 1905. Mackenzie calls it Venner's room in his novel and Magdalen is called St Mary's. I quote from a passage describing a conversation between a group of undergraduates and the long-standing JCR Steward:

'Venner,' said Lonsdale one evening, 'do you remember the Bishop of Cirencester when he was up? Stebbing his name was. My mother roped him in for a teetotal riot she was inciting this vac.'

'Oh, yes, I think he was rather a wild fellow,' Venner began, full of reminiscence. 'But we'll look him up.'

Down came some account-book of the later seventies, and all the festive evenings of the Bishop, spent in the period when undergraduates were photographed with mutton-chop whiskers and bowler hats, lay revealed for the criticism of his irreverent successors.

'There you are,' chuckled Venner triumphantly. 'What did I say? One dozen champagne. Three bottles of brandy. All drunk in one night, for there's another half-dozen put down for the next day. Ah, but the men are much quieter nowadays. Not nearly so much drinking done in college as there used to be. Oh, I remember the Bishop – Stebbing he was then. He put a codfish in the Dean's bed. Oh, there was a dreadful row about it. The old Warden kicked up such a fuss.'

And, as easily as one Arabian night glides into another, Venner glided from anecdote to anecdote of Episcopal youth.

The young men did not appear to work much harder than they had before the Great War. Douglas said that the only time anyone had ever asked him what degree he had got was when he entered the Sudan Civil Service. For that it was necessary for him to get at least second class honours so he worked for it, but most undergraduates with no such testing hurdle to jump didn't bother. Each undergraduate saw his tutor at least once a week for a one-to-one tutorial. Douglas had two tutors, one of whom was called Thompson, previously the Dean of Divinity but now a History Tutor. Thompson had unfortunately believed in one supreme being instead of the Trinity so that Warren had felt it necessary to put the Chapel in sounder hands. He got Douglas his second in spite of the distractions of the river and Gyne's room.

In the afternoons most men were involved in sport of one sort or another, many of them on the river, rowing being then and now the most important sporting activity at Oxford. This didn't necessarily mean being in strict training all the time and indeed the crews only trained hard for three or four weeks before the spring races known as Torpids and the summer races known as Eights. However if you were an oarsmen you might go down to scull any afternoon on the river by yourself, or take out a pair with a friend.

Robert told Douglas that he was interested in playing hockey, but soon discovered that it was a minor sport at Oxford and that he could not play it regularly every day. Douglas claims to have converted him into being an oarsman and certainly he appears in the Magdalen torpid second eight of 1928, only six months after coming up, rowing at number seven. By 1929 he was in the torpid first eight rowing at number three, and in the summer eight as stroke. He was again stroke in the 1930 eight. This was a fair achievement for a man who had never sat on a sliding seat before coming up to Oxford as Marlborough was not a rowing school, although of course he would have been used to pulling on an oar in the waters of Guernsey and Cornwall. Given Magdalen's high standard of rowing, to become stroke within a year of coming up says a good deal about his strength and determination, although Douglas never had too many good words to say about his skill. 'He had once been told by an Australian that ten of the fastest strokes at the end of the race was worth more than nine of the best' he told me. 'Unfortunately, it isn't easy to know when your last ten strokes are about to commence. We didn't win many races but we had an awful lot of fun.'

After the heady heights of the Olympics before the Great War and being Head of the River several times in the early 1920s, Magdalen's rowing, it has to be admitted, was sliding a little. Douglas put this down to the appointment as Dean of Admissions in 1927 of a Canadian don called Oliver Wrong. He had apparently insisted upon merit entry into the College, presumably for the first time ever, so that there were no longer assured places for top schoolboy oarsmen. The college was third on the river in 1928, sixth in 1929 and eighth in 1930, the lowest position Magdalen had sunk to since 1876! They regained the headship in 1932 but Magdalen's near absolute dominance of the river was over. However, all that we need note in Robert's case was his ability to take on a new task and then excel at it by being stroke for his college in his second and third years, and who shall say the gentle slide from head of the river owed much to his unpolished labours? They did, however, contribute to the building of a physique that was to stand him in good stead under the punishing conditions of Coastal Forces warfare.

More than one of his contemporaries remembers Robert as of a serious turn of mind when it came to his work, not a common state of affairs in the Magdalen of his time. Oxford between the wars, though always attracting more than its share of serious scholars, could be fairly described as still primarily a finishing school for the upper middle classes. James Griffiths, later to become a Fellow of Magdalen and ultimately its President in the 1970s, was a member of the boat club in Robert's time and particularly recalls him coming down to the college barge, in the days before a boat house was built, carrying a law book or two and becoming immersed in them before and after training outings in the eight. He may have been remembering the summer of 1930 when Robert's father had just died, a major distraction before his final examinations, and Robert could well have been unusually pre-occupied with his work. However Douglas also remembers the same characteristic and it seems that Robert took his work seriously. This still left him a great deal of time for conviviality and few members of the boat club in those years would have been other than convivial drinkers. Although when they were in strict training alcohol was limited to a pint of beer in the evening, at other times the boat club indulged in the fruits of the college cellars in the days when a glass of sherry or a glass of port cost 6d and a bottle of champagne only 4s. 6d. In that all-male world this generally led to singing at some point in the evening. Douglas has a particularly clear memory of Robert singing a chant, allegedly composed for the boat club by another of their contemporaries, Humphrey Slade, later a London solicitor and father of Julian Slade who wrote *Salad Days*. It started, chanting in E-flat minor, a quotation from a much derided Great Western Railway lavatory notice, 'Passengers are respectfully requested to refrain from putting into the pans articles calculated to cause obstruction, to the inconvenience of the passengers and the closets thereby rendered both objectionable and useless, etc. etc.' It was a refrain still being sung in the 1950s after boat club dinners, led by James Griffiths.

There are regrettably no casual photographs of Robert at Magdalen. The only photographic record which survives comes from the boat club archive where you can see him straining at stroke oar at the start of a bumping race or seated in the middle of a group of nine young men who formed the elite of Magdalen's rowing in 1930. Considering that few of them could be over twenty-one, they look a remarkably mature group, and with a self-confidence bred of a natural assumption of leadership. Almost the whole undergraduate body of Magdalen at that time had been to independent schools of one sort or another, with a high preponderance from the best known public schools. The young men are clearly from a privileged world but it was a privileged world which did not shrink from its responsibilities when the time of war came.

In his third year Robert had digs in the Gatehouse, almost opposite the College on the other side of the High and next to the Botanic Gardens.. In those days the Gatehouse was not a part of the College, though it is today. I was aware of this because my mother remembered going to his rooms there when they were first going out together and Douglas also recalls receiving hospitality at the Gatehouse. However it is interesting that he has no recollection at all of meeting Catherine Enys who was to marry my father in 1931, thus confirming my mother's clear view that Robert liked to preserve his reputation as a misogynist, apparently carefully cultivated from the moment he came up to Magdalen, and thus never permitted her to meet any of his friends, which she thought a considerable bore.

Robert and Douglas were very close at Magdalen but they only saw each other again once after Robert went down in 1930. Douglas went into the Sudan Civil Service and was virtually cut off from England, apart from the occasional long leave. Thus he did not attend Robert's wedding the following year with all the other members of the Boat Club. They did, however, run into each other again in 1942 when 'in some London club or other' Douglas spotted Robert in naval uniform. Douglas was then in SOE, the organization set up 'to set Europe ablaze' after the fall of France. Douglas was impressed to find his old friend with a DSO and a DSC and bar and, after gathering that they had been mostly won in a motor gunboat operating in the North Sea and the Channel, asked whether Robert would be willing to help him to land agents in the Low Countries where SOE were having great difficulty in gaining

11

access. Some weeks later this suggestion bore fruit and Douglas went out one night with Robert in MGB 77 to try to drop an agent on the Dutch coast, a failure due to the brightly lit area that he had selected for the drop off point which made it impractical to get ashore unobserved.

Magdalen is one of Oxford's most beautiful colleges and few who have spent three or four of their formative years there have failed to be profoundly affected by the experience. It is also a college with a long history of tolerance for differences in intellect, outlook and social status. Robert would have absorbed Magdalen's civilizing influence. It evidently had little impact on his impatience, a characteristic he increasingly displayed as he carved his way in the world through peace and war, but it did start to teach him the elements of logical analysis and judgement.

Robert and Catherine met in Cornwall in 1928. Robert was in his second year at Magdalen aged twenty and Catherine was six years his senior. Catherine and Robert were fourth cousins and no doubt when Constance Hichens looked around for a house to buy in Cornwall she would have started to meet Cornish families to whom her husband was related. Harry and Sadie Enys, Catherine's parents, lived barely two miles from Bodrennick at Enys, just outside Mylor, which Harry had inherited in 1912. Their youngest daughter, Elizabeth Enys, always known as Betty, was exactly the same age as Robert to the day and perhaps the two mothers thought that it would be nice if they met. As with so many calculations of that nature, neither parent could have allowed for the attraction that grew up between the much older Catherine and young Robert. Catherine was, of course, of that generation of young women in England whose husbands would normally have emerged from the ranks of the young men who officered the British Army in the First World War, from which virtually a generation failed to return. In Cornwall in the late 1920s there was a distinct shortage of suitable young men. Catherine, good looking, vivacious, quick witted and not at all averse to flirtation, found the prematurely mature Robert quite attractive enough to overlook the difference in age. No doubt scoring off her younger sister, whom she cordially disliked and regarded as the undeserved family pet, would have added a little spice to the situation. However it came about, Robert and Catherine were well away within weeks of first meeting.

12

It cannot have been easy to keep their relationship a secret from their families but they did their best. Catherine had by then become bored with Cornwall and the life of a young women going to tennis parties, garden parties, cocktail parties, dances and dinners, and had with great difficulty persuaded her conservatively minded father to let her go and work for one of their neighbours, a Mrs Stephens, as her social secretary in London, and she was then living at the Basil Street Hotel which her family thought more suitable than having a flat. This allowed the young couple to meet in London and Oxford. Evidently at some point the alarm bells started to ring, certainly in the Enys household, for in the summer of 1929 Sadie Enys, a Philadelphian by birth and very American in outlook, decided to take Catherine, her second daughter, with her on her first return visit for forty years to see family and friends in that great city. It is pretty clear that her motives in doing so were not just to see relatives on whom she had not set eyes, or sought to do so, since marrying Harry in the 1890s. The primary motive must have been to keep Catherine apart from Robert for some months to see whether things would cool off. They didn't.

At this point it is necessary to explain who Harry and Sadie Enys were and how that affected the subsequent marriage between Robert and Catherine. Harry and his American wife were a distinctly unusual couple to be found as the squire and lady of an ancient Cornish estate. The Enys family had lived at Enys since the reign of King John in the early thirteenth century. As was commonly the custom in Cornwall, the family took its name from its land. The Enys family had the habit of marrying well and adding to their holdings so that by the mid-nineteenth century their property extended far beyond the 1,400 acres of farmland surrounding their ancestral home. Successive generations of Enys squires were much like their neighbours and did little more than marry the occasional heiress and breed the next of many generations. Yet when Harry Rogers inherited Enys through his mother in 1912, changing his name to Enys, he was somewhat different from most of his neighbours in the same walk of life.

Harry's father, Captain Henry Rogers, Royal Navy, was the scion of another old Cornish family with its seat at Penrose, near Helston, still lived in by the Rogers family today. Henry Rogers met Jane Enys and married her in the mid-nineteenth century, and she had the good fortune to be the only Enys of her generation to marry.

Her older brother, Francis, left his property to his younger brother John, who had spent the last forty years in New Zealand farming sheep. He in turn left Enys to his late sister's oldest son, young Harry Rogers, on the sole condition that he changed his name to Enys.

Harry had been brought up as one of the very large family which old Captain Henry Rogers had sired when living in comfortable retirement in a substantial house just outside Plymouth. Harry went into the Church and was a curate in Brighton when he met his future wife, Sadie Dufus. Sadie's mother had been a member of the Baldwin family who made locomotives in Philadelphia in the nineteenth century, very profitably it would seem. Sadie was orphaned at a young age and brought up by a Baldwin aunt. She was kept at school however, allegedly to avoid her marrying one of her rich cousins, to the unusually late age of twenty. When she was twenty-one she inherited a modest capital that made her sufficiently independent to leave both school and Philadelphia and travel in Europe. One of her school mistresses had been English and came from Brighton, and it was staying with her old English friend that she met young Harry Rogers. They brought into the world successively one boy, Saltren, and then three girls, Jane, Catherine and Elizabeth. Sadie's small private income must have been an immense benefit to an impoverished clergyman who had nothing from his own father to add to his stipend. However, his Uncle John died in 1912 and suddenly he was the owner of two substantial estates and much town and village property in Cornwall.

The family did not immediately move to Enys, only going down there for holidays in the summers of 1913 and 1914, and then came the Great War. Harry decided that he should stay and serve the people of Brighton, being by then too old to become a military chaplain, and it was not until 1919 that the family moved to Cornwall. No doubt from 1912 onwards the social standing of Henry and Sadie was considerably enhanced by whatever income they felt they could take from Enys while death duties were being paid, and the prospect that they would be translated in due course to the grandeur of their estate, with its substantial William IV house and extensive and beautiful gardens. Nevertheless the children were not brought up in Cornwall and in many respects the family did not all that closely resemble their neighbours amongst the landed gentry of that county. This did not prevent Sadie from cutting a swathe through Cornish society.

Sadie had a strong character. No doubt her odd upbringing had contributed to this. She had a very American viewpoint and would say about almost everything that it was done better in America. She was highly intelligent and put her considerable energies to work improving the life of the Cornish poor and entertaining anyone with intellectual pretensions who came to that not markedly intellectual county. George Bernard Shaw and A.L. Rowse were guests at Enys, as were the officers of every visiting Royal Navy warship to come into Falmouth, including, as my mother recalled frequently, Captain Carpenter VC of Zeebrugge fame, a married man who had a flirtation with Catherine.

With a mother who, in A.A. Milne's deathless verse, 'sat on committees for cleansing our cities' and a father who was a sufficiently keen Mason, as many clergymen of his era were, to have his portrait painted with apron and trowel, the Enys girls must have presented something of a challenge to Cornish county society. The elder, Jane, was an attractive girl, but more conventional than my mother and less sharp witted. Young Betty was generally regarded as a terror, and certainly cut her own peculiar swathe through the young men of her era. They had no help in carving out their place in society from their one brother because he was distinctly odd. His mother always said that he had been run over by a runaway horse as a baby to account for the fact that he never managed to cope with formal education, in spite of a couple of years spent at a particularly broad-minded Cambridge College during the First World War. He was in and out of the Army in a good deal less time than most people achieved, being invalided home from basic training. Eventually his father decided to put him into the Church but the Bishop of Truro wouldn't ordain him and he remained an unordained clerk in holy orders.

The county watched all this amused and said behind their backs that the Enys girls were a little different from everybody else. Robert's first cousin, Charles Le Grice, who appears in the photograph of Loveday marrying Leonard Fletcher at Treriefe in 1927, once said to me that he thought the bravest thing my father had ever done was to marry one of the Enys girls. That probably sums up the view that their neighbours took of them.

Robert was accepted as a future partner of Reginald Rogers, a very long established firm of solicitors in Falmouth and Helston, whose senior partner was his cousin, Percival Rogers, also cousin to Catherine. Percival wanted a young partner who was also a kinsman, and he must have seen the potential in Robert, reading law at Oxford and desirous of staying in Cornwall. By the spring of 1931, when Robert married Catherine, it was settled that he would become an articled clerk with Reginald Rogers for the necessary three year period to become a qualified solicitor himself and then a junior partner. If Harry and Sadie had objections to Robert on the grounds that he was not yet in a position to support a wife, these now finally evaporated and both families accepted the fait accompli presented by the young couple's determination that they should be man and wife.

Robert actually proposed to Catherine in 1929 while cutting bamboos in the Enys gardens, as he recalled many years later in his war time diary. The marriage took place in April 1931 in St Gluvias Church, Penryn, where the Enys family had worshipped for hundreds of years and whose walls are adorned with their memorials. The Magdalen crew of 1930 came down as a body, my mother recalling that they dined at Bodrennick in dinner jackets and at Enys in evening dress, a fact that stuck in her mind because one had forgotten to bring either so had to wear a dinner jacket at Enys and evening dress at Bodrennick, borrowed from one of his friends. Enys was always something of a challenge for the diner because they had a butler who was convinced that you passed the port anti-clockwise and would solemnly march round the table filling glasses in that unusual direction, unnoticed by Sadie who was a teetotaller, as many of her American generation were, and Harry who apparently seldom noticed anything connected with social graces.

They honeymooned in Italy, driving there in an open Lancia which had increased my father's popularity at Magdalen substantially in his last year as he could squeeze the Magdalen eight into it when they drove to training sessions or regattas. Catherine's recollection of the honeymoon was of mile after mile of scorching French and Italian roads, parking on hills because the Lancia did not run to a self-starter and this saved hard work with the starting handle, followed by the blessed peace and beauty of the island of Capri, then years away from becoming a mass tourist destination, where the chief attraction was the absence of the Lancia which meant that they could stay in one place for a few days' rest. Driving to Italy in an open car with a restless driver unwilling ever to stop for more than dinner and a bed was a prelude to holidays throughout the 1930s married to Robert Hichens.

Chapter Two

Cornwall in the Thirties

After Robert and Catherine returned from their honeymoon Robert went back to work as an articled clerk in Reginald Rogers. Reginald Rogers had been established by a member of the Rogers' family in the middle of the eighteenth century and was one of those firms of country solicitors, well known locally and of good repute further afield, which cover rural England with a network of sound legal advice. Robert had almost certainly started his articles, the process by which a solicitor gains practical experience before completing his professional qualifications, soon after coming down from Oxford. The process was one by which the articled clerk, or frequently his parents if they were putting up the money as was the case here, signed an agreement with an established firm and paid a premium, a small capital sum, to be instructed as a solicitor, so that he was ultimately prepared to sit the Law Society's examination. For a country solicitor, part of that time was normally spent with a London firm, where a broader range of work would be met with. Constance Hichens had signed a contract with Percival Rogers which placed Robert under his tutelage for a period of three years, ending in 1933.

As Robert earned no income for that period he remained dependent upon his mother for an allowance on which to keep himself and Catherine. Catherine had a small income of her own. The young couple, rather surprisingly, seemed not able to afford even the most modest establishment in Cornwall and lived alternately at Bodrennick and Enys. This was not a happy period in my mother's memory. She did not like her mother-in-law very much. Constance became bedridden shortly after her husband's death, a mode of behaviour hardly known today but then common enough amongst late middle-aged and overweight women with servants to tend them, and this almost certainly contributed to her own early demise in 1933. Life at Bodrennick was made no easier by Robert's sister, Loveday, her husband, and their son Robin coming to stay on long leave from Burma, before moving back to Guernsey for Len's retirement. Enys would have been a good deal less crowded but was not a terribly welcoming house at that time. My maternal grandfather was an austere man, tight-fisted due to his lengthy apprenticeship in straightened circumstances as a clergyman before he inherited. My grandmother was a good deal better company and certainly more open handed, and she and Robert liked each other, but she was permanently at loggerheads with her husband, generally about spending decisions. Catherine's older sister, Jane, had by then been allowed to escape and have her own establishment. However, young Betty still lived at Enys and no doubt took some pleasure in being a mischievous element in a household where a man she had once coveted was now married to her older sister.

Nevertheless, they got by somehow. The Lancia gave them a means of escape. Finally, the welcome moment came when Robert needed to spend a year with Reginald Rogers' correspondent firm of London solicitors, which I deduce from references in his wartime diary was called Mackrell's. It still has offices in Bedford Square. They rented a small house at Bourne End on the Thames, where Robert could renew his passion for rowing, and they could live in the decent privacy that man and wife naturally desire. Robert competed at Henley Regatta in double sculls, being able to train regularly at Bourne End, and worked at learning the law.

Then everything changed dramatically. Constance died in June 1933, leaving Robert Bodrennick and his half of his father's capital, which provided what must have seemed a very welcome private income. He was master of his own financial affairs at last. At about the same time he completed his articles, starting paid employment at Reginald Rogers, and becoming the junior partner on 1 January 1934, so that their economic fortunes were transformed. They returned to live at Bodrennick and settled down to five years of very happy married life, professional consolidation and sporting achievement.

Bodrennick is a stone-built, two-storey house which stands little more than twenty feet above the level of high spring tide on the

Penryn Creek, with the village of Flushing to the east and behind it and to the west the creek running up to Penryn, muddy and shallow at low tide, but capable of great beauty, particularly on a calm summer evening at high springs. Its garden is not extensive or sheltered and therefore grows little, but the house has its own beach and mooring and is as close to offering life on the water as can be arranged without moving to a houseboat. It was big enough for Robert and Catherine to employ a cook and a housemaid and, when I came along, a nanny, with a gardener coming in daily from the village. The other important member of the family was Komarakul, a large Siamese cat, named after the Siamese cox of the Magdalen Eight. Although only twenty minutes away from his office by car, driving round the Penryn Creek and into Falmouth, Robert preferred in half passable weather to row across to Falmouth every morning where he could tie up his ten foot wooden praam to the steps below his office. Marjorie Lang, then Marjorie Yeo, who worked for Robert and Catherine as their maid from 1934 until 1937 when she married, had previously been a housemaid at Enys. She remembers Robert complaining that his good shoes didn't last very long because they tended to get wet in the boat on his way to work and the salt destroyed them faster than normal wear and tear.

When he inherited Bodrennick, Robert had brought down a sculling boat, designed for the Thames. One would have supposed that it was out of place or even dangerous on the Penryn Creek, by no means habitually calm. Nevertheless, at least for some years, he used to carry it down the steps to our beach and row on still evenings when the tide was up. Marjorie would be summoned to help him put it into the water and get it out again. However, gradually he moved away from rowing to other sporting pursuits. Perhaps the most dominant was dinghy sailing. No longer satisfied with the lug-sailed *Arethusa*, he started to race in International Fourteen dinghies, then a major dinghy class in competitive sailing. Robert had had an International Fourteen called *Venture* in Guernsey which he brought to Cornwall and in 1936 he commissioned a friend to build him a new boat which he named *Venture II*. He used to sail most commonly with a cousin, Jane Cree, resident in St Mawes and we have a fine press photograph of them competing in the Fowey Regatta. He competed in the Prince of Wales's Cup, a very well known event for International Fourteen dinghies, on the Clyde in 1936, Lowestoft in 1937 and at Falmouth in 1938. I still have the replica trophy for the 1936 race in which he was placed fifth. In 1938 he was beaten in his home waters by Peter Scott who, with considerable imagination, adapted the concept of the trapeze which allows the crew to stand up and hang outwards on the windward side of the dinghy when beating, stiffening the boat and so permitting it to point higher. The Committee disallowed the trapeze the day after the race, but it brought Scott victory on that occasion. It is clear that Robert was in the top flight of International Fourteen dinghy sailors and Scott in his autobiography, *The Eye of the Wind*, recalls the number of times that they competed against each other 'in the piping days of peace'.

More occasionally, Robert went ocean racing or cruising. He competed in several ocean races, three times in the Fastnet race. In June 1939, on the eve of war, he crewed in the Channel Race. He joined the Royal Ocean Racing Club. He probably had more fun and satisfaction out of cruising where he was the captain. In 1936, he and John Burnett, an old Marlborough friend, together with Frank Barmby, a member of the 1930 Magdalen crew, chartered a boat called *Thyra* and cruised to the Isles of Scilly. The same crew had sailed to France in 1934 and there are some good photographs of another boat with the three young men cruising off the west coast of Scotland some time in the late 1930s. It is clear that he had quite extensive experience of sailing offshore.

He had an equal passion for fast cars. This is not uncommon in young men and the uncluttered roads of the 1930s made it far more fun than it ever could be today. With his new-found economic freedom, he bought a 1.4 litre Aston Martin touring car in which, in 1935, he took Catherine, Bob and Marjorie on a tour of the Continent. They drove to Austria, staying in both Innsbruck and Vienna before driving over the Brenner Pass, still dangerous with snow, into Italy to visit Venice and then back into Switzerland by the equally snow-choked Stelvio. Marjorie remembers day after day of fast driving but with great confidence in her employer's skill. At some point, there was a Riley which he took hill-climbing, competing at Beggar's Roost in Somerset and Blue Hills in Cornwall. There was a Norton 500 cc motorbike. Robert had had a smaller machine in Guernsey when still a schoolboy. According to Marjorie, he once persuaded Catherine to don breeches and ride pillion behind him. As we never heard her speak of this during our

21

childhood, my brother and I concluded that she must have been so frightened by the experience that she never wanted to think about it again.

However, the great love of his motoring life was a two litre Aston Martin that he bought secondhand in 1936. It was one of a batch of six built for the Ulster TT (Tourist Trophy) race and then entered as a works car by Aston Martin in the Le Mans twenty-four hour race of 1936, cancelled due to the French general strike of that year. This was an altogether different creature from anything he had owned before. It was a car of great distinction and beauty and had the power to compete in serious racing and he took up the challenge. With Aston's help, he made a private entry to the Le Mans race of 1937 and, quite extraordinarily, won one of the major trophies, the Rudge Whitworth Cup. The Rudge Cup is a biennial race, which means that a car has to compete the year before to qualify for a win in the second year. The winner is the car with the maximum number of miles driven in twenty-four hours on the aggregate of the two years, with a handicap allowance based on engine size. As the 1936 race had not been run, the authorities decided that all those cars which had been entered for it would qualify for the Rudge Cup in 1937. Thus Robert inherited his Aston's 1936 qualification and, together with a co-driver who was employed by Aston, Mort Morris Goodall, he found himself competing in 1937 with an ever-decreasing field as cars fell out amongst those qualified for the Rudge Cup. In the end he was competing only with an MG. When that also fell out, it only remained for Robert and Mort to finish the race to win the Rudge Cup. In the early afternoon of a race which ends at four p.m., a valve dropped, damaging one of the Aston's pistons and Robert naturally stopped. Mort, when Robert failed to appear, ran round the track to find him and plead with him to finish the race, so the Aston limped into the pits, waited until shortly before four o'clock, and then set off on a final lap so that it crossed the line as soon after four o'clock as possible, making the most terrible noises. It was a very unusual way of winning the Rudge Cup but win it he did and my brother still has it. It is an object of extraordinary ugliness in the art deco style, made of some form of green stone, with bronze plaques all round it depicting the various dangerous corners of the Le Mans track. I was brought up to regard it as second only in importance to the Holy Grail.

Robert raced again at Le Mans in 1938. They drove out in convoy,

Catherine at the wheel of the family's Rover and Robert's Cornish mechanic, Bill Barbary, riding the Norton, with the future managing clerk of Reginald Rogers, Brian Stephens, on the pillion. Regrettably, at four o'clock in the morning the Aston lost all valve clearance on an exhaust rocker. Robert and Barbary worked feverishly to clear the obstruction. At nine o'clock in the morning the Aston had trouble with its exhaust valve which burnt out. The cylinder head was removed and the offending valve was replaced but some quick footwork was required to get the right tools into the pit, possibly in breach of regulations. Finally, after a three hour delay, the Aston's engine started again but it was not to be for long because a timing chain had been left loose and jumped its teeth and the car never finished the race. Robert raced again in 1939 and this time the Aston performed like clockwork until midnight when valve trouble occurred again. Robert was determined to qualify the car for the subsequent year's race so continued on three cylinders to finish twelfth. Although Robert naturally never competed again, the car was entered in the first post-war Le Mans race in 1949 under my mother's name because it was one of the few cars qualified for the Rudge Cup.

There is little doubt that Robert loved the two litre Aston more than any other car that he ever owned. He continued to drive it until his death in 1943, reputedly utilizing 100-octane petrol, on which it ran beautifully, from the plentiful supply available for his motor gunboats. Since the day he owned it he had looked after it personally, in spite of Bill Barbary's skilled attentions available to him at any time. To my mother's despair, every winter the engine was taken apart and laid out on sheets in the drawing room, to be inspected, mended, oiled and replaced. Robert's knowledge of the internal combustion engine was considerable and he had the natural mechanic's love of taking apart and re-assembling all the moving parts of his beloved car. Shortly after the war, my mother sold the vehicle, a totally unsuitable means of transport for herself and her two small boys. I can still remember its smell, dominantly warm castor oil, when sitting snugly in the front seat with my legs warmed by the engine, faced by an array of little switches and other controls that I did not understand and probably still would not today, as the great car roared down a road somewhere in Suffolk, no doubt fired by purloined MGB fuel, my father's comforting presence beside me. It was a car to die for.

Robert started to invest in houses and land during the Thirties. Perhaps the great crash of 1929 had reduced the attractions of investing in the stock market for that generation. He owned several houses in Falmouth and then in about 1938 bought a farm near Constantine called Treworval. Whether he bought this because he felt that war was coming and he ought to own somewhere safer than Bodrennick, just across the water from the strategic Falmouth Docks, we do not know, but it is where his family moved to at Christmas 1939. From his wartime diaries, it is clear that he greatly loved the farm. Indeed, rather surprisingly, he wondered aloud in his diary whether he would ever return to Bodrennick because of a preference for living at Treworval. I can remember the deep mud and rural squalor of that farm in 1940 as clearly as though it were yesterday, but perhaps he had plans to clear the place up before it became our permanent home.

Robert's greatest love was for simple family life. He had two sons. My elder brother Bob was born in 1932 and I in 1936. He clearly adored both his boys and his love for his wife comes out with rather startling clarity from his diary. There is nothing like separation to make the heart grow fonder, but there can be little doubt that he and Catherine, in spite of the disparity of age and outlook, were a very happy and united couple. There are endless photographs of his children playing in the garden at Bodrennick, sitting in one fast car or another or playing at picnics on one of the many beaches to which we would frequently go in the summer months after Robert had finished work. He also liked to take us as a family to London, normally driving up in the Aston and invariably staying at Browns Hotel. My brother remembers matinees at the circus and J.M. Barrie's play *Peter Pan*. Beach parties were the dominant memory for me. Durgan beach on the Helford with my father frustratingly sunbathing when I wished to swim comes clearly to mind, though I think that memory must date from 1940 and not from 1939 and was probably when he came back on leave from Dunkirk. Nevertheless, it typifies our family life in Cornwall in those days, a pattern which my mother faithfully continued after the war when we were growing up.

I have tried to paint as best I can, a picture of what Robert Hichens was like by the age of thirty when war broke out in September 1939. To understand what happened next, his formative years have to be outlined to see what aspects of his character had developed which enabled him to mutate so rapidly into the assured naval commanding officer, fighting successfully in the front line of Britain's maritime defence in the Channel and the North Sea. I think the dominant characteristic was the seriousness with which he took every job that came his way. I don't think he was obsessive about his work but it came first. When it was done, and for a country solicitor in those days with competent clerks that didn't necessarily mean a very long day, he could free himself cheerfully to do the things he enjoyed most, sailing dinghies, driving fast cars and seeing as much of his family as he possibly could.

He believed very strongly in the importance of physical fitness. He had started a regular regime of body strengthening exercises when still a school boy. He was not a fitness fanatic but he wished to maintain his strength and endurance to deal with whatever challenges came his way. Douglas Dodds Parker's comment that at Oxford he wanted hard exercise every day, couldn't get it from hockey and hence turned to rowing, is evidence of this, as is his record of continued sporting activity on the river, on the sea and on the road. Was it a conscious preparation for war? Until well into the 1930s, his generation didn't expect a second world war and he is unlikely to have had any view different from the majority. I think he just felt that it was an essential part of manhood to be capable of enduring and of putting oneself in the way of activities which tested that endurance. Dabbling with ocean racing and the challenge of the twenty-four hour race at Le Mans are good examples of where he thought his physical toughness would give him an edge. Rowing is essentially an endurance sport and he kept up his rowing right up to the war, even if it reduced ultimately to crossing from Flushing to Falmouth and back most weekdays.

He had one belief which singled him out from the generality of young men. It was that to appreciate life fully one needed to face danger from time to time. Only after regular exposure to serious risks could one comprehend how sweet life was and recognize one's good fortune in continuing to experience it. He sets this view out in his wartime diary but my mother recalled it to mind many times when she looked back on her life with Robert. It may explain part of the attraction of the challenge of Le Mans. He must have expounded this personal philosophy on occasions, such as post operation gin sessions in the wardrooms of his flotilla, because a brother officer, who had borrowed his Norton and found it to be virtually without brakes, expostulated on returning the machine after a close shave: 'I suppose not bothering with brakes is part of your philosophy of seeking danger.'

Nevil Shute, the novelist, in his autobiography *Slide Rule*, quoted his own headmaster at the Dragon School, a keen offshore sailor, as saying:

> If I have learned one thing in my fifty-four years, it is that it is very good for the character to engage in sports which put your life in danger from time to time. It breeds a soundness in dealing with day to day trivialities which probably cannot be got in any other way, and a habit of quick decisions.

This quotation precisely describes my father's philosophy.

Probably his father's early death and his own early marriage and parenthood induced a stronger sense of responsibility at a younger age than most of his contemporaries. He certainly was a highly responsible person, even if his friends wondered quite how that showed itself in dangerous activities such as motor racing. His answer was to take out substantial life insurance to protect his family should the worst occur. It was perhaps that sense of responsibility which made him a particularly popular and successful young solicitor because he felt so responsible for his clients and they in turn sensed this. Later, it would come out in the care he took of his motor gunboat crews to which they also responded with fierce loyalty and affection.

He was a very careful man. That is also a solicitor's trait and one does not know whether a habit of carefulness came from his experiences as a solicitor or whether it was just the way he naturally was. Perhaps the best example of the degree of care he took to prepare himself for challenges was his disassembly of the Aston Martin's engine before the annual pilgrimage to race at Le Mans.

I do not think anyone would have described him as an intellectual but he thought very clearly. This was commented on by quite a number of men who knew him during the war and it can scarcely have started on his entry into the Navy. He had that capacity, which doesn't have a great deal to do with high IQ, to worry away at a problem until he came to a clear, common-sense answer. It was in some measure a reflection of his determined character, of his carefulness and of his sense of responsibility that he wanted to be satisfied that the answer to a problem was correct, so that he thought things through from first principles before accepting that the conventional way of doing things was the correct way or the best way. This undoubtedly contributed to that aspect of his naval career that concentrated on the development of tactics and the design of motor gunboats and their armament.

Perhaps the most powerful or obvious characteristic Robert had developed by 1939, and probably had always had, was impatience. Impatience is a characteristic that is often deplored because it is said to lead to impulsive and ill-considered actions, or indeed in failure to tolerate dissent, tardiness or other minor sins which society expects one to accept with reasonably good humour. Yet the other result of impatience is that it often causes the impatient person to do something about the problem that creates this emotion in him. My father was impatient with everything that didn't work perfectly and, rather than kicking the offending object as I would, he took it apart to work out how it could be made to do its job better. It was a characteristic which he brought to bear on everything for which he found himself responsible in the Navy. It explains a great deal of the success he had in changing the Navy's conceptions about how the war should be fought by motor gunboats.

Where does impatience end and determination start? Determination perhaps implies a steady application of one's skills to the resolution of a problem or the achievement of a goal. Robert certainly had that characteristic just as much as impatience. His pursuit of success in dinghy sailing and in racing his Aston Martin at Le Mans are good examples. Another was his approach to entry into the Royal Naval Volunteer Reserve. At Oxford he joined the Officers Training Corps and gained a commission in the Territorial Army. In the summer of 1930, returning from Oxford to Cornwall, he diverted the Lancia to Bristol to call in at HMS *Flying Fox*, the RNVR divisional headquarters there, because he wished to join, preferring the Navy to the Army in the event of war. He was told that he would be more than welcome but that there was a requirement for an evening a week training in Bristol, and even for Robert the three hours it would take to get him there and three hours back were beyond his capacity. Most young men would have accepted this situation. Robert did not. He applied to the Admiralty, explaining his position and saying that there must be hundreds of other young men keen to be part of the Volunteer Naval Reserve but frustrated by the distance that they lived from an RNVR division. It appears that the Admiralty took what he had to say seriously and, in the end, the RNV(S)R, the Supplementary Reserve, was formed as a list of yachtsmen sufficiently knowledgeable about the sea to be considered suitable for a commission in the Navy in the event of hostilities. He had at least one period of training at sea, serving in the destroyer HMS *Thanet* in the late 1930s, based in Plymouth. After the declaration of war, he expected a call up telegram within a matter of hours. When after a week he had only received a holding letter saying that call up would take time he wrote back to say that if the Navy didn't want him he could always rejoin the Territorials. The result was an order to join HMS *King Alfred* on 27 October 1939, two months after war was declared.

What did my mother make of these characteristics in her husband? She was sensible enough to see them for what they were and that she was unlikely to change them. If as a result there were many aspects of the life she would have preferred to live that were denied to her, she could clearly see that a man who adored his family, worked hard for their future, looked at no other woman and steadily gained the respect of his friends and neighbours as a young solicitor, was not a husband to complain about. When he said he wanted to go into the Navy if the war came, she can hardly have supposed that it was a more foolhardy course of action than remaining as a Territorial Army Officer, particularly with memories of the last war and its slaughter of the infantry. Nor could she possibly have supposed that he could be persuaded that he didn't need to go off to war when war came when every able-bodied man of his age, and indeed a good deal older, amongst their friends and neighbours was doing the same. She probably hoped that the war would not be like the war before, wouldn't last very long and that the Navy would be as safe a place to be as anywhere.

My father departed for his first seagoing appointment from Penryn station in December 1939 after the completion of his training at HMS *King Alfred*. My mother must have expected that he would do pretty well, thinking him well-suited to what he was about to face and that he had as good a chance of returning to her and the family as anyone, bar perhaps the lurking suspicion that he might seek out danger more assiduously than the average

28

volunteer. She could hardly have foreseen how quickly she would find herself as a naval wife, leaving Cornwall, neighbours and the life they had led together behind her, and following her husband into the spotlight which the need for good news in wartime was so quickly to direct on those who shone in action and survived the experience long enough to become recognized heroes.

Chapter Three

Sweeping in the Phoney War
September 1939 – April 1940

Robert was called up on 27 October 1939 with orders to join HMS *King Alfred* and, subject to interview and medical, to become a sub-lieutenant RNVR. HMS *King Alfred* was 'a stone frigate' initially sited in the municipal marina at Hove on the coast of Sussex, just beyond Brighton.

Virtually all RNVR officers went through their basic training there from the date it opened, 14 September 1939, until it finally closed its doors in 1946. Fully trained RNVR officers who had joined before the war were immediately appointed to ships. By early 1940, most of the *King Alfred* intake were CW[1] candidates, that is to say, ratings who had been recommended by their commanding officers as likely candidates for a commission and then sent for an interview before admission to *King Alfred* for training. However, between September and December 1939, *King Alfred* went through an initial phase of dealing with the RNV(S)R, the Royal Naval Volunteer (Supplementary) Reserve, often known as the Yachtsman's Reserve. As noted in the last chapter, Robert was one of those who pressed for such a body to be formed.

In 1936, the then First Lord of the Admiralty proposed that a list should be drawn up so that the Navy would know where to look for additional officers quickly in the event of a war. There is an apocryphal story that the First Lord needed to find something more to say to the House of Commons when introducing the Naval Estimates and asked for ideas from his staff. The Admiral Commanding Reserves sent in this suggestion. The Admiralty was

1. Commissions and Warrants.

then astonished by the speed and scale of the take-up. The list ended up 2,000 long and most of those men passed through *King Alfred* during the first three months of the war.

There was no formal training requirement for members of the RNV(S)R before the war, but a number of men on the list undertook training at their own expense, even getting temporary billets in ships at their captain's invitation, paying for their own messing and travel. Judy Middleton, the author of a monograph on *King Alfred* published in 1986, records that:

> some Supplementaries went so far as to find their own vessels so that members could gain experience handling powerboats. The Admiralty gave moral support but not much else. It was down to the individual to come up with a suitable boat. For instance, *Response* started life as a naval steam pinnace but had been pensioned off and lay in a private yard at Gosport. Then along came Henry Chisholm and Henry Trefusis, both RNV(S)R as well as members of the Royal Ocean Racing Club, and paid £150 for her.

Henry Trefusis was Robert's close neighbour and they joined *King Alfred* together.

The first batch of RNV(S)Rs, 140 men strong, joined *King Alfred* a week after she was commissioned. Robert joined on 27 October. There was no set time that had to be spent in *King Alfred*. It depended upon your knowledge of the sea, and what your training officers thought of you. As Robert passed out in early December he spent only five or six weeks there, whereas a full training period was three months.

The first commanding officer of *King Alfred* was Captain J. N. Pelly and he served in that capacity until his untimely death in 1945. Pelly was initially backed up by a number of retired officers, though later it became the norm for officers serving afloat to be sent to *King Alfred* for a period of a few months each, both to bring their fresh experience to bear on training and no doubt to give them a rest from the stress of constant sea-going in wartime. Perhaps the member of the training staff most vividly remembered by those who passed through *King Alfred* was Chief Petty Officer Vass, 'a short stocky man with a face burned a deep nut brown and a voice like a bull'. Vass was there throughout the war and was responsible for inducting young officers under training into the mysteries of marching, saluting and generally bearing themselves in a smart and naval manner. His greeting of one new arrival may well have been typical. Speaking in a deceptively quiet voice, that individual remembers him saying 'In five minutes you are going to hate me', then in a bellow 'I hate you already'. Vass's bark was worse than his bite and, by the end of a squad's period of training, to most men he was seen as a very necessary part of the experience that they had to go through. A gunnery instructor from Whale Island, where HMS *Excellent* was the Navy's School of Gunnery, Vass brought with him not only a smart uniform and the traditional shiny black gaiters, but also that trick of personality that makes young men remember with pleasure their erstwhile tormentors.

King Alfred's staff had to improvise mightily to be able to accept the first batch of supplementaries on or about 18 September 1939. Van loads of collapsible chairs and tables for use in classrooms arrived with minutes to spare. Hard chairs designed to line the seafront bandstand 'left an indelible impression ' on their users. Part of the underground car park, designed to hold 480 cars on one level, was converted into dormitories with rows of double-decker bunks. Other officers made their own arrangements in the town. There was a restaurant cum-dance hall which was 'turned into a very comfortable wardroom and rapidly furnished with suitable chairs and tables, a grand piano and two billiard tables'.

Supplementaries had no uniforms and they turned up in every type of clothing. In a world not yet used to the shortages to become so common in the Second World War, every tailor capable of making naval uniforms descended upon Hove and soon everyone was fitted out with the appropriate range. The tailors must have done very well out of *King Alfred*. They were able to clothe 1,700 officers in the first seven months of its existence. Robert went to Gieves, the doyen of all naval tailors.

The curriculum must have been rough and ready in 1939. It concentrated on navigation and seamanship, but there were also initial lessons in gunnery, including for instance the stripping and reassembly of an Oerlikon, the 20mm automatic gun, which was just coming into service with the Royal Navy. No doubt much time was spent on teaching the young men the meaning of naval parlance and teaching them what their relationship with their men should be in future, as well as their brother officers. CPO Vass is particularly remembered for taking a leading role in bayonet drill.

When it was all over, sooner or later depending on age and ability and previous experience, most passing-out officers had their photograph taken by Charles the photographer in Palmeira Square, Hove. I have a picture of Robert looking very young, very serious, in his brand new Gieves uniform, starched white collar and brand new cap with its crown and anchor badge as yet unsoiled by seagoing, a single wavy stripe visible on his right arm, the hands being folded to permit its subtle message to emerge from the bottom left-hand corner of the photograph. He looks particularly young because his early baldness is invisible under the cap. The lines which etch themselves into the face of experience are not yet there. They were to come all too quickly over the next two and a half years.

Robert's War Diary starts on Monday, 11 December with the words:

I left Bodrennick this morning, probably for the last time even if I survive this war, as we might like Treworval better and never go back there.

Catherine and his two sons saw him off at Penryn station:

a forlorn little group waving after the train until it disappeared round the bend, better than leaving a wife with no children behind to keep her company.

His travelling companion was his friend and neighbour Henry Trefusis who had joined *King Alfred* with him. They were both returning there for orders to join their first ships.

Robert's first appointment was as a lieutenant with special navigating duties in HMS *Halcyon*, a fleet minesweeper. On his way north to Grimsby to join her he passed through London and called in at Gieves to put up his second stripe, a moment of deep gratification in a naval officer's career. He then suffered a typical wartime journey with unexplained delays, arriving at Grimsby at 5.45 a.m. A bath and a shave at the Royal Hotel made him feel better before he reported at the Naval Base, only to be told that his ship had been sent to Newcastle, so that he journeyed on there and then to North Shields and at last found *Halcyon*. He met his first commanding officer, Commander St John Cronyn:

33

fat and extremely cheerful and pleasant and the other members of
the wardroom. We had many gins. I shall have to find a way of not
having too much of this.

On Saturday, 16 December Robert went to sea for the first time in a
Royal Naval ship in wartime conditions:

Cold east wind blowing but clear and fine for once after all the fog
and filth we have been having on the east coast since I came up. We
did an eight mile run to the swept channel, then a twelve mile sweep
out and twelve miles back. A few minutes after we started sweeping
a mine bobbed up in front of us. We were the second ship in the line.
We avoided it and shortly afterwards our Oropesa trawl cut one. They
were sunk by gunfire. Nothing more occurred until nearly the end of
our sweep when the ship two behind us blew one up in her trawl. The
explosion shook our ship a bit about a mile off and I saw the tremendous fountain of water.

Sunday, 17th December. Out at 6.30. Cold with a fresh easterly wind
and rising lollopy sea. Swept to the south first, then a long sweep
north. We picked up five mines, one of which exploded, all near one
place. We got no others on the way back and therefore thought that
we had cleared the field. In at about 5.30 after much cursing at our
flotilla leader's delays. Had a bath and felt better. This life combines
a fair amount of discomfort, extreme boredom and much danger. A
bad combination, but someone has to do it as it is a vital job.

Monday, 18th December. Out at 6.30. The same northerly sweep.
Nothing until the return journey. Then two mines in quick succession
right in front of us. Only just in time to dodge. One cut by our sweep
and four more shortly afterwards by the other two ships, one
exploding and blowing away a sweep. I was having lunch at the
exciting moment that we struck the field. When the sirens began
blowing to show that mines were cut one of the RN lieutenants
hopped out and the surgeon looked rather scared. The Chief
Engineer, an oldish man sitting beside me, didn't turn a hair. Neither
did I, I am glad to say. It was satisfactory feeling self-possessed and
unaffected in the circumstances, rather like getting through one's first
baptism of fire and knowing that your nerve is alright.

So on went the drudgery of minesweeping with, as Robert noted,

34

its constant accompaniment of extreme danger. The humdrum nature of life must have been all the more marked because almost every evening they returned to harbour and normality. For 22 December Robert noted:

The skipper was very pleasant in the evening. He quoted the famous historic remark 'It was only the small storm-tossed British ships blockading the French fleet at Brest, upon which the Grand Army never looked, that stood between Napoleon and world domination.'[2] It is the same now and it is satisfactory to feel that one is assisting, in however humble a way, in the maintenance of those storm tossed ships at sea.

Robert also reflected on the beauty even of war ships as humble as minesweepers. On 22 December:

A lovely day with a North Sea sunrise, dull grey mist being dispersed by a red sun. A hard west wind. The flotilla looked very fine behind us like miniature battleships with their high bows. We were the leaders today. The 5th Minesweeping Flotilla looked lovely astern with the red rags of the sun lighting up their grey hulls. There is beauty in a grim sort of way in warships at sea.

25th December, Christmas day. Out early and a rather short sweep. But we got seven mines and exploded one. A typical and rather beautiful North Sea sunrise, cold, hard and wintry with some livid red patches just as the sun came up. I really know there is a war on when I am running a minesweeper here while the children are opening their Christmas stockings. Nothing else would keep me from that. Went for a long walk in the afternoon and rang up Catherine in the evening. Very lucky in catching her at once. Then Christmas dinner with turkey and plum pudding, followed by my rum punch which I brewed over the wardroom stove. A very cheerful party considering we were all pining to be at home. The Captain is a delightful and amusing person and I am beginning to get on well with the other officers. Finding my niche.

26th December, Boxing Day. A very hard day's sweeping. Twelve hours solid. Picked up five mines on the long sweep up. It blew up to a northerly gale and got very rough. Luckily my stomach is settling

2. *The Influence of Sea Power upon History,* Captain A.T. Mahan, US Navy.

35

down though I feel queasy at times, which is foul. It is alright on a channel crossing when you know it will be over in a few hours but it is foul when you feel you may have years of it. After the main run we went out to the Eastward and got out double Oropesa sweeps and swept inwards. We picked up several mines, two exploding. One exploded quite near us and it was getting dark and it made a most magnificent firework, clouds of bright sparks. Two ships got mines caught in their sweeps, which was very dangerous. As it was very rough and almost dark they had to cut the sweeps. I went off and watched our sweeps come in from the stern as it was interesting in the big seas. A wild sight, almost dark, with the seas coming up astern and banging all the gear about. The toughest day we have had. There was a bright moon up as we rolled into port, a lovely wild sight with the ships steaming in line ahead.

Saturday, 30th December. Out sweeping. An uneventful day. There was quite a lot of motion on the ship and for the first time today I didn't notice it, which shows that I am getting acclimatised. I do hope so because feeling seasick is the most lousy thing of all. I don't worry about the mines or the aircraft but I shall be mighty glad if I can get my stomach so that it doesn't worry me at all.

At this point a reader without much knowledge of naval warfare as conducted in the middle of the twentieth century needs some explanation of what minesweeping was then all about. It was, as Robert noted, an unpleasant, boring but extremely dangerous job that nevertheless had to be done. In the First World War the Germans and the British had laid extensive minefields off each other's coasts, using broadly the same technology in the form of a moored mine. These mines had positive buoyancy but were attached to the seabed by a cable that allowed them to float just under the surface where a passing ship could strike them. The explosion was triggered by the impact of the hull breaking one of several protruding horns. To clear a path through a minefield the minesweeper was invented. This was normally a relatively small and inexpensive ship, sometimes originally a trawler, which had the unpleasant task of itself steaming through the minefield trailing a length of wire hawser behind it that was held at an oblique angle from the ship's line of advance by a float at its end, known as an Oropesa from the ship that first trialled the system.

36

The Oropesa was so designed that it pulled away from the line of advance of the ship towing it and thus kept the cable well out to one side or other at an appropriate depth below the surface. A 'kite' kept the inboard end of the hawser at the appropriate depth and an 'otter' marked on the surface the position of the Oropesa itself. On the hawser were cutters so that, if the hawser were pulled across a vertical mine anchor cable, the cable was pulled down the hawser until it reached one of the cutters and then, with any luck, was severed, causing the mine to float to the surface where it could be destroyed by gunfire.

The obvious problem was that the minesweeper itself had to steam through minefields with a fair chance of being blown up. Sweepers could gain some protection by working in groups of three or four so that each sweeper steered a course protected by the sweep of the ship in front of it and in turn protected the ship behind. That still left the lead vessel unprotected. If you knew where the edge of the minefield was, you could place your lead vessel just outside it and then each ship astern would extend further into the field, cutting mines while protected by the ship ahead, but of course finding the edge of a minefield was not a precise science. Generally speaking little attempt was made to clear whole minefields but rather effort was concentrated on keeping a well-marked channel swept, up and down, which ships could pass in reasonable safety so long as you kept sweeping it. Continuous sweeping was necessary, partly because you didn't always get every mine you passed over when sweeping, partly because the enemy might come back and lay more mines, often from sub-marines or dropped from the air, sometimes from small surface ships, and partly because mining became more sophisticated and mines could be put in place with a timed release that allowed them to float up to a dangerous height from the seabed only after some days or weeks.

Britain faced a major advance in mining technology in 1940 in the form of the magnetic mine. When the Germans first deployed their version the British were very hard pressed to know how to deal with it. It relied on the magnetic field which every steel ship has, resulting from its construction, to trigger a mine lying on the seabed or on a cable well below the level at which sweeps cut contact mines. Due to a remarkably brave and fortunate recovery of one of these mines very soon after the Germans first started dropping them, its method of working was discovered, and the answer emerged as a process known as degaussing whereby the ship's magnetic field was neutralized so that it no longer triggered magnetic mines.

In joining the Fifth Minesweeping Flotilla Robert found himself in a part of the Navy with a dangerous job to do even during the Phoney War. German strategy was to blockade Britain with mine-fields and U-boats. The job of the minesweepers was to keep swept channels all round the British coast as clear as possible of mines so that warships and convoys could pass along them. It was an unglamorous and daunting task.

Robert's diary entry for Monday, 1st January reads:

> Today we are flotilla leader still as *Sphinx* is boiler cleaning. Pretty thick fog for the first time. We got out and then it came down much too thick for sweeping. So we came back and found it exceptionally thick in the harbour. About one cable[3] visibility. It was interesting navigating up the river to the dock where she was to lie for boiler cleaning.

Robert got leave while *Halcyon* was having a boiler clean and spent it in London at Brown's Hotel, with Catherine and the children coming up from Cornwall. On the first day everyone was taken to the zoo and then off to Trafalgar Square to feed the pigeons followed by 'an exhausting tea at the Criterion'. The next day it was Hamley's to buy toys in the morning, returning to Browns for the children to rest before a pantomime while he and Catherine went to Catherine's dressmaker, Lonval, and 'bought two most success-ful dresses there at the sales'. Then off to the pantomime.

> The show was hardly up to the best standard but Bobby loved it and could not be stopped bouncing in his seat with laughter, much to the discomfort of those behind. Antsie sat on my lap and lasted very well from 2 to 4.30 when there was a bit of an uproar, which we finally beat down to a subdued mutter, so managed to save taking him out.'

Two more days of leave in London followed. On the 5 January his family saw him off on the train back to the north-east.

> We walked up and down the platform, one child each with a hand in

3. A cable is 200 yards.

mine and I couldn't help wondering whether it was the last time I might ever see them. Anyway it's no good worrying about that. We examined the engine and then got back into the carriage. Finally I kissed Bobby and Antsie good-bye in front of strangers and went to the door with Catherine. There I had to talk about business as the only thing to do to make the parting less unbearable. It seems strange to think that my father must have been through just the same experiences and for the same reason. I suppose unmarried people are really luckier in war.

On his return to *Halcyon* on the 6 January Robert found that his captain had been made Senior Officer of the Fourth Minesweeping Flotilla, known as M/S 4. Robert was now a watch keeping officer and assistant navigating officer, a job principally entailing keeping chart corrections up to date, one of the more boring jobs known in the Royal Navy and which particularly required a cast iron stomach when done at sea.

On Tuesday, 9 January *Halcyon* saw more action than normal.

Out sweeping and a nice day. Working at the charts after watch keeping. I felt rather sick in the stuffy hot little chart room but had to stick to it. Then down to lunch. I found the Doctor, Chief Engineer and Number One[4] there. I said we should be cutting mines in ten minutes as we were approaching the dangerous area. Sure enough while I was having lunch the siren began to blow again and everybody shot out except me and the Steward, who proceeded to tell me how he was mined in the last war. Then a mine exploded close by shaking the ship and more siren blasts. Everybody was so excited by this time outside that I thought I had better see what was on. I found that our sweep had cut seven mines and exploded one, all in the space of about four minutes and we were leading ship. Then I heard Number One say that the float had disappeared after having been seen for some little time after the explosion.

It is Number One's job to deal with the sweep. I saw him go aft to the hawsers and then call for the watch to man the winches to get it in. So off I went aft to help and be with him for moral support. It was grim getting in the kite as the trip wire had broken and there might have been a mine in it. But no, it was all right. Then we began

4. Naval slang for the first lieutenant, the second-in-command.

to haul in the sweep wire. It was obvious at once that there was very much greater strain on it than usual. Number One and the sweep man kept on feeling it and saying there must be a mine and a sinker if not two in it. I couldn't help thinking that, as the float had survived the explosion and then gone down, that it was probably the float full of water that was causing the extra strain. But no, Number One and the others were sure it was a mine or two and it was grim slowly hauling it in wondering when it might go up or if it would go up when it was right under us. There were only two other men aft with Number One and myself, the men for handling the cutters. When we got to fifty fathoms[5] Number One stopped. He was so sure that there were mines in it after the clutch we had come across that he went to the bridge to consult with the skipper. He came back with the skipper and it appeared that the latter had decided to veer the sweep again and tow it into shallow water, cut it there and clear it.

I was still standing right aft and Number One rejoined me and veered the sweep to one hundred and fifty fathoms. Then he stopped it. I said to him again that I felt sure it was the float and probably not mines, and suggested that we might haul in and try to see. I don't know what inspired me to be so persistent and careless of danger, but I felt I was right. In the end he suddenly said 'yes we will'. Then he ordered all hands back behind the winch about sixty feet from the stern, and there was Number One and I alone waiting and watching. It was very dramatic and very exciting. Then some little time after, the hauling in must have taken about ten minutes, the skipper joined us. In came the sweep slowly. One couldn't help being a bit frightened of sudden death, but I was so glad to be able to prove to myself that I was able to control myself and be quite indifferent to it. After what seemed ages we saw the otter porpoising about. Still we couldn't see whether it had a mine in it.

Number One had given it as his view that there must be a mine there because without the buoyancy of a mine the otter without a float would be dragging much more directly downwards instead of outwards as it was. Finally we could see that the otter was clear and hauled it up under the stern. Then the float. After considerable difficulty we fixed heaving gear to it and hauled in. When we first saw it it looked as though it had a mine in it. There was something large and black, but as we got it right close to we saw that the float had been

5. A fathom is six feet.

cut in half and one half was being dragged back like a drogue in the water, with its black bucket mouth towards us. So I was proved right after all. We got the half float in with great relief amidst considerable rejoicing. It was a very exciting incident and a lucky one for me.

I have included this diary note in full because it was the first time that Robert had chosen to stand his ground in front of danger in the Navy and pursue the course of action that he thought right. Two years later he would probably not have bothered even to record it but at that particular stage in his development as a naval officer it was a major event for him.

The next diary entry of note is on the 11 January, a foggy day on which they could not go out. Robert was Officer of the Day.

I persuaded the Captain to let me come aft in the event of air attack to be in control of and fight the 0.5 pom pom[6] and the after four inch.[7] This is much better than taking cover on the bridge and having nothing to do.

Friday, 12th January. A very exciting and interesting day. Out at 6am with up to twenty dan buoys[8] and double Oropesas. At once our starboard wire parted. We were lucky in being able to retrieve the float and otter, but it took us about forty minutes. Meanwhile the other two ships swept on and later we heard sixteen curious deep thuds that meant mines exploding at a distance. So the enemy had laid them right in the fairway. Presently we got going. After we had turned back, boom, up went a beauty on our starboard sweep. I was right aft with Number One and it was a magnificent sight. We both thought it was a more powerful mine than anything we had seen before. Then a few minutes later, boom, a mine in the port sweep went up. Then within five minutes, boom, boom, almost on top of each other the ship astern put up one in each sweep. It was an uncomfortable feeling as the tide was getting low and we were on a searching sweep, with no swept water. You felt that the next one might lift the ship out of the water. But there was no time to worry,

6. A 0.5 inch four barrel, quick firing anti aircraft gun. Robert refers to it as a pom pom. *Halcyon* is recorded as being armed with 0.5 Vickers machine guns, not the two pounder pom pom.

7. The four inch gun was a fleet minesweeper's main armament. *Halcyon* had one forward and one aft.

8. Buoys with long upright sticks with flags on them mostly used to mark a swept channel.

the doctor wanted me to check a cipher message he had to get out to the Admiralty, informing them of the mines we were exploding in the so called swept channel. It was vital to get it off at once, as there were convoys going up and down the lane at any time, and it was a sheer death trap. We had already put up eight mines in a short distance. I found he had left out the most vital word 'mines' in the excitement, which meant ciphering over half of it again. While we were doing this there was the biggest explosion of all. In the captain's cabin, where we were working, it seemed as though the ship had been struck and it made one stagger. We think it was two exploding together in the port sweep. Anyway nothing more was seen of the port float and otter.

We got the cipher off quickly after checking it again together. It was exciting and made one feel we were doing very important work, as that information might save thousands of tons of shipping and many lives in the course of the next few days. After that there was an air attack alarm. Aircraft sighted flying low to the westward. After yesterday and the mines today everyone was on tiptoe. The shells were all ready and everyone at action stations in a flash, but the aircraft did not come to us. After this alarm I decided to get to know my guns, and had a good look over the 0.5 pom pom. It's a lovely gun, but I think it is just as well I am taking an interest in it. The gun layer, who runs the whole show, told me repeatedly, in spite of continued and doubting questions on my part, that an ammunition drum would last for two minutes continuous firing. I felt sure this was wrong and have since checked upon it and found that it is used up in precisely eleven seconds. A bit of a difference! I shall tomorrow go into it fully and work out a technique as far as possible.

Saturday, 13th January. I have today sent Bobby his first cheque. A birthday present for his eighth birthday. I hope I may be permitted to send him many more, as all fathers should.

Out very early today. Started a clearance sweep where we had our exciting party yesterday. We hadn't long to wait. One exploded in our sweep as leading ship about ten minutes after the kite was veered, and then they went on, boom, boom, boom all morning. I was working on the charts in the chart room. I don't know why but it's very much more difficult to stand it with equanimity in a confined space by yourself. But I made myself do so. Then there was one terrific smack that threw me on my face on the chart room table. Then I heard a shout that the sweep had parted. So I went down aft to see if anything exciting was on. Only the end of the wire coming in this time, no wire throbbing and straining with the extra weight of presumed mines.

Since I was a boy I have always had a wish that I had fought in the last war. I wanted to know that I could undergo fire and keep cool. Now I have had my experience and I am glad to find that I can. It meant a lot to me and it was a thing you never could tell for sure until it had happened to you. Motor racing was the nearest thing I could get to it in that direction and that proved alright too.

Monday, 15th January. I saw in the Daily Telegraph of the blowing up by a mine of the *Lucinda*,[9] a trawler. She just disintegrated with the loss of all hands in the space of about three seconds. What the paper did not say was that it occurred in the middle of our swept channel, just where we go, almost twice a day. It must have been a delayed action mine. These German mines are terrific. I heard several of the older men who swept in the last war say that the mines in the last war were like pimples compared with these. I certainly have succeeded in getting myself into one of the toughest jobs going in the war and in many ways I am glad. At least one feels that one is on real active service.

Friday, 19th January. Out at 4.15 am this morning as we have to rush up north to sweep a longer convoy of eighty ships through this mined area round the Tyne. So we don our little inflatable life belts and led the way. The other people ought to say 'God bless the minesweepers', but their usual attitude appears to be that we're a bloody nuisance for getting in the way with our sweeps. At least they nearly always seem to make no effort to get out of our way. It was very funny the other day because a merchantman was coming right across our sweep in spite of all our efforts to get him to keep clear, when suddenly we exploded one of these big German mines. I have never seen anyone put about and clear out of it so quickly.

Saturday, 27th January. Out early and found it blowing hard from the south east. A lovely big sea running when we finally got right outside. When I had breakfast I had an active time. First I was pinned by the

9. *Lucinda*, a steam fishing trawler, lost 11 January 1940.

43

table sliding against the ward room wall, then having given that up and tried sitting at the side of the table instead of the end, I kept on sliding down chair and all to the wall, skilfully grasping my coffee and kipper, until in the end I gave it up and remained leaning against the wall. Finally the nearby table, with all the books and papers on it, fell over on my toe. So after that I thought it best to return to the comparative safety of the bridge. But the great thing was that in spite of a really terrific roll on the ship, I felt quite alright, not a qualm. I'm so frightfully pleased about that as I always wanted to be sure that I should get quite used to motion, and I do, and it makes all the difference to your happiness if you are trying to live on the sea.

Thursday, 1st February. At last we were able to go out. When we got to the breakwater there was a tremendous swell where the seas were running in over the shallow water. The ship seesawed and plunged, burying her nose which is a considerable feat with her high bows. We wondered seriously whether we should be able to bring her back if that swell continued, as if she started to yaw in the narrow entrance it might be impossible to stop her before she rammed the breakwater. As we were in the worst of it, with the stern coming right out each wave, the engine room voice pipe bell went and I answered it. I heard the Chief's plaintiff voice 'The engines are racing very badly Sir'. I nearly said 'So what'.

It was a bit better outside and then further off shore it was very rough again. We were doing a special job, sweeping the cruiser *Southampton* out of the Tyne southwards along the War Channel[10] for about twenty miles. It was really much too rough to sweep properly and we should only have gone out for a special job like that. Later in the day we saw the *Southampton* racing up astern through the mist to pass us, as we came to the end of the swept channel. She was a fine sight doing about twenty knots in that big sea.

After the *Southampton* had gone by, we gave the order 'in sweeps'. I went off to assist. It was a fine sight with the waves at one moment well above your head and then you were careering high up with the sweep wires drumming under the sudden strain of the ascending stern. One couldn't help feeling rather stirred that one was part of this life that required toughness to enjoy it and get the work done. You can see how the men like an officer who is there when there are

10. Swept channel from Aberdeen to the Thames.

44

dangerous or unpleasant things to be done. It is a rather curious thing the immense effect that cool officers will have on the men when there is any question of panic. The fact that I can make myself indifferent to danger is the greatest boon, as I feel that I can be really useful by just being with the men when there is any excitement on, such as mines exploding or aircraft attack.

Saturday, 3rd February. The news came in of the *Sphinx* being hit by a bomb up at Invergordon and being towed in by the *Speedwell.* The *Sphinx* was our flotilla leader when we were part of the Fifth Minesweeping Flotilla. So we all know her very well and the officers aboard. We have heard no further news as to casualties or the damage done. We suspect from signals that keep coming in now instructing us about aircraft look-outs, etc., that she was caught napping and failed to open fire before she was bombed. I spent quite a while perched on the 0.5 platform when the worst aircraft scares were going on in order to supervise the fighting of the gun if attacks should start.

Sunday, 4th February. My work will be even more useful for a bit now as today Pilot[11] was smitten with an attack of bronchitis and hauled off to hospital in a distinctly groggy condition. The doctor says he will be there for a fortnight, so now I am flotilla navigating officer pro tem and still more busy.

Tuesday, 6th February. More news came through today of the total loss of the *Sphinx.* Apparently the Captain and four hands were killed when the bomb exploded. She was then taken in tow without removing the crew. She then turned turtle in the heavy seas, probably through a bulkhead giving way and four more officers and forty-seven ratings were lost. A terrible thing after the comparatively light casualty list resulting from the bombing.

I heard today also of the secret and terrible story of the loss of the destroyer *Exmouth.* Apparently she was escorting the *Cyprian* up to Scapa, *Cyprian* having an immensely valuable and vital cargo in the shape of all the new anti aircraft defence equipment for that base. At dawn, as they were proceeding at ten knots, the *Exmouth* was torpedoed and broke in half. The Captain of the *Cyprian* at first stopped his engines and then almost at once went full speed ahead.

---

11. The pilot is the navigating officer in a ship.

He went right through the sinking destroyer and could hear the men screaming on either side, hence the fact that there were no survivors out of the whole ship's company. He was congratulated by the Admiralty on his decision, as the cargo was so vital and the danger of torpedoes was so great had he stopped to help, or even hesitated. It must have been a terrible decision to have to take, with one hundred and seventy men being drowned and battered to death in the water around you.[12]

Just heard another discouraging story. A trawler with a party of mine experts from HMS *Vernon* managed to pick up a German mine and get it on board. Subsequently she was found still floating but with everything in her blown to bits, including of course everybody on board. While she was steaming home the mine must have exploded for some reason and just wiped everything out on the ship. People ashore don't realise what a grim war we are waging at sea with the Germans. A cold blooded war, in a way I think requiring the maximum of bravery from the men on both sides in the long run, as it is so ceaseless and intangible. You just don't know whether the next moment will be your last, and it's surprising how untroubled by it most people manage to be.

Wednesday, 7th February. We swept fifty miles north to clear the War Channel for the cruiser *Sheffield* to come south. It was a long tiring day on the bridge. It got dark about 5pm and we weren't in until 7pm. I had been handling the ship most of the day and was doing so as it became darker. First we had to negotiate a convoy and numerous ships without light or with very little light. Finally I brought her successfully towards the Tyne entrance and there we could hardly believe our eyes; as we approached it looked more like Brighton in peacetime than a blacked out port. Finally we realised that it was a huge convoy of probably eighty ships anchored in a cluster all round the entrance to the Tyne, with their riding lights showing. Fortunately with my good sight at night I was able to pick up our entrance and then suddenly we found ourselves surrounded by black hulls. It was most difficult. The night being pitch dark and the riding lights bright, one could not see the hulls or tell how near you were to them until you were almost on top of them. I kept on handling her, expecting the

12. *Exmouth* was sunk with the loss of all hands by *U22* on 22 January 1940. The Admiralty enquiry confirmed that the Master of *Cyprian Prince* was right not to attempt to pick up survivors and he was so informed, though with reluctance.

Captain to take over at any minute, as I had hardly ever handled a large ship before in traffic and it was a very difficult ordeal getting through this. I managed to zigzag her through the anchored ships going very uncomfortably close at times. Then the Captain said 'are you alright because I haven't quite got a hang of this yet'. He couldn't see our way through as well as I could.

Finally I brought her triumphantly through and right up the river to the dock, the first time I had done it and in the dark. It certainly was rather nerve racking. As we were tying up alongside with the ten inch searchlight playing on the quay, accentuating the great sheer of the bow overhanging the wharf, I had that rather peculiar and pleasant feeling of lassitude at being able to stand still and do nothing, watching others tie up, after the intense strain of the preceding half hour.

Another boiler clean for *Halcyon* was due. Robert was rostered to stay aboard but Catherine came up from Cornwall to be with him.

Tuesday, 13th February. I read in the paper today that on good authority it is proved that in the transport of the Polish population out of the Corridor into the centre of Poland, great numbers perished of the cold and lack of food. The Germans probably intended it. In one case when a cattle truck was unlocked it was found that the occupants, thirty Polish children, were all frozen to death. It makes me see quite red when I hear of cruelty to children. Just think if Bobby and Antony had been in that truck. And it's exactly the same as if they had been, as children all the world over are the same. I am glad I have read that as nothing will now stop me from doing all I can to avenge those children, and that will help if things get tough. One can't help being afraid of death though one can control it, but the thought of what one is fighting and if necessary dying for, the extermination of things like that, will I think make all the difference.

Wednesday, 14th February. I was much interested in doing my first pay for the men. Each man's name would be called and everyone below the rank of a petty officer would come forward and take off his cap and hold it out and I would put the pay envelope on it. It seemed almost feudal. Some of the older men had a priceless way of coming forward the few paces to the table in a kind of forced run, lifting their legs rather high. Hard to describe but evidently the idea being to come forward at the double even though you have no distance to do it in.

Tuesday, 20th February. The Captain had taken the opportunity to arrange to have us docked and the oil tank put right. Accordingly we waited for the tide until 12 o'clock and then in a thick fog came into the dock and thence into the Royal dock by the great tower. The professional pilot who took us in was very funny calling out to his pals in the tiny little tugs. One was called 'Perce'. I remember 'Touch ahead Perce' and then with a masterly waggle of his bottom he would indicate to Perce that he was to give her a touch to port or starboard as the case might be.

Robert's turn for leave now came up. Catherine had come up to Grimsby to be with him for a few days, so they journeyed home together.

Wednesday, 21st February. We had decided to go to Cornwall for my leave at all costs. I was relieved therefore to find that there was nothing to prevent me getting off. Indeed in the end the Captain travelled down to London with us. On the way into the station I asked him if he would give me my watch keeping certificate. I thought that as I had just finished successfully my term of office as full flotilla navigator it was a good moment before I made an utter balls of something. He said he would give it to me. I was highly pleased.

Thursday/Friday/Saturday/Sunday, 22nd/23rd/24th/25th February. As this is a diary of my war experiences I shall not set down in detail my doings during these four days of leave. I shall merely comment for my own satisfaction upon my outstanding impressions.

First of course the children. A lovely impression. They both seemed so lively and cheerful and enormous and full of life. Bobby was so much improved. Physically better looking and much fitter and less skinny, and so much more sensible. Very much the schoolboy. Antsie copying him in every way, very tiresome but very loveable. A vivid remembrance of perpetual rough and tumbles on our beds with both children sitting on my head, of uproarious joy at this, of sudden peace when I would read to them and they would sit one on each arm of my chair. Of little Antsie singing 'I'll see you in Scotchman', (a reference to the fact that I had said that if I went up to Scotland they would perhaps come up there to visit me) of him crying because I was going away in the evening before my departure, and of his complete unconcern (luckily for my peace of mind) on the actual night of leaving. They were very delightful and one of the hardest things of this war for me is being away from them.

My other vivid impressions are of my joy at seeing Cornwall again and realising more clearly than ever what a lovely place it is compared with the east coast. Of sitting in that delightful old room at Treworval[13] with Catherine in the evening, of waking up in the mornings and looking out from my bed right over that lovely peaceful countryside away to the Helford river, or the Dodman with the sun rising out of the sea behind the high land. I loved those early mornings, hearing the first little chatter of the children and knowing that soon they would come bustling in ready for the fray. So different to my little cabin with its closed porthole. It was fun too seeing one's friends but rather difficult in some ways to talk to them, because four months in a minefield changes one's point of view so much.

Finally the sad parting. A sad little evening meal in spite of a bottle of champagne, a last look at the children fast asleep in bed after hours of playing and reading, a rather desperate drive to the station with practically no lights thinking we were rather late, then a few minutes on the platform in the dark with Catherine clinging to my arm. Then it was all over, except for a lovely memory.

Monday, 26th February. Having some gins with two RNVR officers off another boat they told me of a new A.F.O.[14] that had just come out asking commanding officers to recommend RNVR officers for commands of trawlers, MTBs, armed yachts, etc. They said they were going to try to get a recommendation and I decided to also, but I thought I had better see that I got my Watchkeeping Certificate first.

Tuesday, 27th February. The Skipper had seen the A.F.O. about recommending RNVRs for command and had talked about it to the Secretary who came to see me. Apparently the Skipper said to the Secretary that he would give me a recommendation if I asked for it, but that I was so useful he didn't want me to go and that he thought

13. Catherine and the children had moved to Treworval, the farm near Constantine that Robert had bought in 1938. Bodrennick was leased for the duration of the war.
14. Admiralty Fleet Order.

49

I might be wasted. Then the Secretary said that the Skipper had told him to get out my Watchkeeping Certificate and he was trying to find out whether we (RNVR officers) were allowed to have them after only two months at sea whereas RNs had to have three months at sea first. Finally he gave it to me though they weren't sure whether the time was too short or not, which was very nice of them I thought.

Monday, 11th March. Work on the charts and lots of QZ's[15] in the morning. In the afternoon we were told that the Duke of Kent would be coming aboard. So after lunch we all changed into our Number Ones[16] and put on clean collars and in some cases shirts. I looked round next door into the doctor's cabin and found him rolling up his shirt sleeves. That was his method of preparing for the 'Duke' as his cuffs were dirty. Finally, when we were all teed up, had missed our golf and had waited for ages, we were informed that the Duke would not be coming but had sugared off to Liverpool!

I know that I must see the Skipper about being recommended for a command and about the volunteering and I went down to my cabin to consider the C.A.F.O.[17] again and to make a final decision, as the consideration of the children was still worrying me and I hate being undecided on any important matter. While I was below Catherine's letter arrived saying that she hoped I'd get my MTB and sink all the Germans I could. This seemed to me a coincidence arriving just as I was pondering a final decision. It fell in with my wishes and I decided to go forward with it all.

So I went to the Captain and volunteered. He was surprised and said 'Are you sure?' I said I was. Then I asked for a recommendation for a command, especially for MTBs. He said he would give me one and to tell Scratch[18] to see about them. So that was that. I saw Scratch and we worded up a recommendation for me for an MTB especially on the ground of my knowledge about engines and experience of high speed. In the recommendation for special operations we merely said 'he is of good physique' which is what is required apparently.

Friday, 15th March. I was sitting writing to Catherine about six when the last person in the world that I expected was ushered into my

15. QZs were ever changing convoy routes along swept channels.
16. Number Ones are officers' and men's best uniforms.
17. Confidential Admiralty Fleet Order.
18. Naval slang for the captain's secretary, normally a paymaster lieutenant.

cabin. Henry Trefusis, beard and all, looking very flourishing. We had a lot to talk about so spent the evening together and in the end got rather sozzled. It was great fun seeing him. He is so much more communicative than he used to be. He seemed to be enjoying life in his destroyer very much, though I gathered that he was suffering from the same complaint as all of us, namely not enough responsible work to do. He hadn't been so lucky as me in stepping into things, very naturally in a larger ship, and he isn't allowed to touch the charts or QZs, so his navigating is nil.

On the 18 March Robert went down with German Measles. He spent an uncomfortable week in hospital but then enjoyed the bonus of recuperation leave in Cornwall.

Tuesday, 26th March – Thursday, 4th April. The joy of waking in the morning to see the hills of Cornwall going by in bright sunlight, with a glimpse of the sea at Par and St Austell Bay. I cannot describe how lovely it all seemed to me after the east coast. It makes me realise how desperately fond one gets of Cornwall.

Then Catherine, the children and Jenny[19] all looking out of the car when they arrived. The children rather shy and Catherine rather upset at being late. Then my old clothes and comfort and just the joy of being home. It is worth living in the discomfort of a small warship at sea in the winter in wartime to get days of leave like this.

The children get better than ever. Making the most wonderful mess of themselves out doors. One little incident stands out. I was pacing up and down the room talking with my hands behind my back, as one often does on the bridge or the quarter-deck. Suddenly I became aware of little Antsie by my side pacing step for step with me, his hands behind his back, very long strides to keep up with me and turning just as I turned. It was delicious. I engaged him in serious conversation as we paced!

Then it was back to *Halcyon*.

Friday, 5th April. The same old dull train journey back to Grimsby. I could not help thinking how strange everything was. I was going back to the war, mines, bombs and machine guns. Recognition signals,

19. Jenny, if memory serves, was a sheepdog.

CBs,[20] QZs, and all the paraphernalia of the British Navy at war. That seemed already to be the most natural thing for me. The past week was an interlude. A peaceful happy experience in a rather grim but exciting life. The children playing, Catherine knitting or dealing with her little domestic problems, a dance, old Smith discussing at length the fearful problem of whether a client should pay five shillings[21] a year or ten shillings a year for his use of a water supply. All the old usual values no longer usual. Wiped out and replaced already in my mind by the fierce wastage of war.

I got a shore boat almost at once and arrived at the ship by about 6.10. After parking my bag I went up to the chart room and found Pilot very busy making out supply and receipt notes for all the chart room equipment. Cronyn was to take over *Niger* and he had decided to take his whole ship's company with him.

Saturday, 6th April. Went into the lock and docked alongside *Niger* who had entered before us. My last trip in *Halcyon*. One feels quite sentimental about leaving a ship you have lived in even if only for a short while.

Niger had picked up the day before a peculiar little pear shaped black mine which the Germans had just started to lay for the purpose of cutting our sweeps by blowing them up. It was hanging by its tail from one of the float winches on the quarter deck. I noticed an RNVR Lieutenant, who came aboard with *Niger*'s Captain, go and examine this mine. Being interested I stepped over to see what was going on. It appeared that the RNVR man was an expert on mine destruction but, as this was an entirely new thing, had had no experience of the type. He undid a top nut which held the whole guts of the mine and withdrew this mechanism leaving only the empty shell. He proceeded to examine it and said that he thought there was some explosive there but did not wish to try and take it to bits unless ordered to and he would get in touch with Glenny, one of *Vernon*'s[22] experts who had taken the first magnetic mine to bits. So he and the Captain left, telling a sentry to see that no one touched it. That of course did not apply to an officer. So I proceeded to examine it, in a curious way fascinated by the idea that it might blow up.

20. Confidential Books.
21. Five shillings is today 25p but with the purchasing power of perhaps £10.
22. HMS *Vernon* was the Navy's centre for mine expertise.

A Chief Petty Officer called Ramsby off *Halcyon* was also there, and he was by way of being knowledgeable as he had done a short course at *Vernon*. So he examined it with me and we spent about an hour with it, fiddling about and trying to work out theories. When we had pulled and pushed and unscrewed all we could and generally kicked it around the deck we had finally arrived at a theory that there was no explosive in the part we had, and that it was only the release and firing mechanism, the explosive being elsewhere.

Sunday, 7th April. The change-over proceeded. We got our cabins changed over today and slept aboard *Niger* tonight for the first time. The hands are marvellous, rushing around grabbing all they can for their own ship as a matter of honour. For instance, in the end we changed everything in our chart room over except the parallel rulers and sextants because everything of ours was better and kept up to date better, except as I heard him say in the most matter of fact way 'we haven't got a sextant on *Halcyon* and they have two parallel rulers and a sextant on *Niger*, so I left those'.

I heard today of the narrow squeak that *Sutton* had. She is one of our flotilla. She was pulling in her sweep when she found she had a mine in it. Then the First Lieutenant rushed forward with everybody and told them to slacken out and go full speed ahead. As he did so the mine went off about ten feet astern. Luckily they were all forward of the winch. The explosion was terrific. Everything breakable on the ship went. Number One said he was knocked down twice. Once by the force of the explosion and just as he got up he went down again with the weight of water landing on the deck. The decks were knee deep in water for some time. The kite, a piece of iron weighing a good half ton, was chucked clean over the bridge and landed in the water about one hundred yards ahead of the ship. Actually she was lucky not to sink. She managed to creep in and she is so badly damaged that she will take about eight weeks to repair. Lucky blokes.

We find to our pleasure that *Niger* has about 650 hours in her boilers, well over the due amount, so that we shall have to boiler clean right away. It is to start on Tuesday, and I of course will stay and look after the ship.

Monday, 8th April. I spent the whole morning settling the chart room in. Finally I had got everything to my satisfaction and went aboard *Halcyon* for a last gin in her ward room. Here I found the RNVR mine officer called Armitage talking to the Captain. It appeared that Glenny of *Vernon* was coming up to take the mine to bits and that there was three pounds of hexanite, the most devastating of German explosives, in it. That made me laugh when I thought how we had decided that there was no explosive in it and had kicked it around for so long. Especially as hexanite is a notoriously unstable explosive. I couldn't help thinking of the hushed tones with which the Romney Foxs[23] had mentioned the fact that Andrew Le Grice had nearly been with a party who had been examining British mines for instruction purposes one of which had blown up, and how his wife wasn't being told that he had nearly been in danger. It was all very funny. Before turning in tonight I made notes and diagrams of what I had learnt on rendering a German mine safe and pinned it up in my cabin. You never know when it may be useful in this job to be able to step forward as an expert and render a sausage safe if need be. Or try to. There's one thing, you wouldn't try unsuccessfully more than once.

Tuesday, 9th April. At 12.45 I came down from the chart room and was called in to the Captain's cabin. There he was having a drink with *Sutton*[24] and in a high state of excitement as he had just heard the news of the attack on Norway. He clearly thought that we might be going over to Norway at any minute. Later in the day we got a signal to say that all ships of the 4th and 5th M/S Flotillas were to take on coal,[25] stores and a full complement of dan buoys and stand by to sail for Norwegian waters. We received a demand to know how quickly we could close down our boilers and be ready for sea if necessary. I said about twelve hours.

All this was frightfully exciting and Scratch and I are thrilled at the prospect of going to Norway. To our surprise no one else seems to be. We must be very belligerent or something but anyway we are both so longing for it that we shall be bitterly disappointed if we don't go.

Wednesday, 10th April. Feverish work on the charts in the morning coupled with a lot of dashing about to the docks arranging that the degaussing should be finished earlier than promised. Then the first news began to come through on the wireless of the smashing of the

23. Romney Fox of Trewardreva, of Quaker descent and thus a non combatant.
24. The captain of a ship was sometimes referred to by his ship's name.
25. Most of the Fourth and Fifth Minesweepers were 'Smokey Joes', coal burners. *Halcyon* and *Niger* burnt oil.

German Fleet by the Navy.[26] Scratch and I could hardly contain ourselves. Our desire to be in it is terrific. The only consolation is that with any luck we may be off in a day or two. It is funny this terrific desire to be in the thick of it when anything exciting is going on. I would have given anything to be in the fray at Narvik yesterday.

Thursday, 11th April. Armitage told me an interesting story about how poor Baldwin had met his death. Baldwin was one of the men who took the magnetic mine to bits and one of the chief experts in *Vernon*. He was killed when a mine exploded on a trawler and blasted the whole of the guts out of it. Apparently an RNVR officer had survived long enough to say what happened and had then died. They had swung a British mine on board. These are quite safe once the mooring wire is cut unless a considerable pull is put on the mooring wire again to make contact. The horns had been broken when it was swung over the side and when Baldwin was not looking a hefty trawler hand (knowing nothing about mines) had jumped up to steady the mine which was swinging from the gallows, by holding on to the end of the cut mooring wire. He missed the first time but caught it the second time and his weight coming on to the wire made the necessary contact and, the horns being broken off, up went the mine. I think it is the most infernal bad luck on Baldwin to die as a result of that silly mistake after all the risks he had taken in mine destruction work.

Saturday, 13th April. About dinner time the Captain arrived. He had been at the Admiralty for some time while he was on leave. We are not going to Norway, at any rate for the time being. We were returning to routine at Grimsby. A bitter pill.

Wednesday, 17th April. I heard a rather interesting fact today. Apparently after Zeebrugge the Admiralty allotted so many VCs to the expedition and one was to be given to the Vindictive. The second-in-command under Carpenter,[27] I forget his name but I think it was Morgan, and Carpenter were the obvious people to give it to as being in command. So the ship's company voted on it and everyone was supposed to vote. Well Morgan voted of course for

26. The German Navy lost many destroyers at Narvik but did not lose their fleet.
27. Captain Alfred Carpenter, VC, RN, another admirer of Catherine's so none too popular with Robert. I have a signed copy of his book, evidently a present to my mother.

Carpenter and when the results were brought to Carpenter the numbers were exactly equal for both of them but Carpenter hadn't voted. His C-in-C told Carpenter that he must vote, but Carpenter, knowing that if the numbers were equal he would have to get the VC as senior officer, refused to, because of course he ought to have voted for Morgan. In spite of protest he refused to vote and so got the VC. A pretty low piece of work in my view. Apparently Morgan was the man who deserved it as he had led the party onto the Mole.

Thursday, 18th April. Still standing by for Norway, lying at anchor in the stream. I started my training of the 0.5's gun crew. It was quite successful as a start and I won over the Chief Gunner's Mate, which is important. At first he viewed me with suspicion. I shall cut their reloading time down from about five minutes to forty seconds, in time.

Friday, 19th April. It was blowing hard and rough outside. I put my 0.5 crew through their paces as I thought it would do them good on an unpleasant day. They got on quite well. It was fine up there on the high gun mounting with the ship careering about and the gun firing. It was exciting. I made them fire about 400 rounds and got the gun into good trim, which it wasn't before.

Monday, 22nd April. The Captain told Number One the other day that I had better take over all the gunnery. Rather flattering, but a tall order for me with no training and all the other work I have to do. I have no doubt however that in time I could effect great improvements. It is really incredible the slackness and lack of preparation for action that I find. It is illuminating that I, an utterly untrained (so far as gunnery is concerned) RNVR officer should be the only person to get anything done.

Later this evening, about 23.00, we have just had quite an excitement. There was an air raid warning from ashore and enemy aircraft reported over Spurn Point about four miles off. The 0.5 gun's crew was ordered to be closed up. So I popped on a coat and went up. It was a wonderful night with a low full moon and a hard east wind blowing out of a clear sky. The tide had swung us against the wind, so we trained the gun aft towards Spurn Point and waited. There were about twenty searchlights from ashore working all over the sky. It was really a wonderful sight and very exciting standing there by the gun with its four muzzles feeling that at last I had made something of it. We were not nearly ready for them but at least nearer than a few days ago. Presently the searchlights died away and we all went below.

Sunday, 28th April. Four magnetic mines were blown up by magnetic sweepers round the Chequers buoy after the German aircraft raid last Tuesday. As we went around that buoy about three times (and either side) immediately after the mines were laid, it looks as though the degaussing gear may be fairly hopeful.

Tuesday, 30th April. We are standing by today while two of the flotilla are making a searching sweep off Yarmouth, a long way out, where the SS *Cree* was mined. If she finds mines we go, if not we revert to ordinary routine.

As it turned out fine I had a game of golf with the Captain and played very well, beating him handsomely. When we got back to the club house at the end of the round the steward came running out for the Captain saying that Scratch was on the 'phone for him. The news was that *Dunoon* had struck a mine during the searching sweep and was sinking. We got a taxi and dashed back. We are off tonight at once as soon as the tide serves. She has *Elgin* standing by. Everyone seemed surprised at the news. Personally I was not. I think we have been lucky not to be sunk like some other sweepers. That is the second ship in our flotilla to be mined, but *Sutton* got home without casualties. I wonder how many will be lost with this sinking.

Skippy told me this morning that now that I had applied for MTBs and volunteered for dangerous work, and as I should get one, he knows that at the beginning of the war the intention was to use them in an attack on Wilhelmshaven. We should indeed then be death and glory boys! I think after motor racing and the strange way that I feel quite impervious to danger now, I should welcome the job. Anyway what I feel is that Englishmen have got to do this work now to defeat Germany, and I must be one who does the worst work as I am fitted for that particular type of fighting. If I was killed on such a job my sons could at least feel proud of me, and is that not better than dying of old age in one's bed with your children tired of you?

The latest signal from *Elgin*. She says *Dunoon* is sunk with her stern showing, and that she is returning to Yarmouth with forty two survivors. If there were no other ship there and that is all the survivors it is a terrible loss of personnel. It brings it home to you when you knew all the chaps well and only saw them yesterday.

Wednesday, 1st May. I am writing with the ship at anchor in the middle of the North sea. It seems such a strange place to be at anchor. Not at all friendly with the thought of enemy aircraft and submarines. When we got the news from "Elgin" it appeared that "Dunoon" had hit a mine forward and that it had blown most of the forward part of the ship away, including the bridge. Consequently all the officers on the bridge had been killed. These included the Captain, the navigator and the assistant navigator and Hill who I had seen a lot of at Hove and had liked very much. He also was a solicitor and being in my squad at Hove[28] we had made rather special friends, and I had seen quite a bit of him since as he was in our flotilla. In fact I had had a drink with him only two days before. It made me think how much chance one's continued existence was. Our names both began with 'H' and I might just as likely have been in his place yesterday as where I am now. We were each allotted to a ship and now he is at the bottom of the sea.

We had not long been sweeping however before signs of the lost ship reminded us vividly of her fate. First clothes and barrels began to float by, then parts of the bridge and superstructure generally. There evidently must have been a very violent explosion forward as we saw part of the chart house float by. This was presently vividly confirmed by the presence of charts floating by. First a few, curiously unreal floating face up. I remarked to the Pilot 'There goes part of the tidal atlas'. Then more and more until whole folios were floating by still with their strings tied. There must have been a great eruption in the chart room. My special sanctuary!

We swept for some hours and then as it was growing dark about nine o'clock we anchored off Smith's Knoll, one of the sand banks in this part of the North sea.

Thursday, 2nd May. We started sweeping at daylight with a long day ahead of us. It appears that *Elgin* and *Dunoon* had cut or exploded about six mines before the latter was blown up. They were doing a searching sweep endeavouring to ascertain the western limits of the minefield. We were now instructed to do a clearance sweep out to three miles beyond the War Channel. The captain of *Elgin* felt sure

28. HMS *King Alfred*.

that we should not find any mines in this area as they were all further out to the eastward. But the Admiralty policy was to clear for certain a sufficient area to make the channel quite safe, and then leave any mines that might be beyond in the hopes that submarines coming back later might blow up on their own field thinking that we had cleared it.

At dusk we anchored again off Smith's Knoll and so left poor *Dunoon* to her fate and the remaining mines. I am sorrowful for poor Hill. He had had no chance of having a wife and children. If I am to be blown up, I shall remain for ever thankful that I have been allowed these advantages. They are the only great things in life worth having, and the only thing that can in any way ensure that something of oneself remains behind.

Sunday, 5th May. A lovely day. We went into a small church service, held in the herring sale room of all places, in memory of those lost in *Dunoon*. It was rather an attractive and touching little ceremony. Only sailors there. Even the padre had been a Lieut. Commander (G)[29] before he heard the call. As the dead men's names were read out it seemed so extraordinary that they were gone. This day a week ago I was laughing and talking with two of them. They were nice chaps too. Anyway they are alright. It is the people they leave behind.

Directly the service was finished we went out sweeping. There has been a 'blitzkrieg' of magnetic mines. They have exploded eleven in magnetic sweeps in the last few days. It is rather disturbing to find that in the latest mine obtained when the plane crashed at Clacton they have reversed the polarity of the switch. Therefore unless our degaussing gear is correctly calibrated, neutralising our magnetism, it will be increasing the risk for us. We have reason to believe that it is not correctly calibrated, as this is difficult and requires time.

This evening after dinner I was listening to the wireless and they had a rather attractive programme of all musical comedy hits. They brought home to me what a gulf was fixed between my present existence and pre-war life. I find that somehow mentally I have made a clean cut. I have in a sense blanked off the past. I suppose instinctively I have found this necessary in order to steel myself for death at the worst or laborious days cut off from all I love at the best. The comfortable pleasure loving pre-war self has had to be cut clean out,

29. Gunnery specialization.

so that I can dedicate myself entirely to the cause of destroying the enemy. I feel that very strongly. Englishmen have got to be brave now and be willing to make the supreme sacrifice of death. I have fortunately been able to make up my mind fully to that idea, and so I wish to press on to my MTB and throw it and myself if necessary at a German warship if thereby I can feel that I am really wrecking the enemy in greater proportion than ourselves. It is a funny feeling to be like this and in many ways very satisfactory. One feels in some way that thereby one is being true to a tradition that is more worthwhile than anything else in our little lives. But in order to be able to be like that the past has to be cut out. And so this evening the music cast disquieting shades of the past over me. Especially when someone sang 'Lover come back to me'. I remembered that it was Catherine's favourite during the time of our engagement.

What lovely times we have had together. And what lovely children we have created. I often think of them all. I loved Antony's remark when chanting 'What shall we do with the drunken sailor',[30] 'Mummy, how do you drink a sailor'. Most logical for his little mind which knows nothing of intoxication. Sometimes when I think of them I wonder whether I should not try to preserve my life a bit more by at least not pushing myself forward for dangerous work. And then I reassure myself by the knowledge that I am fitted for the work and that England needs those who are fitted, and also by the knowledge that Catherine would not have me hold back, in just the same way that she would not try and restrain me from motor racing. A thing I have always greatly admired in her.

The Phoney War came to an end in April with the German invasion of Denmark and Norway. The invasion of France and the Low Countries in May followed close on its heels. The pattern of work for the 4th Minesweeping Flotilla varied very little until the order came to head for Dunkirk and assist in the evacuation of the British Army. Thus this is the point at which we should look back at Robert's experience in the Phoney War and take stock of what it meant for him.

In the course of just over five months it had turned him from a very green young RNVR lieutenant, joining his first ship, to a respected member of that ship's company, holding a Watchkeeping

30. A sea shanty much sung by Robert.

Certificate, responsible for the ship's gunnery, and quite able to take the flotilla navigating officer's place when he was ill. He had found his feet thoroughly in the wardroom and had something of a reputation amongst both officers and men for courage and determination. His commanding officer had recommended him for the command of an MTB. He had endured the brutal winter of 1939/40 at sea, one of the coldest of the century, and he had endured the danger and boredom of minesweeping.

To be in minesweepers during the Phoney War was, to many thoughtful officers and men, a surreal experience when they came ashore and back to normality, as they did almost every night. At sea they endured the worst that the weather could throw at them while undertaking the dangerous but meticulous task of keeping swept channels around the British coast clear of mines. Returning on leave, to a place as remote from the war as Cornwall, must indeed have been a peculiar sensation.

I have recorded Robert's innermost thoughts drawn from his diary, not because I would not normally wish to respect his privacy, but because I believe it is important to understand how tentative the first steps may be in the creation of a reputation for determination and courage. The confidence necessary to achieve both objectives does not spring fully formed to a man's aid. Both qualities are built on experience, and it is important to understand the doubts that assail the bravest of men until they know themselves to be thoroughly tested. I think it also important to understand how much his family meant to Robert and how that sustained his belief in where his duty lay. Throughout his narrative he comments to himself on how much he would have liked to find himself where greatest excitement was afoot, for instance bemoaning how much he missed being at the Battle of Narvik. He was shortly to get all the excitement he craved.

Chapter Four

Dunkirk
May – June 1940

It is clear from Robert's diary entries in late May 1940 that the Royal Navy was, by then, fully aware that it was about to face one of the most hazardous and complex operations that it had ever been called upon to perform. The defeat of the French Army in May 1940 created the need for the evacuation of the British Expeditionary Force, most of which had fallen back to the coast of Northern France. This force was accompanied by many thousands of French troops cut off from the main body of their army by the blitzkrieg tactics of the German Army driving for the Channel. The evacuation of armies by sea in the face of the enemy is an extraordinarily difficult thing to accomplish without very heavy losses. The British Expeditionary Force in France numbered over 500,000 men of whom some 300,000 were falling back on Dunkirk, and it is hard to think of an operation on a comparable scale that any navy has ever tackled.

The operation was organized by Admiral Sir Bertram Ramsey, supported by Rear-Admiral W. F. Wake-Walker and Captain W. G. Tennant, from underground quarters in the cliffs above Dover. In the end the plan for Operation Dynamo, as it was officially called, boiled down to nothing much more than sending everything that would float across the Channel to pick men up from the beaches and carry them away, under what was expected to be both bombing and shell fire, while committing in support lighter units of the Royal Navy capable of carrying larger bodies of men from Dunkirk harbour. The famous 'little ships' of Dunkirk, although making a sterling contribution to the lifting of the troops from the shore, actually carried very few troops all the way back to Britain. The great majority of the 338,226 troops which were evacuated returned by warship or the many other ships and craft which were manned by the Royal Navy. The Navy quite rightly decided that it could not risk serious losses amongst larger ships so nothing larger than a destroyer took part in the evacuation, other than some AA covering fire from a small number of cruisers. Given the already all too obvious fact that the Navy was desperately short of escort vessels, it could hardly regard the risk of losing a significant number of destroyers with anything other than horror. Because of the imperative need to keep swept channels open round the coast there must have been some hesitation in sending the fleet minesweepers, but they were available, not far distant, and they went.

Robert's own account of his experiences at Dunkirk must have been written in snatched moments between action and sleep in the immediate aftermath of the evacuation, which makes it an exceptionally fresh record of what he saw and felt. I think it is sufficiently important that I have not edited it at all after the entry on 29 May.

Friday, 10th May. '7.30am. Sir, it's a fine morning, Sir, Germany has invaded Holland and Belgium, Sir.' I was awakened with these words by my servant. Momentous words I consider! I said 'Christ' and leaped from my trap.

And so the 'blitzkrieg' has started in spite of Stephen King-Hall,[1] and the Government have been justified in their action over Norway in spite of Lloyd-George. What an incredible moment in history this is. Upon the outcome of the next few weeks' fighting, the future history of the world for generations will depend.

There is a thrill of excitement in the ship. We started out on our routine sweep. At 10.30 we were north of the Outer Dowsing with the Captain below listening to the news and myself in sole charge of the bridge. An order from the Captain's cabin. 'In sweeps.' That meant some special operations. In the circumstances one could not help being thrilled and excited. I hoped and felt sure that it meant we were going down to Dover.

Presently another cipher message came through to say that we were to proceed to sweep a fifteen mile channel for our submarines well

1. Commander Stephen King-Hall RN retired. A political journalist and one time boyfriend of Catherine, so much disliked by Robert.

offshore in the North Sea opposite Harwich. It will be a two day sweep, anchoring out for a couple of nights. I had so hoped we were bound for Dover and now it looks as though we may go back to Grimsby when the sweep is over. However we may see some aircraft on this line and have a pot at them.

I heard the news this evening. Mr Chamberlain's resignation came as a shock to me. I believe in him. I am glad he will be in the Government. He was much moved and most moving. His final indictment of Hitler was strangely stirring coming from someone who is so calm and restrained.

It is now midnight and we shall be anchoring shortly. It is eerie on deck. Black shapes occasionally going by, quiet and dark. An occasional lamp flashing out. I hope no tube will find us tonight. I had a last look around the 0.5 and its crew. I must get there as soon as I can if there is an air attack.

Germany has once again thrown Europe into misery. I hope Hitler will soon suffer the hell he has let loose on the Low Countries.

Saturday, 11th May. We had quite an exciting night. Planes continually droning by and once a submarine slipped past some distance off in the dark. We did not challenge him as being at anchor we could do nothing. Was he friend or foe?

A lovely day. Bright sun and a fresh north easterly breeze. We swept all day. Several times during the forenoon and early afternoon we had single German planes flying high overhead. Action gongs went and twice I had to jump from my lunch and leap up the 0.5 ladder, which somewhat interfered with my digestion.

Then in the evening just as we were getting the sweeps in and were hampered hopelessly by having both still over the side we suddenly saw ten dark spots in the eastern sky flying fairly low straight towards us. I nipped to the 0.5 at once and for the first time put on my tin hat in earnest. The crew were all there ready and silent. The squadron split into three flights slowly spreading out and coming straight at us at high speed. It was an extraordinary moment this waiting. It seemed an eternity. I suppose in fact it was only about three minutes. I felt certain they were German planes. They looked black with a wide wing span, they were coming from the east, and why should any British planes come straight for us opening into battle formation and without giving the recognition signal. Besides had not German reconnaissance planes spotted us sweeping that afternoon?

With our inefficient A/A weapons ten planes making any serious attempt would finish us for certain. We were fifty miles off shore, out of range of our fighters and with no air escort. One could not help feeling that anyway we would try to sell our lives dearly. It is impossible to describe that period of waiting as the ten black sinister specks grew steadily larger. When they were only about a mile and a half away I wondered when the Captain would open fire with the 4 inch guns. I think he should have done so sooner for a ranging shot. The crew on the 0.5 were very good and steady. Silent. I thought the layer, who I am not sure of, showed slight signs of panic. I made him start laying the gun although they were still far out of our range.

Then suddenly out shot two lights from the leading aircraft. A white and green. They were British. The relief was a curious and interesting sensation. I made the layer go on laying the gun and I could see by looking through the other sight that he was being pretty inaccurate, probably through the nervous tension. I shall have to watch him and take his place if I have any reason to doubt his ability to lay the gun in action.

Monday, 13th May. I am on the whole glad that Churchill is Premier. It seems somehow fated that he should lead the nation at this supremely critical moment, after having failed to be Premier through all his long and brilliant career. It seems as though he has been held back from the position purposely to come there now. Much depends on his drive and energy and ruthlessness. We must be prepared to sacrifice our fighting forces if these barbarians are to be beaten. To give them their due they are prepared to sacrifice themselves and their High Command is utterly ruthless in doing so. Until we are prepared to counter this by equal sacrifice I do not believe we can hold them. I think most of us who think seriously about the issues involved in this war are prepared to die if thereby a useful contribution can be made to the ultimate crushing of Hitlerism. I know I have made up my mind to that effect, hence my application for MTBs.

Tuesday, 14th May. A truly glorious day again. We went out to the Aldeburgh light vessel, and as it was fairly thick and it was very necessary for us to have an accurate position to be sure we swept the area where mines had been seen, we used taut wire gear from the light float to our position. Then we proceeded to sweep. The first line up

65

in unswept water was the most dangerous moment for us as leading vessel, more especially as the mines, if still there, were known to be laid shallow, as they had been seen from the air just below the water. So I offered to go aloft and keep watch from the crow's nest at the top of the mast. I climbed up with my glasses. It was most tiring as the ladder was a loose and wobbly wire one and the mast inclined backwards. However I got there and rather enjoyed the view of everything from my eyrie. I did not see any mines though we swept all day.

We had other excitements than mines however. A fog came down for a few hours. While we were in it we just caught sight of two MTBs slipping past. Were they German or British? We were a sitting target for them. We had our usual quota of aircraft alarms but nothing very threatening luckily so far. I hope our luck holds as we are God's gift to the German aircraft just off the Dutch coast with our sweeps out. Then in the late afternoon we beheld a pillar of smoke in the east; taking a bearing we made out that it must be the Hook of Holland on fire. The smoke hung about in the form of a cloud all the evening. Very gloomy and forbidding it was.

Once to our astonishment a large shell splashed into the sea about a mile ahead of us. I wonder where it came from and at what it was aimed?

If anyone had suggested that I should be sitting at anchor twenty-five miles off the Dutch coast all night in war time I should have laughed, but here I am. There is something very impudent and comic about it, but what else can we do. We have the job to do out here and we cannot waste our time sojourning to and from a safe spot. We should never get it done.

Wednesday, 15th May. I had finished breakfast and was sitting talking at the table when the alarm gong went. I dashed up to the 0.5 and as I arrived I saw a German plane dive out of the clouds and drop a salvo of four bombs on *Hussar*, one of the ships in our flotilla. It appeared as though two fell close one side of her and two the other. It was very good shooting anyway.

Then there was pandemonium. We all steamed about at full speed, circling around, and banging off our 4 inch guns whenever we saw an aeroplane. There were three I think, though there may have been more, and I gather they dropped about twenty bombs, none very near

66

us. We had one zooming fairly low and near to us and we gave it a short burst from the 0.5. He turned away and a number of people said that they saw smoke coming from one of his engines. It was most exciting while it lasted, circling around, firing. The noise was terrific. I think we did quite well to drive them away without suffering serious damage as they caught us nicely in line with our sweeps out, just the most dangerous time.

Well when the firing had died down we discovered that *Hussar* had been holed by a direct hit on her starboard quarter, but luckily the hole in her side only extended to about a foot above the waterline and, as the sea was fairly smooth, she was in no danger of sinking and could steam and steer alright, which was very lucky. Apparently about ten bombs had burst all round her in addition to the hit aft and the flying fragments had torn her about badly, killing two men and the First Lieutenant, badly injuring two and injuring about eight others to a lesser degree. We lowered our boat and sent Quacky[2] over to *Hussar* to tend to the wounded. Then we formed up and started home. We had swept the required area and had to see *Hussar* home before the weather deteriorated as the glass was falling fast. We also escorted a little Dutch minesweeper home. We had come across her earlier, about 6.30 and she had said 'Can you tell me the way to England'. We could see that her decks were crowded with refugees, women and children mostly. I had suggested that they put me on board to navigate her home, but the Captain wanted me to go aloft and so decided to tell her to wait until we had finished. We had heard the news that Holland had capitulated that morning. The little huddle of pathetic refugees brought home to us very vividly what that meant. I remembered the cloud of smoke over the Hook of Holland the day before. The refugees must have had a fine view of our aerial battle and they must have been well pleased to have some British warships to escort them home.

We got home to Harwich without further incident, in glorious and almost oppressive sunshine. I had a bath and feeling desperately sleepy turned in about 9.30. At 10 o'clock just as I was about to go to sleep I heard the sound of gunfire all down the river. I hopped out of bed as the alarm gong went and put on my dressing gown. As I went up the aft gangway to the 0.5 the air was alive with tracer bullets, looking like a firework display. Someone was firing low over us and

2. The flotilla doctor.

several tracers just seemed to flip over my back as I climbed the ladder. Luckily I got to the gun first and trained on the only aircraft in sight, which had navigation lights on and was flashing the identification, and was obviously British. However nearly everyone else in the river seemed to have lost their heads and were loosing off like hell at it. The next door ship loosed off the entire four belts of the 0.5 and several rounds of 4 inch, the latter strictly against local rules, and the former in spite of the fact that the plane was well out of range. Luckily I had our gun, as otherwise I am sure the enthusiastic gunner would have loosed it off. So when the excitement had died down, I went to bed and soundly to sleep.

Friday, 17th May. The news is very bad this evening. Three German mechanised divisions have penetrated the Maginot line and have formed a bulge in it. I suppose our parents had to withstand such news and such days as these. I often remember hearing my mother talk of them. Now we must stand up to them, but our parents were never fighting such devils as the Nazi gangsters. A defeat would be far worse now than in 1870 or 1918. It is inconceivable that the Lord should be on their side.

Saturday, 18th May. The news was worse this morning. The 'bulge' has increased, Gamelin has ordered the French Army to die at their posts now rather than retire and the British have had to fall back west of Brussels in order to conform with the dented French line. This news gives one a terrible feeling of gloom. If the Germans were to break through, turn the Maginot line and give the French a crushing defeat, everything that we hold worthwhile would be gone. That is why I think we are going through the darkest days that any Englishmen ever have.

We are standing by again today. It is glorious weather. It would also be for the bloody German airforce. We had a naval funeral for the three men killed in the bombing the other day. We had a long walk of two and a half miles through the lovely country along the banks of the Orwell. The funeral was very striking in a beautiful little cemetery overlooking the river. In the little naval cemetery I happened to stand next to a tombstone in memory of Lt. Richard Boase, RN, aged 25, who was drowned when the submarine *C16* was lost on the 17th April 1916. He came from Penzance. These bloody Germans creating these needless wars.

Tuesday, 21st May. The news this evening is very bad. The Germans are in Amiens and Arras. Will anything stop them? At least they can't drive tanks across La Manche, the blessed Channel. If France is knocked about badly we shall just have to hang on until we have got such an air fleet that the Germans will be unable to get in the air at all. I think we shall be able to do that. We always work up and scrap best when we have our backs to the wall and the British pilots can do it alright if we and America can produce the planes in time.

In the meanwhile it is La Manche again, and those distant storm tossed ships. etc. It is difficult not to be gloomy at times like these. I manage not to be when I'm with other people but when alone it is well nigh impossible. That I suppose is what is meant by morale, and we have got to keep it up.

Surprisingly, on the 25 May *Niger* received orders for a boiler clean and Robert spent the 26th to the 28th on a quick leave in Cornwall, Catherine returning with him on the night train to London.

Wednesday, 29th May. We had a good journey up and had breakfast at Browns Hotel. Then we wandered around and bought the children some incredibly cheap toys at a little shop behind Leicester Square. Then we saw 'Gone with the Wind'. We only had time for some sandwiches after that before leaving to catch my train. On the platform we met the Captain who at once informed us that the B.E.F. were being evacuated by Dunkirk and that we were off at once to help. The news of the position of the B.E.F. had been so terrible to me that I was only too glad to hear that a real effort was being made to help them, and that I should have a chance of doing my share. On the other hand the prospects of a sticky end were strong and so our leave taking, although we said nothing to indicate it, was I think a special one for us both.

I left Catherine at the end of the platform. While I was waiting for a minute or two before the train started I could see her standing there. I think we both wondered whether we should ever see each other again. These times require courage, mercifully we have our fair share of that, as have most of the British people.

Thursday, 30th May. We steamed steadily down all day. I spent a hectic day getting the charts up-to-date specially in the Dover/Dunkirk area. I had the first watch to myself. It was rather fascinating plunging along lost in the darkness. It gave one a great feeling of aloneness. The only snag was that if we weren't alone we were as like as not to collide suddenly with another ship using the War Channel.

I turned in at midnight when I was relieved. One's state of tense excitement was increasing as we got south. We had shortly before received orders to proceed from the North Goodwin light vessel direct to the beaches at La Panne, about eight miles east of Dunkirk and just across the Belgian frontier.

Friday, 31st May. I awoke about 5am and dressed and went on deck. Or rather I was awoken to go to action stations as we were already in the danger area. When I got on deck I found that we were already proceeding eastward along the Dunkirk channel, which is narrow and close to the shore. The coastline was about a mile off, looking forlorn in the dull morning light. The sky was overcast and rather misty and a fresh north-west wind had got up. There was an indescribable air of desolation about the scene. Here there were numerous fires ablaze, thick smoke pouring from many places and houses all along the sea front, gutted and knocked about.

But I think it was the wreckage in the sea that struck one most. At about every quarter or half mile one would come across some large wreck in the channel or stranded in the shallower water nearer the shore. Every conceivable kind of flotsam was in the water from up-turned ship's boats, to life belts, tins or stores or bodies. There was the continual thud of gunfire from ashore. Altogether a dismal scene. I went up on the 0.5 and could see that the hands were a bit nervous, and so tried to cheer them up with a bit of chat.

We passed Dunkirk, already a mass of flames to the westward, and began to see and pass along the now famous beaches. There were batches of troops dotted along these long low beaches and all sorts of small to moderately large craft along the shore side of the channel at anchor. Some seemed to be sending boats ashore. Others did not seem to be doing much about it.

We came to our position about seven o'clock and dropped anchor as near in as we could. We naturally expected that boats would be plying from the shore to bring the troops out to us. We also expected that they would come pretty quickly as at anchor we were exception-ally vulnerable to aerial attack. But nothing happened. There seemed to be no organisation ashore for bringing troops off. So we lowered our motor boat and two whalers and sent them in for troops. The troops were queuing out along a rough pier built of army lorries placed side by side evidently at low tide.

We waited. Periodically a German plane came over and we loosed off at him with the 4 inch guns. One of the most extraordinary and striking things of the whole situation, to my mind, was the lack of aeroplanes over us, both our own and German. I expected it to be a continual aerial battle, but it was nothing of the sort. It struck me that our chaps must be doing good work elsewhere in holding the German Luftwaffe down.

As time went on and we got no boats back we got more impatient. With the fresh north-east wind blowing there was a decent bit of surf beginning to run on the beach making things difficult. We could see that one of our whalers had already been capsized by the soldiers trying to get into it. So we signalled the motor boat to come back to the ship and I said I would try and get things going better. I got ashore with one whaler and two other ship's boats that I had picked up on the way. I got the motor boat to lay off while I went on to the improvised pier and began to organise the boat parties.

Never have I seen such chaos. There was a very nasty surf running in by now and the lorry jetty was a very tricky thing to get boats to and from without damage. The unfortunate soldiers were the most awkward ham handed stiffs I have ever seen near a boat, poor things. I was so sorry for them. They were so tired and so pathetically helpless with the sea, with all their equipment, but here and now I will take my hat off to their discipline.

Not once but time and again I had the greatest of difficulty in getting the men out along to the end of the jetty and into the boats because they said that it was not their unit that was embarking at the moment. As the others could not get past them to the boats along the rickety little pier I had to make them get in. But I admired them very much for it. These boats and the waiting ships meant England, life and their families as opposed to Heinkel bullets or bomb casings in their guts if they stayed much longer on the beach, and they were so tired which must have made it harder. But there was no rush, not a single man did I see panic the whole of my time on the beach, and as I say time and again they were trying to make way for each other.

I got on the jetty and spent the next three hours jumping about like

71

a monkey getting boats alongside, getting them filled, getting them off, shouting to the soldiers to pull here, or shove there, or to sit still or get in, until I was hoarse. But I did succeed in getting things going and I must have got off twenty or so boats where none were getting off before. For the first time in my life I had found my ability to act quickly and surely in small boats, a quality I have developed in myself since I was six years old, of great value in saving the lives of others. It was a most satisfactory and exhilarating feeling. The fact that we were occasionally machine gunned or shelled I didn't notice. I was so busy. I was the only seaman on that part of the beach and it was wonderful being there and knowing one's job when all these men needed one so. It cannot be often that a man is given such a lucky break for feeling himself useful to others.

I expect Catherine will remember the sort of picnics we used to have which involved landing from the dinghy in a praam and perhaps from a motor boat, with children and baskets galore in a swell. And she will perhaps remember that somehow or other I used to manage it all, or perhaps rather she will have noticed that it was a bit tricky and disorganised if I wasn't there to row, and hold on and hand things. Well it was that sort of ability in small boats that I was able to exercise to the full in these far more exacting circumstances and I think it was the most exhilarating moment of my life.

As the tide began to go down and the wind to get up, the surf became more and more difficult to deal with. Rowing out from the jetty became a matter beyond the skill of the soldiers and few sailors in the heavily laden boats. I saw that the only thing to do was to get some of the smaller motor yachts cruising around to anchor as near in off the end of the jetty as possible and to try and get a rope ashore from them to the pier. Then the boats could be hauled out to the yachts along the ropes, a thing that even soldiers could do quite easily. So as each boat came alongside and I got them filled and away I told the men to get their captains to organise this rope idea. I fear my earnest exhortations fell mostly on stony ground, but in one case a boat was manned by two RNVR ratings who were obviously gents. I besought them and they seemed good chaps and, as you shall hear, on this occasion the seed fell on good ground and bore fruit.

In the meanwhile conditions were getting worse. It was becoming more and more difficult to get boats off under oars. No signs were showing that anyone was making any effort to adopt my suggestion which was the only hope for the continued evacuation of troops from the beach. I began to realise what was, I am afraid, the truth all too often, that these smaller craft were not going to take any chances or make too much effort if it involved them in loss or danger and that I must rely on myself if I was to get anything done.

A whaler had been waiting alongside full of soldiers for some time, tossing up and down trying to get away but unable to because there were no sailors on board and none of the soldiers knew how to take control. So I decided to take her off to *Niger* and see what I could do about organising the rope party. So I hopped in the whaler, told the officer on the jetty that I was going to try to organise my idea which I had explained to him, and that I would be back. I got the whaler out to the waiting yachts and got towed off to Niger. When I got aboard I was horrified to find that I was just being recalled as we had been ordered to take what we had back to Dover and then come out again for the final evacuation that night.

The Captain congratulated me on my work, but that was no help. I explained my plan, said I thought I could get lots more off if I could work it and pointed out that anyway I had said I would be back and that they were relying on me ashore. I said 'couldn't you leave me behind to do it, if you really can't stay until I have organised the rope?' So Skippy said he would leave me and that I must try to find my own way home. It was a grim thought, being left on the beach in the same position as the soldiers, especially as we understood then that the final evacuation was to be that night from Dunkirk, (though this proved to be wrong) which appeared to mean that the Germans were close. But I had promised the soldiers I would be back and they so pathetically needed a seaman ashore there. I'm glad I stuck to it. I thought of Catherine and the children and then remembered that we had agreed it was no use being afraid of death. It will come to me when it's my turn and I have never avoided risks before and I knew Catherine would not wish me to in these circumstances. So I rushed round the ship and seized all the rope available, cast it onto the yacht that had towed me off and cleared off. It was a rather great moment. I think the chaps on my ship thought well of me for it.

I found the skipper of this yacht quite hopeless and totally unwilling to take any chances in co-operating. So I yelled at a passing motor yacht, also RNVR, and they seemed more helpful. So we came up alongside and transferred me, all my rope, and a bloody awful old dinghy that I had acquired in the course of the morning. There was so much sea running by now that the two yachts crashed against each other tremendously in the process. The skipper of my first yacht was very agitated. I didn't care a damn and could only think of the soldiers waiting hopefully and patiently ashore.

My general impression of this period is of the intense effort and blasphemy required to get anybody else to see my point of view and make any effort towards my plans. But I slowly succeeded. At last I got this second yacht anchored reasonably near in and then I began to go ashore in my boat with the rope. A nice young RNVR sub said he would come with me and was most enthusiastic and helpful. We only had paddles in the boat so we could do no more than direct her as well as we could towards the pier. When we had got as near as possible I told him to hang onto the rope and pay it out to me and I hopped over the side and swam to the end of the pier with the rope. I had a hell of a struggle to clamber along the broken jetty all crashing about with the impact of the waves but I succeeded in getting to where a soldier could clamber out to meet me and pass it on. Again it was a very exhilarating moment, this fierce fight to get along the jetty with the rope, with all the soldiers watching hopefully. I find I take to these rather desperate ventures well. I suppose I get my blood up with action.

Well, we got the rope fixed and cleared and the boat in and then troops began to haul themselves out. It was a good moment for me when I saw some of these chaps getting off by my method as it was by this time quite impossible to get soldiers off by rowing, the surf being much too much.

Presently I saw some other sailors rowing like hell and I saw that they had a rope in tow. They had a hell of a job. I recognised them as the RNVR ratings whom I had impressed with my plan. They were trying to put it into execution from their yacht. Presently I saw one of them just tin hat and large cheerful face beaming above the water trying to tow the rope in. So I went in again up to my face and tin hat, and went out to join him and together we got the rope ashore. It was good and heartening to have these cheerful chaps there too to give a hand. We began to get boats off by this rope too. We got a good many off but not as many as I had hoped before the tide beat us.

With the dropping tide various lorries dotted about began to be disclosed. Alas our ropes both got caught under a lorry. Before I could get out to clear one the rope had parted. The other one was caught some way out and the position of the yacht to which it was attached was such that it would cause it to catch repeatedly unless the yacht was moved a little further east. I decided to try to row or swim out to the yacht and get her position altered and then to come back and clear the rope from under the lorry. I realised that, as it was then nearly three o'clock, low tide would be along soon so it was really our last hope for keeping the embarkation going. So I collected the only little boat available that we might be able to row, straightened one of the rowlocks which had been crushed, and collected the sailors to make a crew. Four of us. We took six soldiers with us while we were about it and I told the officer on the jetty that if I didn't succeed in my project the only thing for them to do was to go to Dunkirk for the night evacuation. Actually the Germans were held for longer than expected and the evacuation from the beach lasted for another twenty-four hours, though we could not know that then.

We started to row. The boat simply broached to in the sea. So two of us got over the side and pushed her out until we were up to our necks. Then we hopped in and rowed like hell. I took one oar and after pulling for ten minutes I thought my arms were going to drop off. It was then for the first time that I realised how much I had been taking out of myself during the last nine hours on the beach. The excitement keeps one going until physical exhaustion is just around the corner. Slowly, almost imperceptibly, we pulled out of the surf, getting tremendous set backs with some extra big waves and then slowly going ahead. Finally we were out of the surf. With another ten minutes pulling we were near the motor yacht that had the line from the shore. As I got near enough to hail I looked round and to my horror I saw that the captain had let go the rope, having attached a grey life buoy to it. I yelled at him and he smugly replied 'I had to let go as we were near to grounding, but I buoyed it'. Of all the fat headed asinine remarks for a seaman to make I think that takes the cake. What the bloody hell good it did to buoy it when the whole flaming lot would drift ashore in a few minutes the lord only knew. I knew I could do nothing more on that tide and that if we went ashore again we should not have the strength to row off again. So I went along to the other yacht, *Chico*, which the ratings with the other rope had come off.

We got aboard and found them in a poor way as they had mucked up their engines by getting ropes foul of the screws. They had to try and get back to Dover where they were operating from and as I had to rejoin *Niger* I thought that it was the best thing I could do, as there was nothing further I could do on the beach as you could not row soldiers off and I had no more rope to attempt to renew my scheme.

I had realised when I was on the beach that we were being machine gunned from time to time and hadn't taken much notice, being too busy, but I had entirely failed to notice that we were being shelled from Nieuport, further east. It appears that the weather having cleared about noon, a German battery at Nieuport had opened up. Anyway shells began to drop all around the *Chico*. They have that unpleasant 'wheeze' and then bang. They straddled us in every direction but luckily never hit us, as a shell would have finished the little *Chico*. Meanwhile I was helping hoist the anchor and finally by being lowered over the stern managed to clear the rope off the propeller fairly well, so that she was able to proceed at a slow speed, about five or six knots.

I felt pretty bad about leaving those soldiers on the beach, but I had done my best and could do nothing further and I had at least told them what to do. I think I must have got about five hundred to seven hundred troops off that day through my exertions, who might never have embarked otherwise. It seemed really a worthwhile effort, but as I lay on the deck of the *Chico* resting it was not the thought of the shells falling around that worried me, but the haunting spectacle of those soldiers quietly waiting for help. It is nice to know now that those that were not killed on the beaches were ultimately taken off.

We slowly proceeded west and had got about half a mile when suddenly the worst bombing attack of the day took place. About twenty German bombers came over and dropped about forty or more bombs, I should judge. They were evidently aimed chiefly at the beaches but fell short in to the edge of the water, causing a terrific noise and clouds of smoke along the fringe of the beach.

Some British fighters appeared almost immediately and a dog fight ensued. Presently two planes crashed, one with terrific violence into the sea and the other over the land. Two parachutists dropped, one into the sea and another behind the sand dunes. I could not be sure whether they were both German planes but at any rate the Germans left us again promptly. It was exciting while it lasted.

The next little excitement was that a fat and cheerful member of the crew leaning against the guard rails suddenly caused a part of it to give way and in he went with a splash. We picked him up alright. After that we made our slow way back without further incident, arriving in the submarine basin at Dover about midnight. It was quite like being back in the old yachting days on *Chico*, everything was so informal and small again. They were a nice lot of chaps too. I got a bath at the Grand Hotel and slept on a sofa, as the whole of Dover was full.

Saturday, 1st June. The next morning I kept an eye out for *Niger* and she came in and tied up at the Admiralty Pier about 10am. I got a naval car along and came aboard. They were all very glad to see me back, as they were by no means expecting to. They had run another trip that night after resting in Dover during the Friday afternoon, and apparently they had been lucky in getting away before the main aerial attack had taken place.

A destroyer, the *Keith*, had been sunk and machine-gunned and also another ship, with considerable loss. But worst of all the *Skipjack*, one of our lot, and a sister ship to *Niger*, had been hit by a dropping magnetic mine and had simply disappeared in the explosion. No survivors. So they were all rather prostrated and shattered. We were told that we were off again at 6pm that evening for another final evacuation from the beaches. So we all rested up and got what sleep we could. A post arrived which brought me letters from before my leave, including one from little Antsie, and a nice one from Bob. One of Antsie's remarks I loved 'The horse is outside and the rocking is inside the attic'. It is a wonderful relief and pleasure to turn one's mind to one's family at times like these.

We were off to work again at six o'clock. We had an uneventful passage over and began to arrive off the coast as it was getting dark. It was an awe inspiring sight. Dunkirk was burning fiercely. Some oil tanks had been caught afire and there was a great pall of smoke spreading away down the coast. The flames looked livid and evil against it. There was much heavier gunfire now both from the forts of Dunkirk still holding out, and from the enemy artillery a little further inland. The noise was tremendous at times.

I said, 'Mussolini[3] ought to take a good look at this. It might have done him some good.' How anybody can be such a swine as to plunge people deliberately into this sort of thing, I cannot understand. There were occasional shells falling around but we got safely past Dunkirk and anchored as ordered about one and a half miles beyond, close to the beach at Malo-les-Bains.

We were informed that everything would be organised tonight. That there would be plenty of boats operating from the shore. However, as usual nothing seemed to be happening. No boats were about. So we lowered our motor boat and whaler, and another ship's boat that I had borrowed from the SS *Urere* in Dover thinking that this might happen. The Captain had nearly stopped me, saying that everything would be organised, but I didn't trust it and I was right. Knowing the lack of initiative of seamen on their own and fearing that there was no organisation ashore, I suggested that I should go in in charge of the boats and see what I could do. The Captain agreed and I slid down the boat falls into the motor boat just before she cast off.

It was a dark night luckily, though one got a certain amount of light from the flames in Dunkirk. We went ashore and I could see nothing. No troops, no shore organisation, only a lot of large derelict boats. So I told our boats to wait for me and hopped over the side. It was a chilly shock and I found the water up to my chest, but I soon got over that.

I waded ashore and started along the beach towards Dunkirk. About a quarter of a mile along I found a large number of French troops drawn up in platoons. I tried to get them to understand that I had boats ready for them, but they didn't seem at all inclined to move. I kept on having a bayonet pressed into my belly and told not to go by. Finally I found an officer who spoke a little English. I explained to him that we could take off a large number if they would wade into the water. He said they could not move until the commanding officer had given the order. By this time I was getting very fed up with all the delay and trouble, but I agreed to go and see him. So I was taken up into the town and there met the commanding officer. He agreed to start embarkation. So after interminable delays, efforts and coaxing

3. Mussolini took advantage of the German defeat of the French Army to attack France from the south, declaring war on 10 June. Robert cannot have known this on the 1 June! Perhaps Mussolini's aggressive intentions were well understood or perhaps he wrote this down after 10 June.

and pushing I got some poilus[4] to wade out and get into the boats. I think they were slightly put off by the fact that I had persuaded them to pull out and relaunch another boat that was lying on the edge of the water. I filled this boat up, and tried to get them off but I found that I couldn't, the further out we got it made no difference, she still seemed aground. I discovered then that she was holed badly and the soldiers were gradually beginning to sit in the water. However, finally, after much blaspheming I got our three boats off full and got them safely onto the ship.

I had a bad moment when I came back from the town as I could not find the boats anywhere and it took me ages, or what seemed like ages, of shouting before I got in contact. That happened on several occasions that night. As we were again informed that it was the final evacuation it gave one an unpleasant sensation to feel that the Germans were at your back and no boats in front, a sort of nightmare sensation in the dark.

Meanwhile one load of British soldiers had been brought off by a lifeboat, the only boat apparently there, apart from a paddle minesweeper which was running its rowing boats in now. From this lifeboat we were informed that there were some British troops farther to the east. So off we went rather more in that direction. It was terribly difficult to get in contact in the dark with the shallow beach, because the boats could not come close in at all for fear of grounding in the slow surf. So I went ashore and found more French troops perched like brooding birds along an improvised jetty. But they were quite unwilling to go. They had orders not to. One admires their discipline in the circumstances with the German guns sounding ever nearer.

I found three British sentries who said that the remaining British troops, the rear guard, were not through yet and they could not say when they would arrive. As I had three boats of my own waiting and there were two other larger ones waiting from the paddler, I asked a sentry to take me to the commanding officer to see if I could hurry things up. So off we went. One kept on falling down in the dark, as the beach was covered in debris and pitted with shell holes or holes dug for taking cover.

I found a Colonel up among the houses. I asked him if he had

4. A *poilu* in the French Army is a private soldier; hence a general term in English to describe French soldiers.

more to come off. He said he did not know when the rearguard would arrive, or whether it would arrive at all. I asked him if there were any other British troops to take off. He said 'Oh yes, there is a street full here', and there sure enough were a large number of troops waiting among the houses, several hundred of them. So much for organised evacuation from the beaches! I told him we were waiting, so he ordered them to start embarking. Off I trooped again with the soldiers following, falling flat on my nose every now and then and knocking my tin hat over my eyes. Bob would have laughed.

Then we really began to get the embarkation going. We got off about three hundred troops before dawn when we had orders to leave for fear of aerial attack. I had to get them to wade out to their waists to get them into the motor boat and it was a hell of an effort pulling these heavy men in over the side with all their equipment on. One trip we got a dog, the regimental dog. He was heaved aboard, and then later I saw him over the side again. I thought he had fallen over and said 'Hey', and someone said but we can't take him into England from France. But the poor dog, scrabbling round the boat trying to get in, was so pathetic that I heaved him in. I hope he is alright. I saw him safely into *Niger*.

One incident of the night illustrated how near comedy is to tragedy in this sort of work. On one of the trips the boat from the *Urere* had been overfilled. I could not chuck the chaps out, so I tried to take up the tow gently from the motor boat, but the soldiers were clumsy and when she began to heel a little as the tow came on before she finally straightened, they failed to balance her and over she went. I had the motor boat full and so could not pick them up. I went back and saw that they were all holding on to the boat. I told them to hang on while I emptied the motor boat and that I would come back for them. I did so as quickly as possible and picked them up. Just as we were about to leave the overturned boat one of my hands heard a sound from under the boat. We came back alongside and I leant over and shouted into the bottom of the boat and the following unique conversation ensued:

Me (very loud and clear). Is there anyone there?

Muffled Voice (from under boat). Yes. Help.

Me. Well swim out from under the boat and we'll pick you up.

(I had already tried to see if I could tip the boat back, but could not.)

M.V. How can I?

Me.Get to the side of the boat and duck under the edge.

M.V. Which side?

Me. It doesn't matter, either side.

There then ensued a pause and then a sudden spluttering and gurgle on the other side of the boat.

Voice (no longer muffled but very spluttering). Oh my God, what a bloody awful nightmare!

Whereupon we got hold of him and heaved him in, where he lay prostrate and belching. He was nearly all in. It was extremely comic in a way, but very near to tragedy for that poor sod.

As dawn came I was ordered to hoist the boats. I had told the poor chaps anxiously waiting up to their waists in water that, if we could not take them all in time, they must go to Dunkirk where the final evacuation was bound to take place. But again one had that horrid experience of leaving people behind.

It does seem to me incredible that the organisation of the beach work should have been so bad. We were told that there would be lots of boats and that the embarkation of the troops would all be organised. All we should have to do would be stand by to take the chaps aboard. That was what all the little shore boats were being brought over from England for. But to our knowledge only one boatload was brought off that night to us apart from our own efforts, and that lifeboat did nothing more. I yelled and yelled at it on several occasions to come in with us and load up, but it just sheared off and did nothing. One can only come to the conclusion that the civilians and small boats packed up and went home with a few chaps instead of staying there to ferry to the big ships which was their proper job. As for the shore organisation, it simply did not exist. I never once saw any sailors ashore organising and I am certain that, if I had not made the efforts I did to get in contact with the troops, our night would have been wasted. It makes one a bit sick when one hears the organisers of the beach show being cracked up to the skies on the wireless and having DSOs showered on them, because a more disgraceful muddle and lack of organisation I have never seen and could not have contemplated. Of course it may have been good during the first few days, but at the end it was as I have written. If a few officers had been put ashore with a couple of hundred sailors and the boats that I know were over there from time to time, the beach evacuation would have been a different thing. Thousands of troops would have been got off quickly and methodically. However the improvisation of the ferrying boats on the spot seems to have done fairly well in the end, combined with the fact that the defence of Dunkirk was more effective than anticipated which enabled thousands of troops to be taken off during the last few nights from the eastern mole in a way that had not been imagined.

Sunday, 2nd June. When the boats were finally hoisted I found that I was very tired and very hoarse as well as soaking wet. So I had a drink and then changed. I had an artillery officer in my cabin who was very interesting. They all seem to have been very impressed by the dive bombers and the vast number of them, and by the general efficiency of the German forces. The soldiers are not very encouraging, but they were very tired which always makes one pessimistic, and they had been out of touch for a long time. This officer did not even know that Churchill had replaced Chamberlain as Premier.

When I got in touch with the ship's company again I found that they had been shelled a certain amount, some shrapnel falling aboard. I must say I had been so busy all night that I did not know that any shells had fallen near, though I do seem to remember hearing some of the well known 'wheems'. Apparently one of the pieces of shrapnel had hit our old O.A.[5] in the behind, inflicting a slight wound. Now the O.A. is a very frightened man at the best of times, and he was seen running along the decks with his hand clasped to his bottom, whereupon the Captain, so the story goes, to cheer him up, clapped his tin hat over his bum and said 'There. That'll make you safe'.

An RNVR Lieutenant called Mead[6] who was in the lifeboat to which I have referred got a bad shrapnel wound from one of the shells and was brought aboard in a bad condition. He died soon after. Apparently the buzz got round the ship that an RNVR Lieutenant had been brought aboard badly wounded and they all thought it was me. Luckily they were wrong!

We got back to Dover without further incident. Dover made a stirring background somehow to these extraordinary days. Coming back from that low mutilated shoreline to the towering white cliffs

5. Ordnance Artificer, a senior rating in charge of the maintenance of the guns.
6. Lieutenant R.H. Mead RNVR from HMS *Excellent*.

that seem almost to enclose you in Dover harbour, gave me a great sense of security and power. The strength of this seafaring race of ours and its will and power to defy attack seemed typified by those lovely sheer cliffs. They always looked their best too when we were leaving in the evening. With the sun sinking behind them they were outlined stark and majestic, with deep shadows at the base. I shall never forget them.

Well we all went to sleep and woke up to find that our instructions were to arrive at Dunkirk at one o'clock that night and go alongside the eastern mole and embark troops. I wrote a note to Catherine, had a bath and a good dinner and then we started about 8.30pm. Waiting to go on one of these trips was rather like waiting for the start of a motor race, once you are off you feel alright. Pilot was a bit touchy on the way over and would be rude to Skippy, but I endeavoured to keep the peace and succeeded pretty well.

Monday, 3rd June. As we got towards Dunkirk we saw the most incredible pall of smoke that I have ever seen. It was like a vast cliff of blackness. Luckily it extended along the southern edge of the approach channel and not across it, or we should have seen nothing. As we steamed south straight in to it, it looked, in the dark, just as though we were going slap into the foot of an overpoweringly high black cliff. It was most awe inspiring, like the wrath of God, or like Tweedledum and Tweedledee's crow, 'as black as a tar-barrel'. I couldn't help thinking of Lewis Carroll's famous verse. Then, as we came to the channel, we turned east and went along the edge of our black cliff, which was useful in that it most effectively screened us from the shore. In the dark we had some narrow escapes from collision as there were numerous ships coming from the other direction.

Dunkirk was, of course, still well alight. I had no idea a town could burn for so long. We arrived at our appointed time and entered and after some to-ing and fro-ing came alongside the eastern arm. I was looking after the wires aft and we were told to run the wire along forward. In the process the ass who was paying the wire out let a number of coils slip over the stern and it got under the ship and jammed. I thought it had been caught in the starboard propeller. I got another wire out at once, and heaved the ship in with that, and let go the first wire and started to try to clear it. It would not heave in and so I brought it to the winch and began to heave. At first it would not budge and then at last to my intense relief it began to come slowly and finally cleared itself. I think it was the most awful moment I had on the party, because if one screw had been jammed we could never have turned and got out, and might easily therefore have lost the ship. We were assured that tugs would be there for us as this class of ship needs them badly for turning. But there was no tug there, another good example of the organisation!

As soon as I had cleared the wire I dashed up forward to where the gangplanks were already out and French soldiers trooping in. We were one of the later boats as dawn comes about 3am and all the British troops had already been taken off. So we got a mass of poilus. The trouble was they would all follow each other up the first gangplank. We had two others out that were not being used. One or two of our sailors were on the mole trying to induce them to use the other planks as well. So I went on the mole and tried likewise, but they couldn't understand and no amount of pulling or pushing would do it. They struggled on the gangplank to follow their comrades. Finally I hit on the only way to do it. I jumped on the gangplank they were using and stood with my arms out. So that they either had to knock me off or stop. Then once they had stopped they saw we were indicating the other planks and passed on. I had to keep on jumping off and on like a monkey as the traffic required.

It was a fascinating scene, all lit up by the flames of Dunkirk. The graceful hulls of the ships, the mole outlined against the sea and the steady line of steel helmets pouring along the mole and across our little planks to safety. All to the accompaniment of bursting shells, though these were fairly few, almost continuous gunfire and anti-aircraft fire, the tracer bullets looking like a firework display. The sort of scene that is impressed on one forever.

Finally *Niger* seemed to be seething with bodies and the Chief Gunner's Mate came to me at the gangplank and said that the mess deck and all below were full up and the decks getting crowded. I tried to find the Captain but could not in the mêlée. But I found Pilot and together we decided to remove the gangplanks. We did this with some difficulty and then slipped our wires.

We backed out and then came the anxious moment of turning. It seemed as though she would never go and we were getting nearer and nearer to the shallow water. A French smack banged into our bows and bent the stern a little. Then she came back and banged us again, whether in anger or to apologise we don't know because she proceeded to sink. The crew were picked up by another small craft. By this time the anxiety was over and we were pointing outwards and proceeding slowly. The rest of the journey was uneventful and consisted in dodging other vessels and leaving that appalling line of smoke astern.

We went into Folkestone, which looked very peaceful and English in the morning sun. The French soldiers, about seven hundred of them, seemed quite cheerful in spite of the bloody time they must have had. I had a long talk with one large headed giant who was much interested in the depth charges and the gear 'pour enlever les mines'.

Then we went back to Dover and anchored outside and got our heads down ready for the evening's show, which we understood was really to be the final party. I was woken suddenly about 1pm thinking I was in an air raid at Dunkirk. What had happened was that they had been sweeping for a magnetic mine dropped the night before and they had exploded one quite near to us. They make a tremendous detonation.

We got off this time at 10pm. We were one of the last ships to enter Dunkirk waters. All went well until eleven o'clock when suddenly, when I was on watch alone, a thick fog came down. We had to reduce speed and crawl along as we were going into the returning line of traffic down the swept channel from Dunkirk. The fog persisted and we nearly had one crash. By twelve thirty we were still two hours steaming at full speed from Dunkirk and no signs of the fog lifting and so we had to abandon the trip as we could not go there after daylight.

Tuesday, 4th June. We turned round and steamed slowly back. Then, when we had picked up our bearings by a bell buoy, we anchored out of the channel. When it was light, about 4.30am, we proceeded and found a lot of other vessels beginning to go ahead too, some with soldiers on, the earlier ones, and some without. We got back slowly to Dover and tied up to a buoy seemingly right under the cliff itself.

And so ended the battle of Dunkirk. I only wish we had been one of the earlier ships and had got in on the Monday night as well. I would not have missed it all for anything.

My general impressions are three in number.

1. The almost incredible freedom on the whole from enemy aerial attack during the considerable period I was over there. There were occasional raids but I had expected continual air attack. Many naval officers complained that the RAF were not there, and perhaps they should have kept a continual patrol of a few aircraft there all the time, as that might have saved some of the ships that were sunk by bombs. But on the whole the RAF must have been doing their stuff somewhere to hold the German Luftwaffe off as they did.

2. The extraordinary lack of any effort at organising the boat work on the beaches. Typical mess and muddle and people managing to get away with it somehow by extra effort and muddling through. This, mind you, is an impression from Friday onwards only. There may have been organisation and efficiency on the beaches before this, and I think the work in Dunkirk itself was very well organised.

3. The quiet steady ranks of soldiers waiting their turn. They were wonderful. Thank God we got them off.

We had a sleep and then went ashore for dinner at the Grand Hotel, Dover, which was pretty poor. Then a night in, the first for a week.

Chapter Five

Invasion Threat
June – September 1940

On the 5 June 1940 *Niger* returned to Grimsby and minesweeping. Most of the ship's company were sent on leave to recover from Dunkirk but Robert was left with the small retard party on board.

Friday, 7th June. Had dinner with the Captain at the Royal in the evening. He asked me whether I would like to take over as First Lieutenant. He said he did not suppose I would want to give up the idea of an MTB, but that if I did and would like to be his Number One he would get in touch with the Admiralty at once and fix it. I was flattered but did not accept because I prefer navigating and think I should very much like an MTB if I can get one. He says he will try again.

I got through to Catherine on the 'phone. It was lovely to hear her again. I hope for a few days leave when the others come back, but it isn't certain. I heard from her of Andrew Le Grice's death in France. Poor Andrew and Ann and the twins. It brings it all home to one. I like the fighting when I get it, but this sort of thing is so sad. Aunt Dorothy and Uncle Harry will be devastated. I hope they don't lose Charles too.[1]

There is one thing I am happy about. If I am killed I know Catherine will bear it very bravely; she is like that over big things and she knows she has the children to fend for, and the children are too young, bless them, to grieve very much.

---

1. Andrew and Charles Le Grice were Robert's first cousins. Andrew was serving as a lieutenant in the Duke of Cornwall's Light Infantry in France and was killed in action on the retreat to Dunkirk.

Saturday, 8th June. The Captain completed his report on our part in the Dunkirk action. It was short and to the point. As it is probably the only time I shall ever have a chance of being mentioned in dispatches, I quote the part that deals with my day ashore:

'Lieut. R.P. Hichens RNVR was left behind. He moored two yachts as pontoons, secured grass lines to the pier of lorries and organised the boats pully-hauly on these lines. I was later informed that his work made the most tremendous difference to the rate of embarkation of troops, apart from making it comparatively safe and avoiding the risk of drowning soldiers which was extremely high in the early morning when boats were capsizing frequently.'

There was also a short description of my activities on Saturday night in getting in touch with the troops and getting them off.

Monday, 10th June. Italy entered the war this evening. Expected but still a shock. One could not conceive that they would either be so foolish or such cold-blooded jackals. It might mean the Straits[2] for us. I hope not, I'd rather be in on the party at home, and there will be a party, and I can keep in touch with my family better.

Tuesday, 11th June. We must pray for the French and help them all we can. They must be going through hell. The German armoured columns have reached Rouen. To think that soon they may be rumbling up that lovely road that we have flown up so often in the Aston to the Café de la Foret. Will Monsieur and Madame be still there, or will they have fled?

Wednesday, 12th June. A quiet day sweeping. We cut four mines towards the end of the day. The first we have cut for ages. Again quite like old times peacefully sweeping up mines instead of Dunkirking. I think that in many conditions minesweeping is as dangerous as a trip to Dunkirk, but one doesn't think so as the danger is so much less evident.

We got back late in the evening to Grimsby. I suppose tomorrow we shall start on Operation Dagger,[3] the patrolling of our section of the east coast to give warning of invasion and then to attack the invader. Skippy and I worked out orders for our patrol during the

2. Presumably Straits of Gibraltar, i.e. to the Mediterranean.
3. The operation for protecting the coast of Britain from invasion.

three days Dunkirk leave and it is to start as soon as any necessary mine clearance is effected.

My work on the charts today involved the erasing of a great number of lights all around the coast, preparing for invasion. Le Havre light vessel and the Royal Sovereign light vessel were amongst them. It was only about this time last year that I rounded them in our triumphant Channel race in *Marie Victoire*. It gives added point to the phrase 'The lights are going out all over Europe'. I too am afraid it will be a very long time before they are lit again.

Thursday, 13th June. The thirteenth is always my lucky day. I came into the wardroom about 10 o'clock expecting to go to sea at any moment and was suddenly confronted with a signal from the Admiralty: '*Niger* is to be taken in hand tomorrow the 14th for a refit.' Everybody began fixing things and I agreed to splitting leave so that we could all have the maximum time possible, especially as I hadn't been out for the short leave. So I went off at four o'clock and caught the last train to town, thereby saving me a whole day extra in Cornwall.

Friday, 14th June. I arrived home to find Barbary ominously awaiting me. From him I gathered that Catherine was not too well and when I got home I found that he had indeed not exaggerated. Poor Catherine had gone down the night before with pneumonia and was feeling like nothing on earth after having the terrific cure that they give nowadays and which Dr Lanyon had luckily applied very quickly. Added to that the news in France was getting graver and graver, so that prospects of fun and gaiety on leave were not exactly promising. But the children were in exceptionally good form. It was very hot and we bathed repeatedly and poor Catherine sweltered. And in the background was the horrible feeling, 'would France pack up?'

Saturday, 15th June. If it was unlucky that Catherine was ill, it was a very good thing that I did get leave at this time. The 'phone went at about nine o'clock this morning and who should be on it but Loveday. She was pretty astonished when she heard me. She and Robin were leaving Guernsey by 'plane on Monday. I was to book sleepers and arrange for them to go out to the farm right away. All very exciting though sad for Loveday. It was nice to feel that I had somewhere suitable for them to go.

The Germans are entering Paris today. There is to be no miracle of the Marne this time. I wonder if the French can possibly hold together.

Sunday, 16th June. Very hot again. Been bathing twice with the children and had a good look round the farm. Somehow I have an uncomfortable feeling that France is going to pack up, reading between the lines in the news. The suspense is horrible.

I rang up Loveday and she said there was no room on Monday and she would be coming either by boat Wednesday night or by 'plane on Thursday.

Monday, 17th June. The eight o'clock news said that Reynaud had resigned and Petain and Weygand virtually taken over. That seemed to indicate that the army had taken over and one hoped, but at one o'clock the blow came. How could Petain[4] and Weygand do it? Poor France! Somehow I feel better now I know. I wonder why it is, but uncertainty is always worse than the actual news however bad that may be. Now we know that we have got to look to ourselves only. I have an idea that England will respond wonderfully to this setback. She is always greatest in taking reverses.

Tuesday, 18th June. The 'phone went at about six thirty this morning. It was Len to say that he was trying to get Loveday and Robin off by boat that night, but that things were difficult and if he couldn't manage it, would it be possible for me to do anything about it. I said I thought I might and would see about it and he was to let me know as soon as he got anything fixed, or if he wanted me to come over.

I thought of all the people I might get a boat from and decided that the only hope was a fishing boat from Porthleven or Mousehole. I went into Falmouth and met George Angove[5] who told me that he understood that they had all been called up by the Admiralty and were lying in Falmouth waiting to go, and that volunteers were being called for to take them to France. So I thought that this was my chance and went along to the base and volunteered to go to France provided I could get back by Thursday when I had to rejoin my ship. They kept me waiting a long time and then said that the boats would

4. Marshall Petain, hero of Verdun in the First World War, formed a new Government and sought armistice terms from the Germans.
5. George Angove was a fishing boat owner who lived in Flushing.

not be going yet, but that they would probably have another job for me soon. So I gave them my number and left.

Churchill made a fine speech in Parliament today. The bit about Dunkirk I thoroughly endorse, although I have heard many naval officers disagree with me. The thing that impressed me most about Dunkirk was the lack of German aircraft, taking things all in all. The other piece concerns our particular job in 'Dagger'. We patrol to intercept an invading force. Our primary duty is then to give warning by wireless and when that is accomplished to attack the enemy regardless of odds. I fear we may suffer heavily before the main British supports can arrive, but it will be a rather glorious affair, and if it occurs I can think of no way in which I should prefer to meet my end, and meet it some day I must, a thing one is rather inclined to overlook in one's youth. We are in a tight spot, but we are relying on no one now except ourselves, and so we know where we are, and I think at bottom we are rather thankful.

Wednesday, 19th June. The 'phone went again at six thirty. This time it was Len to say that he had got them off by the boat the night before. I promised to let him know they arrived safely.

Still very hot. At twelve o'clock the 'phone went again. This time of all incredible things it was Mort[6] on the 'phone. He was waiting at Falmouth station having just arrived from France. He looked well on the whole and as red in the face as ever. I spent a hectic two hours with him, seemingly almost totally connected with beer. I took £2 worth of beer up to his men who were sitting in the hot sun near the station. The second case I left in the car with Bob, while I went to speak for a moment with Mort, and when I returned I could not see the car at all for the pack of soldiers. All that was visible was Bob's head sticking out of the sunshine roof, handing out bottles as fast as he could. He didn't seem a bit frightened and I thought he did very well.

Mort left and the next excitement was Loveday and Robin arriving. After a good deal of dashing about I finally got them only about an hour late, which really was very good considering the number of troop trains operating. Considering that Loveday is really a refugee, I thought she was wonderfully cheerful. One could hardly realise that she had been forced out of her home, leaving virtually everything she

6. Mortimer Morris Goodall, Robert's co-driver at Le Mans.

has behind, possibly never to see it again. It seemed much more like a visit somehow. Robin was in great form, bicycle and all. I finally deposited them at the farm about ten o'clock of a lovely moonlit night.

Thursday, 20th June. The last day of my leave. Still glorious weather. We had a lovely bathe at Durgan.[7]

The time for the train seemed to tear round and alas the taxi I had ordered just did not come. So I had to take a most hurried and blasphemous departure in the Rover which of course elected to break its throttle connection on this particular occasion, with the result that I shot into a completely full up 1st class carriage just as the train was going, with my hands covered in oil and sweat pouring from my brow. I think I was more concerned than my fellow passengers, who had all just arrived from France and could not be surprised at anything.

I must break Robert's breathless narration of the effect that the fall of France had on him while on his leave in Cornwall. Almost every reader will remember that the collapse of France followed hard on the heels of Dunkirk. It was all over at Dunkirk on the 4 June and the Germans entered Paris on the 15 June. Petain signed an armistice on the 17 June, ending the fighting. Falmouth was an obvious destination for many refugees from France, including that part of the BEF that had retreated westwards rather than to Dunkirk, and Robert found himself in the thick of it during his leave. The coincidence of the arrival of his old co-driver from Le Mans days, Mort Morris Goodall, apparently accompanied by some of his soldiers from France, must have made an extraordinary week seem even more amazing.

Friday, 21st June. We were an hour and a half late into London, but I had my grilled sole at Browns Hotel soon after nine even so. A tribute to the GWR[8] in these troubled times. London was looking lovely in bright sunshine, but with a fresh cool breeze. Regent Street, with all its flags flying, was looking as only Regent Street can. It is the only big city street that I can think of with a curve in it. I think perhaps that is why it is so fascinating. But London was ominously empty.

7. Durgan beach on the Helford River.
8. Great Western Railway, the railway company for the West of England.

Nelson's prayer:

May the Great God, whom I worship, grant to my country and for
the benefit of Europe in general, a great and glorious victory; and
may no misconduct in any one tarnish it; and may humanity after
victory be the predominant feature in the British Fleet. For myself,
individually, I commit my life to Him who made me, and may His
blessing light upon my endeavours for serving my country faithfully.
To Him I resign myself and the just cause which is entrusted to me
to defend.

I know of no prayer more appropriate for the present times. It seems
exactly to fit the position of the Navy today. It is interesting and
encouraging to think that England was in just the same danger then
and that Nelson realised the vast implications of his defeat or victory
at Trafalgar. The same will apply exactly when we meet the invasion
of the German and Italian (+ ? French) fleets and fight it out, as now
seems almost inevitable. Let us hope we shall be granted another
Trafalgar.

I arrived at the ship about eight thirty, to find her in dry dock. The
trouble is we are all expected to go ashore when an air raid warning
goes and go into the nearby shelters. These are just concrete rooms
on the surface with nothing in them and therefore frightfully uncomfortable. As the air raid warning usually lasts for about four hours the
prospect is pretty bleak.

Saturday, 22nd June. Sure enough there was a proper air raid. The
siren went about eleven thirty. I went with the rest to the nearest
shelter, but after about twenty minutes, nothing very much having
happened, I returned to my trap. I'd rather risk being bombed than
sitting in such discomfort for hours. It is very true that shelters
should be made as habitable as possible. Soon after I had dozed off
the bombs began to drop. It was a rather uncomfortable feeling
because if one had dropped at all close, the blast would have knocked
the ship off her struts and she would fall over in the dry dock and if
she came on my side it would kill me. So whenever a bomb dropped
near I would hop out of my trap and go and stand in the middle of
the ship until all seemed quiet. A tiresome performance. Two salvoes
dropped pretty close; out in the river I should guess. The all clear
didn't go until about 4am. How everybody in the shelters stuck it I

don't know. They must be very frightened of bombs.

Thursday, 27th June. An order has come out that naval officers may not keep a private diary, I presume for fear lest it should fall into the hands of the enemy and prove of use to him. Alas therefore I must give up my diary. I propose, however, to jot down notes on happenings of interest and my personal thoughts and reactions to them, avoiding any reference to matters that would be censurable.

Fortunately for historians, the order that officers should not keep diaries was widely ignored, the best possible example being set by General Sir Alan Brooke, shortly to become Chief of the Imperial General Staff, who kept arguably the most important diary of a serving officer in the Second World War, without which our understanding of what really happened at the highest level of decision-making would be far more deficient. Robert felt that he had to obey at least the letter if not the spirit of the order, so that we have an entirely different narrative, commenting on the events around him and his experiences but without dates. It is inevitably hard to follow the precise sequence of events, but Robert remained in HMS *Niger* until the beginning of October 1940, a period in which, although *Niger* continued to conduct her normal duties as a fleet sweeper, she was also part of the initial naval response to any German invasion of the British Isles, known as Operation Dagger. The threat of that invasion dominates the narrative.

The diary proper resumes on Monday, 24 December 1940 when he was given command of *MASB14*. Presumably by then whatever sense of discipline had caused him more or less to obey the order finally evaporated and he resumed his private journal. Perhaps widespread disregard of the order had come to his ears.

July 1940:

My last bit of refit leave went pleasantly and all too quickly. It was lovely out at the farm, and being there I saw much more of Catherine who was still unable to do anything much. The air raids on Falmouth began while I was there. It was interesting to see the reactions of all the people I knew, and who as yet had not been touched actively by the war. I felt quite like an old campaigner. It was extraordinary the way the German bombers came over our farm. There I would stand in a field, goggling up at them and quite helpless. Almost a dispassionate observer, because one felt they would not bomb a farm when they had Falmouth in view. The children, of course, were thrilled, and knowing nothing about the terrors of bombing, looked upon it all as a great excitement.

The last day is always rather terrible. And then going round to see the children just before leaving for the train. They are always asleep and look so attractive. It is unlikely that life can provide much worse partings than these. With the invasion of England so imminent and in the position I am, so to speak in the very front, the outer line. And yet I wouldn't have it otherwise. To be safely in a shore job would be impossible now.

The journey up to London was good and I slept well. It seems to me a great tribute to our air defence that the train was so well up to time, more than three weeks after the collapse of France. Breakfast as usual at Browns. After spending sometime at Mackrell's, I went to Hatchards[9] and bought the family presents, books seeming the most sensible things these days with them out at the farm and winter coming on. Altogether I spent quite a long time in the shop and was served by some nice old men of about seventy-five, just the sort of people you would expect there. One of them, while suggesting books, said 'Do you like Robert Hichens?' He was much impressed when I said that I did not much, perhaps because I was his nephew. We then had quite a long chat about him as he is well known there evidently. It was a rather attractive little interlude in a lonely day in London. It seemed to take one back to pre-war days and beyond. Talking of my family to these nice old men, and in my uniform, on my way to sea, in I suppose England's darkest hour. It seemed to make vivid the contrast between the present and the past.

Back on the ship I found myself very busy again at once. Lots of chart work to get on with. As I did chart corrections today the sun was shining and there was a hard wind. The country around looked lovely, in spite of being low and flat. 'Coot Club' country, and I couldn't help being reminded of Bobby's book and the description of the country. I thought of my last reading in bed to him. In these days when death for me may come suddenly from above or below at any moment, those times are incredibly precious. It is impossible to put one's feelings into words. It makes one put first things first, and realise how at bottom the only thing that really matters to you is your

9. Hatchards, the famous bookshop in Piccadilly.

family. Everything else could go provided one was left with their company. At any rate it makes it easy in a way to fight and if need be die in preserving them.

The strong wind outside reminded me suddenly of the same strong wind almost always blowing at Treworval. How it blasted round us in the fields while we were pulling the plants a week or two ago, and how if Bobby pulled one just windward of me, the wind would often blow bits of the earth off the root into my eyes. And then a destroyer would come by at speed and I was brought back to reality. She looked a fine sight though on that bright morning. Whenever I see a destroyer I think with joy how Hitler must dislike ships and the sea.

I still revel in the feeling of being in sole charge of the ship especially at night. It was fun too swinging her for compass adjustment. I found I could handle her very well, it making all the difference in the world to have a little head or stern way on before putting the other screw astern or ahead. It is fun that feeling of control of a biggish (to me) ship. You feel isolated high up on the bridge and lord of all you survey.

The other night I had the first watch during Churchill's speech, and so did not hear it, which was rather tiresome. Afterwards the Captain came up and told me all about it. I suppose our position is about as dangerous as is possible in view of the threatened invasion, but I couldn't help being full of joy at being in that position. Being on the bridge of one of HM ships, being talked to by the Captain as an equal, and knowing that she was to be in my sole care for the next few hours. Who would not rather die like that than live as so many poor people have to in crowded cities at some sweating indoor job. There is perhaps a peculiar irony that I should be able to appreciate my good fortune even now, but it is better than being glum. Furthermore it does one's companions good.

It is a funny life this wondering almost academically how long one is going to survive. I bought an expensive bottle of hair oil in London some months ago, the first I ever have. It is nice because it is spirit and therefore not at all sticky or greasy and it has only the slightest of smells. Every morning when I take a drop I wonder whether I shall live to finish the bottle; a sort of feeling of academic interest.

I record this funny little fact, because in days to come if we do survive to peace again, it will be interesting to look back to and analyse one's main impressions and reactions while living in these times. One of the chief things that impresses me is that I am not afraid of death and therefore I welcome any action. The only sort of feelings of fear that I get, (if you can call it fear, it being more a sort of pessimistic and disturbing wondering) is when say I am lying in my bunk and I think supposing the torpedo, or the mine, or the bomb comes now. Would it twist me up in the folding shattering metal, or would it knock me out mercifully at once without feeling? Would there be agonising moments while one was drowned in a trap or while one saw the blood leaving one with an arm or a leg torn off? It is no use speculating on these things and it only occurs when not in action. But one cannot help thinking of them sometimes. The matter is so important and ever present. One will never know the answer in time to set it down for those that come after.

Until I knew something of the workings of these things I thought that people got DSOs and DSCs and VCs for being outstandingly brave and devoted to duty in the face of danger. I find now that the great majority of them are just handed out to fairly senior officers once there is a war on, entirely regardless of whether they are particularly efficient or brave or not. The Captain of the dan-laying trawler who used to follow us when we were sweeping up at the Tyne got a DSO when that field was cleared, although his was the one ship that was absolutely safe, as it simply followed where the sweepers had cleared the water and dropped dans. Then I find that the Captain of the *Halcyon* got a DSO for Dunkirk, when in fact he was actually on leave at the time and never went there. They meant it for M/S 4, our Captain, and thought he was still Captain of the *Halcyon* and leading the flotilla from that ship. It just shows how much notice they take about enquiring into people's conduct if they can actually dole it out to someone on leave.

With the prospect of increased fighting, both aerial and surface, the Captain has appointed me Flotilla Gunnery Officer. I take it as a great compliment though it will mean a good bit more work for me. He is trying to get a fully qualified Gunner and in the meantime I must do my best, with little or no training. Fortunately it seems that my common-sense will take me quite a long way and has done so far. I shall have to go round to the other ships in the flotilla and try to shake things up a bit. I have also had my Watchkeeping Certificate sent in, and the Captain has said that I am qualified for watchkeeping in a destroyer if need be. So I feel that I am beginning to be quite a useful member of the Navy, a thing that seemed a very long way off six months ago, soon after I joined my ship.

End of July:

Today we went forth to swing compasses. We were starting up from anchor in the roads. I was in the chartroom correcting charts, the Captain was ashore and Pilot was in charge. Apparently a trawler got under way rapidly with her anchor ball still up and made a blackguard rush at us, ramming us just opposite the wardroom and making a large hole above water. I came out of the chartroom, just before the crash, to see about a signal to do with the recognition signals that I deal with. I saw the trawler very close to just as Pilot started his avoiding action. I cannot help thinking Pilot must have seen it after he should have, but the trawler could have avoided a bad crash by turning to port or going astern, both of which he apparently failed to do.

Anyway the result was that instead of going on patrol and thence to Harwich where the rest of the flotilla were congregating to sweep mines laid by German E-boats, we had to be in dock for nine days undergoing repair. I got a week's leave and went straight to Cornwall where I have all that I love, my wife, my children and my land. It is so heavenly there by comparison with being at sea in this war that one goes into a sort of daze as the time goes by, hoping so much that the time will not pass that you almost cannot appreciate the joy of being there.

I had a glorious week working most of the time on the farm. That is the life for me if I can ever get back to it. I drove the tractor to cut two of our fields of corn. I loved it except for the time when the poor little rabbits were caught at the end. I used to wonder sometimes whether my dislike of inflicting pain or anxiety or even seeing it done on something helpless was a sign of being a rather soft sort of man. The more normal one, who didn't seem to worry about the feelings of a fox or a bird or a rabbit was a tougher and braver man who would be more use than me in a tight corner. My motor racing experiences began to make me see that it was not so and my war experiences have now convinced me. Cruel and so-called tough men are not usually brave when it is their bodies that are threatened. The man with finer sensibilities has the finer spirit and can stand up to it better when it is he that is in danger. I am convinced of that from my present observations. I hope my sons will not be cruel, but will be brave. Those two traits cover half the duty of man I think.

On returning from leave I had my usual breakfast at Browns and then went to the Admiralty. I saw a very nice Lt. Commander who implied that I was doing a useful job where I was. I said I was enjoying my present job alright but that I was very keen on MTBs and what chance was there. He said he couldn't promise anything, but that I was on the list of people recommended and had a pink mark against my name which meant that I was thought specially suitable. I have at least satisfied myself that I am well on the list and specially marked and that is the best I can do. I must wait until the boats are built.

Back at Grimsby again I very quickly slipped back into the old routine with a lot of work to do. I have come to the conclusion that if the guns are to be used effectively on this ship it is entirely up to me. I must push everything on and get training forward. I took the 0.5 under my wing and fitted it and trained until I think it is one of the best equipped about. Now I must do the same with all the rest of the gunnery, including the controlled side of it as opposed to high angle stuff. I got protection put at all the guns which pleased the men very much and gave them more confidence. I got their sights made right and fixed rapid action control at the gun in case of sudden air attack with no warning. All these things have pleased them and given them confidence so that I feel we are coming on.

The air battles over Britain are intensifying and I believe that they will prove to be the crux of the war. Sixty-one German planes downed yesterday, with seventy-eight, one hundred and sixty-nine and seventy-one in the previous three days. Can they stick it? One feels an immense joy at being British, the only people who have stood up to the air war blackmail. We've got to take it and beat them at their own game. I keep training my guns' crews and if I get tired or fed up I think of that. We may be able to bring some down if we get efficient. Who knows? The Navy's role in the war can be summed up in the reply Joffre[10] made to a question as to 'Who won the battle of the Marne in 1914?' (meaning which commander). His reply was 'I don't know who won the battle, but I can tell you who would have been blamed if it had been lost.'

10. General Joffre commanded the French Army in 1914 and fought the defensive Battle of the Marne which prevented the Germans from reaching Paris.

That is the position of the Navy. The RAF may seem to win the war for us in the end but the Navy would have lost it if it failed to do its stuff.

When we were at our buoy with *Salamander* alongside us, I was sitting sprawled in a chair in the wardroom with a gin as I was pretty tired. In came Price, the doctor of the *Salamander*, and rather a friend of mine. As he came in he shook hands with me and said 'congratulations'. I didn't know what he meant and thought he was being funny. Nothing more happened for some time and then he said quite casually 'What does it feel like to be a bloody hero', or something like that. I said I didn't understand him, and then he said 'Surely you've got a DSC. I'm sure I saw your name in the list'. He dashed off to get the Times when he gathered that I knew nothing whatever about it, and sure enough there it was. The Commanding Officer and Engineer Officer of *Salamander* had the DSO and DSC respectively so the two ships started a party. I remember rather little of it I fear. My last recollection was taking a beautiful shot at a teed up glass with a mashie, and I understand that I was sitting happily for sometime with people knocking glasses off my head. I do not remember this, but I am assured of its truth. However these things don't happen everyday.

Everybody seemed to think that I had well deserved my decoration, though I am inclined to doubt it and certainly had not expected it for a minute. They have been very liberal with them and I heard a number of the other decorations much criticised.

Apparently my efforts are being appreciated by the guns' crews themselves, because the Chief Gunner's Mate was talking to me yesterday and asking whether I could do anything to get the crews trained in *Hussar*, a ship in the 6th MSF which is working with us at the moment, because he had been aboard there and they were complaining that they were getting no instruction. He then said that he thought our crews were getting on very well and feeling quite different about air-attack and much more confident because at last they had mastered the idea and technique of modern A.A. firing and felt that they could do something. It makes all the difference to morale once they get that sort of interested hopeful attitude, instead of the uninterested, bored outlook I had to deal with first of all.

I think that to have got this result is the most satisfactory thing I have done so far in the Navy. A real concrete result. As the Captain said when we were discussing my DSC over a glass of port, 'Although you thoroughly deserve your decoration for the Dunkirk affair, I think really your work in training the guns' crews is more deserving'. I am a very lucky man, as I do not consider that I did more than thousands of others, and some poor sods got killed for their efforts instead of decorations. But then so much of life is luck!

Another night out with sweeping at dawn. We also practised night sweeping. I like these nights at sea. There is a solitude and quietness which is pleasant and not possible to find during the day or on land. There was a bright moon from two o'clock onwards and I was on watch. I walked up to the extreme bow of the ship. It is always lovely in that position. You feel isolated and can only hear the murmur of the water on the bows. We have one quite young lad on the flag deck, a future yeoman of signals. He is a very good type. He does his work well and never complains. They are the backbone of our Navy, chaps like that. They have nothing but discomfort and danger, and very little to look forward to, but they just go on cheerfully doing their work. They are the real seamen that England can count on.

There is one lovely story of Dunkirk that I have just been told. As it is true I must put it on record. I was told it by the Captain of a corvette. He was returning from one of his trips to Dunkirk and came across a lifeboat packed with soldiers. It turned out afterwards that they had been afloat for thirty-six hours and had lost their way. As the corvette drew past them to stop ahead the Captain sang out 'Haven't you got any oars aboard?' A cockney voice replied immediately. 'We ain't got no (wh)'ores aboard, but we've got a fucking sergeant major'. That's the sort of spirit that is going to give Hitler his quietus. Those men had been through it before ever they got into the boats.

Out again at 18.30 on Sunday. We went down to the Downs by night and swept up through the channel until dawn. It was rather exciting sweeping at night. You couldn't of course see if you were cutting mines. One has some rivalry with the signalmen as they are trained all their lives at spotting things through glasses and our yeoman is very good. It is very tiring being up all night and on the lookout. We had all guns closed up for fear of E-boat attack.

This is the second reference that Robert makes to E-boats, his ultimate enemy once in MGBs. They were about 110 feet long, capable of nearly forty knots and armed with both guns and torpedoes. The Germans called them *Schnellboote* (Fast boat). The British called them E-boats, the E being thought to be short for Enemy!

We swept all day. We swept the Southbound convoy through and the Northbound convoy back. We took them to and from the mouth of the Thames where the greatest air battles of history were going on. They were big convoys with a lot of large ships, all going to and from the port of London under the noses of the Luftwaffe and within forty miles of their air bases. It seemed very impudent and it made one realise how vital sea power is compared with almost anything else. It would have taken train upon train to carry the contents of one of those big steamers. Germany would give a lot to have one of those convoys in a week from the outer world and we have two a day into London alone. It makes one realise what a potent long term weapon the blockade is.

When we had finished with the convoys we went to search another area farther offshore about thirty miles out where it was suspected that E-boats had been laying mines. While we were on this search we had double Oropesas out and about four thirty I was on watch alone. I saw what looked like a bit of wreckage floating about a couple of miles off on the starboard bow. I took no more notice until about eight minutes later something suddenly sat up in the bit of wreckage and started waving and shouting. It was a little rubber float with an airman in it. I reported to the Captain and went hard astarboard and began to get in our sweeps.

Even after he must have realised that we had seen him the poor chap went on waving and shouting. When we had got our sweeps in we lowered a whaler and the Captain sent me away in the boat armed with a revolver in case he was a balmy Jerry. I was to wave my hat if he was English, and just wave my hand if he was German. We rowed up to him. He had a flying coat on and his face was all queer and twisted so that I could not tell at once whether he was German or British. So as we approached I got my revolver ready in case. I sang out to him and then waved my hat.

He was rather a ghastly sight because when he crashed he had broken in the right hand side of his upper lip below the nostril and one half of his lip was in place and the other half all smashed in. However he

102

was able to climb into the boat and we returned towing his rubber boat. He seemed quite normal and calm and I was amazed to find that he had been in the boat since two o'clock on Sunday night. It was then 5pm on Wednesday. He had been in the boat for sixty-three hours, wet and with this wound and yet he could talk and behave coolly and normally and climb the monkey ladder into *Niger* without help. His name was Pilot Officer M.S. Burberry, RAFVR. Apparently he was returning from a bombing raid over Hanover on Sunday night and was getting quite near Harwich and was coming down to see the sea when he thinks he must have dozed at the controls because the next thing he realised they had crashed into the sea. He scrambled into the boat and saw nothing of the rest of the crew except one man who was swimming wildly away shouting 'mercy, mercy'. He could do nothing and thinks the man was badly concussed and understood nothing. This was on Sunday at 2am. When it got light he found that the boat was attached to some of the wreckage of the aeroplane and as he went to remove it he got a nasty shock because he found the head of the other pilot bobbing about just below him. He said it was the one time he felt really sick.

Then he proceeded to drift about for sixty-three hours. He had some iron rations and a little water and a flask of rum which he was reserving for the last to get really tight on when he thought there was no more hope. He was wet and cramped and could get no sleep because he had to bail out frequently. He saw a number of ships in convoy but some way off and no one saw him. Towards the end his rubber float began to leak and he realised that it could not last much longer. Altogether I should surmise that I have never been so welcome to anyone as I was on that occasion. Poor devil he must have had a hell of a time, but I take my hat off to him. He was cool and quiet and answered questions normally and without exaggeration, and physically I think he was marvellous to be able to clamber about after all that. We took him straight in and landed him about eight o'clock. He sent off wires to his people who must have known that one of our planes had not returned for several days.

I was just turning in very tired at about nine thirty having been up and feeling bloody with this inoculation since three o'clock in the morning, when Bang! There was a loud explosion which shook the ship. I had to put my rubber boots and mackintosh on over my pyjamas and go up to the 0.5. I found the whole of Parkeston Quay lit up with a fire raging on it. The bang had been a bomb dropped just astern of us. I went to the 0.5 and waited there with the crew. There were a number of searchlights, about twenty, all playing over a patch of sky to the north of us. Presently they got the plane and held him there firmly. Guns went off and there were quite a number of bursts near him. Meanwhile we appeared to be in grave danger as a lot of silly trawlers alongside Parkeston Quay were firing right over us and as the plane sank lower the bullets were getting quite close. You could see the tracers just over our masts. I thought if someone made a slip or the plane got any lower we should be for it. Presently the plane went away seawards dodging and some British recognition flares shot out showing that fighters were on his tail.

We now go to instant notice for speed each night and that's about all we do. It's most trying this hanging about waiting for something to happen. I wish they would lay some mines or send us on patrol. I hate not being at sea. And there is no prospect of anything else except Purge.[11] If that happens, as it well may any night, I am afraid our chances are poor. What with the invading German forces, the dive bombers, and our own guns ashore, we shall have a poor time. I suppose really we are just a bit of an outpost, so to speak. The intention is that we should engage them for a little while and destroy as much as we can before we are ourselves destroyed, while the big stuff is coming up from more distant and safer parts. I wonder whether they will invade? If they do, I do not think they will succeed, but I rather doubt if I will survive to know.

Meanwhile we just wait. The air warfare is pretty intense. Last night was the first real large-scale bombing of London by night.[12] It was bound to come sooner or later if Hitler's other plans did not succeed. I think it is a sure sign of weakness and that his other plan of going for military objectives has failed.

We sometimes almost continuously hear aircraft going overhead, and on moonlight nights you will suddenly see the dark and ominous shape of an aeroplane appear silhouetted pitch black in a rift in the clouds. They look like some evil bird of prey at night, especially if seen close to amongst dark ragged clouds flying across the face of the moon.

11. Purge was an anti invasion plan for destroyers based in east coast ports.
12. The first large-scale night raid on London was Saturday, 7 September 1940. Some 300 tons of bombs were dropped and about 2,000 people killed or seriously injured.

We often go down off Ramsgate and the flak (A.A. fire) at night visible over London and the French coast is fascinating. Every now and then it flares up to a crescendo of fireworks, large flashes, orange flares and clouds of red and green incendiary bullets. Bob would love to watch them.

Well another and one might think particularly crucial week has gone past and so far (touch wood) no invasion.[13] The weather is now turning our ally. This perpetual standing by, and calls to instant notice in the middle of the night, become rather wearing. One would rather have a good battle and get it over with! I wonder if we shall live to be old men and tell our grandsons how we stood by day after day, week after week and even month after month waiting to fight the Germans if they should dare to entrust themselves to the sea. I wonder if we shall, or if they will. The answer to one is probably dependent on the answer to the other!

A sudden flap this morning. We are all to sail forthwith for Sheerness, a very unpleasant prospect these days. Well we sailed and I found it very interesting at last proceeding up the entrance to the world's most famous river. I have sailed in most of the waters around England now, but not here. It is in a way attractive, quite high cliffs alternating in a curious way with low lying marshes. There were a lot of H.M. ships in Sheerness. It is good to see the concrete signs of Britain's resistance and sea power in the shape of large convoys moving regularly in and out of the Thames in spite of the Nazi's boastful nonsense.

Well we hadn't been there many hours when the purpose of our visit was made apparent to us. There is to be a sort of Zeebrugge blitz on Calais and Boulogne. Two large oil tankers have been prepared and each filled with seven thousand tons of oil and kerosene. These will be taken, manned by seven brave men, into the respective harbours and set fire by explosives on a time fuse. The explosives will blow out the sides of the ship and all the oil will spread flaming over the water and be taken up into the harbours on a flood tide. If all goes well we shall see such a blaze as never before and one which will burn up everything in the basins and docks. We minesweepers have been split into two groups of three ships each, one group to sweep each fire ship into a port. We are for Boulogne.

13. Given that Robert was appointed to HMS *Osprey* on 6 October 1940, we can date this entry to about 20 September.

It is just like the old story of Drake's fire ships burning the Armada off Calais, only the party will be just about one hundred times more terrific than in those days. The seven men after setting their fuses in the entrance to the harbour will leap aboard an MTB and hope to make a clean getaway.[14]

We have chiefly to contend with shore batteries and what the Germans call 'Flakshiffs' which are hulks fitted with heavy A.A. and low angle armaments which are stationed off the entrance to harbours. The RAF are to co-operate and almost the entire bomber command are turned onto the job of working the bombing of the two ports up to crescendo at the time we make our entrance. It is very thrilling and ought to be a magnificent spectacle. I wouldn't miss it for anything. We are to rendezvous off Dungeness with the oil ship and some destroyers at about midnight to start our sweep in, we, of course, heading the 'party'.

During the afternoon, making the final preparations, it is all rather tense. The CBs (confidential books) have to be landed. Great bags of them. We get all the charts teed up and then try to get a little rest. I was reading 'Flowering Wilderness' by Galsworthy and happened just to come to the part where Dinny Cherwell falls in love with Wilfred Desert. It is very well written. Dinny reminds me so much of Catherine. Beautiful in a very unusual and nymph like way. Attractive to men but not wishing to attract them physically and therefore finally falling in love much more spiritually and mentally than physically, though capable of real physical love if it is finally brought out. She falls in love with Wilfred at once. She realises that she is thrilled by him in a way that she has not been by any other man.

I suppose being in a state of tension and excitement at the evening's prospects one's thoughts become more vivid and roving than usual. Reading of their falling in love and proposal about a fortnight after meeting and having always seen the resemblance of

14. This was Operation Lucid, first planned to take place on 26/27 September 1940. The aim was to attack Calais and Boulogne where invasion craft were being assembled by the Germans. Fire ships were to be sent in carrying 7,000 tons of petrol and 2,000 pounds of explosives. It was postponed twice due to bad weather and started again on the 7/8 October only to be halted again due to the mining of a participating destroyer. It was finally cancelled, presumably because the diminishing threat of invasion had to be balanced against the high risks. Denis Jermain, a distinguished MTB commanding officer, was detailed off to pick up the fire ship crews inside Boulogne and was heartily glad of the cancellation.

Dinny to Catherine, I began to think of our courtship. It took about the same time. I remember asking Catherine quite suddenly, as Wilfred does, to marry me while I was cutting bamboos at Enys.

I kept on thinking of our first meeting at the Sycamores[15] and trying to analyse my feelings exactly. I was tremendously stirred, but I suppose would not have admitted at the time that I had fallen violently in love at first sight because I was so young that the idea seemed rather precocious and I never for a moment imagined that she would fall for me. I wonder whether Catherine felt thrilled by me at once, like Dinny, in a way that she had not been by other men. It is a funny thing, but very real, this intense attraction which in cases like ours, as portrayed by Dinny and Wilfred, is almost entirely a spiritual rapprochement only helped by a natural physical urge. I am convinced that it is infinitely deeper and more violent than cases of great physical attraction only. Galsworthy has put it very well.

Well I had to turn from these pleasant thoughts to sterner things. We slipped and proceeded at sixteen thirty and after a long run through the Downs in the gathering darkness, rendezvoused with the tanker and destroyers correctly at midnight off Dungeness. Then at zero hour we started out, got our sweeps out and led off. I went around and gave final instructions to the closed up guns' crews. It is hard to portray the tense excitement of such a moment as this.

Then suddenly one of the destroyers bustled up alongside and sang out through their loudspeaker that the operation was cancelled.[16] It was a bitter disappointment to me and the anti-climax after being so keyed up was terrific. We do not know the exact reason yet. It may have been that the other party failed in some way or that the direction of the wind was not quite good enough. There was rather too much east in it. There we were, well on our way over and all stopped! I gather we have to wait for some nights till we can try again.

I navigated her back to the Downs. The moon got up and it was a lovely night. We had to creep along in order to look after the old oil ship, which could only do seven knots. The white cliffs of Dover looked magnificent and very defiant in the moonlight, and away over to starboard twenty miles off the German flak was flashing away and

15. Colonel Sycamore and his wife lived just outside Flushing on Trefusis Point, about fifteen minutes walk from Bodrennick.
16. This suggests that Robert was present in *Niger* on the 26/27 September when the operation was cancelled at sea.

every now and then there would be a very bright glow where some bomb had found a likely target. In spite of the disappointment, an unforgettable night. Better luck next time. They had to have three attempts before they pulled off Zeebrugge (in the First World War). We dropped the oil ship, the *War Nawab*,[17] at Sheerness, and after waiting a few hours, we were ordered to move on to Harwich. They never leave concentrations of ships about when these operations are on, as it might give the fact away to the enemy.

The new Captain[18] came aboard today soon after we got in. He seemed quite a nice chap from the very little I have seen of him so far. An absolutely different type to our present skipper. With all his faults, some of which at times were tryingly patent, I can't help being sorry at seeing the last of Cronyn. He has been very good to me and was in many ways an excellent introduction to the Navy. By his great powers of conversation and considerable experience of the Navy, (he went to sea when he was thirteen) I have learned a great deal of the real guts and inwardness of the Navy. Probably more than anyone in the RNVR could hope to learn normally, for which I am duly grateful.

Today there have been big aerial battles again. So far one hundred and twenty-five German planes brought down. But I have also come across the other side of it. Leading Seaman Crick, one of our best deck hands, had a wire this evening. 'Come home, house bombed' was all it said. He is to go first thing tomorrow. He lives at Maidstone. I do hope his family are alright. He has a wife and one child at home. Another boy in the Air Force. He is an exceptionally nice man. I offered to help him with money, but he refused gratefully. He was obviously glad to talk to me though and unburden himself a little (I being Officer of the Day). It is surprisingly pleasing to find that one has the men's confidence. I know few things in life that have given me more pleasure. It was clear from the way he talked that I had his.

I have always held the opinion that the best officers were not those who barked loudly at the men, or tried in other ways to show off their superiority and efficiency by sharp remarks and sarcasm, which is all too common. I think that being helpful and pleasant to them, as long as you are firm, and especially by a good example, that is by working hard yourself and not getting drunk or abusive, you get the

17. *War Nawab* was a Royal Fleet Auxiliary.
18. Commander Harris, an Australian, replaced St John Cronyn.

confidence of the men much more and can lead them much better in difficult circumstances. I was pleased to find my views confirmed by a passage on discipline in K.R. and A.I.[19] summing up the correct attitude for an officer, thus: (Talking of the Captain of a ship) 'While upholding the legitimate authority of all the officers under his command, he will check by timely reproofs any tendency he may notice to abuse of power, recommending by his example that firm but conciliatory manner of conducting duty, which is the surest way to gain the respect and confidence of the men.'

At this point Robert's diary ends for three months. Some notes at the end of the diary refer to his appointment to HMS *Osprey* where he started his time in Coastal Forces.

---

19. Kings' Regulations and Admiralty Instructions. The definitive guide to the law applicable to naval service and guidance on conduct.

Chapter Six

First Command
December 1940 – February 1941

On 6 October 1940 Robert was appointed to HMS *Osprey* at Portland for training in MASBs. Prior to the commissioning of *St Christopher* at Fort William, Coastal Forces officers trained at Portland. His service record then shows him appointed 4 November to command *MASB 16*, replacing her sick captain, and then *MASB 18* on 18 November. Both boats were building at Hythe so he was 'standing by' them. *MASB 18* was a seventy foot Napier-engined boat with a top speed of only twenty-seven knots and thus considered too slow for fighting E-boats. Once this problem was recognized, however, plans were laid to change the Napier for the new Packard engines imported from the USA, which would give her front line capability but which delayed her completion. Perhaps due to this delay Robert was ordered off to Command *MASB 14* on 23 December 1940. He was not appointed to *MGB 64* until February 1941.

MGB 64 and *MASB 14* were very similar boats. They were both the product of George Selman's design, the chief designer for British Power Boats, and were both seventy feet long. They were hard chine, that is to say their underwater design allowed the boat to ride up on the crest of its bow wave at a critical speed and plane over the water. Depending upon the engines this could give them a top speed of up to forty knots, which *MGB 64* enjoyed, having three Rolls Royce Merlins. From mid 1941 the standard power units for new MGBs became the Packard.

MASB 14 was very lightly armed, with two single Vickers 0.5 inch machine guns and depth charges, having been originally conceived as an anti-submarine craft, hence their name, Motor Anti-Submarine Boats. Shortly after the start of the war the Admiralty noted that the Germans did not appear to be using their submarines in coastal waters, the only area suitable for MASBs to operate in, and it was then decided to convert the MASBs into motor gunboats, which meant that they were re-armed and re-engined. *MASB 14* had been earmarked as a training boat at *St Christopher* until she could be converted into an MGB.

MGBs were heralded as the answer to the E-boat which had wreaked considerable damage on British convoys ever since the fall of France and the Low Countries had placed German bases close to the British coast, transforming the strategic situation. E-boats, operating at night, were attacking British convoys inadequately guarded by the very small number of destroyers and corvettes available for escort duty. E-boats were a difficult target to hit at night in the days before radar controlled gunnery. With a top speed of thirty-eight to forty-two knots, a length of 115 feet, two torpedo tubes, a 37mm gun, plus two 20 mm guns and two machine guns, E-boats had real teeth. They were also used for mine laying.

The longer term solution to the E-boat problem appeared, to the naval authorities, to be the building of new classes of boats. These included Steam Gunboats, Fairmile 'C' and 'D' type MGBs and a new class of 'short' MGBs, British Power Boat built and seventy-one feet six inches long, roughly the same size and design as motor torpedo boats but not armed with torpedoes in order to concentrate their capacity to carry weight on heavier guns, as their task was to attack the E-boats rather than larger enemy shipping where torpedoes would have been essential. They also retained two or sometimes four of the depth charges which had been fitted for their anti-submarine role and these turned out to be, in effect, their only heavy weapon, though delivering depth charge attacks against surface warships was one of the most dangerous acts that the Royal Navy was called upon to undertake.

Throughout the narrative that follows, both in Robert's diary and in his unfinished account of motor gunboat warfare, *We Fought Them in Gunboats*, are to be found essentially two themes. Firstly, that MGBs were too lightly armed to make much impact on the larger and almost equally fast E-boats and hence the struggle to persuade the Admiralty that they could and should carry the additional weight of heavier weapons. Secondly, that in spite of their specialist role in fighting E-boats, they often saw opportunities to use torpedoes against larger targets and there was no reason why torpedoes should not also be fitted, their weight compensated for by removing unnecessary equipment such as anchors, substantial stocks of reserve ammunition and heavy powered mountings for guns which could perfectly well be hand trained and as such were more reliable. Much of Robert's determination was required for success in both projects against entrenched opposition from the naval authorities, in spite of support from British Power Boats and George Selman, and indeed from his senior officers up to the level of Commander-in-Chief Nore.

Monday, 24th December 1940. Here I will resume after a gap of shore-going. Well yesterday morning (Sunday, 23rd December) I was all set to spend the day at Power Boats[1] and then slip off the next day to spend Christmas in the bosom of my family, which even then seemed too good to be true. It was not to be.

I was late over there and arrived with a signal to take over MASB 14 forthwith at Milford Haven. My hopes were dashed. Prospects of an infernal railway journey followed by the difficulties of taking over a fresh job with entirely new people just over Christmas time when one does like to see familiar faces. I must admit I was sad. I had so counted on seeing little Antsie opening his stocking, the first I should have seen as he was really too young the year before last. Also the thought of reading to the children in the evening and of Antsie snuggling against my arm while we had the Milne poems and of Bob's eager little face listening to the Arthur Ransome books was rather saddening.

However, I had to get busy. I got back to Southampton and got my ticket and found out the trains. Six fifty from the Central station. Then I had lunch and went back to Lucy's.[2] I packed my things into two suitcases. It was difficult to know what to take in view of the word temporary in my appointment. Was it for a week or months and what sort of work was it to be? Then I sat down and wrote a long

1. The British Power Boat Co Ltd at Hythe who were building *MASB 18*. Power Boats were also building *MASB* (later *MGB*) *64* and the other Rolls Royce Merlin engined boats who were to constitute the Sixth MGB Flotilla, which Robert joined in February 1941.
2. Lucy Carden, Robert's cousin and longstanding friend from his Northamptonshire childhood. She lived near Hythe then and must have provided a welcome relief from the naval world.

screed to Catherine for Loveday to take back and another long screed to Campbell[3] with instructions on lots of points. I also put calls through and actually got Catherine's call just before I left at six pm. I'm glad I did because it would have been even more disappointing to her if she had expected me in the car the next day.

Finally I had a large tea of sprats, said goodbye to Lucy who had been more than kind to me during my time at Hythe, and then got off with Loveday in the Rover.[4] It was bitter cold and freezing. Luckily I took food with me. We arrived at the station at six twenty-five and as there was an air raid on I told Loveday to go away again at once. Then I proceeded to sit on the station until seven forty before the train came. There was no food on the train and indeed no light. I finally arrived in Milford Haven at about two thirty in the afternoon the next day. A monumentally unpleasant journey on Christmas Eve in extreme cold. I stood it better than I should have expected and did not feel too tired. There I reported to the base, who told me to have lunch. This I did at the Lord Nelson and then had a shave and came back. I was then told that a motorboat would come for me to take me to No. 14 which was lying at Pembroke Dock a few miles up the estuary. I waited for the boat and finally, after a very cold journey in a speedboat, reached my ship at about four pm..

I was relieving Shaw, a Lieutenant RN, who I knew as he was in Fitzroy in the 4th MSF. I discovered then that he had been appointed to No. 63 an Anti-E-boat[5] which made it look as though they were putting me into 14 temporarily until they had another suitable person and until 18 was nearer completion. At least I hope that is the case as I don't want to be stuck in a training flotilla for long. I was also informed that they were on their way round to Fort William to the training flotilla and had taken five weeks to get that far from Portland owing to defects and weather. I was to sail as soon as possible and get up there with all despatch as the boat was badly needed.

I was taken ashore to spend the night in the RAF barracks there, where they work Sunderland flying boats. I was glad to be able to get

3. Lieutenant Robert Campbell, always known as Boffin, was to be Robert's first lieutenant in *MGB 64* when he joined the Sixth MGB Flotilla. Robert and Boffin were standing by *MASB 18*.
4. His sister, Loveday Fletcher, must have driven up from Cornwall in Robert's Rover, expecting that they would return to Cornwall together before Christmas.
5. These were seventy foot British Power Boats, built as MTBs for France but requisitioned and converted into MGBs.

a bath and meal. We decided to turn over the next day, Christmas morning. As I was feeling rather forlorn it being Christmas Eve and knowing no one and feeling very tired, I thought I would put a call through to Catherine and hope for the best. I was surprised and delighted to get through very quickly. It was nice to talk to my family, I spoke to Bob and Ants too, and I heard that Loveday had just arrived as I was speaking, which was good news. But in a way it made it feel all the bleaker when I had to ring off. The only thing to do was to think of all the people who were worse off than me and nowhere in touch with their home at all. That is the worst of being so devoted to one's family. Then I went to bed and slept soundly, as I was very tired.

Christmas Day 1940. I woke and looked at my watch. It was seven ten. I at once thought of the children just about to get busy with their stockings and I could visualise the whole scene. I suppose one of the most attractive memories of any parent who is fond of children.

We handed over early. Then I settled down to my charts and worked out a suggested plan. I aimed at getting to Peel on the west coast of the Isle of Man on the first day's run. This had every advantage as if the weather was bad I could duck into Holyhead. If I succeeded I should be certain of doing it in three days, barring accidents or very bad weather, as I had a shortish run then into the shelter of the Mull of Kintyre and I could have gone on there on the third day by the Crinan Canal if need be. Or if I was lucky I could make one bold day of it and go right on by the Sound of Islay past the Isles of the Sea (lovely name) to Fort William.

I had an early, rapid and lonely lunch of turkey and jelly. But I think I was lucky to get any turkey at all in the circumstances. Directly afterwards I hopped off to the base at Milford Haven in a speed boat and saw the Commander there. I fixed to start early the next morning and try to make Peel in the Isle of Man. I got my recognition signals and route and off I went. When I had squared everything up for the night aboard, I went ashore with my charts to work out all my courses as navigation is hopeless while under way in these boats.

To my great indignation I had been left by the late captain with no parallel rulers. So after ringing up Catherine and hearing about the children's Christmas, I sallied forth to the RAF operations room and worked there using their rulers. By the time I had finished everything and written a few essential letters as to my doings, it was eleven o'clock before I turned in.

It was nice being able to get through to Catherine again on Christmas Day, a sort of homely feeling when you're with strangers, but in a way it makes you almost more homesick, because you can visualise just what it is like at home, and you do so wish you were there and there was no blasted war on. However there it is. Thus ended my Christmas Day, the second of the war. My first saw nearly the start of my naval career in minesweeping. My second saw the very start of my active service in HM Motor Boats, because we made a signal at 08.00 on Christmas Day to the effect that Lieut. R.P. Hichens, DSC, RNVR, had assumed command of HM *MASB 14*.

Wednesday, 26th December. Boxing Day. We got off in almost pitch dark at 08.00. It was tricky finding my way down the long reaches of Milford Haven. It became light as we got outside. And then we opened up to our regulation 1800 revolutions and headed north.

It was lovely at first flying over the calm seas and the prospect was good, but over-clouded. Presently when we were off the South Bishop light and headed for a one hundred mile run out of sight of land, the wind freshened rapidly and dead ahead. We were in an area fiercely marked on the charts with overfalls. I very soon learnt what life at sea in a fast Motor Boat was to be like. I did not want to reduce speed because I was running to a schedule and I could not possibly risk making Peel in the dark and therefore if I had reduced I should have lost a whole day by having to go into Holyhead. So we kept on batting.

It is an indescribable sensation going fast into a steep head sea in a speed boat. The feeling of shock preponderates, closely followed by the feeling of leaving your stomach behind as at the start of a scenic railway drop. You see a big sea coming up ahead. You have the sickening sharp drop, followed by the sudden shock bending your knees and making you hold on hard. All this is almost instantly followed by a shower of solid water which lands on your head as you crouch in the dustbin.[6] Catherine would not like it!

Well we stuck to it and after about four hours conditions got better. By this time I was soaked to the skin, because it is impossible to do

6. The open bridge of a MASB, MGB or MTB was always known as the dustbin.

anything in the way of changing when the boat is bumping severely. By this time I expected to see land at Holyhead, but it was thick over the shore way, so I headed in to try and get my position, hoping that I had not overshot the mark and was ploughing on towards Liverpool. The visibility was only about a mile or two and I was getting anxious as I should have been near land by this time. But my reckoning was very difficult. I had never taken the boat to sea before. I had only the supposed speeds per revolution counter marked on the navigating notebook to go by, and the ASDIC dome[7] had been taken off since these notes were made, which was bound to affect her speed. Also I did not know the effect of the bumping in reducing speed through the water.

At this moment we sighted a destroyer who challenged us. I asked him my position. The reply came back 'South Stack 036 fifteen miles'. I was on the right course but fifteen miles short of my reckoning. Either the previous captain was all to glory with his notes on speed or the bumping had checked us more than I expected. A bit of both I expect.

So on we ploughed and presently the high shoulder of the South Stack loomed up ahead quite high above us. The visibility was very poor. I had rather a difficult decision to make then, because we were one and a half hours back on our schedule by then and if I could not make more speed than heretofore it would be dark before I reached the Isle of Man. The alternative was Holyhead and the loss of a day. The sea was calmer by then and I decided to risk it. We opened up to 2000 and roared on north. The sky cleared and the sun went down on the most perfect bright horizon such as you get in midwinter in northern latitudes. The Isle of Man loomed up well on schedule this time. The extra two hundred revs had made a lot of difference. That run in towards the Isle of Man, lit by the last rays of the sun sinking behind us, was one of the most lovely I have had. The high mountains of the island looked beautiful. We reached Peel, a little harbour on the west side, about five thirty with the last of the light. Peel has an old ruined castle at the harbour entrance. The red western sky was just behind this as we entered and showed off the old embattled walls to perfection. It was an unforgettable sight.

7. For her designed anti-submarine role *MASB 14* was equipped with an ASDIC (Allied Submarine Detection Identification Committee), predecessor of today's SONAR (Sound Navigation and Ranging), for detecting submarines.

We tied up alongside a Dutch minesweeper. After getting out of wet things and putting them on the engine (our only drying apparatus) I went ashore with the First Lieutenant in my best uniform. I had to ring up N.O.I.C.[8] at Douglas and arrange my sailing signal for the morrow. We found our way up the funny little town in the dark, it reminded me rather of a little Swiss town, and were directed to an hotel. There I rang up and fixed to sail at 09.00 with the light. We asked for dinner and they said they had none, but the kind old lady of the house took pity on us and said she would produce a meal. This she did and very good it was. Soup, pork, plum pudding and cheese and biscuits, for which she would only take the sum of two shillings. We stuffed ourselves as we had had practically nothing since breakfast. She was a dear old thing and chatted to us as she brought the courses in to us in front of a big fire in their private room. She said how she had a sailor son who had just been back on leave to 'bear' a son, I thought she said; so I said cheerfully how nice, etc. and was rather overcome when she said 'buried', realising that I wasn't on the right tack at all.

Outside in the bar meanwhile the local inhabitants were making merry it being Boxing Day. They were singing heartily and it was rather nice to hear them. We went out and had a beer and then returned to our ship to bed. Altogether we took a good view of the Isle of Man and the Manxmen.

So ended Boxing Day. Quite an eventful day which finished amidst decidedly damp sheets and pyjamas, a condition which I now realise is likely to be remarkably permanent with me for the future. I have no doubt the human frame will get used to it!

Thursday, 27th December. We were off with the light. There was a fresh N.W. wind blowing straight into Peel harbour causing us to bump about considerably but as we neared the Mull of Galloway, with the sun rising gloriously behind the high hills of the Isle of Man, the sea seemed to ease down, though the wind freshened. It was a lovely day with a clear sky. We were very lucky as it made all the difference to pleasure and navigation. The next bit of land we sighted was the Mull of Kintyre, looking high and fine, and just a misty glimpse of Ireland on our port bow. I was pushing her along all the time at 2000 as I wanted to try to make Fort William before dark.

8. Naval Officer In Charge.

With a fine tide under us we were making twenty-six knots over the land. The fastest navigating I have done yet by far, but I hope to do faster yet.

After that we slipped across to Jura and went through the Sound of Islay. It is only about two cables wide in places and going through it at about thirty knots with a ripping tide under us was exciting. All the people at the lighthouses as we passed came out to wave.

Then we roared away up towards Oban careering along on the tide race. We were very lucky carrying the tide with us the whole way, with the result that we arrived in good time at four forty-five. The last bit in from Oban up Loch Linnhe through the narrows to Fort William was fine. It seemed strange to see a large convoy anchored opposite Oban. Apparently the place, which until recently had hardly been aware of the war, was shaken up by the bombing of a convoy on Christmas Eve, three ships being sunk and five more hit.

I was mighty glad to arrive at Fort William after two hard days. Given bad luck or bad weather it might have taken me a long time because it is four hundred miles in notoriously dirty waters. My predecessor had taken five weeks to get from Portland to Milford Haven, a matter of about two hundred and fifty miles only. It was also lovely to have a bright day in which to see the lovely Scottish scenery as we came up.

When we arrived we went off to a buoy over the far side of the loch from Fort William and I had to get a boat and go to see the C.O. of the base. He is one Commander Welman, DSO, DSC, with multitudes of bars thereto. A great C.M.B.[9] man in the last war. We had a priceless talk as I had had a decent bit of gin with some friends who came aboard and he asked me my opinion on things, and being rather ginned up I said I thought this was the worst place in the world for a training base as you had none of the things you had to contend with, namely heavy weather and bombing. I added that I thought Motor Boats were being mucked about as we were all anxious to get cracking and never got the chance. Much to my surprise he agreed heartily.

Friday, 28th December 1940. We came alongside early and then proceeded to do nothing except remove all detonators from depth charges, except two. In the afternoon we cleaned the ship and I saw

9. Coastal Motor Boat, introduced into the navy in 1916, carrying one or two torpedoes in a stern discharge trough. They were designated CMBs to avoid revealing their role as motor torpedo boats.

to a lot of correspondence that needed attention. Very cold and damp aboard. No heating whatever. Everybody assures me that the paraffin heaters are all burnt out and won't work.

Saturday, 29th December. Went ashore for a long walk along the north western side of Loch Linnhe. It was lovely. Very wild, just a fringe of cultivated land about an acre wide and then wild rough mountainside towering up. Just before lunch, while I was waiting by the loch side for my little boat, I saw a telephone booth in the adjoining hut. It surprised me in such a wild spot. I wished to ring Catherine and thought I would try it, thinking I might at least find out if there was any chance of getting through to Cornwall in a few hours. Within five minutes of picking up the receiver I was through to Treworval and could hear perfectly. Certainly the most wonderful telephone call I have so far achieved.

On returning from my walk I did some work and remained shivering and damp and turned in early. I don't think I have ever been so uncomfortable in my life. I suppose I shall get used to it. Water drips onto one's bunk and settee. Everything has to be kept in a suitcase or it gets soaking.

Sunday, 30th December. A day of training. Out morning and afternoon with officers and men swarming over the boat. In the late afternoon when we had finished as I was returning to the trot where we moor at about twelve knots, we struck some submerged object good and hard with our centre and starboard propellers. We were not near land or rocks and in seven fathoms, so suspect it was a barrel full of tar. Several of these have come down the loch and they may float completely submerged. It is most unfortunate as I'm afraid it will put us out of action and necessitate a trip up the Caledonian Canal to Inverness to slip her, as they have no slipping arrangements here.

Monday, 31st December. New Year's Eve. We got underway in the morning for training purposes, but found the vibration on the shafts too bad to make it worth carrying on. So we came in and made a report. Perry,[10] the training officer, who was at Power Boats and who knows more about these ships than anyone, was very helpful.

10. Lieutenant K.H. Perry, known as Pop, subsequently became the Engineer Officer of both the Sixth and Eighth MGB Flotillas on base staff at Felixstowe and was a great support to Robert. He had been in the Navy in the 1930s, resigned to work at British Power Boats, and rejoined in 1940.

Still remarkably uncomfortable, but I have gone into the question of the heaters. I have got one to work now which makes all the difference. Goodbye the Old Year. I saw it out in my damp little trap. It certainly has been a teaser. I hope I shall never live through a worse time than May to September, after which we knew the Germans could not wipe us out as they had the rest of the Continent. Thank God for the Channel.

Wednesday, 1st January 1941. I went ashore this morning and tried to get some heaters. The Paymaster was most helpful, but there were none to be had in Fort William. All the training officers seemed to be suffering from the effects of a pretty cheerful New Year's Eve, Hogmanay as the Scots call it. It appears to be the greatest day for getting drunk in Scotland.

Friday, 3rd January. I went to dinner with Perry and we talked shop. He told me that he had been asked to pick out another officer to assist him in teaching the handling of these boats, and that he had noticed that I could handle them and he wanted to know whether I would help him. It put me in rather a fix because I didn't want to refuse to help him and yet the last thing I want to do is to get stuck in this training job. So I said I would provided it did not in any way prevent me going back to operational work. He said it wouldn't and in fact would be good for me as it would get me known as an efficient chap and that when the time came in the Spring for the big Motor Boat offensive I should be able to go back to operational work for certain. I hope he is right.

Saturday, 4th January. A quiet day, still waiting and hoping for orders to proceed. I am slowly getting a bit more work out of my crew. I got the bilges properly cleaned out this morning. They could not have been fully inspected before because very few of the bottom boards would come out without a terrific struggle.

It is extraordinarily beautiful up here at times. In the morning while the sun is still below the mountains to the east, the first of the light begins to pick out the western mountain tops and with the snow on them they look a mysterious bluey green. It is most fascinating and extraordinary, but mighty cold.

Sunday, 5th January. This morning we were called up by lamp from

Fort William and told that Commander Welman wanted to see me that forenoon. So I went off in my best suit and had a pleasant interview. He has, alas, appointed me to assist in the training. I said I hoped it would not prevent me from going back to operational work very shortly, at which he rather took offence and indicated that he had no wish to keep anyone back from operational work. Which only made me the more suspicious.

He then said that I could start off up the canal to Inverness the next morning. So I went away rejoicing at getting going at last, but rather anxious about getting involved in a training flotilla.

Then I put a call through to Catherine. She sounded much more cheerful and well and herself suggested what I had been longing for but was afraid would be too much for her, namely that she should come up here with Antsie as soon as Bobby had been settled at school. She said she would come and sounded excited about it and that Bobby would be at school on the 17th.

I finished the day by doing a splice in a big mooring rope and going for a long walk and then writing a long letter to Catherine. She often says she doesn't believe I love her. I suppose its because I'm not effusive and often abusive, but if she knew how thrilled I was at the prospect of her visit she would never be worried about that again.

Monday, 6th January. It was a lovely day and the prospect of the trip up the canal was pleasing. We got into the first lock at Corpach at about ten thirty and then started our slow progress up. There are eleven locks in the first two miles after leaving the sea and they take a long time. So we were still within sight of Fort William at two o'clock after hours of hard work. When we got to the top of these locks we found there was quite thick and unbroken ice on the canal which we could not possibly break without ripping our bottom up. It looked as though we would be stuck there for the day until they could send the ice breaking tug from Fort Augustus, but luckily a Dutch iron merchant ship was coming through the ice a few minutes after we had arrived at the top. It certainly was a bit of luck. The children would have loved to see her crumpling the thick ice in front of her with a great cracking noise.

Even then it was tricky going for us. We had to go dead slow and I had to keep a very wary eye out for heavy pieces and often stop her as one nasty bang would have holed her. We had a pretty seven mile

121

stretch then from Banavie locks to Gairlochy locks. After that we were in Loch Lochy, the most beautiful loch I have ever seen. The mountains come steeply down to the water and it is quite lovely. We went quite close passed a lovely Georgian house which had a large glass front door. I looked at it through the glasses and saw a lot of little children crowded at the door watching us. We did a bit of mutual waving. They are certainly safely refugeed here.

At the end of the loch are a couple of locks called Laggan locks. The light was going when we arrived and so we stayed the night there. There was a nice lock keeper. I went to his house to 'phone the base and saw his two little girls. I said I had two little boys in Cornwall.

It was an exceptionally cold night. I went on deck just before turning in. A full moon was lighting up the whole countryside and glinting on the water, and ice was already forming tight round the ship. I took one more look at the snow covered hills blue in the moonlight and retired to my trap, kept beautifully cool by being only divided from the freezing water by one inch thickness of wood. It would make a good place for cooling champagne!

Tuesday, 7th January. In the morning we found ourselves firmly embedded in ice and the reach stretching away from us solid. You could throw heavy stones on it and not break it and there had been no ice there the night before. It must have been a terrific frost last night. We had to wait until the tug could reach us from Fort Augustus, which meant several hours as she could not be there until about two o'clock.

I went for a long walk in the mountains and observed the funny mountain sheep closely. They certainly have the most magnificently warm coat provided by nature and the funniest little black faces. Then I talked to the lock man and learnt all about 'maggots' which apparently breed very free and large in Scotland as a result of the bluebottles. Then I went to a funny little shop near the lock and found two (the last) lovely tins of sweet biscuits which I bought for the children. I thought Bobby would like to take his to school.

Finally the tug came and went on west leaving us to force our way through broken ice. This wasn't too bad through Loch Oich, a funny little narrow loch, but after that the last few miles to Fort Augustus were awful. Thick heavy blocks of ice, broken but covering the water. We had to push our way through dead slow. Start and stop for ten seconds at a time. It was very tedious, but we finally arrived at Fort Augustus somewhat exhausted but unhurt except for loss of paint. We were lowered down the five locks into Loch Ness as it was growing dark, free of ice at any rate on the eastward passage.

The old lockmaster, a regular old Highlander, came aboard and knocked back neat whisky as though it was lemonade, delighted to find somebody who got it cheap.[11] When he had succeeded in squeezing himself out of our diminutive hatch we went up to the Lovat Arms for a bath and dinner. The bath was the best I have had for ages, so long I couldn't reach the ends lying at full stretch.

Wednesday, 8th January. We arose to a thick fog, but I was determined to push on. The exit into the loch was easy and after that the course was straight and no obstacles except other craft. If our compass was not accurate, as I suspected, we should only come close to the sides of the loch where there was deep water and we had a cable's visibility.

It was rather eerie after we got fairly launched in the loch. We might have been in the middle of the Sargasso Sea instead of Loch Ness. We had been informed by our bibulous friend of the night before that the local opinion about the Loch Ness monster was that it was all tripe and a newspaper romp, but highly convenient to themselves for trade purposes. No local had ever seen it, even in his cups. This was comforting as otherwise one could imagine it rearing out of the fog.

After we had proceeded cautiously for about an hour, we saw the shore to starboard dimly and straightened up along it. Soon after the fog cleared miraculously and we proceeded at about thirteen knots down the loch, which is attractive, with one lovely old ruined castle on a point. Then we went through narrow Loch Dochfour, and another loch and then along the last seven mile stretch of the canal, the dullest of the lot and so to the five locks at Inverness. There we had to wait for two hours while a couple of merchant ships came up. Meanwhile I walked into the town and reported my arrival and sent a signal to Fort William. When we got to the bottom of the locks I found that we couldn't get out of the sea lock that night as the tide was too low. So we tied up at the end of the canal and had a somewhat convivial evening with a Scotch engineer who was working

11. The Navy gets its wines and spirits duty free aboard HM ships.

in a naval office nearby. He also appreciated our cheap whisky.

Thursday, 9th January. I had arranged to get through the sea lock early and cover the two miles round to the slipway by ten o'clock in order to catch the morning tide for getting on the slip. I had to have a pilot. I suppose it's an old custom so that these chaps can get a living. As it was I was glad because it was a thick fog. So thick that at one moment the pilot said he thought we had better anchor, but I was determined to catch that tide and we went on and luckily picked up the little post that marked the narrow entrance to the river.

We were quickly slipped and the damage revealed as a couple of propellers damaged, as I had suspected. The P^{12} brackets and shafts were intact. It seemed likely that the work would not take long and that we should be ready by Monday or Tuesday. So I reluctantly decided to give no leave and to give up hope of any for myself. I had hoped to get down and see Bobby off to school for the first time.

I took up my abode in the Douglas Hotel. It was nice to be warm and dry again in bed. They have plenty of eggs and butter up here too.

Saturday, 11th January. A morning sloshing around in the ice and snow of the yard watching progress. Then at noon I rang Welman at Fort William to report the probabilities of the finishing of the work and at the end of the conversation got a great surprise when he said 'The Number One of your new boat is up here, Campbell'. I thought at once of *18* and said 'Good, I hope he can be with me while I'm here'. I puzzled over that all afternoon at the yard. Did it mean 18 or something else. It was exciting anyway as anything was better than the training flotilla. So I tried to get a 'phone call through to Campbell to hear the buzz and almost as I was doing it he appeared at my hotel. We had a breathless talk. It appears that, DV,[13] I am to take command of *64*, an MGB with three Rolls-Royce Merlin engines and to be in Howes' flotilla. Howes was an R.N. Lieutenant whom we saw a lot of at Hythe who is to be flotilla leader of the Sixth. Above all we were to be together and to do our working up at Fowey.

The prospect was altogether too dazzling. It was what we had always aimed at. Campbell brought a letter from Shaw saying that he

---

12. Metal bars providing stability to the exposed end of the propeller shaft.
13. *Deo Volente* meaning God Willing.

had seen the signals and that when asked by R.A.C.F. (Rear Admiral Coastal Forces, Piers Kekewich) whether he could spare any officers Welman had said yes, Chesney and Davidson,[14] two who were in disfavour through cracking up their engines by allowing them to freeze, and that I was to be retained as assistant training officer The reply to this from R.A.C.F. was that I was required to take the crew of *18* to *64*.

We knew that Perry and Welman wanted to keep me and we were desperately afraid that our dreams would be shattered by him getting at R.A.C.F. and saying that I was needed here for training. So we rang through to Howes at Fowey and told him the position and he said he would do all he could to ensure that things went through. Actually I have heard from another source that Howes asked for me in his flotilla, which is fine because I'm sure we'll get on and I think he will make a most excellent flotilla leader.

Tuesday, 14th January. The end of our visit to Inverness is in sight. We hoped to get her in the water this afternoon and succeeded. As I suspected with the correct distribution of pressure coming on her hull, the shaft took up correct alignment and so in the evening, after a rather long and anxious day, I went off to report the good progress to Welman, as I was anxious now to get back.

He was pleased with my efforts and so I asked him when he thought I should be going to *64* as I wanted to know what to do about my wife coming up for a visit. He said he thought I should be off within a week or two at the most, whereat I rejoiced mightily as it meant he was not any longer trying to stop me going. Or so I hope. He also said that Campbell would be arriving that evening to accompany me back. He arrived and we went cheerfully to bed that night.

Wednesday, 15th January. We ploughed through the Inverness locks and then had a rapid run up Loch Ness which was great fun. She was going well. Campbell enjoyed the trip and the handling very much. We worked up through the five locks at Fort Augustus and arrived at the top as it was dark. It gave promise of a very cold night to come, so I arranged with the tug to take us on the next day the whole way, starting with the light at 09.00. Then we had a drinking session with

14. The Commanding Officer and First Lieutenant of *MASB 15*.

him and our old friend the lock master. The latter was quite boozy when he left and had great difficulty in heaving his large bulk out of our little hatchway. Then we went and had dinner at the Lovat Arms and so to bed.

Thursday, 16th January. It certainly was an exceptionally cold night. In the morning we were firmly frozen in and the ice was very thick. Then followed a very anxious period of ice breaking, following the little tug which was unfortunately narrower than we were. I must say I was worried by the ice. If it had holed us or bust our propellers it would have been the limit. So I took extreme care. Campbell was a great help and the trip has polished up my handling a great deal.

We got clear of the ice again at Lochy and had a beautiful run down there in sunshine. It is by far the most beautiful loch I have seen so far. Then we had ice again, only much lighter, right down to the sea lock. It was a beautiful clear field of ice covered in snow and looked whiter and smoother than anything I have seen. It was fascinating watching the tug crash through it, the whole white floor rising at her bow and then splitting suddenly a few feet further aft into small bergs.

We reached the sea lock at five forty-five after a long anxious day. I was not sorry to be back and so ended our adventurous and interesting trip through the Caledonian Canal in mid-winter.

Friday, 17th January. I've been darned lucky to get *64*, a Rolls-Royce boat.[15] I am working hard on these engines now, getting all the details up and it is work that I love and am fitted for as I do like engines so. Three Spitfire engines whose welfare is entirely up to me! What could be more suitable. Perry apparently was asked by Welman how he thought I would get on in a Rolls boat, as I am the only RNVR chap to be given one so far, all the others being RN. Perry said he thought I was one of the few chaps he had met who might be able to keep one running, which was rather a nice write up. Being the only RNVR boat in the Sixth MGB flotilla, Campbell and I will have to be on our metal!

Today Bobby went to school. I thought of him much this evening. I do hope he will be happy; happier than I was. I think he will be. Poor little Bob, starting out in the world. It's a funny world just now to start out in too!

15. The marine version of the Merlin, the engine that powered the Spitfire.

Saturday, 18th January. Training classes in the morning. Very dull except that it is blowing up hard from the N.E. for the first time since I've been up here, which made the handling more interesting. It is nice having Campbell up here. There is also a very nice RN Sub. called Scott who is training with us for a Higgins[16] boat. He is most amusing and we three have great fun together. Scott is a triplet, having two perfectly healthy sisters born with him. Most unusual. It is going to be a dirty night.

Sunday, 19th January. It was a dirty night. As a result I passed it sleeplessly. The banging of the waves on the boat, which being hard chine is like a drum, was most disturbing in itself, added to which our mooring in this direction of wind allows our stern to be within about thirty yards of some rocks and with a really hard wind my anxiety lest we drag was enormous.

I rang Catherine just after lunch and had a nice long talk. I was delighted to hear that Bob had gone off very happily and contentedly to school with a large new Meccano, which appears to have brought him instant and undeserved popularity. I'm awfully glad about the whole arrangement.

Then I went for a long walk with Campbell in the snow and biting north east wind, which set me up no end. I am very pleased to find that in spite of my age, thirty-one, the maximum age for these boats being supposed to be twenty-five, and the very bad weather conditions, I am settling down to living in this tiny ship in damp and cold and am now thoroughly liking it and feeling well. I wouldn't live ashore now if I could, except to be with Catherine or doing some dockyard repairs.

Monday, 20th January. On with the training. I am learning a great deal from Perry about the ships generally and the engines in particular, so I am not wasting my time here. One useful thing I learnt was never to allow any of my hands in the mess deck, which is forward, while at sea in a wind over force four. One hand had been killed by it. He went down there to get something and was thrown to the floor by the bumping, broke his knee, and they found him half an hour later a battered carcass, because once he was incapable he was thrown like a ball all over the place and of course hit his head continuously.

16. Another type of MGB purchased from Higgins in the USA.

Wednesday, 22nd January. *MASB 15* arrived with her new engines. I am now assistant training officer and have to do the training in my boat, Perry going in 15. We had great fun today as we roared down to Oban together doing flotilla manoeuvres by flag hoist. Campbell and I had a pretty tricky time as we had no signal rating with us and it was the first time we had kept formation at high speed. We learnt a lot and enjoyed it. But all the time we are longing to get to 64. It is so irksome not to be able to get down to it yet. We heard today that we, that is the Sixth MGB flotilla, is to be based at the Nore and that we are the last but one boat of the flotilla which is to start forming up in February.

Our trouble is that at present, until they are produced, we have no heavy guns at all, nothing but rapid firing 0.303 weapons. Our job is to hunt E-boats and they have four Bofors guns, being rapid firing two pounders.[17] It is a poor outlook trying to tackle them with such disparity of weapons. We shall have to rely on speed, the dark and the fact that the Hun is not generally very brave in the face of determined attack at sea. I hope we may get better guns before long. It is always the same with England, no weapons until the third year of the war.

Thursday, 23rd January. More training. Today we stripped 0.5s and Lewis guns with Scott who is very good at them and taught us all about it. I was very glad to get this knowledge safely tucked away, because now I can tackle my guns with certainty and see that my gunners keep them well, instead of being led by the nose by them. It is also very interesting work. I am certainly glad of all this training, which we are very largely organising for ourselves.

Friday, 24th January. Campbell and Scott came off and spent the evening aboard and we had great fun, stripping 0.5s and Lewis guns again. I got the record for stripping and putting together the 0.5 lock easily in two and a half minutes. We drank quite a lot of gin and laughed a great deal, as we all have much the same sense of humour, and Scott is really very funny. A very enjoyable evening, the first I hope of many in our tiny wardroom.

Sunday, 26th January. Went for a long walk with Campbell and Scott this afternoon up Glen Nevis. When we got out of the town we did

17. In fact they had only one 37mm gun.

fleet manoeuvres as we walked, giving flag signals by word of mouth as we needed to learn these. Blue, Red and White turns and Orders 1 to 6 being freely given, interspersed with Freddie and King and Formation and Disposition orders. It was great fun and we enjoyed our zig zag progress very much. The few passers by thought we were quite mad and laughed considerably as we turned abruptly and walked into the river only to do a Blue 9 just in time to save us. It may stand us in good stead on a dark and stormy night at forty knots!

Monday, 27th January. Training work again. Campbell is splendid at getting the hands down to things. They don't like it much after weeks of idleness. How glad I shall be to get away from this bloody training base.

Wednesday, 29th January. Today we went to sea. It was a nice day and we got a few hours of slight bumping when we got out, which gave the troops some idea of what it may be like. I was overjoyed this morning by news from Perry. He went to see Welman to point out that I ought to be down at my boat as there were alterations going on to the engines and I ought to know all about them. Welman said that he was still hoping to keep me. He had been down to R.A.C.F. and had asked for me and Kekewich had said I was wanted for *64*. Welman's attitude was that he had tackled him at the wrong moment and might still be able to wangle keeping me. So luckily Perry tackled him and said he thought it was all wrong that I should be held back, that I was one of the few people really suited to running a Rolls boat and that I would be wasted being kept here on Napiers. Mercifully Welman agreed and promised to send a signal suggesting I go down to stand by my boat and watch the engines. So the prospects of going soon are brighter.

We got back about four after annoying old Chesney in *15* by going a bit faster than he could go flat out, and we were at cruising revs. He wrecks his engines by opening up from the cold. I am most careful, being fond of engines and the result is that we are a lot faster. All the silly young asses out training think it is clever to roar off opening the throttles up wide and suddenly, but the laugh is on the other side when it comes to doing any real hard running with the engines.

When I got in I had to go up and see Welman, who was apparently intending to bottle me because people had been asking not to be trained on my boat, but on *15*. I convinced him that if they had been it was because they were made to work on my boat and to do jobs that they didn't have to do in 15.

I spent the evening in the *Aberdonian*, the base ship, getting all my CBs and SPs[18] squared up. A.J. Villiers, the famous sailing man who wrote 'Falmouth for Orders', etc., was CB officer and I had a most interesting evening with him. Andrew Le Grice sailed with him to America once. He was loud in his praise of Andrew. Everyone always was. Andrew must have been an awfully nice chap to be liked so much wherever he went.

Thursday, 30th January. Perry showed me a signal today saying that 64's crew were to be at Hythe on Saturday. I'm afraid that does not mean that I will be there as they are sending a signal enquiring who is to relieve me. But it is encouraging.

Friday, 31st January. Campbell and the crew were off today at two forty but needless to say not me. It is very disappointing but at least I see my way to going now.

In the evening I went ashore and gave dinner to Perry and his wife. I like them and I must say I think I owe a lot to Perry. We shall miss young Scott.[19] He is one of the most delightful and amusing young men I have ever come across. To hear him rendering a Petty Officer's instructions in a Funeral Firing Party drill when slightly intoxicated was one of the funniest things I have ever listened to.

Saturday, 1st February. Said my adieux and caught the bus. It was rather fun seeing the canal and the lochs that I had striven up and down in the boat from the comfortable seat of a bus. It is a lovely run and it was a lovely evening. I have been very lucky in my weather up here, but how glad I am to be rid of that place, with its atmosphere of back biting and trying to keep men up to the pitch without the incentive of real work to help.

We arrived at seven. I got my ticket, applied for a sleeper for the night train on Sunday and then went to the Douglas Hotel, had dinner (I was very hungry) and then a bath and so to bed. I hadn't had a bath for a week and that and the unwonted comfort of a good bed seemed the height of bliss. Hard living is good for one's soul, and I certainly have been through a strain lately. And now for *64*!

18. Confidential Books and Signal Publications.
19. Commander David Scott RN died in September 2006, sadly before I knew where to locate him.

Chapter Seven

MGB 64
February – July 1941

Robert's diary continues with his journey south to stand by *MGB 64*, building at British Power Boat's yard at Hythe.

Monday, 3rd February. I had a good journey down from Inverness. I decided to stay a few hours in London and deposited my baggage at Browns Hotel, which seemed exactly the same as usual. London was wonderful I thought. Apart from a few horrid gaps, as though a building was being pulled down, it seemed exactly the same as ever, except for a sort of spirit of sadness. It all seemed so quiet, as though the great old town was in mourning. I shall hope to live to see her reinstated.

I bought Catherine a little present of scent and some books for Antsie at Hatchards, which seemed just as usual. I caught a train on to Southampton, which was very late. There I met Catherine and Antsie and we just managed to catch the last boat to Hythe. It was lovely seeing them once again. Poor Catherine is not looking well. I shall have to do what I can for her.

4th, 5th, 6th, 7th, 8th, 9th and 10th February. These days present a memory of intense activity at Power Boats. Campbell and I straining every nerve to get things done and learn about our new engines and guns. All this interspersed with reading to Antsie in the evening at the hotel and talking with Catherine. A visit to Portsmouth rustling up missing stores, a day at Lucy's getting my gear from there and then Monday the 10th, a terrific struggle storing the ship and getting as ready as possible for commissioning. We are to sail for Fowey as soon as we are ready! Glory be!

Tuesday, 11th February. I commissioned my first ship today at ten o'clock. The struggle continues. It is such a job getting everything in and anything like ship shape. Campbell works magnificently but gets over-enthusiastic and expects too much of the crew. This is inclined to lead to tooth-sucking by the sailors and I shall have to go carefully. It is over-eagerness by Campbell but tactless.

Wednesday, 12th February. Still striving to settle the ship in. Went to F.O.I.C.[1] Southampton this afternoon and received orders to sail to Fowey tomorrow at 0900. Catherine and Antony went off today. Shall we ever get ship-shape?

Thursday, 13th February. Thick fog in the river[2] this morning. No chance of sailing. It was flat calm however and obvious that the sun would disperse the fog by 1200 or 1300. Ideal for a fast run to Fowey thereafter. However at 1130 they cancelled our sailing and of course the fog cleared perfectly by 1300. Very annoying as I badly want to get down to Fowey as we may only have a short time there.

As a result of the extra day here I got a small lamp for my cabin and a lovely rotary pump and hope that will make all the difference to the job of changing the oil in the engines. I went ashore late in the evening to get this pump at dead low tide, to make sure of not missing it the next morning. I had a hell of a time and ended up by getting into the mud and water up to the 'muddle', like Doctor Foster. I just got pig-headed about it and determined to do it and not be stopped by the mud. Ended up by washing my trousers on deck in the gloaming in my pants.

MGB 64, along with two sister boats, *62* and *63*, had just been finished by British Power Boats and given orders to join the Sixth MGB Flotilla which was forming and training at Fowey under the command of Lieutenant Peter Howes, RN,[3] a young man of forceful personality and considerable ability. The full flotilla consisted of eight boats numbered *58* to *65*, all except *64* and *65* commanded by RN lieutenants or sub-lieutenants. *65* was the last to join and was commanded by another RNVR officer, Lieutenant Alan Gotelee, known as Goaters.

Peter Howes had a difficult task. Over the previous five or six

1. Flag Officer in Command.
2. Presumably Southampton Water.
3. Peter Howes, a distinguished signal officer, was to become, in due course, Rear Admiral P.N. Howes, CB, DSC, Flag Officer Middle East.

months two fast motor gunboat flotillas had been formed, the Third and Fourth, from boats requisitioned while building as MTBs for foreign navies. In these boats the British Power Boat design had been modified to provide a fast, light craft, carrying guns but no torpedoes, specifically tasked with the job of countering the threat posed by E-boats to the coastal convoys. Whether or not the Germans had foreseen the likelihood that they would capture ports in the Low Countries and on the northern French coast early in any conflict with Britain, they had designed and built their own fast light craft. Their impact on coastal convoys in night attacks had been very considerable. Recognizing the need to counter them with boats of comparable or greater speed, and which would represent a much smaller investment at stake than risking destroyers, the MGB had evolved. Unfortunately, the project, which was an emergency measure using such boats as were available, had not been thought through with the care that it deserved. The early MGB flotillas had had virtually no success, with a very high rate of self-inflicted wounds in the form of broken boats unfit for operations.

Small wooden craft, seventy feet long with powerful petrol engines, were a grave temptation in the hands of the young naval officers assigned to their command. Few understood the limitations on what could be expected of the engines, particularly if they were driven at full speed in any kind of a sea. Yet they were so driven, with the inevitable consequence of ruined engines and strained hulls, leaving the early flotillas extremely short of operational boats. They were also armed extraordinarily lightly. This was due to the unavailability of more suitable weapons, but to send boats like this to sea to fight E-boats, armed in some cases only with 0.303 machine guns, was asking a great deal of them. Another fundamental problem was the noise they made. Fighting almost invariably at night, due to the need for the cover of darkness to protect them from aircraft attack in coastal waters, the MGBs were so noisy that they could often be heard ten to fifteen miles away. This was unhelpful if they were seeking out an enemy who, himself, was reluctant to give battle even to these small and weakly armed adversaries, as his principal task was to attack convoys. Their small size also made them unstable gun platforms in any kind of weather. In such conditions they also could not use much of their speed.

Thus by February 1941 there were quite a few senior officers in the Royal Navy who were wondering whether the new MGBs had any utility at all in the fight to maintain control over the coastal convoy routes in the Channel and the North Sea. Peter Howes had the formidable task of trying to prove that the MGB could be a valuable tool in the right hands.

Rather than continuing with Robert's diary, which in any case ends shortly, at this point the book he wrote during the war and never finished, *We Fought Them in Gunboats*, picks up the narrative of his introduction to MGBs.

MGB 62, under Lieutenant P. Whitehead, RN, and *63* under Lieutenant D. (Arty) Shaw, RN, were ready at the same time as *64* to sail for Fowey. The morning we were to go, the 14th February, dawned ominously, with a red sky and a gusty south-easterly wind. It really did not look good enough, but we were determined to go. We had to arrange R/T call signs before we left, and we discussed these on the deck of *63*. Shaw's was to be 'Dave', his Christian name, Whitehead's 'Percy'; I could not think of anything suitable for myself. 'Why not 'Hitch'? said Shaw in his slow way, and so it was; ever after in Coastal Forces I was known as 'Hitch'.

We slipped and sped down Southampton Water at thirty knots. The wind was south-east, and when it is in this direction the full force of the sea is not apparent until well clear of the Needles on a course for Anvil Point. As we thrust out to sea through the narrow neck by Hurst Point, treading on the short steep waves kicked up by the ebb-tide, we could see the angry line of water several miles to the southward, sharp jagged peaks with breaking crests, and in between a seemingly smooth stretch of water under the lee of the Needles. But this was deceptive; though the broken water of the wind-whipped Channel was still some way off, the swell driven on by the sea running offshore was sweeping in quiet but steep undulations round the southern extremity of the Needles. We were all inexperienced and the height of the sea was hard to judge. On we sped at thirty knots until, suddenly, we reached the top of the first big swell. it was a breathtaking sensation as we dropped off it; the boats fell so sharply that men were left two feet in the air. There was a sickening drop as you left your stomach behind, and a shuddering bang as the fore-part of the boat hit the hollow of the wave.

We had none of us done this before. We were all pretty startled.

Automatically throttles were brought down and the unit slowly pulled itself together at about twenty knots. In one case the harm was already done; *62* dropped farther and farther back, her lamp beginning to speak: 'Coxswain's back severely damaged, returning to harbour for immediate medical attention.' The poor man, when coming down to earth, so to speak, had missed his footing. He was in hospital for many months.

My coxswain, Curtis, had also injured his leg and had to relinquish the wheel. It had been a surprise, but a useful one. We had learnt our lesson. *62* receded into the distance, *63* and *64* ploughed on, now right out in the full force of the sea. It was blowing hard and there was obviously worse to come, but luckily we had it on our beam and in a short while when we rounded St Albans Head it would be on our port quarter. Had the wind been ahead we should have had one of our worst trips.

Gaining confidence with the wind and sea well aft, we increased to twenty-four knots, and a wonderful sight those little boats were, close to the race off Portland Bill. The wind had risen to almost gale force, at least seven or eight; with the effect of the race on the sea, there were some very sharp and, for us, large waves. We jumped through them like porpoises, at one moment entirely hidden from each other by the crest of a wave, or by solid sheets of spray, at another exposed to view well down to the under-belly of the ship, with a third of the boat's keel forward clear of the water, like a large fish leaping from a wave.

It was an exhilarating and satisfying experience. Slowly, as we plunged and thrust across West Bay, my admiration for the sea qualities of these little boats grew and grew. We were wet, yes, soaked, but what other little ship could go through this at twenty-four knots and not be drowned? The stability of the boats was wonderful, the way they adapted themselves to the tumbled surface of the sea a joy, and there grew up in me a confidence and pleasure in my gunboat that I have never lost.

As we neared Start Point the weather thickened and visibility reduced to a few miles. Presently we just caught a glimpse of the land, then it closed down again. Being a West-countryman I knew this coast well. Shaw stopped and asked whether I had recognised the land. I told him I thought I had sighted the entrance to Salcombe, a black gash in the high cliffs, all made indistinct by the driving mist, as though a veil had been partially torn aside. He suggested I should lead.[4] I went off confidently, shaping a course, as I thought, to clear Prawle Point, and suddenly saw towering above me the cliffs just to the southward of Dartmouth. In that glimpse I had mistaken the entrance of Dartmouth for the entrance to Salcombe.

'Hard a port.'

We swung round into the teeth of the wind. Two or three shattering bumps in quick succession brought our speed down to a mere crawl, ten or twelve knots. We had indeed learnt our lesson. The sea was piling up in here, short and steep. Due to my mistake we had four miles dead plug into it before we could square away round the Start. Where were those Skerries Rocks? The rocks between the Start and Dartmouth. I slid down from the dustbin to the wheelhouse, my oilskin trousers having no means of support visible or invisible, slipping down and binding my legs as though I were a contestant for a sack-race. I hastily consulted the chart, looked blankly at the wheelhouse windows perpetually covered in sheets of spray, and hoped that my course would clear the danger; forced my way back into the dustbin, hitching frantically at my trousers, and saw with a sigh of relief the Skerries buoy close on the starboard bow.

This was sifting the crew already. My leading stoker, Punton, a wonderful man, later to prove the tiger of the crew, was on the wheel. Momentarily I considered why he was there, then seeing the quiet satisfaction in his face as he exerted his strength and skill, I wondered no longer. Start Point bore squat and solid on the beam. 'Starboard Wheel.' We could bear away at last and stop that maddening spray slapping, slapping into one's eyeballs.

In a very few minutes, with a west-flowing tide, we were abreast of Prawle Point and, with one of those magical changes that are not infrequent in the West Country, the whole scene was metamorphosed. The driving mist was swept away for good. The wind dropped to a whisper, and, clear of the sheer black cliffs, the steep sea steadied out miraculously into a smooth undulation.

Tentatively we lifted the throttles, eighteen knots, twenty-four knots, soon we were sweeping west at thirty knots, bouncing and swooping, cleaving the waves in unending sequence and inevitable

4. At the beginning of the war, any Royal Navy regular lieutenant was automatically senior to any RNVR lieutenant, regardless of time served in the rank. Thus Shaw was senior to Robert and so was leading the unit.

impermanence. Past the Eddystone Lighthouse, always to my mind like an enormous candle surrounded by a sea of its own grease, the latest droppings of which show white and foaming at the foot; until we could see the sheer black outline of the Dodman, tremendously impressive against the watery sinking sun. Where was the entrance to Fowey? As ever there seemed to be no opening in those grey Cornish cliffs. Ah, there was the Gribben day mark, like a man, a giant, silhouetted against the skyline. The cliffs closed in on us and we slowed to a crawl to pass the boom gates, a strange reminder of war in these, to me, intensely familiar surroundings.

We had made our first passage. The immediate need was to release Edwards. We had been warned that our Boulton & Paul turret, an electrically worked aeroplane turret housing four 0.303 Browning guns, our main armament, reacted extremely badly to salt water, that the base filled up and shorted all the power. So we had to insert the gunner and seal up all the openings with a special plastic compound and tape. This we had duly done and poor Edwards had spent the six hours of the trip sitting stiffly in his cramped seat, observing with some alarm the threatening approach of the steep quartering sea, and probably muttering to himself:

'Christ, why did I ever leave a f*****g battleship.'

As we steamed slowly up the Fowey river, past the huddled grey houses rising steeply to the skyline, we ripped off the tape and released our gunner.

Howes greeted us with surprise; we were just a little bit proud of ourselves as another member of the flotilla, who only had to come from Dartmouth, had not been allowed to sail because of the weather.

I shall pass very quickly over our brief stay at Fowey. We thrashed about in the open waters off the Udder Rock, doing shoots and manoeuvres and learning to keep station, the most necessary qualification in a gunboat officer. Looking back on it the thing that strikes me most is the fact that we had no idea of what our fighting would be like, so that our preparation was mostly wrong; we had to learn our correct tactics in the hard school of night actions at sea.

Where we should have been devising and practising the correct formations and special tactics required for high speed, close-in fighting with E-boats, we were going solemnly through the various naval fleet formations, from Order 1, line ahead, to Order 6, sub-divisions in line abreast to starboard, columns disposed astern. We hauled flags up and down with the boats doing thirty knots over a long Cornish swell that every now and then gave us a rude jolt, and many were the concentrated panics aboard 64 when the appropriate flag couldn't be found or worse still the leader's hoist couldn't be read or understood, while the sharp-eyed seagulls floated serenely along, keeping close station without moving their wings. So keen were we on flags that we even produced tin ones which could be held sideways to the wind, and so read at high speed! Mercifully in our case, all this make-believe was very soon to give way to the sterner realities of war.

One evening, after we had been there for ten days, there came the whispered rumour of a job. 'All available gunboats to sail the following evening on a special job, half from Dartmouth, half from Fowey.' That was the effect of it. Were we to go? The three of us that had recently arrived had done no night work as yet. Would we be allowed to take part? Luckily there were only one or two of the operating flotilla based at Fowey able to work, so they needed us. We sailed to Dartmouth that day, received our orders and prepared for action for the first time. Little did we think what arduous work we should have to go through before we had our first real fighting.

I shall never forget our get-away that evening. We were the only boat of the three tied up to the Kingswear jetty, the others having fuelled and moored to a buoy in mid-stream. We were slipping at dusk, and being T.A.C. ('Tail arse Charley' as we called the junior boat) I was to follow in behind the others as they sailed down the river. In good time I gave the order to start up. The self-starters ground. Nothing happened. This went on and on. Presently the First Lieutenant and others were delivering short and concise messages to the engine room; still nothing happened.

61 and *58* burst into throbbing life and let go. I could see them begin to slide slowly down past the town. I had no means of explaining my predicament; my feelings can be imagined. My very first operation and unable to join because the engines wouldn't start, a thing that had never happened before. Nothing worse could occur to an untried C.O.; they might think anything of one. At the last moment one engine, by the grace of God the starboard one, the inside engine, started.

'Let go!'

They would be out of sight in a minute; I had to risk manoeuvring on one engine. Turning hard aport with the starboard engine running we just managed to get round inside the line of ships moored the length of Dartmouth harbour, dragged in our other engines and, accelerating rapidly, took up our station as though nothing had happened. It is hard to define the reason, but it remains one of the most anxious moments of my life.

Our job for the night was to act as a covering force for some mine-laying destroyers which were distributing their deadly load somewhere on the enemy convoy route near the Isle Vierge along the north coast of France between Ushant and St Malo. We were to sweep down to the eastward of their course and the Fowey unit to the westward, until within a few miles of the French coast, then turn to the eastward, sweep along the coast and back fairly close to Pleinmont Point on the south-west corner of Guernsey.

This we did without incident, but how we managed to keep together as a unit I do not know. We had had no night experience and it came on to blow from the south-west force three to four with driving rain. Howes had not yet learnt the tips we subsequently practised of getting a unit off in difficult conditions and of giving warning of a turn; nor did we have a shaded stern light in the rain, which later would have been the case. We did thirty knots under way the whole time; I can still remember vividly the anxiety we went through in the blinding rain near the French coast when we seemed to have lost the leader at the turn. We hung on somehow and we had our compensations in the morning. There was the impressive high land behind the Start with a bright, clear dawn and a rapidly freshening wind, very beautiful to behold; and had we not accomplished our first operation successfully? And did we not anxiously spell out a semaphore signal from the S.O.,[5] as the great hills of the Dart valley enclosed us once more, 'Well done'? We had only achieved the least that was expected of us, but we had been inexperienced and he knew what we had been through.

The Fowey unit had not fared so well. After stopping for a while in the low visibility caused by rain, their S.O. had suddenly, with the minimum of signalling and no time to be sure that all engines had started, dashed off at thirty knots. The others, *62* and *63*, had shot after him, creaming up his wake with wide open throttles, hoping to

5. Senior Officer of the unit.

see him and having only an indistinct wake to follow. The S.O., finally noticing that his unit was not with him, stopped as quickly as he had started; *62* coming on him suddenly at thirty-six knots, swerved to starboard, slammed down throttles and stopped; *63*, close behind, unluckily chose to swerve to starboard also on sighting the S.O., and rammed *62*. *62* was seriously damaged, luckily above water, and had to limp home alone. This was very largely if not entirely due to lack of method in handling a unit at sea. It was a persistent fault of many of the young R.N. Senior Officers that they would not take sufficient care and precautions to enable the following boats to be handled safely. In this case, had the S.O. given his unit plenty of time to start up and gone slowly until he had seen that they were in formation, there would have been no accident. This should have been more especially his care since he knew that neither boat had had any night experience.

Subsequently the S.O.'s boat developed stern gland trouble and filled her engine room with water; *63* made endless efforts to tow her, which were fruitless in the increasing weather conditions. Finally a destroyer had to come for her and tow her in, finding her only after her dead reckoning position had been altered fifteen miles by a sight taken by a French officer acting as navigator, probably the only occasion when a sun sight has been taken and used successfully from a fast gunboat.

This, I should imagine, was a fairly good example of the type of operational result that made senior officers ashore dislike gunboats. Two seriously damaged, out of action for weeks, and a destroyer engaged for fifteen to twenty hours to assist, exposed the while to the danger of air attack.

We were held at Dartmouth for a week unable to rejoin the rest of the flotilla at Fowey on account of strong westerly winds. While there we were entertained at the College, and in return Howes arranged to take a large party of cadets out in the boats to show them what they were like. It was a fine evening with a strong westerly wind and there was a heavy swell sweeping round the Start across the entrance to Dartmouth. We each had about twenty boys aboard and when we were well outside, to my horror, Howes led right into the sea and opened up, evidently to show the little boys what we had to take. We started leaping and banging and taking the spray over heavily.

Many of the small boys began to turn peculiar colours, and some of them, having no room anywhere but on the open deck, were clinging on for dear life. I began to get really anxious, but was greatly heartened by the sight of C.E.C. Martin, the racing motorist, Number One of *59* which had joined us at Dartmouth, standing with his back to the turret aft with his arms outstretched 'fielding' for any of the passengers who might begin to be bumped sternwards.

The next day we returned to Fowey and immediately received our sailing orders. 'The Sixth Flotilla to sail forthwith for Felixstowe.' This was exciting news indeed. Many rumours began to circulate as always on these occasions. The East Coast convoys were having a bad time; the E-boats were swarming in that area; a destroyer had been sunk and they wanted the special anti-E-boat weapon. There was some truth in these whisperings. The East Coast convoys were suffering very severely at this time and the culminating blow that cut short our working-up period and caused us to be rushed to Felixstowe, was the torpedoing of the destroyer 'Exmoor', at the end of February, by E-boats.

The day before we sailed, a German aircraft, in broad daylight and with no opposition, dropped mines accurately in the narrow entrance to Fowey. Aiming at bottling up the gunboats, they had done this before with success;[6] but early on the morning of the 6th March, 1941, in bright winter's sunlight, we slid out close to the high black eastern cliffs and headed for our operational base.

Of the journey round there is little that needs telling. Suffice it to say that three boats of the five that sailed from Fowey arrived after several days. Two had fallen by the wayside, at Portsmouth to be precise, but the trip had shaken the crews still further into shape.

Quite incidentally also we had been under fire as a flotilla for the first time. As we were jogging past Anvil Point in flat calm and sunshine, all five of us in tight arrowhead formation, a stick of bombs came down with a sibilant sigh, just audible above the roar of the engines, and burst in the water a hundred yards astern. None of us had seen the aircraft dip suddenly out of the clouds. I remember

6. Vice Admiral Sir Fitzroy Talbot in his privately circulated autobiography, *Old Rope*, records the use of part of the 3rd MASB (later MGB) Flotilla, which he commanded in July 1940, being ordered to clear acoustic mines dropped in the entrance to Plymouth by passing over them at top speed, about thirty-eight knots, in the hope that the subsequent explosions would be safely astern. This optimistic view was just sufficiently correct to avoid total disaster but the boats suffered severe damage.

poking my head into the wheelhouse and asking why the W/T was oscillating so, as the bombs whistled by. This little incident drew attention to two factors concerning attack by aircraft. One that, denied the normal method of detecting the proximity of 'planes by the sound of their engines, we should have considerable difficulty in obtaining warning of attack; the other that, even when taken by surprise, a large tight formation at speed was difficult to hit with bombs.

Two incidents remain in my mind: one, an air raid at Portsmouth. I was standing by my after turret to control the fire. Suddenly the turret of the boat alongside, *61*, roared into life, its four Browning guns with their high muzzle velocity and bright tracer shattering the night air and spitting a bright path of light low across the forecastle of my boat, where several of the crew were standing. They fell flat and by the grace of God no one was hurt.

I leapt across to the turret yelling at the occupant; the only result was another terrifying burst of fire on exactly the same bearing. It was time for deeds not words. The guns did not speak again. It transpired that the quaking victim was a stoker who wrongly thought he understood the turret; he thought that you trained the guns by pressing a certain little button. Actually you fired them by so doing. A sad case of misplaced zeal.

The second incident was a good deal more alarming. While at Portsmouth we lay right inside the cats[7] at *Hornet*. It is a very tricky place, as you have to execute a sharp one hundred and eighty degree turn round the end of the cats from the inner position to attain the outer channel, with very little sea-room to do it in. It definitely means swinging your boat by going ahead and astern respectively on your wing engines.

All five of the Sixth Flotilla were packed close together in the inner berth on the morning after our arrival, and there were several MTBs moored on the outer side of the cats. We were changing plugs on my port engine and checking magneto points on the centre. Thus it was impossible to use either of these engines in a hurry. Suddenly there was a cry of fire. One of the MTBs[8] on the outer side of the cats had had an explosion in her engine room and was almost immediately

7. Catamarans or floating jetties.
8. On 7 March 1941 *MTB 28*, a new seventy-two-foot Thornycroft boat in the 3rd MTB Flotilla, was destroyed by fire at *Hornet*.

ablaze from stem to stern. Several of her personnel were blown clean out of her on to the cats; it was soon clear that the fire could not be controlled. It was seen at once that we should be in grave trouble if the war-heads of the torpedoes or the air bottles of the tubes should explode. We all proceeded to start up and endeavour to get out of the inner basin as quickly as possible. Having only one engine available it was impossible to get my boat out, and being tied alongside 58, we arranged that she should try to swing both of us together out around the end of the cats to safety. It soon became apparent that she could not do it against the northerly wind blowing us all the time towards the mud on the *Hornet* side, where we should lie helpless, no more than one hundred feet from the blazing MTB. Every time we began to get round, another boat, manoeuvring to get out, gave us a nudge back in the wrong direction. Finally *58* gave it up, let us go, and got out of it. By this time all the others had got away and the MTB was a mass of flames burning steadily to the water line, with streams of 0.5 shells bursting out from her with the curious 'pheet-pheet' of unenclosed bullets igniting. The situation seemed sufficiently alarming; the heat generated round the air bottles and the war-heads was terrific, the metal was glowing a dull red. We were helpless, unable to turn with only one engine, and being blown steadily on to the mud. The only thing to do was to clear away, let go the anchor, and hope for the best. Boffin was ashore getting stores; I jumped on to the foredeck and superintended the clearing away of the anchor, casting an anxious eye from time to time at the burning hull. She was getting lower and lower, the war-heads would soon be submerged. I began to feel that all was over and we were safe. Just as we were letting go the anchor, the port engine burst into life.

'Hold on. Stow that anchor.'

I nipped back to the controls and took her gently out, our pro-pellers churning up thick patches of mud where we had been nearly aground.

Within three minutes we had berthed alongside the others, a cable from the blazing remains. As the order was given to stop engines there was a shattering explosion and a black cloud covered the wreck. An air bottle had exploded with one of the loudest bangs I have ever heard. Large bits of metal landed in Gunboat Yard half a mile away, and the front of *Hornet* was blown in, killing one Wren. It was fortunate that the casualties were no worse. We were indeed lucky.

143

Had we not got out just three minutes before the explosion we should have been in the immediate line of the blast, which was directed across the inner basin towards *Hornet*.

We arrived without further incident in a thick fog, after some extremely accurate navigation by our temporary S.O., Dicky Richards in *60*, and some even more dashing leadership. Doing thirty knots in the approaches to Harwich through fog patches in which you could not see the leading boat farther than half a cable, opened my eyes to things to come, and some of the chances we were later to have to take.

We were arriving at our proper theatre of war and we were glad of it. It was to prove a long struggle; a struggle not only or even primarily with the enemy, but first to understand and conquer our temperamental craft, and then to acquire the necessary equipment and discover the essential operating tactics without which success would have been impossible.

The first three boats (*MGBs 60, 63* and *64*) of the Sixth MGB flotilla arrived at Felixstowe on Sunday, 9 March 1941. The rest arrived in April. No one was quite sure what to do with these new boats. To say that they had been designed to fight E-boats would be significantly to exaggerate the thought that had gone into modifying their design and armament. All boats had two twin .303 inch Lewis guns, sited, amidships, while *MGBs 58-60* had a 20mm Oerlikon aft. These had run out by the time *MGBs 61-65* completed, resulting in their receiving a Boulton & Paul aircraft turret, with four .303 inch Browning machine guns as their main armament. Thus a degree of optimism prevailed over the size of weapon that could make much impression on such an enemy, matched by an equal amount of pessimism as to what weight of weapons such boats could carry and still attain the high speeds that were thought essential to their chance of finding and engaging the enemy. No one seems to have thought much about how the enemy were, in fact, to be located and brought to action.

The East Coast convoys had been hard pressed by E-boats throughout the autumn and winter of 1940/41. Their destroyer escorts had found it very difficult to fight off the fast moving, low silhouette German warships attacking at night. The early models of radar could do little more than give warning of an E-boat's approach. Gunnery was not radar controlled in the sense that it would be later linked to a radar. All that a destroyer could do in those circumstances was to fire star shell in the hope of seeing the attacking E-boats. A number of destroyers had been sunk in such actions and the loss of merchant ships in convoy had been significant.

My first impression of HMS *Beehive*, Coastal Forces base at Felixstowe to which we were attached, were favourable. After the chaos of Fowey, where there was no proper accommodation for crews who had to live in their boats, with the town, where the officers lived, a great distance away, and repair shops and slipping facilities insofar as they existed, scattered around the harbour, the comparative compactness and comfort of *Beehive* was a great asset.

As I climbed up the oily gang ladder of the dock wall for the first time in the rapidly gathering gloom of a foggy winter evening, I was greeted by the First Lieutenant with the news that my crew could have accommodation ashore; I was so surprised at this that I asked him for confirmation more than once, until I called down upon myself an acid rebuke for my temerity in doubting the good news. This was followed by a good dinner in the comfortable surroundings of the RAF mess, where the naval officers were for the time being housed in the surplus accommodation provided by a beneficent Air Ministry for the 'balloonatics', as we called the RAF personnel looking after the Harwich balloon barrage. The dinner was made even more memorable by the quantities of port generously provided for us by the First Lieutenant who was determined to welcome us royally. And royally he did us and himself too, accompanying our libations by a magnificent if slightly incomprehensible account of the commissioning of a cruiser.

But things deteriorated pretty rapidly, at least so far as Boffin and I were concerned, in the ensuing days. We had arrived in admirable condition, except that one of our propeller shaft stern glands was leaking and required repacking. This, I now know, is an easy job and can be done without slipping the boat, but having no experience of the trouble at the time, and being advised by the base staff that the boat should be slipped for the purpose, slipped we were.

The slipping at *Beehive* is done by means of a giant crane lifting a cradle on to which the boat is floated. The crane driver was a notorious character by the name of Bill, the slipping party being in the charge of a remarkably tired Petty Officer, under the supreme control of the shipwright officer, Lieutenant-Commander Lillycrap, of whom more anon. The responsibility for slipping was out of my hands, so I only did what I was told. My surprise and chagrin can therefore be imagined when, after the interminable shouting and strife that always accompanied this operation, the boat finally having left the water and swinging poised in the air like an enormous cod hooked at last, it was discovered that the after chocks were taking the weight on our wing propeller shafts, and that they were bent like two gleaming long-bows. The cradle had not been correctly measured and adjusted and, in the process of finding the proper positions for the chocks empirically, we had suffered severely.

And how we suffered. Within the first seventeen days of our time at *Beehive* we were slipped and un-slipped no less than five times in an endeavour to correct the misalignment of shafts, stern glands and P brackets which ensued. Only a gunboat or MTB officer who has experienced these things can appreciate fully the labour and discouragement involved in all this continual slipping; taking down the mast and aerials, removing guns, de-ammunitioning the ship, and so on, with no chance to get on with our training and final working up, and all at a time when we were particularly wishing to make a good impression.

Well, we did not make a good impression, however hard we tried; just the reverse. But I have more than a suspicion that our case was largely prejudged. Had we not wavy rings on our arms?[9] Was I not in command of a boat, the first RNVR to be so appointed? Naturally everything would be inefficient. What else could you expect? I am sorry to have to record that as the atmosphere surrounding us. I have already remarked upon the young RN officers, six of them in our flotilla, how well they treated us and how easy and pleasant we found it to work with them. I have invariably found it thus throughout the sea-going personnel of the Royal Navy, except on this occasion.

Led by the Captain of the base, a red-faced, paunchy individual, a retired officer with a DSO, and DSC, earned in CMBs, the Coastal craft of the last war,[10] there was a clique of young RN Lieutenants in

9. RNVR officers wore wavy gold stripes on their sleeves instead of traditional straight Royal Navy gold braid.
10. Commander R.H. McBean, DSO, DSC, Royal Navy retd. He evidently made Hitch's initial months at *Beehive* unpleasant.

command of MTBs who thought very highly of themselves and nothing at all of their lowly brethren with wavy stripes, who were struggling to perform a difficult and serious task. There were, of course, several notable exceptions, RN officers who gave us all the help they could and treated us as their equals, but the general atmosphere was hostile. They did not make allowances for our difficulties caused by lack of knowledge and experience of a specialised nature. They were all too ready to trip us up, get us into trouble, and cast us down both mentally and physically.

This was only a passing phase and my book will have failed of its purpose if it does not faithfully record the happy co-operation that later ensued between the few RN officers retained in Coastal Forces and the ever-growing stream of RNVRs; but at the time it was a real and disappointing difficulty that we had to face.

For three or four weeks after we arrived we were not operated. I do not know why, but suspect that it was because the operational authorities at the Nore were either unaware of our existence or did not know how to try to use us. Anyway it caused us to 'suck our teeth' to no small tune. Day after day of suitable quiet weather passed us by and still we were not sent out.

At last they made up their minds to use us in conjunction with destroyers. At this time one method of using destroyers for defending a convoy against E-boats was to have two of them weaving up and down at twenty-two knots to seaward of the convoy during the dark hours. Using their, at that time, somewhat primitive RDF (radar) for picking up E-boats, they were able sometimes to 'flush' a unit of the enemy coming quietly into the attack. But being much larger than E-boats, they were nearly always seen by the latter first, who, having considerably more speed than the destroyers, disappeared forthwith making smoke, so that it was unlikely that the destroyers could do more than disturb them. The idea was to have us as, so to speak, a projection of the destroyer patrol. They would find the quarry with their RDF,[11] and we, having a few knots more speed than the E-boats, would be released and sent off to chase and endeavour to destroy the enemy. The snag from our point of view was that they made the mistake of putting us between the two

11. At this stage of the war no MGBs or MTBs had yet been fitted with radar. Hitch got his first set in July 1942.

destroyers instead of behind both, and from the destroyers' point of view they reckoned without our intolerable noise, which being audible for many miles, gave away the presence of the whole party to E-boats proceeding on silent engines, as they would be when approaching a convoy. Thus having plenty of audible warning the E-boats would be able to avoid the, to them, thoroughly objectionable patrol and make their attack from another quarter.

However we started out for our first operation on a lovely spring evening in early April unaware of these difficulties. The boats were Dicky Richards (SO) in *60*, and Boffin and I in *64*. We were to rendezvous with the two destroyers on the convoy route a few miles north of the Shipwash, and to take up station in line ahead behind the leading destroyer and followed by the second one. This meeting duly took place; we dashed into position in fine style, rather showing off our high speed to the interested crews of the destroyers, who had not seen these peculiar noisy midgets on the East Coast before.

Then began one of the most terrible ordeals of my life. It was all right while the light lasted, but as soon as it got really dark it was awful. Sometimes the second destroyer would be a decent cable or so astern, but it is very difficult for us to keep an exact throttle setting and so a constant speed, when keeping station on another ship; frequently 60 would drop slowly back, forcing me astern until the destroyer's bows were almost overhanging my transom, all this in the dark at twenty-two knots. It was literally terrifying; the strain on one's nerves station-keeping under these conditions was intolerable. Every now and then Richards, having ridden up a bit too close to the leading destroyer, would throttle down rather rapidly. Up we would surge and to avoid a collision swing out to port or starboard, get on to his pressure wave and ride irresistibly forward almost level with *60*. This in its turn would necessitate rather violent deceleration on my part. I would drop back to clear 60's stern and find the seemingly vast and terrifying bows of a destroyer literally overhanging my stern. To make matters worse we were continually weaving around, often turning 180 degrees, and this frequently resulted in the second destroyer nearly cutting us in half, which they would have done on occasions if we had not violently accelerated to get out of the way. All this was a tremendous nerve strain to inexperienced officers such as Boffin and myself, but there was real danger as well. The destroyer was not aware of the great likelihood of our engines or underwater gear developing some defect during a long run of this sort, so he kept up close, seeming almost to delight in menacing us. There was an almost fifty percent chance of such a breakdown in the then unreliable state of the boats and, had our speed suddenly dropped on this account, there was the extreme probability of the destroyer's bows splitting us in half like a coconut; in such circumstances few of the ship's company of 64 would have survived.

However we were spared this fate. The fierce drumming of our engines continued unabated. Two diminutive noisily activated cockleshells, we swept along beneath the threatening black silhouettes of the destroyers, the white waves hissing back unendingly from the beautiful lofty down-swept bow. Boffin and I managed to keep awake and alert by talking and joking in a strained sort of way, when at 0400 we began to sweep slowly to port out of the line. Remonstrances with the coxswain proved unavailing. The steering had jammed; we executed a magnificent curve out and away until the others were lost to sight. Then we stopped and examined the gear to locate the jam. This was easily done, (bottom boards had entangled themselves with the steering gear) but we had completely lost our party.

Oh, the joy of the peace and silence! We had been underway in the conditions already described since five pm the evening before. That is eleven hours on end of continuous nerve-racking tension and noise. This is nothing exceptional for an MTB or MGB officer. I have often since done as much as sixteen or nineteen hours on end under way in our little cramped dustbin, two feet six inches by five feet, subjected to the tension of station-keeping at thirty knots much of the time in the dark, where an instant's inattention or lapse of judgement might mean disaster sudden and devastating. I am inclined to think that this is the greatest physical and mental strain that a serving officer is subjected to as a matter of normal routine. I have not flown on long bombing flights. Doubtless these can be very exhausting, but they are rarely so long, the officer is sitting in comparative comfort, he is not subjected to the intense noise and rush of cold air and often continuous spray, and above all he is not undergoing the strain of close station-keeping. The noise, vibration and flow of air remind one of an open racing car. I have raced repeatedly in the twenty-four hour race at Le Mans in a small open British car and not found it so exhausting as a bad night in a gunboat.

This feeling of utter physical and mental exhaustion has to be felt

149

to be understood. I do not believe that the majority of people have ever experienced it. I certainly had not until I operated gunboats. The last few hours as the light makes, the tension of night station-keeping relaxed, searching the horizon for a landfall, are almost the worst of all. Though it is easier, this very fact makes it more difficult to fight off the clutching hands of sleep and, curiously, the younger men invariably nod off. Shapes appear wherever you look on the horizon, you have to tell yourself all the time: 'I'm only seeing that', because after you have experienced the reality you know that it is different from the images. When you are ashore and it is all over, the relaxation is complete and overwhelming. You feel quite a different person, either stupidly happy over a drink, or irritable and depressed, small difficulties seeming desperate and insurmountable. One's natural stability is largely gone. Finally you get to bed and understand for the first time that sleep really is a vital chemical process. It literally does renew you; after ten hours you come back, a normal man again. And one other thing you have learnt, that you have been fussing unnecessarily because you have lain abed often before with sleep evading you. If you are sufficiently exhausted sleep will come, willy nilly.

Mercifully for us the destroyers did not like that devastating experiment. I suspect that the unceasing noise was not to their liking, and they guessed, no doubt, that it would give the E-boats fair warning.

Then started a grind of patrols. Flogging endlessly up and down a patrol line at either twenty-four or thirty knots, until it slowly dawned on all and sundry that this was not a good thing to do. It wore out our engines, it wore out our boats, and it was inclined to wear us out too; this maybe would not have mattered except for one decisive factor; it came to be realised that our chances of interception were almost nil. We pointed out that we could only see an E-boat a matter of a few hundred yards from a gunboat under way, but that if cut we could hear them for a very considerable distance in quiet weather, that is operational weather.

So they thought up a new method of using us. We were to go out at dusk and rendezvous with an ASDIC trawler off the convoy route in a likely position for E-boat interception. There the trawler anchored and we tied up astern. This was a delightful modus operandi, as far as we were concerned, since we could get plenty of rest, it being necessary only to have one officer on watch. It was quite a sound scheme, too, combining as it did the ability to listen for engines by ear and propellers by ASDIC.[12]

One of the early 'trawler patrols' indirectly resulted in our first brush with the enemy. It happened this way. We were lying astern of our trawler in a position 090 degrees five miles from the Aldeburgh light vessel, when reports began to come through of E-boats on the convoy route. This went on so continuously and enticingly that Howes finally decided to move up towards the area of strife. We slipped, the three of us, 60 with Howes in her leading, 59 on the starboard quarter, and 64 on the port, and sped away northward at thirty-six knots.

Presently the destroyers began to put up star shell to seaward of the convoy. We swept in a great semi-circle round the perimeter of the area lit by star shell. I shall not easily forget that run. The sea quiet, the port side of the hulls lit up by the greeny, white glare of the star shells, the wake creaming aft under the high pulsing beat of the engines opened up to their maximum continuous effort; men were on tip-toe, it seemed that the enemy must be near, and the steady fierce rush of the wind in the face kept them alert and expectant. Abruptly and yet almost unperceived the thing we were expecting was upon us; I saw a swirl of wash to port and noticed the leader going hard aport. I looked back and there it was, unforgettable and vivid in my mind now, my first sight of the enemy at sea. The moon was to the southward, astern; silhouetted in the moon's path, about a cable astern, was the black malevolent shape of an E-boat's bows, crossing at rights angles to our line of advance, heading for the convoy.

'Hard aport', the order shouted into the voice pipe was drowned by the high-pitched deafening crackle of the four Brownings aft. Edwards had got his teeth into them without hesitation. We swung round close alongside 60, opening up as we did so and gaining on her. The E-boats, there were at least three of them, were turning away, accelerating; the next moment our whole world was blotted out. We were in dense smoke doing forty knots and close alongside another boat. There was nothing to be done about it except carry on, hope

12. Within a few months, Coastal Forces craft were fitted with portable hydrophones, lowered over the side, to hear distant propeller noise.

for the best and aim to come out up-moon of the smoke screen. Tearing through this dense smoke cloud, unable to see even the bow of your own boat, was a harrowing experience. Luckily I remembered to give the coxswain a course at once. After what seemed like an age, actually I suppose about three minutes, the smoke began to thin, and suddenly we were out in the clear moonlight again. There was a thick line of smoke billowing away to port, looking like an ever elongating and enlarging caterpillar. Turning quickly round, I could see a black hull tearing along three hundred yards on our starboard quarter. The opportunity I had dreamed of, to have obtained adequate bearing on an E-boat for a close-in depth charge attack, seemed within my grasp.

'Stand by to let go starboard depth charge.'

Boffin scrambled over the whaleback and dropped down close to the large drum like weapon. His head reappeared close to mine and in a horrified shout he informed me that he did not know how to set the depth charge to fire. An entirely unmoved voice replied from the wheelhouse in measured tones:

'Press the key in and turn to the right, sir.'

The coxswain was always at his best in these moments of crisis. Boffin never again forgot how to set a depth charge!

There flashed across my mind a doubt. Was it one of our own boats? I had gone into the smoke still a little astern of *60; 59* was well back. I didn't think it likely that I had got ahead of Howes, and I doubted if *59* could be up so close. Still better make sure. I flashed our recognition lights; back came the answering flash at once. It was *60* after all. We had led out of the smoke. I had nearly depth-charged my Senior Officer. Still we had proved one thing, the effectiveness of the display signals. No challenge and reply could have been dealt with in those conditions of high speed and necessity for split second decisions. We were ever to remember that lesson, it was invaluable to us. Through using the more correct but cumbrous procedure of the ordinary challenge and reply, two coastal force officers and one rating in another flotilla from a different base lost their lives in an engagement between two of our patrols; I am convinced that had the display signals been used this tragedy would have been avoided.

Immediately we were again enveloped in thick smoke; go where we would we were plunged in dense patches of the wretched stuff, thrashing our way eastward in pursuit of the fleeing E-boats. We none of us saw them again, though we nearly rammed and engaged

152

59, saved once more by the rapid use of the recognition lights.

We had all engaged them for a brief moment or two before they made smoke; they had replied, but very half-heartedly. At that close range we must have hit them to some extent, and when starting for home we had observed a large orange flash some miles to the eastward. Thinking it might be *60*, who had not rejoined, we turned and went back eight miles in the direction of the explosion, but could see nothing. It was not *60* and we do not know to this day whether it was an E-boat blowing up, or what it was.

We had made a beginning. We had driven at least one unit of E-boats away from their attack and given them a fright; we were pleased at that. Howes gave the troops a speech, told the boats engaged to put up a star on their wheelhouse, which they did with enthusiasm, and the whole episode bucked the flotilla up considerably.[13]

It is interesting to note that Hitch's instinctive reaction to seeing a boat he took for the enemy was to depth charge her. The Brownings they carried were an inadequate weapon for destroying an E-boat, no matter how much damage they might do to her deck personnel. The Oerlikon could damage an E-boat but *64* had only Brownings.

After completing a number of trawler patrols without further luck, we were started on another type of operation. The listening patrol having been established, it was proposed to use us for this purpose off Brown Ridge.

Brown Ridge is the only considerable bank in the southern part of the North Sea in the latitude of Lowestoft, where the bulk of the E-boat attacks took place. It was almost exactly in the centre of the sea and thus was a very suitable Tom Tiddler's ground for the opposing forces. On account of the soundings and because there was a lighted buoy there, we were almost certain that E-boats must use this bank as a check on their navigation on the way over and even more probably on their way back. So we were sent to do listening patrols off Brown Ridge and very pleased we were, since it took us further afield. It was the thin end of the wedge towards fully fledged operations on the other side.

About this time an incident occurred that brings into sharp relief some of the difficulties we laboured under, nearly two years after the

13. This action took place on the 19/20 April off Harty Knoll.

153

war had begun. Out of the eight boats of the flotilla three had single Oerlikons, 20 millimetre guns on a heavy mounting aft. The rest of us had four 0.303 Browning guns in the electric Bolton & Paul turret, because there were no more Oerlikons available. A heavier gun was really essential against E-boats since they had two Oerlikons and we could not expect to stop an E-boat with 0.303s. The three Oerlikons were therefore the pride of the flotilla and greatly cherished. It has been an everlasting source of wonder to me that extremely costly gunboats should be produced and run, at great expense, without making any provision for supplying them with suitable guns. It has still more surprised me to observe how, when guns were finally available, these comparatively large vessels weighing thirty-five tons should be considered incapable of carrying more than one Oerlikon and four 0.5 guns; whereas a Spitfire weighing five tons has been found capable of carrying four Oerlikons.[14] The reason for this apparently inexplicable situation lies in the method of approach to the problem. The correct outlook is to treat these planing boats like aircraft, since weight is as important to them as to their airborne counterpart, but this has been beyond the capacity of DNO's[15] department. In their conception, if a single 20 millimetre gun is to be carried weighting 160 pounds, it is necessary to mount it on a stand weighing 1,530 pounds, instead of numerous light gun positions in the boat as part of the ship's construction, and to carry a great weight of ammunition which is unnecessary. Thus weighted down by a needless load, our boats subjected their engines to unnecessary strain and succeeded in carrying one 20 millimetre gun only as our main armament.

Anyway, Greece at this particular moment was in the process of being evacuated, and three days before the papers announced that our troops had been got away, we received a signal ordering us to pack up our three precious Oerlikons and send them forthwith to Liverpool for shipment to the Mediterranean to assist in the evacuation of Greece.

This was a bitter blow. We felt that we had just started to achieve some results in our job. We had made our presence felt by the E-boats and were eagerly hoping for another chance soon. The removal of these three guns almost put the flotilla out of the running for

14. The Spitfire, in fact, carried the lighter Hispano 20mm cannon.
15. Director of Naval Ordnance.

'killing' an E-boat for the time being. We could see fighters flying about all the time with four 20 millimetre guns in each and they had comparatively little to do in England at that time in the Spring of 1941. We felt it hard that the success we were trying so diligently for should be jeopardised for the sake of three guns which could by no conceivable chance arrive in time to help the evacuation of Greece, though doubtless after weeks of cold storage in transit they might be of use to ships in the Mediterranean. We had the E-boats there and then on our doorstep and we thought our job of sharing in the protection of the convoys an important one.

There was no appeal; our guns went. We were determined not to be defeated. Dicky Richards, Boffin and I started a predatory search for fire arms. We combed the local gun stores. There was nothing available. We had high hopes of the nearby aerodrome at Martlesham, where they had some thirty or forty Hispano guns which they were fitting into Hurricanes, four in each. We tried to persuade them that one gunboat flotilla was more important than one Hurricane; that all we needed was four of these guns; and it would be possible to have four without lowering the operational efficiency of the fighters, because there must always be at least one 'plane being serviced whose guns we could have. We even considered the possibility of salvaging, surreptitiously, four guns from a Hurricane that had just recently crashed in the water near Walton. But they would not, or could not, listen to us.

They did one thing, however. They put us in touch with a secret experimental depot at Orfordness. Thither we repaired to be greeted suspiciously by some civilian scientists. We were naval officers no doubt but our story seemed almost too incredible. During the second year of the war, a gunboat flotilla and no guns!

But our persistence and obvious sincerity slowly made its impression. Gradually suspicion changed to pained interest and finally to active co-operation. They were good fellows those scientists. Their job was to test our machine guns and ammunition with similar guns and ammunition captured from the Germans against German armour, with a view to improving the penetrative power of our shells. They took a chance on us and lent us four guns, the only weapons they could possibly spare. One was a whopping great 38 millimetre single-shot COW[16] gun (two-pounder); one was a 20 millimetre

16. Coventry Ordnance Works.

Hispano, just what we wanted; the other two were old Vickers 0.5s. We returned in triumph. We built a special cradle for the COW gun and mounted it on the Oerlikon pedestal in 60. The Hispano was installed in *59* and one of the 0.5s in the place of the Oerlikon removed from *58*. As one of the leaders of the search party, I got the spare 0.5 and set it up on a little tripod in the bows of my boat. This was early proof of the operational officer's opinion that a gun forward could be used effectively and was badly required. We had nothing with which to shoot forward. The more knowledgeable personnel ashore, who decided these things, did not share this opinion but it was subsequently proved to be correct by the success of the two-pounder mounted forward in the later seventy-one-foot-six inch MGBs.

Thus the Sixth Flotilla went to sea again, with its guns motley but its ardour undiminished. Shortly afterwards plans for a proper rearmament of the flotilla were arranged. After considerable consultation it was decided that all boats should be refitted, as the material became available, with a single Oerlikon aft in place of the Boulton & Paul turret, and with two power worked Frazer-Nash turrets mounting two Vickers 0.5 guns in each. These power turrets were to be placed on either side of the 'dustbin', replacing the twin Lewis guns, previously the only side armament. Boats were to go one or two at a time to Brightlingsea to be dealt with. *63* went first, early in April, and was kept for an unconscionable time; *61* went next, then *62*, finally *64* in mid-July.

The early summer drew on, with a continual run of patrols, though little further incident. Even if few excitements befell us at this time, there was always the fascination of the boats. Life then was not altogether easy for us at the base, and for that reason we enjoyed our sea time the more. To get out on one's own in the North Sea beyond the convoy route, to know that for the next twelve hours at any rate you were your own master, within the limits of the operation ordered; to see a North Sea sunset and a North Sea dawn, to feel the rush of cool air in one's face as the little boats creamed over the smooth sea; these were circumstances of never-failing delight, never to be forgotten.

Alan Gotelee, another rather elderly solicitor, arrived in *65* with a Canadian, George Duncan, as his first lieutenant. Otherwise of this period, the period up to the time that my boat went away to be rearmed and I came back to take over the flotilla under a new

Captain, I have little more to say. But there were a few patrols that deserve comment. The first was an air-sea rescue trip.

There had been a fairly strong northerly wind which had died away, leaving a long bumpy swell. We were all busy at ten o'clock in the morning, cleaning guns, checking W/T, testing steering and compass lights, all the usual preparations in anticipation of a job that night. Suddenly a shout along the dockside.

'All gunboats prepare for sea forthwith.'

A quick look round, a word with the coxswain and motor mechanic, and I knew that we were ready. Howes was coming along the dockside; I reported all ready to him. He said:

'Right. You take *64, 60* and *62* with you. Slip as quickly as you can. Get your clothes and come to SOO's[17] office for orders.'

I gave a few brief orders to Boffin and the coxswain, and ran up for my seagoing gear, which included my old Guernsey. I had had that old blue jersey since I was a boy. It had been with me on all my more adventurous sailing trips. I had worn it always at sea throughout the first year of the war in a minesweeper and at Dunkirk, and I had begun to look on it as my lucky mascot. Sailors are notoriously superstitious; there is something about the risks at sea and the fact that luck plays so large a part in the success or failure of any seaman's activities, that lends itself to the development of this way of thinking. Be that as it may, by this time I was firmly convinced of the importance to me of this old jersey, and I would not have gone to sea without it unless utterly impossible to do otherwise.

I remember rushing down, donning my garments, and speculating as to the cause of this unexpected and urgent call. SOO had our orders ready. We were to search for five airmen, the crew of a large bomber, who had been in the sea now for three days and nights. The HSLs (high speed launches), the RAF air-sea rescue launches, had been out after them all this time, but had had no joy so far, in spite of aircraft reports of the men's position. So the gunboats had been called in. It was a challenge to take up.

The engines were running, splitting the silence in the confined space of the dock. We jumped aboard.

'Good luck', from Howes.

17. Staff Officer (Operations), responsible for issuing operational orders transmitted from the Commander-in-Chief Nore's staff to an operational base.

'Let go'.

'Ahead port'.

The boats were gliding to sea, accelerating, the engines throbbing louder and louder, until they attained a steady roar as we settled down to thirty-four knots in open water. This was my first chance to study the chart and consider the position given to us.

'What a hell of a long way', was my first comment.

The little cross I had marked on the chart was to the north-east of Cromer, right out in the North Sea, one hundred and fifty miles away.

We were out on the convoy route and at thirty-four knots were bumped considerably in the northerly swell. We had a long run up the coast before we left the convoy route; this would give us a good opportunity of checking the accuracy of courses by the buoys. The effect of bumping on the compass can throw the course out by many degrees. It was a matter of care and judgement to ascertain the exact compass course to steer in bumpy conditions in order to make good any required course. I remember swearing to myself, as I studied the tidal streams in relation to the direction of the wind and swell, that I would put everything I had got into the navigation. Did not five men's lives depend upon finding that little cross, or such other little crosses as we might be given to reach?

On we roared. We left the convoy route and our last navigational aids. We ate our sandwiches. I told the coxswain that everything depended upon the accuracy of his steering. He stuck to the wheel all through that day. He was a magnificent helmsman. At 1300 we received a signal ordering us to sweep a line a little ahead of where we then were, to a position fifteen miles away from our original goal. They were evidently getting aircraft plots of the men. We were told there were reports of two rubber dinghies. The buzz spread from the W/T cabin and interest quickened. We altered course slightly and spread to visibility distance, thus covering a searching lane of at least fifteen miles.

Presently *62* flashed Harry, meaning a breakdown. We had a long way to go yet and probably many hours of searching before us; we had to retain our speed and could not afford to keep a boat with two engines only and a speed of eighteen knots. I ordered her to return independently. On we went at our thirty-four knots; our search was reduced to a ten mile strip.

At 1500 we reached the second position ordered and stopped. I

158

considered what to do next as *60* closed. The obvious thing seemed to be to proceed to the position originally ordered, which was fifteen miles away, in case it had been the right one. Suddenly there was a shout from Punton, the leading stoker, aft.

'Making water fast, sir'.

This was unpleasant news. We were a long way from home. I went to inspect. There was no doubt about it. The starboard P bracket had broken its retaining bolts; the propeller, on the unsupported shaft, was being allowed to swing up against the boat, and had cut a hole the size of a dinner plate in the bottom. The after compartment was flooding rapidly; if the bulkhead to the engine room failed, nothing could save the boat. The only hope was to keep her going fast, so that the self-bailers acting by the suction of the boat's speed through the water, and helped by the lift of the hull when planing, could keep the water level down.

'Start up'.

I explained the situation to *60* by semaphore and moved off, accelerating to thirty knots, shaping a course for the original position. We couldn't give up the search at this stage with five men, maybe quite close, in the drink. We kept an anxious eye on the after compartment. It kept a steady level of water, about eighteen inches deep, as long as we retained our speed.

We spread again and continued our search. Three aircraft came over, took a look at us and passed ahead in the direction in which we were going. They did not seem to know where to go either, and gave us no lead, such as we had hoped for. We were within a mile or two of my first little cross, or so I reckoned. I was wondering what to do next, as we could not stop, when the problem was solved for me by a further signal from the Nore.

'Proceed to position – .'

Eagerly I plotted my third little cross. It was thirty-five miles away in exactly the reverse direction to that in which we were proceeding. Round we wheeled. Anxiously I checked the tide. We had been under way now for six hours and had covered some one hundred and eighty miles. Could we keep our DR accurate?

'What are you steering, Coxswain?'

'South 74 east, sir.'

'Make it 76.'

'Aye, aye, sir.'

Well, I couldn't do more than check the figures and sea conditions as carefully as possible.

We were joined by an HSL, which hove over the horizon coming on opposite courses. She asked permission to join up with us, as she had lost herself. I agreed, spread her on my port side, *60* being stationed to starboard, and gave her my estimated position. On we went. The men were silent now. They had had a tiring time already, keeping their eyes skinned; the first excitement and enthusiasm was wearing off. Mercifully our starboard prop kept going and the water held its level, though I was expecting to have trouble with the shaft at any moment.

We received another signal.

'After completing existing sweep, search for fifty miles 270 degrees.'

Another fifty miles to the west, and then one hundred and eighty miles home. Christ! Would the boat stand it? That meant another seven or eight hours running at thirty knots. We should have to go into Lowestoft. Lucky we started with a high fuel load. We were getting near to the end of the run down to the third little cross. A mile and a half to go.

'Object in the water fine on the port bow, sir.'

It was the port Lewis gunner who saw it first. Eagerly we scanned the sea. Yes! There it was, and it was a rubber dinghy too. We rushed towards it, slowing as we neared. There were no signs of airmen, though. As we slid alongside we saw the tragedy at a glance. There was one man in the dinghy. He had evidently fainted from wounds and exhaustion, and had slid down into the base of the dinghy, which had a foot of water in it. His head had fallen back and was under water. He was dead. The excitement was gone. Sailors are quickly moved from cheerful anticipation to depression. Everyone was silent.

'Signal the HSL to pick up this dinghy. We will continue the search.'

The telegraphist passed the signal. The HSL had special gear for picking up purposes and anyway we could not stop, as already our after compartment was filling dangerously. We moved on. I looked round for 60. I had stationed her three miles on my starboard beam. She was slowing up. Yes, definitely, and beginning to flash.

'Am closing dinghy with four airmen in.'

A cheer went up when this was announced. I called for the R/T phone and made contact with *60* that way.

'Are the airmen alive?' I asked.

'Yes, why?' came back the surprised reply.

I realised then what a silly question it was; but our recent disappointment had made me cautious.

'Have you seen another dinghy?' came from Richards. 'Airmen inform us that their captain was wounded and put in one dinghy by himself for comfort. Dinghy broke away last night and was seen drifting to the northward.'

I told him of our discovery. A pause.

'Did you say he was dead?' from *60*.

One could imagine the survivors' anxious query.

'Yes.'

I closed and circled *60* while they were getting the men aboard. There was nothing more to wait for. We set course for home and sent a signal informing the Nore of our success. I congratulated Curtis on his steering and felt rewarded for my special care over the navigation, or was it luck? Mostly luck, in matters of this sort and we had indeed been lucky. Each boat had brought up one dinghy right ahead.

We had an uneventful run back in a beautiful flat calm summer's evening. The glossy surface of the water was broken at one point by numerous bits of floating wreckage, black and ominous against the golden sheen of the sea gilded by the setting sun. *60* sent a signal.

'Am running out of oil, have you any to spare?'

The motor mechanic was consulted and said that he could let them have five gallons.

'We can let you have five gallons. Will this do?' was flashed back.

'Yes, just' came the reply.

But we could not stop. How to transfer the oil at thirty knots? The motor mechanic hit on a bright idea. He put it in an old ten-gallon drum and sealed the top. Over it went, and *60* stopped and picked it up while we circled. The only other distinct memory I have of the return journey is of Boffin and I sipping sherry with extreme enjoyment as we neared the Shipwash. We had had nothing to eat or drink since our sandwiches at noon – it was then nine in the evening; that sherry tasted very good. The first time we had had a drink on our bridge.

We had sent a signal requesting to be slipped immediately on arrival. We roared up to the examination vessel, who made his usual signal, 'stop'. He must have been somewhat astonished to receive our reply, as we swept round him in a large circle at thirty knots.

'If I stop I sink. Request permission to enter.'

The assent came at once; in a few minutes we were in and over the slipping cradle. We had done twelve hours under way at thirty knots and over, seven and a half of them with a large hole in our bottom, and the starboard prop shaft, unsupported, describing weird and wonderful arcs beneath. Even if we did have breakdowns in our highly strung little boats, is it to be wondered at that we grew to be very fond of them?

We had been very lucky. Lucky to find the men at once, and lucky to get back all that way with the boat in this condition. That good fortune, the secret of which I hoped lay in my old jersey, had not failed me this time.

We kept many morning rendezvous at Brown Ridge, hoping to meet the E-boats returning at dawn. Howes achieved this on one occasion with *61* and *59*. They were on their way home when they saw high-speed boats approaching. Realising they must be E-boats as they were heading east, Howes turned round and started to cut them off. There were two of them, one larger than the other. They joined battle proceeding to the eastward at thirty-seven knots. Exactly what happened I do not know, but *59*'s engines early gave out and she dropped behind. Howes held on until almost in sight of the enemy coast, but his 0.303 weapons were unable to inflict serious damage on the enemy and soon jammed, whereas the E-boats began to cause him considerable discomfort with their two Oerlikons. He had to turn back in the end, with only one Lewis gun firing. At that the E-boats turned too and it looked for a moment as if they were coming after him.

'I took the lowest view of that,' he said in his humorous way, 'as my engines were pretty well red hot, and the Browning barrels drooping with exercise. Luckily they changed their minds.'

I met him when he got back. He was very disappointed, but there was nothing else he could have done. He had a few minor casualties and a great number of shell holes in his boat, but luckily no very serious damage. Considering the unfair odds in armament he did remarkably well to chase them away.

Soon after this we started to go over to the other side for patrols, to back up the MTBs and look for convoys. At this time there seemed to be practically no shipping on the Dutch coast at night. Neither the MTBs nor ourselves ever found anything except a very occasional fishing vessel. We often found ourselves quite close to the other shore at dawn due to some delay or other and, as SO of the unit, I used to wonder what I should do if we suddenly sighted German destroyers. With only 0.303 and a depth-charge there would be only one proper course of action in daylight. To keep clear and shadow, reporting the enemy's position, course and speed. But I was sufficiently inexperienced then to think it was my duty to attack whatever the odds, and I believe we should have tried a depth-charge attack if the situation had arisen. The problem used to bother me a lot because I realised it would be virtual suicide; yet was it not my duty? Luckily the chance never came, otherwise foolhardiness, born of lack of experience, might have ended many lives prematurely and unnecessarily.

On another occasion, near the Dutch coast, heavy British bombing raids were taking place. We were patrolling slowly on a flat calm sea; the night dark and moonless. Every now and then there would be bright orange flashes to starboard followed by tremendous thuds as heavy bombs landed in Holland. Suddenly a large plane, travelling from east to west, flew low over us with flames coming out of her exhausts, an intermittent popping and banging audible above the drone of our engines. There was a poignant pause. We all realised something was very wrong with her. Forty seconds later there was a crash a mile or so to port, followed instantaneously by a bright flash of flame and a horrible report.

There was no need for comment; we turned to port and opened up. Within three minutes we were on the spot. Large bits of floating wreckage surrounded us. Tanks, bits of fuselage, clothing, pieces of wing, and a half-blown-up rubber dinghy. This latter we investigated at once and hauled aboard 64 with some difficulty, all lending a hand. Of the crew of that plane we found no trace, or rather, alas, only one trace. That dinghy was covered in entrails, and the smell, a deathly smell, clung to our hands in an uncanny manner. I remember washing and scrubbing for days afterwards before I could get rid of all traces.

At the time we were much distressed. The plane was clearly British. In a matter of seconds five brave men, living, warm and happy like ourselves, had been dashed to destruction, almost within our reach; now there was nothing left, nothing but a contaminating smell. Such experiences happen all too often in war to many; it was not my first. Nevertheless they cannot but have a sobering effect. We set sadly home with our pathetic remnants, honouring afresh the men who nightly risked such a fate.

Hitch ends this chapter of his book at the point at which the Sixth MGB Flotilla had essentially completed its novitiate. Officers and men had learnt how to operate their boats and had started to form sound theories about the best way to find the enemy and bring them to action. Very little had been achieved beyond morale raising skirmishes but the illustration of Peter Howes' pursuit of two E-boats with a single gunboat, armed with nothing heavier than 0.303 guns, and most of them temporarily out of action, illustrates the extraordinary esprit de corps of the Royal Navy generally and the young men in Coastal Forces in particular. So does Hitch's theorizing of how he would have had to tackle a German destroyer in daylight, had he had the misfortune to meet one. In spite of the inadequacy of the boats and their weapons there was a determination to reaffirm the Royal Navy's control of the Narrow Seas after the German Navy had bid to seize it in the wake of the fall of France.

This time also marked the point at which most of the regular Royal Navy lieutenants were being withdrawn from Coastal Forces and sent to larger ships where their professional training was of far greater value in those infinitely more complex vessels and weapon systems. Their places were being taken steadily by young reserve officers, most of them fresh out of a few weeks of training, who had to be rapidly forged into competent seamen, navigators and, ultimately, commanding officers.

Chapter Eight

Sixth Flotilla
July – November 1941

Hitch had almost completed the rearmament of *MGB 64* at Brightlingsea in July 1941 when he was telephoned by Peter Howes:

His voice came sharp and incisive over the line:

'Hullo, Hitch. I'm going on a long signals course, starting at the beginning of September. I think you're the right man to take over the flotilla; will you?'

'Can't you get out of it?' I temporised.

The idea of losing Howes, with his strong personality and powers of leadership, seemed devastating. I was happy enough commanding a unit at sea, but the idea of taking on all the strife ashore was an altogether different matter. In a flash I remembered how often I had been sheltered in matters large and small behind the secure barrier of his responsibility as Senior Officer.

'No. Not a hope. I've tried everything. It's bloody.' The staccato sentences drove home the full realisation like hammer blows.

I said nothing. All the difficulties, the responsibilities, my own lack of knowledge and incompetence in many matters of naval routine, the mere fact of having to follow in the footsteps of such a fire-brand as Howes, above all certain difficulties with the Base Captain, these things revolved desperately before my mind like a kaleidoscope of bad dreams.

'Well, will you take it on?' The voice was insistent. I must make an instantaneous decision, a decision that would certainly vitally affect the rest of my naval career.

Could I cope with it? I did not know the answer, but I knew deep down that it was cowardice and therefore a fatal mistake to refuse additional responsibility and work, provided I thought I understood my job in its essentials.

'All right, I will,' I said. 'Good. See you in a few days.'

There was a faint click as he replaced the receiver. I was committed.

All too quickly Howes' last ten days passed. The weather was rough and *64* was being re-engined in the hangar. There was only one trip and that was disastrous. There had been a big bombing raid and several returning planes had crashed in the North Sea. Though it was blowing hard from the south-west the gunboats were ordered out to search early one morning. Howes took four boats and, as he was going down wind on the way out, he went further than he had realised, and when he turned back into it, he had a hell of a passage home. They came in at midday soaked to the skin; three out of the four boats were 'gash';[1] it was many weeks before they were running again.

Howes left at the end of August, departing in a blaze of glory and with his large blue Bentley stuffed to the hatches with luggage. Just before he left he was awarded a D.S.C., fully merited. His attitude towards this was accurately summed up in his remark to me when I first saw him wearing the ribbon and went up to congratulate him:

'Well someone's got to hoist it for the flotilla.'

He had worked hard, fought three engagements with inadequate weapons, and given gunboats their only sound start. We were all sorry to see Howes go, I most of all. I had a natural shrinking feeling at the thought of stepping into his shoes. He had held the centre of the stage so completely and so fittingly, he was so much liked and respected by the sailors as well as the officers that I realised it would be difficult to follow on, particularly as I had not that *je ne sais quoi*, that inexpressible something, that goes, or is supposed to go, with straight stripes.

Though we did not know it, the wavy stripes were at the dawn of their day. Howes had handed over to an RNVR, showing that he at least had an open mind. The first Captain of the base had handed over to Commander Kerr, who had a still more open one. We had got on well with our RN officers, but most of them were leaving now. Whitehead and Dixon went, and very soon Johnson also to

1. With defects making them unfit for operations.

command the Fourth Flotilla. They were replaced by RNVRs, mostly our early first lieutenants.

Hitch was appointed Senior Officer in command of the Sixth MGB Flotilla on 25 August 1941 and was promoted to lieutenant commander the following month. He was the first RNVR officer to be promoted to Senior Officer of a flotilla. He then set out to form the officers and men into the most effective fighting unit that he could contrive. In this he had the full backing of his new Base Captain, Tommy Kerr, who had taken command at the end of July 1941. Kerr was an avuncular commander RN, brought back from retirement when the war started, who therefore cared not what their lordships thought of him but cared a great deal for the success and safety of the young men whom he was there to support and serve, and send out to fight the enemy. Everybody who served under Tommy Kerr liked him. His tall, thin, angular figure was always to be seen on the pier head at Felixstowe when the boats went to sea, waving them goodbye, and he would be there when they limped back, as so often they did, tired, strained and, all too often, with their dead and wounded. He never failed to support Hitch in his demands for changes in motor gunboat armament, invariably resisted by the Admiralty until proven beyond all reasonable doubt and perhaps further than that. He also turned a blind eye to young RNVR officers who did not always comply with King's Regulations and Admiralty Instructions but got on with the war in their own enthusiastic but unorthodox ways. Perhaps he felt that they had enough to learn about the sea and the enemy without worrying too much about less urgent matters such as their dress, their discipline, and even their tendency to intoxication when not required for duty.

Indeed these young RNVR officers, some of them now captaining their boats for the first time, had much to learn. Most had only been in the Navy for between twelve and fifteen months and none for more than two years. They had a fair idea about how the Navy did things by then, even if they didn't always agree with it, but how to handle their highly strung little warships in order to bring them into battle with the enemy still required a great deal of practice before success would come. When motor gunboats had first been designed there had been no tactical doctrine as to how they should be handled. It was the development of this doctrine that was perhaps Hitch's greatest contribution to the success of his own flotilla and ultimately, by example, to all other MGBs in service. Hitch was all too aware that the Navy was none too sure that seventy-foot fast motor gunboats were the answer to the E-boat challenge. Their record to date had been indifferent at best, their unreliability notorious, and such success as they had achieved in deterring E-boat attacks on coastal convoys hard to prove in the absence of sunk or captured enemy. Hitch became aware that official thinking about the replacement of the first generation of MGBs was moving to larger but slower motor gunboats, capable of carrying heavier armament, ultimately to be known as the 'D' or Dog class. Hitch did not agree. More of that later in his own words.

There still also remained at this stage of the war doubts about the basic competence of RNVRs in command, with their undisciplined ways and lack of experience. The resentment felt by men of Hitch's age, over thirty and with two years of hard warfare behind them, to the assumption of innate superiority by those with regular commissions comes out again and again in his book and his diaries. Probably it would have evaporated with time, as it did for most other RNVR officers who survived the war and look back on their time in the Royal Navy with deep affection and great respect for their regular colleagues. After all, by the end of the war over 85 per cent of all officers in the Royal Navy were either RNVR or RNR so that it was hard to feel one was the underdog in a world dominated by one's own kind. In 1941, however, that feeling lingered on in spite of the support from men like Tommy Kerr, and the small number of sea-going regular naval officers remaining in Coastal Forces. RNVR officers who suffered from a tenuous grasp of KR and AIs, with the resulting bruises from conflict with authority, were inclined snidely to refer to straight stripers as 'state educated', an allusion to the fact that Dartmouth was a government school in an era when the self confidence of the men who had attended public schools or the great independent grammar schools caused them to joke about their social equals in the Navy enjoying a subsidised education. 'State educated types' were particularly those RN officers who enjoyed quoting regulations at their irregular colleagues.

Hitch felt the weight of responsibility as the first RNVR Senior Officer of an MGB flotilla. If his inexperience led him into manifest error, would that close off the same opportunity for other equally suitable candidates for the role?

Though Howes undoubtedly left me a fine legacy in the Sixth Flotilla he also left a trail of difficulties. Most of the COs went with him. This left me with a set of new officers, admittedly officers I knew since they were our original first lieutenants, but untried in command of boats. Then the boats themselves were in the most unfortunate condition. *65* was away rearming, *62* had been sunk (more of this later), *67* was undergoing lengthy repairs to her bow as a result of collision with *62*, *58*, *59* and *61* were all out of action for some time as a result of damage received in the recent rough trip looking for airmen. This left me with *64*, *60* and *63* only, one of which was always sure to be out with minor defects. The flotilla had never failed to produce a unit when required; I particularly did not want it to fail immediately after I had taken over.

More important than this there was a malaise spreading through the flotilla. Most of the more go ahead and keen officers were getting unsettled and were on the verge of applying for a transfer to destroyers, or some other branch of the Navy, where they considered that they were more likely to see action. This was due to several causes. The breaking down of the boats, the long spell, over two months, without any contact with the enemy or seemingly any likelihood of it, chiefly due to the fact that the E-boats were not operating in the North Sea at that time of year, a growing doubt as to whether the boats ever would be efficient enough tactically and materially to do their job. The immense difficulty in catching the E-boats coupled with the unreliability of our boats was becoming apparent and disaffecting many even enthusiastic spirits.

Perhaps Hitch's greatest challenge at this time was the maintenance of his boats in a state fit for operations. He was quick to acknowledge the important part played by those who supported him in this crusade.

At the other end of the scale was Chief E.R.A. Pavey, the Sixth Flotilla Engine Room Artificer; a wiry, humorous faced little man with twinkling eyes. How that man worked. He never relaxed. No make and mend,[2] no weekend leave, no pipe down[3] at 1600 for him. No nonsense about his work; no sticking to the letter of the law and so holding a boat back from sea. The boats were wanted. They kept on coming in with trouble. They must be repaired somehow and got to sea again. Hours of labour in hot engine rooms, upside down with his head in the bilges, sweat pouring down his face, his bottom as like as not against a hot manifold. Pavey was no chicken. He stuck to it and he made those boats work.

At that stage of the war, making the boats operate reliably had marginally higher priority than fighting the battle with the Admiralty to get them more effective weapons and reduce the noise they made. In turn, both these struggles were pointless unless the problem of finding the enemy, other than by pure chance, could be solved in those pre-radar days, or rather before radars were fitted to small Coastal Forces' warships.

Howes's departure, followed soon after by the rest of the RN officers, created an inevitable disturbance which Hitch sought to settle in his own way by regularly bringing his officers together to discuss what they should be doing to train their crews and prepare their boats to fight the enemy.

I can remember so well our evening discussions in the tiny wardroom in one of our boats, working out over a bottle of port the details of operation Fanny or dwelling, somewhat optimistically no doubt, upon the great possibilities opened up by mine laying trips far afield.

The officers of the flotilla were to be all RNVR from this time on; the boats were manned as follows. I had *64* still, Campbell took command of *67*, and Head was my first lieutenant. Sub-Lieutenant Cowley, a Manxman, late first lieutenant of *61*, had *58*. *60* went first to a Canadian called Kirkpatrick and after a short while to Sub-lieutenant Ronald Carr. David James, late first lieutenant of *63*, got *61* and George Duncan took over *65* from Gotelee, who wanted a larger boat and went to the first D Class MGB to be built.

I have said little of the crews as yet. Individuals have been mentioned, but no generalisations. Our gunboat crews fall into two periods and categories. The early period when we had a majority, or

2. A make and mend is a Royal Naval informal day of rest which, in the days of sail, allowed the crew to make or mend their clothes.
3. In the Navy, a boson's pipe announces changes of routine, including the end of the working day, thus piping down.

at least a healthy sprinkling, of active service[4] hands, and the later days, starting from the time I took over the flotilla, when any new crews arriving were entirely 'Hostilities Only'[5] personnel, in many cases men who had never been on the sea.

The 'Hostilities Only' crews were truly amazing. They were so keen to do their share in downing the Nazis that they could be knocked into good crews in a matter of weeks. Raw boys, from the machine shops, the lathes, the potteries, the railways, the farms, they put up with that most dreadful of scourges, sea-sickness, in smelly engine rooms and stuffy W/T cabins, and they acquitted themselves like seasoned men in the face of the enemy.

But in the early days we had mostly active service men. I had some particularly good ones in my boat. I have mentioned Punton before, my leading stoker. He was a tiger. He had been in MTBs in China before the war. His one idea was to get to sea and at the enemy if possible. I wish he could have been with us later, when his wish would have been fulfilled. The way that man sweated in an engine-room, with a temperature of one hundred and ten degrees, undergoing muscle-aching contortions, changing a set of plugs in order to keep 64 available, was a sight to inspire a cynic.

Perhaps the most serious element of the new training regime introduced by Hitch was the need to establish tactical doctrine so firmly in the minds of all officers that, when presented with the opportunity for action in a fast moving and confusing situation at night, they would be of one mind as to how to tackle it. Again he describes how he went about this.

As the reconstituted flotilla settled down, I introduced one other element in our communal life, which was to be a success and prove of value to us. It was known as 'the tactical talk'. It originated in this way.

Shortly before Howes had given up the flotilla, while *64* was still at Brightlingsea, there had been a slight disaster. A unit had gone to sea consisting of *62, 60* and *67*. They were going over to the other side. *62* was leader. When nearing the Dutch coast they had suddenly

4. Active service ratings were regular Navy.
5. Those conscripted into the Navy for the war were referred to as 'Hostilities Only'. Some ratings had been in the RNVR before the war but once war broke out all those joining for the war only were classified as 'Hostilities Only'.

come upon a small fishing boat under sail. They had closed at speed and *60*, the nearside boat, getting excited, had forged ahead and opened fire. The leader, realising that here was no fair game for a gunboat, had called off his ships and ordered them to follow him, at the same time turning away to starboard. In the resulting confusion *67* had rammed *62* severely, knocking in her bow to a distance of several feet and damaging her so seriously that she rapidly filled with water and had to be abandoned. Her crew were taken off and she was sunk by gunfire. Such accidents must inevitably happen when operating fast boats at night in war conditions, with no lights and often in the presence of the enemy. But in this case I considered that the accident was largely due to the fact that there had been no pre-arranged plan for dealing with the eventuality that had arisen, namely the discovery of a small and inoffensive fishing vessel. *60* had been too hasty in attacking and had thereby caused the confusion. She could not be censured however as everything was left to the initiative of the C.O. and he could justly claim that he was exercising his initiative, albeit somewhat mistakenly.

I had always been of the opinion that a mistake was being made in not having pre-arranged plans for dealing with different situations. Hard and fast rules could not be laid down, but the best method of attempting to deal with the various types of enemy craft that might be met could be discussed and postulated and the different COs would then at least know upon what lines the leader would probably be thinking. I was determined to formulate some clearly defined plans of attack and tactical dispositions. With this in view I decided to have a weekly meeting of all the officers in my flotilla, to discuss these matters and work out our schemes and, because originally our idea was to get at the correct form of tactics for our warfare, we called it the 'tactical talk'.

I think it was one of the most useful training developments we had. In the early talks we got out our first clearly defined forms of attack to meet all the situations we could visualise. In some instances our original ideas proved to be wrong, but we had made a start. As we fought and gained experience, and talked with others who had done likewise both in this war and the previous one, we amended and altered tactics until we arrived at a really sound fighting technique. I can affirm unhesitatingly that the tactical talk helped very considerably towards this end. It not only got us together and allowed of everyone's ideas being put forward and considered; it enabled any officer, however junior, to air his grievances or put forward his query in open counsel. It is said that Nelson's captains were a 'band of brothers'. Though on a humble and undistinguished scale, we were also such a band, and without a doubt it contributed much to our success.

It was frequently frustrating for both officers and men to work with the delicate instruments they were supplied with. An MGB was, at that stage of the war, little more than a fast pleasure craft turned into a miniature warship by adding light armament which, though inadequate in the early stages of the war to stop E-boats, still tended to stress their hulls more than their original design allowed for. These fast, lightly built, high-powered boats, handled by men with little prior experience of the sea or marine petrol engines, were inevitably going to have more than their fair share of troubles. Hitch's strong sense that they must never fail to respond to the call for an operation put even greater stress on both men and machinery, raising the risk of breakdown, often as not at a critical moment.

Though we slowly pulled ourselves together mentally as a flotilla again, we had no luck with the material and physical side of operating until the action of the 19th/20th November. The two or three boats that we could muster were always on the edge of breakdowns because they could not be spared for maintenance. On one occasion we started out with three boats to act as an escort for the minelaying MLs off the Hook of Holland, one dropped off a few miles from the Harwich boom, another twenty minutes later, just as we were heading east from the convoy route.

I was angry by this time, all the more determined that the Sixth should not fail to carry out a patrol when ordered. *64* went on alone and a few minutes later the telegraphist reported that our W/T set had broken down beyond repair. Thus alone and out of touch we carried out our patrol off the Hook. It was a case of anger rather than wisdom and during the later and more lonely watches of the night I rather regretted my decision; but the Sixth had not failed to obey orders.

Soon after, on a rather rough night, 63 carried away both her wing engine pendulastics.[6] In the sea that was running her centre engine alone could not drive her fast enough to retain suction on the salt water pumps, so that engine over-heated and had to be stopped. Helpless, she had to obtain towing assistance and was ultimately taken into Lowestoft by a trawler.

The worst trouble we encountered resulted from rough weather trips in October. They gave valuable experience as to the capabilities of our boats, but were incredibly unpleasant and frightening at the time.

The first was brought about by an air-sea rescue trip. The unfortunate crew of a bomber crashed into the sea twenty miles from the Dutch coast halfway between Flushing and the Hook. It was at night and there had been a very strong westerly wind which had eased to force five or six. The sea was piling up on the Dutch coast and it was not known whether the crew survived the crash. All that had been received was a W/T signal just before the bomber had landed in the water, giving an approximate position and calling for help.

The only boats that could possibly make it were the gunboats; they were sent. It was bright moonlight and we were going down wind. As we drew away from the land at thirty knots the seas began to mount and break, the boats to swoop and stagger in their flight. I looked apprehensively at the little white ensign at our yard arm. It was flying out stiffly ahead. We were doing thirty knots. That meant a thirty-five to forty mph wind. Not good enough, I thought, and looked still more apprehensively at the rising seas. The boats were beginning to surge badly now; drawing up sharply as the stern lifted to a steep following sea, the engines grinding and jarring as the revs came down despite their thousands of horse-power driving and thrusting the hull into the hollow of the wave. The next moment, like a racing car released by the starting gun, they would be hurtling forward at what seemed to be break-neck speed, on the foaming crest of a wave, the entire forward half of the boat clear of the water and the spray flying mast high from the wide thrown bow wave.

The decision whether to go on or not in circumstances such as these is one of the most difficult I have had to face. To go on close to the enemy coast with a strong on-shore wind and sea was to risk our boats seriously. The return journey, banging into the waves,

6. The pendulastic in an MGB was the coupling between the engine and the gearbox, prone to malfunction.

1. Robert Hichens aged about seven with his sister Loveday at St. Mawes, Cornwall during the First World War.
2. Loveday's wedding at Trereife in 1927. Robert is on the left of the first standing row.

3. Robert aged about twenty in his sailing clothes in Guernsey.

4. Magdalen College First Eight, 1930. Robert seated centre.

5. Enlargement of Robert as stroke of the Magdalen Eight.

6. Catherine Enys at the time of her engagement to Robert.

7. Robert in his International 14 dinghy on the Penryn Creek.

8. The Aston Martin's engine laid out for its annual maintenance on the drawing room floor at Bodrennick.

9. Robert racing the Aston at Le Mans in 1937.

10. HMS *Halcyon*, a fleet minesweeper, in 1940; Robert's first ship.

11. Robert sighting *Halcyon*'s anti-aircraft gun.

12. HMS *Niger* coming in to Dover with troops evacuated from Dunkirk.

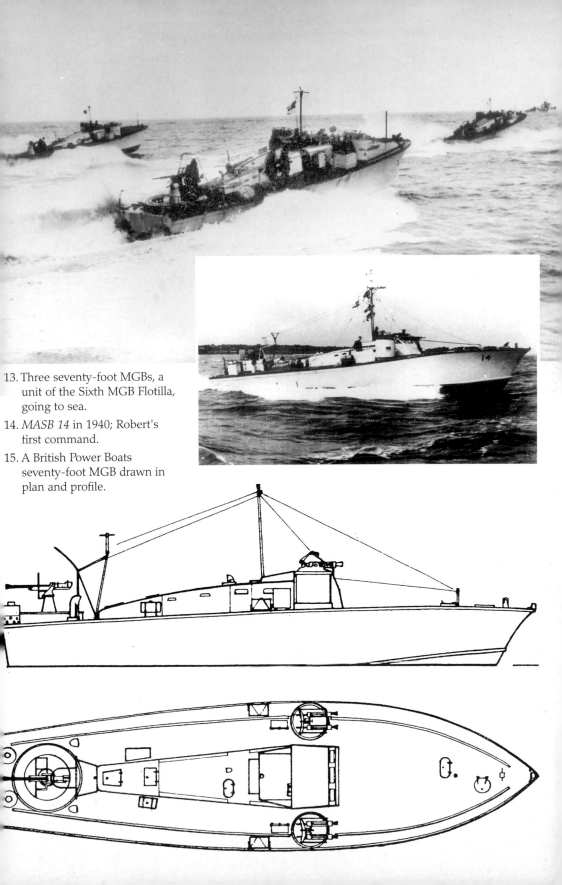

13. Three seventy-foot MGBs, a unit of the Sixth MGB Flotilla, going to sea.

14. *MASB 14* in 1940; Robert's first command.

15. A British Power Boats seventy-foot MGB drawn in plan and profile.

16. *MGBs 64, 67* and *65* passing a trawler March 1942. AB Buckett is manning the Oerlikon. A unit of the Sixth MGB Flotilla.

17. Hitch on board *MGB 64* after sinking an E-boat, *S41*, on the night of 19/20 November 1941.

18. Hitch in 1941.

19. To the British an E-Boat, to the Germans a *Schnellboote*.

20. *MGB 77*, a second generation seventy-one-foot-six boat, working up at Weymouth before joining the Eighth Flotilla.

21. A British Power Boats seventy-one-foot-six MGB drawn in plan and profile.

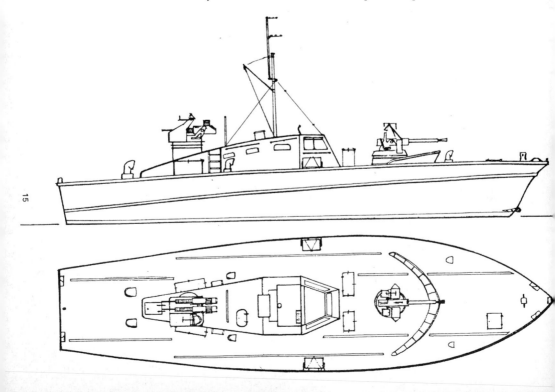

22. The crew of *MGB 77* in Dartmouth after sinking the tanker off Alderney in July 1942. Hitch is standing centre with Francis Head behind his left shoulder and PO George Curtis next to Head. AB Barnes, who won the CGM that night, stands on the left of the line beside PO Mechanic Vic Stay.

23. MGBs tied up behind MTBs in Harwich.

24. A seventy-one-foot-six MGB at speed.

25. Hitch briefing his officers before an operation at HMS *Beehive*.

26. Hitch with Peter Dickens
at HMS *Beehive* in 1943.

27. Tubby Cambridge (left) and
Boffin Campbell.

28. David James.

29. Hand-trained twin Oerlikon.

30. Hitch in seagoing clothes with Bob (left) and Antsie (right) 1943.

31. *MTB 414*, previously *MGB 77*, heading for Poole in 1945 to pay off.

32. Catherine at the unveiling of Peter Scott's portrait of Hitch in 1947 at the RNVR Club.

33. Bob Hichens wearing his father's medals on his right side at the Standing Down Parade of the Coastal Forces Veterans Association in 2007.

imposes the severest strain on hulls and machinery; it is the time when engines, transmission or underwater gear are likely to go, and it is likewise the time when, if any of these do fail, the boat and crew would be lost. Also, the chances of seeing a rubber dinghy in those conditions, assuming there was one to be seen, were about a thousand to one.

But there might be men in a dinghy, their condition branded itself upon the imagination like a cruel vision, without hope except for our efforts. There was no passing the responsibility. Unless we tried no one else would or could. Moreover going down wind with a bright moon we had, comparatively speaking, good visibility. There was just that outside chance of seeing something, if we took the risk.

We kept on. As we neared the Dutch coast the big seas were piling up, steep precipitous declivities with angry breaking crests. The 'climbing' (as we called the laboured struggle of the boat from the trough to the summit of the wave) and the forward surging was becoming intensely pronounced, making station keeping a matter of great difficulty and danger. At one moment a following boat might swoop right by, as the leader struggled up the back of a wave, at another he might be dropped two or three cables astern as the other lurched madly forward on a steep irresistible pinnacle. When it is realised that it was impossible to prevent the boats yawing between an arc of thirty to forty degrees, the grave danger of collision will be appreciated. Collision in those conditions must almost certainly have produced fatal results.

Every now and then a boat would take off on the top of a wave, career along at thirty-five to forty knots, without warning drop sharply into the trough ahead, the bluff bows thrusting solidly into the opposing wall of water. The boat would shudder throughout her length, in the dustbin men would be flung violently against the forward bulkhead, a great wave of green water would roll solidly along the foredeck and break against the wheelhouse coaming, filling the dustbin and sweeping away along the open decks on either side.

Thus we swooped and staggered to the eastward. At one moment foaming along on a crest, at another seemingly stopped and stumbling in the depths, the wet decks glistening in the moonlight, the dripping gun barrels glinting darkly against the moon-path, the tumbled seas forming fantastic patterns of light and shade as the cold light was thrown back to the eye from one wall of water and cut off

175

from another, leaving a black gaping pit; at one moment divided by a sharp peak from all sight of the other boats, at another lifted on high and maybe looking down on the swept decks of one's companions. With this opposing sequence of physical sensations came alternating exhilaration and anxiety of mind. At one moment exalted and excited by the wild beauty of the scene, the pricking sense of adventure; at another filled with apprehension and misgiving, fumbling ceaselessly but indecisively with the manifold risks and hazards of the situation.

We carried on well past the position given. There was nothing more we could do. Reluctantly we turned and instantly our whole world was about our ears.

Revs were cut to the minimum; at any speed above ten knots the boats would have dropped off a wave and broken their backs. Visibility virtually ceased. Spray and solid water continuously sheeted the hulls mast high. It was at least seventy miles before we could hope for any lee. Seven hours of physical hell and intense mental strain. We were soaked at once, nothing could keep it out effectively. The boat reared and dropped, seemingly struck by an endless succession of giant hammer blows. Every now and then the violent upthrust had a twisting corkscrew effect, and the boat landed with a shattering thud on her port side, the wind being slightly on the starboard bow. It seemed that the port turret must come through the deck. It seemed that the bottom must be stove in. It seemed that the engine holding down bolts must shear under the succession of grievous shocks to which they were subjected. It seemed impossible that the pendulastics could stand it. And anyway, where were we getting to? With the compass card thrown through ninety degrees, and the impossibility of judging what speed the boat was making through the water, sometimes apparently stopped short by a specially vicious crest, the dead reckoning position was a matter of guess work.

Though the mind played with the difficulties and dangers of such a situation, raising in endless succession images of the disasters that could occur, it was one form of the physical discomfort that provided the culminating blow. Headed into the wind the eyes were facing a fifty-mile-an-hour gale. Spray, hard and solid, was coming over continuously, driven viciously with the full force of the wind against the forward motion of the boat, slapping, slapping, slapping against the eyeballs. However you looked, attempt to dodge it how you would, your eyes were stung and stung hard. It hit you until the sheer physical pain of it made you so angry that you would swear out loud and senselessly, as one turns round in a rage and kicks a stone over which one has tripped. But the slap, slapping may go on for five, seven, maybe ten hours on end.

The autumn wore on with rough weather and no success, until our piece of luck in November. I hope that this brief outline of our beginnings in gunboats will have shown why that action, not specially noteworthy in itself, was of considerable importance to us in the position we were then in. It gave us new confidence in ourselves. More important still, it revived outside interest in the small fast gunboat at a time when this had nearly vanished.

One of the most significant design defects in the early MGBs, and indeed in MTBs for a more prolonged period, was the noise they made. How could they ever expect to surprise the enemy if they could be heard coming ten to fifteen miles away on a quiet night? Did they have to make a din like the hammers of hell just because they were capable of very high speeds? Perhaps it didn't matter when they were going very fast but it must be possible to go more slowly quietly. Hitch turned his engineering imagination and his knowledge of MGB operations on to finding a solution to this problem.

To make the changes he wanted Hitch had to do battle with 'Bath', as the office of the Director of Naval Construction (DNC) was always known due to its wartime location, which had the power to approve or veto design changes.

We had to devise a means of silencing our boats, at least to a reasonable extent. DNC, not of course the great man himself but one of his myrmidons detailed to supervise the choice and construction of small craft, had not thought it necessary, if he thought about it at all, to silence our boats. This may not have caused any inconvenience at Bath, where this worthy department resided immediately after the outbreak of war, but it used to worry us quite a lot when we careered along the enemy coast, advertising our presence a long time before we arrived, by no means observing thereby the first principles of warfare. An early but abortive attempt at silencing had been made by means of S pipes. These were extensions of the exhaust pipes curving from the stern of the boat into the water down to the level of the bottom. This gave reasonable silence at slow speeds, but as soon as the boats started to plane the exhausts drummed on the water, as they shot hard as a board from under the stern, and the noise was as bad as ever. The pipes could not be lengthened because they would have carried away at speed, and, anyway, numerous troubles developed with the engines because of the exhausts being permanently connected to an underwater outlet; if at any time an engine kicked back when starting it was flooded with sea water and ruined; condensation led to valve and piston trouble. The plan was dropped.

For silencing at slow speeds we devised a modification of the old S pipes which proved satisfactory and led to reasonably adequate silencing of the Sixth Flotilla. We put a trap on the curve of the S pipe which could be opened or closed quickly. This meant that we could operate the boats normally with loud exhausts, and merely shut down to silence for the few hours required when we were closing the enemy coast at relatively low speed. The scheme had its objections, the slow speed tended to cause oiled plugs, the silence was by no means complete and the unfortunate engine-room crews were several times gassed by exhaust fumes until we took steps to deal with this; but it worked, *faute de mieux*, and it enabled us to do many things, NID[7] work and mine laying support, which would have been impossible otherwise.

No one interested in making important changes in the teeth of opposition from officialdom can entirely disregard what officials thought of them, but at least their Lordships' displeasure would not blight any RNVR officer's long term career. Hitch was prepared to risk fighting for his views with those senior to him in the hierarchy if he thought he had any prospect of winning the argument. Yet at the start of this particular debate he must have felt he was a voice crying in the wilderness. 'Here were these little boats', the Navy seemed to be saying, 'manufactured of wood which we don't understand, seldom fit for operations, generally unable to find anyone to fight, and when they do unable to stop them, officered by a bunch of rank amateurs whose views we are not bound to respect. Why should we listen to their arguments for change and improvement? We have probably made a mistake in ever putting these fast midgets into commission. Let us not waste

7. Naval Intelligence Division, responsible for clandestine operations such as putting agents ashore in enemy held territory.

more time and money on them and go back to building more substantial patrol craft which will at least regularly get to sea and safely carry the guns they need to make a difference when they meet the enemy.' It was obvious to Hitch that he needed to prove beyond all doubt what his boats could do before he was going to win serious arguments about improving them.

Chapter Nine

First Blood
November 1941

In *We Fought Them in Gunboats* Hitch starts the book with the description of his first unambiguously successful action against E-boats. I have included almost everything he wrote, in spite of the fact that he starts by introducing both his boats and their crews to the reader who, if he has read this far in this book, knows something of them already. Nevertheless I felt it right that his own description should dominate this chapter and have added only some notes of explanation and a postscript.

It was the night of the 19th-20th November 1941, at HMS *Beehive*, a Coastal Force base. There was an early moon with a flat, calm, glassy winter's night. An ideal night for E-boats. Rain or sun, cold or heat meant little to us, the weather was divided into operational or un-operational conditions. These were perfect.

The Sixth Motor Gunboat Flotilla had been working hard. Still recovering from a holocaust of boats due to a recent air-sea rescue trip in a hard wind, there were only four boats out of the eight operating at the time. These boats were seventy foot long, carrying a single 20-millimetre gun, an Oerlikon and two 0.5s in twin power-operated turrets on either side of the bridge, the 'dustbin' as we called it. They had a speed of from forty to forty-five knots and made a hell of a noise. The Sixth Flotilla was one of two flotillas of fast MGBs covering, or trying to cover, the East Coast convoy route.

On this particular night the boats were standing by at short notice, ready to move at once if E-boats came over. Moreover, we were being held for a special job scheduled for the following night, to escort MTBs to look for a convoy off Terschelling, one hundred and fifty miles away.

It was a little after eleven o'clock when the telephone went in

SOO's office. 'E-boats operating on the convoy route. A unit of the Sixth Flotilla to proceed forthwith to a position ten miles off the Hook of Holland.'

I shall explain something of our tactics and difficulties later on. Suffice it to say here that making contact with small fast craft in the comparative vastness of the North Sea at night, when as a rule they would not be visible farther than five hundred yards, is a difficult task. Such was our job as E-boat hunters.

In search of some method other than the one-in-a-thousand chance of making contact, we had put up the idea of placing gunboat units close off the enemy's ports from which it was known that they might be operating. The gunboats would wait there till first light, then proceed slowly away, fanning out as visibility increased with the growing light. Into this diverging fan it was hoped that the enemy would converge. Hence we called the operation 'Fanny'. The name pleased us a lot.

The Sixth Flotilla was to proceed forthwith to the Hook of Holland and there endeavour to engage the returning E-boats at daylight. Three boats made up the unit, *64, 67* and *63; 64* was my boat, the flotilla leader; *67* was under the command of Lieutenant L.G.R. Campbell, RNVR, otherwise known as 'Boffin' and *63* was commanded by Lieutenant G.E. Bailey, RNVR, or 'George'.

Boffin, though thirty-three at the time, a year older than me, had been my first lieutenant in *64* for the past nine months, because we had been through our preliminary courses together and he, having no previous sea experience, had to be a Number One to begin with. He had just taken over his new boat, *67*; this was his first operation as a C.O. As things turned out, it was lucky that he had been with me so long and knew all our little ways. Boffin is a fire-eater. Rather slow to learn, but extremely sure; he became the best station-keeper in the flotilla and one could be certain that Boffin was on one's tail, if no one else. Very comforting it was at times, too. Red faced and rather bluff in speech and appearance, he always gave the impression of just having had a most satisfying meal; he generally had.

George Bailey (or Beeley of *Beehive* as he was called, having been overheard answering the phone in his slightly Scottish accent by this rather high-sounding title) is dark, with an India-rubber countenance and a great flair for making everyone laugh. He also at the time had not long been in command of his boat and had had uncommon bad luck with engine failures at unfortunate moments.

To complete the introduction of officers going to sea in these boats, Bailey's first lieutenant was a young Etonian called David James, also Scottish, from the Isle of Mull. A seaman by nature, who had sailed before the mast in square rig before going to Oxford, he found it impossible to feel the slightest qualm however disturbing the motion. A devotee of the ballet, with a surprisingly active mind, he was quite incapable of noticing if he had a large smudge of ink on his face or had rent the seat of his trousers.

Francis Head was my new Number One. Tall and dark, if not exactly handsome very nearly so, he turned out to be God's gift to the elderly C.O. such as myself in that he was a highly trained signalman, having been 'bunts'[1] in a cruiser before he got his commission. He could read flashing if it was humanly possible. Finally we had two Dutch midshipmen, who were training with us, Pontier and De Wey, and myself, a somewhat bald-headed solicitor of thirty-two. A solicitor, a tea-planter, and an insurance agent, rather like 'the butcher, the baker, the candlestick maker,' but instead of putting to sea in a tub, we were setting sail for the Hook of Holland, or so we thought.

The water of the dock, still as ice, looked black and sinister. Everything was quiet, the boats like somnolent Leviathans in the half moonlight, half opaque shadows thrown by the sheds and cranes along the dockside. No sound except the smothered tinkle of a radio from one of the hulls.

With the alarm given, noise rises in a crescendo. At first only the clatter of the few duty hands roused aboard, the slamming of hatches, the muttering of sleepy curses. Then the sound of running feet as the crews arrive. The first lieutenants can be heard giving orders. 'Clear away those springs – jump to it.' 'Uncover guns.' Then a tremendous roar, followed by another and another, shatters all hope of speech as one after another the 1,100 hp engines bang into life and cough their poisonous gases into the confined quarters of the dock, until the whole air is a throb and it is impossible to hear a man speak unless he yells in your ear. Then the hurly-burly of departure begins. The COs get their orders and any parting instructions and admonitions. They come aboard and on go the navigation lights. The S.O.

---

1. Bunts is naval slang for a yeoman of signals. In earlier years most naval signalling was by flag hoist. Flags are made of bunting.

hopes that everyone is ready, because in the prevailing din it is very difficult to make sure, and the first hull slips out to seaward.

'Let go.' 'Ahead port.' 'Port wheel.' 'Ahead starboard.' 'Midships.' 'Steady.' 'Ahead centre.'

In an unhurried, even sequence the orders are given for getting away, almost invariably the same. Slowly at first, the unit forms into line ahead, making for the boom gate, their dim navigation lights like creeping glow-worms. The boom is reached. 'We're at the boom, Number One. What's the first course?' Two sparks of light come from the leader, the throttles are lifted. The spray flies away broad from the bow as the fore foot lifts and the boat begins to plane; the noise from the engines settles to a steady roar. The unit is at sea.

On this particular night we were lucky in our weather but not in our reliability. When we had barely left the Cork Light Vessel, four miles from the boom, 63 flashed 'Harry', the signal for a breakdown in main engines. It proved to be an excessive quantity of water in the carburettor and filters of the starboard engine. Several attempts were made to clear it, but we could not afford much time, so regretfully Bailey had to be left to spend the night alongside the Cork Light Ship. Boats 64 and 67 went on at the usual cruising speed of thirty knots, crossed the convoy route, and set a course direct for the Hook.

The time was now about midnight, the moon still up, the sea flat calm. In such conditions motor gunboating can be sheer joy. Station-keeping is easy; the boats seem to fly along with a tremendous sense of speed; they are very beautiful. I think one of the most lovely sights I have ever seen is a gunboat unit at speed in moonlight, with the white pluming wakes, the cascading bow waves, the thin black outlines of the guns starkly silhouetted, the figures of the gunners motionless at their positions as though carved out of black rock; all against the beautiful setting of the moon-path on the water.

Upon this occasion, the satisfactory sense of wellbeing induced by these ideal conditions was rudely disturbed by the smell of burning, always alarming at sea, pressing now, the pungent smell of hot rubber. This was immediately followed by the apparition of my motor mechanic, like a cheerful genie. He was the most admirable person, named Stay, Vic to his friends, whose appearance was almost invariably the prelude to a beaming smile and the remark 'Everything on top line, sir.' You only need to be a gunboat officer for a week to know that this is the most desirable quality a motor mechanic can have. So many report with an overcast countenance and the statement that the vibration is awful. Now Vic was forced to admit that all was not well, that the horrid smell was due to a 'pendulastic going'. This rather fantastic word represents another source of tribulation to a gunboat officer; it is the coupling between the engine and the gearbox, which has an awkward habit of packing up on inconvenient occasions. The pendulastic on my centre engine was now running true to form at this critical moment in the history of motor gunboating. We were forced to stop. Meanwhile, the telegraphist had been receiving and passing up a stream of E-boat reports. 'E-boats bearing 080 degrees from Gorleston.' 'E-boats bearing 050 degrees from Southwold.' 'Am engaging E-boats in position …' etc., from a destroyer. It was obvious that E-boats were on the convoy route in large numbers, and the night was perfect. Should I go on? It was very tempting, but there were grave objections. We could only do eighteen knots on two engines; we were a long way from the scene of action and certainly could not now carry out our instructions to proceed to the Hook of Holland. We were required to be in readiness for an important job far afield off the Texel the next night, and if I carried on for hours on two engines there was a considerable possibility of damaging them. On the other hand there were the enemy in large numbers. It was a difficult decision, the sort that is often presenting itself to naval officers in some guise or another.

I knew what I wanted to do; it's not every officer who is lucky enough to have a Stay at hand ready to salve his conscience. I consulted him, 'We've a long way to go, but it looks as though it would be well worth trying. How do you think she'll do on two engines for six or eight hours?'

'She'll be all right, sir. I'll keep a good eye on them; let you know at once if any sign of trouble develops.'

It was settled. We went on. The little hand lamp flashed white, two longs and a short. The peace of the night at sea was rent by the throaty roar of five engines. The lamp sparked again twice, the boats slid away. We were roughly over the Outer Gabbard Bank. I decided to move to a position approximately twenty miles to seaward of the area in which the E-boats were operating on the convoy route in a direct line to the Hook.

'Steer North 48 degrees East.'

'North 48 degrees East, sir.'

My coxswain, Curtis, had been with me for nearly a year and he was an expert at steadying a gunboat on her course, even in bumpy weather; a difficult art. When the boat bangs the compass flies around. If you follow it the boat begins to swing violently and your wake looks like a tremendous series of S's. It requires great skill and restraint to leave the compass to swing and yet keep your average course correct. Tonight Curtis had no difficulty.

'Steady on North 48 degrees East, sir.'

We were doing eighteen knots now. I calculated anxiously how many hours it would take to reach the chosen position.

'How far is it, Head?'

There was a muffled sound from the wheelhouse, a pause while he consulted the chart, then a face appeared in the little doorway leading from the wheelhouse to the 'dustbin' and a voice shouted: 'Forty-three miles, sir.'

Just over two hours. Well, we should see how she settled down to her two engines. I checked the compass course and the boost pressures, looked round to see that the faithful 67 was close on the starboard quarter, noted that the moon was beginning to get low, that the visibility was decreasing. A slight mist was beginning to form low over the water, often the case in very quiet weather. We got more reports of E-boats. Evidently they were moving a bit farther north. Was my position going to be the best guess? 'E-boats bearing one hundred and three degrees from Gorleston.' That was more like it.

There were probably two groups out working. I wondered in what strength they were as I helped myself to a bull's-eye and handed one to Head. 'Antsie's comfits,' I called them. Antony was my younger son, at that time aged five. He used to prepare a little bag of his sweets for me every time I was going to sea – and very comforting they were.

Probably six in each group, I thought; they usually worked in sixes.

'I wish to God we could catch those bastards tonight', I said to Head.

'Just the night for a battle, except for our eighteen knots, and we've got the place to ourselves,' he replied. We were the only patrol well off the convoy route.

'It's nice to know you can hit anyone at sight,' I said. The moon was going rapidly and with its departure the mist was thickening.

'Shan't see much soon. It'll be damned difficult to spot them,'

185

observed Head.

'We shouldn't see them much more than half a cable, or a cable at the most, but it's a lovely night for hearing them.' I replied. 'The only thing to do is to cut and hope to hear them returning.'

'There seem to be plenty out tonight,' said Head presently, when further signals had been passed up giving more positions of E-boats. 'They seem to be all on the convoy route in the area roughly off Lowestoft; at least one destroyer has flushed some of them already and had a crack at them.'

'Yes, I think the position we've chosen is the best; nip down to the engine room and see if they're all happy.'

There was a short pause, followed by the appearance of Stay, looking somewhat dishevelled, but cheerful.

'Everything on top line, sir! They're taking it perfectly.'

'No sign of trouble?' 'No, sir.'

'They sound all right. They'll have about six more hours to do at any rate, even if we make no contact.'

'They'll be OK, sir.'

Thus encouraged I settled back into the normal state of watchfulness accompanied by a rather blank mind that seems the least tiring method of passing the long hours under way – often as many as ten or fifteen on end. The continuous peering into an unending depth of darkness seems to shroud the mind and keep it in a state of suspended animation, which may go on for hours, until brought back to sudden and intense activity by some alteration in the apparently interminable sameness of the conditions. A real or imagined shape looms into view, a light blinks in the distance or from your companions, a signal is shouted into your ear, that continuous deafening roar of the engines changes its note infinitesimally. The suspended animation is gone. You are thinking fast.

If nothing occurs to distract attention, the one thought that keeps recurring is: 'How much longer?'

'How much longer, Head?'

A short pause, then:

'Fifteen and a half minutes, sir.'

Half minutes matter at thirty knots. Though we were doing only eighteen, the habit of accuracy was there. Watchfulness and suspended animation again.

'Two minutes to go, sir.'

'Right, let me know when there's thirty seconds.'

'Aye, aye, sir.'

'Thirty seconds to go, sir.'

I signalled to the other boat. We slowed down. There was the flip of the revs. as the engines came out of gear, then silence as the order to cut engines was obeyed.

What a relief that silence is after the hours of noise. Together with the silence comes relaxation from the tension imposed by the swift rush through the darkness. You feel that you must have ample warning of the enemy's approach in such an exquisite absence of noise, though this may well not be the case. On such a quiet night as this, every sound comes clearly; the dull thud of a hatch banging closed in a nearby ship, a deep laugh from the after magazine, a muffled shout from the engine room. On this occasion, a call from Boffin:

'How is she going?'

'Seems all right. What revs. were you doing on three?' I shouted back.

His answer confirmed our estimated speed.

'I think this is the best place to hope for an interception', I said.

'I should think so. There seem to be a hell of a lot out tonight,' said Boffin.

'I wish the visibility wasn't quite so low.'

It was now after two o'clock in the morning; reports of E-boat activity were still coming in from the convoy route. That meant that we were not likely to have our chance of catching the enemy on their way home for at least another hour or two. We settled down to our usual listening vigil.

Here I must explain briefly two developments that had fundamentally altered our E-boat hunting tactics. One was that we could lie cut, that is with our engines stopped, for hours, even in fresh winds, and still remain within a few hundred yards of each other. This has been an everlasting source of amazement to me. Having followed the sea since I was a child, I thought I knew something of the ways of small ships in the water. Accordingly, on the first occasion that I operated in a gunboat, when we cut about sixty miles south of the Start in a force three wind, rain and low visibility, I thought: 'How on earth are we going to keep in contact with each other?' To my astonishment the boats, though making at least a knot of leeway in that wind, stayed almost completely still in relation to one another. I was never more surprised and relieved.

The other important discovery we made, though it seems a trifle obvious looking back, was that it is useless to patrol to catch E-boats. The only chance is to cut and listen. You could rarely see an E-boat at more than three or four hundred yards, but in quiet conditions – that is normal operating conditions – you could possibly hear them up to ten or twelve miles. On this occasion, according to the lessons we had learnt, we cut and kept a listening watch in a position about forty miles from Lowestoft, at 0214 on the morning of the 20th November 1941.

All was quiet; at 0330 I went below for a doze and left Head on watch. The reports had died down, which meant that the E-boats had left the convoy route. If we were to have any luck, we should hear something before long. Head was to rouse me at the first sound. I reckoned our zero hour was between 0430 and 0500.

At a quarter to five Head shook me.

'Distant sound of engines, sir, bearing about west.'

A tremendous moment! Were we at last to have our chance? I was on deck in a few seconds; sure enough there was just the faintest murmur away to the westward. The night was absolutely still. Not the gentlest catspaw to stir the water, not the faintest sound to break the absolute silence, except that distant murmur. At long last, music to our ears! Had we not flogged the ocean for nearly a year and never succeeded in engaging them fairly and squarely? The faint rumble was increasing – yes, music to our ears. But eighteen knots, and in that visibility. How could we hope to do it? Was the exhilaration to turn to bitter disappointment again because it was misty and we had only eighteen knots? Probably so.

Head was watching the compass.

'Bearing's about west south west now, sir, getting louder.'

'E-boats all right; they're moving east. We'll have to wait a bit to get some accurate idea of course and speed from the change of bearing. I'll plot it.'

'The bearing was due west as near as no matter when you first heard it, wasn't it?'

'Yes, west, sir.'

A pause:

'Lucky we picked them up well to the westward, it has given us a chance to head them off. Damn the eighteen knots, we want our full speed.'

'Perhaps we shall have some luck,' I said. 'It's time we did.'

We did.

The murmur had grown to a rumble, then to a deep growl. It was eerie, very thrilling to peer into that impenetrable dark to hear the deep thudding mutter grow stronger, more vibrant, knowing that it was our mortal foes approaching, all unconscious of us lurking in their path. In their path? Well, in a manner of speaking! But the North Sea is wide, the night very dark and misty. There is many a slip 'twixt the sound and the ship. 'In their path' would have to mean that they would pass us within one hundred yards, and they were well to the south. How far away were those exhausts, drumming insistently and tantalisingly in our ears, and how many of them? How many didn't matter, how far did. Was it two miles or three? It was hard to tell in the absolute stillness.

'They're bearing about South 50 degrees West now, sir.'

Head was again at the compass.

'Yes, what's the time?'

'0453.'

'That means we've heard them for eight minutes. I'll plot them allowing twenty-seven knots; that'll be nearly four miles.'

By this time all hands, though not yet called upon, were at action stations, listening silently, intently, peering into the darkness. So near and yet so far. It was a great moment for me, my first chance of contact with the enemy as Senior Officer of the flotilla. Could we do it with eighteen knots? That was the question that pounded in my head as the precious minutes slid by and I pored over the chart. Well, I couldn't risk waiting long to check their course, or I wouldn't have a hope; another six minutes and we should be on the beam of their line of advance.

One last look at the rough plot, so much a matter of guesswork, and I had made up my mind.

'Start up. South 25 degrees East, Coxswain.'

The engines roared. The little dimmed blue light flicked – we didn't want any chance of them seeing a flash. We were off, 67 creaming along close on the starboard quarter.

'Steady on South 25 degrees East, sir.'

The minutes went on. Our eighteen knots seemed a paltry crawl.

How were they bearing? No good asking in that crashing roar. You couldn't see them until you nearly rammed them; you could hear nothing except your own infernal uproar. But how were they bearing? I must know. It would be one chance in a thousand to have hit off an interception to one hundred yards on the rough estimate of course, speed and distance judged while listening to their approach. How to get another bearing to check our intercepting course?

We stopped again to listen. The blue lamp flashed, the throttles were slammed down; Boffin, taken aback by the unusual violence of our deceleration, surged up level and stopped too. Time was vital. Stopping to listen was the only solution. It had the disadvantage of still further jeopardising our chances of cutting them off with our slow speed. The immediate insistent roar of our own engines subsided quickly; there to the southward was the distant deeper throb like a malignant echo. It was much louder now.

I looked anxiously at the compass. Was the bearing the same as when we had started up? If so, our course was accurate. It had altered a little to the eastward. That meant we were losing bearing on them, only slightly though. If we altered to the east a bit, it might be all right; they were clearly very much closer.

'Start up. South 50 degrees East, Coxswain.'

'South 50 degrees East sir.'

The crash of the starting engines, so loud it seemed they must hear us, and we were off again.

'Steady on South 50 degrees East, sir.'

'How long was that, Head?'

'Two and a half minutes between courses, sir.'

'Not bad at all; we shall have to get it quicker. We must be getting close to them now.'

Seconds went by. Should I stop again? It would mean that we had missed them unless we made contact in the next two or three minutes. To stop meant the loss of precious time. If they once got ahead, with our eighteen knots we would never catch them. Should I stop

'Flashing light on the port bow, sir.'

Yes, there it was, a little blue light winking quite close to port, then the faint outline of a hull in the mist. Though I knew E-boats were very close, I must identify before attacking. I flashed the challenge. The reply, faintly made, was indecisive. I fired a two-star cartridge, a pyrotechnic we and aircraft had as a quick method of recognition. It happened to be two red lights for that time. In the lurid red glow given out we could see five E-boats, long, low, white-painted hulls clustered together, almost stopped, or moving very slowly, obviously rendezvousing.

Four were disposed in a close group to port, the fifth being a little further off, and almost in our course. It had been but ten seconds from their first flash. We had got them; our first big chance.

'Hard aport, Coxswain,' I yelled, as the guns crashed out to port and starboard, engaging the boat ahead, now to starboard, and the boat that had challenged us. Boffin kept magnificently on our quarter, pumping shells into the starboard E-boat – now only fifty or sixty yards away – with all she had got.

The E-boat to port was only the same distance off and receiving severe punishment from our 20-millimetre, our big guns. You could see the shells exploding on her side and upper works. As yet the Germans had hardly realised what had happened. I could imagine the confusion on board as guns were hastily manned, with men falling wounded and officers shouting orders. A third E-boat loomed up right ahead, moving slowly to port across our bow.

'Port Wheel.'

'Port wheel, sir.'

The coxswain was wonderfully calm. We drew out parallel to this boat and 67, slightly to starboard, couldn't have been more than twenty yards from her. We gave her the most tremendous broadside as we went past and turned to starboard across her bow. She did not reply. It is doubtful if any of her deck personnel survived that blast at short range.

By this time the enemy had recovered themselves somewhat. The E-boats farther away were firing fiercely, some of it hitting us, most passing whining just overheard. As they began to gather way their fire increased, became more confused: brilliant bouts of tracer splitting the darkness in every direction.

Coming round to starboard, we could see a fourth boat about one hundred yards away gathering speed, heading the way we were going. This boat had probably been unhit as yet and the exchange of fire at that range was brisk. Part of the stand was blown from beneath our Oerlikon gunner's feet, the starboard 0.5 turret was smashed and put completely out of action. Still nearly all of it was passing overhead and, best of all, no one was badly hit, an incredible bit of luck.

It is hard to describe the confusion of such an engagement. The pitch darkness, the swift moving hulls, lost to sight almost as soon as seen, the brilliant streams of light from the tracer criss-crossing like comets in every direction; above all, the incessant noise. The nearby ear-splitting crack of our own guns, blending into the more distant gunfire and roar of the engines.

The E-boat turned hard away to the starboard with a fire starting aft, giving great promise, but seeming to blot out suddenly.

'Hard a starboard.'

'Hard a starboard, sir' from the imperturbable Curtis.

'Midships.' I had forgotten the faithful Boffin, who still close on the starboard quarter had found this sudden turn too much for him and was riding up into us. We made the turn more gently, sweeping in a wide circle back to the position in which we had found the E-boats originally.

They had all scattered. Which way to try?

I suppose the general disengaging direction would be the south-eastwards, towards the Hook of Holland. We steadied in this direction, peering intently into the misty darkness for the first sign of a hull.

Although we had suffered no severe casualties, by this time we were in poor shape as a fighting gunboat. Our starboard turret had been completely knocked out, the 20 millimetre gun, the main armament, was badly jammed, and Edwards, the gunner, was desperately working to clear it. Thus we had nothing with which to engage on the starboard side except a stripped Lewis, a hand-controlled 0.303 weapon. As leading boat, we had attracted almost all the effective fire; 67 was unscathed, with three 0.5s and her Oerlikon still working.

Suddenly we saw a misty shape to starboard. It was an E-boat on approximately the same course as ourselves. I roared aft in the hope that Edwards was ready again with his Oerlikon; nothing happened. The 0.5 turret was hopeless. The sense of frustration that I experienced at that moment is one of the liveliest and most vivid memories of my life. After a year's search for the elusive E-boat, to have one ranging nearer and nearer alongside at point-blank range, and be unable to fire anything at her except a rifle bullet was utterly exasperating. Besides, one had the uncomfortable feeling that at any moment there would be a hail of 20 millimetre shells from her, which could hardly fail to hit, with no return fire to keep her gunners jumping. The E-boat was strangely silent, perhaps she had not seen us yet, or hoped that she had not been seen. I yelled at the gunner with the stripped Lewis to fire. There was a sharp crackle and a stream of bright white tracer went tearing straight into the E-boat, by this time no more than one hundred yards on our starboard beam.

Things happened quickly. Boffin evidently had not seen the enemy until the Lewis gun opened up. He let fly with 0.5 and Oerlikon; the E-boat, stung into violent activity, fired back wildly, turned hard to starboard and opened up to full speed. In a minute she was out of sight. With eighteen knots we could do nothing.

We went on south-east. What to do next? How to find them again? We had given them a good deal to go on with; *64*'s Oerlikon, before it had jammed, had got off four pans, two hundred and forty rounds at close range, a great proportion of them hits, while the enemy were still hardly firing, and both twin 0.5 turrets had fired one thousand rounds in similar conditions before having to reload; *67* had done likewise. Those E-boats would not forget us in a hurry; we were shortly to have proof of this.

After proceeding for a few minutes, I decided that the only thing to do was to stop and listen again to see if we could get a bearing by ear of the enemy's movements. We stopped. Again the sense of relief from tension, from the ear-splitting racket to which we had just been subjected. At last there was a moment to think without distraction. We listened intently. The silence seemed complete. A further relaxation from tension; there was no enemy near at hand. I jumped up on to the canopy.

'Any casualties, Head?'

'Nothing serious, sir. Edwards has a splinter in his leg. It's only a scratch and Taylor has been scratched too; it's nothing.'

Taylor was the starboard turret-gunner.

'We're lucky,' I said. 'Check up for any damage below decks.'

'Aye, aye, sir.'

'Are you all right, Boffin? I yelled.

'Yes, quite,' came the reply. 'No casualties, no serious damage. I bet the E-boats aren't. We must have given them a bad time in that first five minutes. Expect they thought we were another E-boat and were all sucking a cup of tea. Probably thought it most unfriendly. Wonder where they've got to? One or two of them might find it hard to get home,' added Boffin.

'I'll send an amplifying signal and suggest fighters go and deal with the stragglers, when it gets light.'

It was about 0545 by this time; still pitch dark.

We had sent an immediate enemy report on turning in to engage, simply:

'Am engaging E-boats in position ___.'

I now sent a further signal.

Have engaged five E-boats in position ___. Lost contact. Suggest fighters search at first light. Two E-boats severely damaged.

Telegraphists in these boats lead a hard existence; very lengthy periods of watch in a tiny W/T cabin. I had an exceptionally able Scottish leading telegraphist named Roberts. Besides being a good tel. he was a good fighter; he was always to be found trying out the guns. His greatest pleasure was to send off such a signal as this.

As he put it:

'For once we're somebody and they're listening. They're stopping the other traffic to get us.'

Most gratifying to a telegraphist's self-esteem.

Head had reported several shell holes in the hull; nothing serious. I was beginning to wonder what the next move was to be, when the coxswain said:

'Do you think you hear something, sir, over there' – pointing to the south-west.

I told everyone to be quiet and listened. Very, very faintly one seemed to hear a low muttering, or was it imagination? Vividly there came to my mind the scene more than two years before in the surgery at '*King Alfred*', when the doctor had suddenly ceased to listen to my heart and had put his mouth to my ear and made the most inaudible of sounds. For a moment I had not been able to think what he was at; the reason was clear now.

'Do you hear anything, Boffin?' I shouted.

'Yes, think so, to the south-west. Not very certain though.'

'I think so, too. Let's go and see.'

The engines roared into life. We swung round to south-west and steadied. Feelings of intense exhilaration were shot through with pangs of apprehension, hard to keep completely subdued. Edwards had not yet been able to clear the Oerlikon. A round had got hope-lessly jammed up the barrel; he had the gun in pieces at the moment.

194

That left us with the 0.5s to fire to port and nothing but a 0.303 to starboard. Were we to light upon a re-formed and thoroughly aroused pack of E-boats? If so, we weren't going to be so lucky. However, we might find a disabled one; the gunboat officer's dream!

The first preliminaries of dawn were beginning to have a faint effect upon the hitherto intense darkness. For no apparent reason there seemed to be a little more light; the mist was thinning. We had been going for about fifteen minutes when suddenly, very dramatically, we saw a low hull lying black and lifeless in the water, a cable on the starboard bow.

'Vessel bearing green forty-five, sir,' came in a shout from the shattered starboard turret position, and in less correct phraseology from aft:

'There's one of the f*****g bastards!'

I shouted to the telegraphist down the voice pipe, 'Make flag three to Boffin.'

Boffin was Campbell's R/T call sign, flag three means 'Attack with depth charges.'

We carried two depth charges each, the minimum setting being fifty feet. At this depth, but no deeper, they could have a profound effect on even a shallow surface vessel, such as an E-boat. The charge goes off five seconds after dropping, therefore full speed must be used, otherwise you would blow off your own propellers. With 64 having only eighteen knots available, I had to order 67 to do the attack; she proceeded to do so most efficiently.

While we slowly circled the strangely silent E-boat, 67 turned away, gathering speed. She was lost to sight momentarily, then reappeared with a creaming bow wave, thundered by us at forty knots and seemed almost to run up alongside the stricken E-boat. There was a five-second pause as 67 disappeared into the darkness, turning hard to starboard, followed by the distinctive shaking bump of the depth-charge explosion against the hull of the boat. The E-boat was lost to sight in a high column of water, reappearing apparently unscathed, still utterly silent. I wondered what this could mean. Were they completely cowed, or had they no guns left firing? They couldn't be all killed. Anyway we must board, but we must be careful as they might be laying a trap for us.

Meanwhile from the direction in which 67 had disappeared there came the flash of tracer and the crackle of gunfire, shortly sustained, but distinct. That puzzled me again, but I was more concerned with the prize within our grasp and intended to make sure of it. The E-boat must certainly have been stopped for good. She was low in the water.

I sent a signal:

'Have E-boat stopped in position 090 degrees Lowestoft thirty-eight miles. Intend to board. Send assistance.'

Suddenly *67* roared out of the gloom. I flashed her to slow and stop and was greeted with a burst of Lewis-gun fire. Evidently some gunner, excited by the night's events and too easy on the trigger. Slowing quickly, she stopped. The roar of engines ceased; I could hear the unfortunate gunner still receiving the full benefit of Boffin's tongue.

The E-boat was lying two hundred yards to the eastward, black and silent. The first of the dawn was by this time taking effect. She was clearly silhouetted against the growing light in the eastern sky. The moment was exhilarating in the extreme.

'We must board,' I shouted.

'Yes,' said Boffin. 'She doesn't seem to have much life left in her. We didn't get fired at as we went by; I came on three others making off fast to the east, when I was turning after the depth-charge attack.'

'I wondered what the firing was,' I said. 'We can't catch them now with my centre engine gone. I've suggested aircraft; very likely they'll catch them. We'd better concentrate on this chap.'

So in the early glimmering light on that calm and peaceful sea we made our preparations. She was obviously hopelessly crippled; there was no fear of her suddenly departing. It was therefore worth taking what precautions we could. We got out all our tommy-guns and revolvers, we arranged to approach one on either side, with 64 to starboard, so that her only 0.5 could be brought to bear, yet so that we should not fire straight across the E-boat at each other. All guns were to be trained on and used to the full if she showed the slightest signs of fight. Boffin was to use his searchlight; one of the Dutch midshipmen, Pontier, was to hail the enemy, calling upon them to surrender.

Everything was understood.

'Start up.'

The order was given, the silence shattered. Slowly the gunboats closed on their prey, the engines throbbing, the guns trained, every man strung up with excitement. No sign from the E-boat. The light was making steadily but it wasn't enough yet to see any details on the enemy decks. Were we going to get a withering blast at the last minute, or what were the Germans up to?

Fifty yards, twenty-five yards. Still no sign.

'Do you surrender.' Pontier's voice carried ringingly over the quiet sea. No answer.

This was passing strange. A brilliant finger of light shot out from *67*; played on the decks of the E-boat. A deserted shambles. Bullet holes everywhere, gear lying about, no signs of life; at the yard arm of her diminutive mast, the ugly German naval flag with the Swastika and the Iron Cross hung lifeless in the air. Was it an ambush? Were there men hidden, guns trained waiting until they could not miss, for one last desperate stand? It was impossible to tell in the grey dawn. The hard light and dark shadows thrown by the searchlight was no better.

'Ahead port.'

'Starboard wheel.'

'Steady.'

'We'll come alongside port side,' to Head.

'Aye, aye, sir.'

'You will lead the boarding party. Shoot at sight if there is any opposition.'

The last orders were given, the last dispositions made.

'Stop port.'

Head jumped for it while still a foot or two off. There was a crash of gunfire.

'Christ, they were there after all.'

Then I realised it was our own Oerlikon, put together again now, ripping across the decks of the E-boat. Edwards had tripped over the firing stand where it had been shattered; in so doing he had pulled the trigger. The shells had gone perilously close in front of Head. He jumped aboard, made straight for the Nazi ensign and lowered it forthwith. My boat was made fast alongside; 67 quickly joined her. At once we realised what had happened. It seemed incredible we had not guessed it before. The German crew had been taken off, obviously by the three boats Boffin had encountered after his depth-charge attack. They had heard us coming while they were in the process of scuttling the boat and had beaten a very hasty retreat.

Leaving a few hands on the gunboats, much to their chagrin and loudly sucking their teeth, the rest swarmed aboard the E-boat. A motor mechanic was detailed to report on the engine room and see if there was any chance of closing the sea cocks.

Head, who had gone on to enter the wheelhouse, reported a destruction charge laid down the companion way from the wheelhouse, the charge at the foot of the ladder. Everyone was kept back. De Wey, the Dutchman, and I approached the charge. There was the fuse line leading down the ladder, with a peculiar wooden handle at the firing end. Had it been lit? Well it must be a long fuse if it was. The Germans had left some fifteen minutes ago at least. Then De Wey saw on the handle the words in German: 'Remove handle to fire.' Without more ado he picked up the charge and threw it overboard. There are advantages in knowing the enemy tongue!

We discovered a mysterious wire leading up to the war head of one of the spare torpedoes, which had been opened up, the explosive exposed, into which the wire had been inserted. No ticking or other alarming symptoms could be detected; we decided to leave it alone.

Meanwhile it was obvious we could not save the boat without help. The engine room was full of water and diesel and the water levels were rising fast in other compartments as it was impossible to get at the sea cocks to close them. I sent a signal asking for towing assistance and a pump, inwardly doubting whether anything could arrive in time; it was exasperating.

'Bring them back alive,' had been the orders, reiterated again and again. The authorities wanted an E-boat, none had yet been captured; here we had one, yet it seemed it was going to be beyond our power to bring her in. Heavy as she was with water, it was impossible to tow, we should merely have ruined our engines. Lacking a power pump there was no hope of keeping her afloat unless assistance arrived within the hour. I doubted if she would last longer.

The order was given to gut the boat. Sailors swarmed all over her, appearing from all the hatches with arms full of equipment. Roberts removed all the W/T equipment, gunners took what guns they could detach and pans of ammunition, charts, books, logs, compasses, searchlights, revolvers, even pictures of Hitler were bundled into the gunboats. Someone came up waving a long German sausage. They had found it all spread out, half-eaten, on the mess-deck table forward, sausage, black bread, sauerkraut. A confirmation of our earlier prediction that they had been 'sucking a cup of tea'.

She began to settle by the stern. She was wallowing, very heavy now. With men everywhere below, I had to consider very carefully how long I could hold on, at the same time trying to make a mental note of all the important features of the boat. A particularly unpleasant wallow accompanied by a downward lurch aft decided me. Smoke was coming from the smoke apparatus where the decks were awash, water was swishing through the large crack in the deck caused by the depth-charge explosion. Only forward was it possible to go below.

'Abandon the E-boat. Get back to your boats.'

The order was quickly though reluctantly obeyed. We let go and stood off fifty yards to watch her end.

Roberts came up to me with a request to take the dinghy and have a last attempt to get some more W/T gear that had so far resisted his endeavours. Barnes, the port 0.5 gunner, volunteered to go with him. I agreed provided one stayed near the hatch to listen for a warning shout. The dinghy was lowered, they rowed off to the E-boat and disappeared below, presently to reappear with further pieces of equipment which they put in the dinghy. Still they worked on. Suddenly she gave a sickening lurch, downward by the stern. A cry of warning went up. Quickly Roberts and Barnes reappeared and jumped into the boat.

Only just in time! She was going rapidly by the stern. Her bows were lifting, lifting, until for a few seconds she hung vertical, her stern under water, her bows pointing upwards, as if in supplication to the sky. Then quickly she sank and disappeared from view. A cheer went up, but it was a feeble one. There is something awe-inspiring and a little saddening about the sight of any ship, however small, however much hated, going down. It is so very irrevocable; in its setting of apparently limitless water, impressive.

Somehow, with the passing of the boat, there was a relaxation of tension. We had been through an exciting three hours since we first heard the enemy. The ludicrous sight of one of the crew falling in while getting the dinghy aboard was hailed with shouts of delight. We got under way and headed for home. We reported the sinking of the E-boat. Two MLs sent to our assistance with special pumps turned back. We ploughed on in a state of blissful reaction.

There is no feeling so good as that experienced after a successful engagement, if you have been lucky enough to escape casualties; the only comparable experience that I have had is paddling back after a win in a racing eight, or cruising round to your pit after getting the chequered flag in a motor race; even these glorious moments do not come up to it. Unfortunately these feelings are generally marred by concern and sorrow over casualties. In this case there was nothing to spoil our pleasure. It was our first real fight. It was perhaps excusable.

As we reached the convoy route we met the destroyers returning to harbour. They had had engagements with E-boats, too, had received our signals, were interested to hear what had happened. We hoisted the Nazi flag under the White Ensign and sailed rather proudly down the swept channel. One destroyer signalled us to close; we stopped close by as her captain wished to question us. When he had finished I noticed that Edwards, always a humorist, had collected a crowd of sailors at the side of the destroyer much interested in him. He was demonstrating a large picture of Hitler with appropriate gestures to the great joy of his audience.

We proceeded into harbour with something of a triumphant entry, the crews of the destroyers and trawlers as we passed waving their caps and cheering, a never-to-be-forgotten tribute from men such as they, culminating in the entrance to Felixstowe Dock. The news of the capture of the E-boat had got round, the whole dockside was lined and most enthusiastic. The gunboats had worked hard, wearily, and a long time for this; the feeling that one had done something of value at last was all the more welcome for that. The Captain, who had so often wished us luck and seen us off, was there, seemingly as happy as we were; I believe he was.

I went ashore to make a preliminary report, leaving the booty to be sorted out in the presence of an Intelligence expert, lately arrived from town. We were told that fighters had found three E-boats limping home and had engaged them most effectively; it was possible that we had got two out of the five.[2] At least we knew that two had been beaten up pretty badly at point-blank range, two others roughly handled.

I had to settle down to the more humdrum business of getting out a report and preparing for the big job of that night, the long-awaited trip to the Texel. *64* was out of action, *67* could go and we could raise one other to make a unit; all the time at the back of my head there

2. They had. Both *S41* and *S53* were lost that night according to German records. *S41* was the E-Boat boarded.

was the cheering thought, 'Motor gunboats have begun to justify their existence. We have made a start. Can we keep it up?'

That afternoon we were off to the Texel, but we could not expect another favour from fortune so soon; the weather broke and we had ten hours' bitter drenching plug back into the teeth of a south-westerly gale; 'A f*****g sight worse than fighting E-boats,' as a member of *67*'s crew so rightly observed.

Hitch's action on the night of the 19th/20th November was the first success that MGBs had had in their struggle to drive E-boats off the coastal convoy routes. Thus it marked the moment when the argument over the type of gunboat to send after E-boats and their armament started to swing back in favour of fast 'short' boats but armed with heavier guns. Note that *67* was ordered to destroy the stationary E-boat with a depth charge before it was realized that she had been abandoned. 20 millimetre Oerlikon shells on this occasion may well have holed the engine room that resulted in her abandonment, as Hitch's subsequent Report of Proceedings opined, but the MGBs carried no gun heavy enough to ensure an E-boat's destruction. A post war intelligence report suggests that the abandoned E-boat had also been in collision, presumably in the confusion created by the ambush from the far weaker unit of only two MGBs, one limited to eighteen knots.

Note also how close range the action was. Visibility was no more than one cable so all gun fire was at this range or less and much of the fighting was within half a cable. Perhaps not yard arm to yard arm, but closer than any other naval action of a period when distances for effective fire were steadily lengthening. This was not the clinical destruction of the enemy at long range. Fighting at night with quick firing light weapons was closer to Nelson's dictum 'No officer can do far wrong if he lays himself alongside an enemy', than anything the Navy had seen for a century. It was a miracle that the two MGBs suffered no casualties. Next time they would not be so lucky.

Hitch was awarded a bar to his DSC, Midshipman De Wey was Mentioned in Dispatches. Leading Seaman George Curtis, Hitch's coxswain, received the DSM, the Distinguished Service Medal. Able Seaman George Edwards, *64*'s Oerlikon gunner, was Mentioned in Dispatches, as were Barnes, Roberts and Vic Stay, entitling them to wear a bronze oak leaf on the relevant campaign ribbon.

201

Chapter Ten

Winter Operations
November 1941 – April 1942

A seventy foot wooden boat, no matter how well designed and well crewed, has limited operational capacity in bad weather. The Sixth Flotilla could go to sea and did so in appalling conditions from time to time when emergencies, as often as not connected with air-sea rescue, compelled them to. However, in much above a force four wind, when waves are for the first time breaking in white foam on surface of the sea, they became highly unstable gun platforms. Indeed, their sister ships, the MTBs, had exactly the same problem in launching their weapons in anything worse. The E-boats, 115 feet long and somewhat better in rough weather, nevertheless took much the same view of the limits that weather placed on their operations and were not to be found on the convoy routes other than in reasonably calm conditions. Thus from the end of November 1941 to the end of March 1942 it was not to be expected that MGBs would be in action to any significant degree, other than in those relatively short periods of good winter weather. One such period included the night of 19/20 December 1941 when Hitch took a patrol of the Sixth Flotilla in the direction of the Dutch coast. The initial visibility was only half a cable with fog and the MGBs did not get clear of the convoy route until after 2300. They then set a course for their patrol position, but off the Aldeburgh Light Buoy they had yet again one of their technical setbacks when 63 stopped, having lost a blade off her centre propeller, which set up a vibration causing her P bracket to break away. The rest of the patrol did not notice that she was gone for a short time but then returned to look for her. Failing to find anything in the fog, they set off again on patrol.

Hitch was in *65* as Senior Officer, where Sub-Lieutenant George Duncan, RCNVR was now the Commanding Officer. He had in company *MGB 67* under the command of Boffin Campbell. The fog gradually cleared and the two MGBs reached their operational area just after three o'clock in the morning. As usual, they cut engines and lay in wait listening. At 0315 they caught sight of three boats about 300 yards away, two probably 140 foot R-boats, the German equivalent of an ML, and the third an E-boat. The MGBs engaged, at about a cable, passing down the side of the three German boats at high speed twice before losing contact in the dark. Contact was made again half an hour later with a further exchange of fire, but with their light weapons the MGBs only inflicted superficial damage. Again they lost contact so stopped to listen. They had overshot the R-boats who, in due course, came up to the MGBs lying silently in their path. Hitch then ordered *65* to make a depth charge attack but, as she ran in, three more enemy vessels came on the scene, so *65* crossed the bows of the leading boat and dropped its charge close ahead of her, probably causing damage. The two MGBs continued to search for the enemy, finding them again at 0435 and engaging, again dropping depth charges. The two MGBs then lost contact with each other but both separately sighted enemy units, engaging once more. Observing each other's gunfire in the dark the two MGBs came together again at 0455 but found no further sign of the enemy.

It was an inconclusive engagement but that was not surprising in a pitch black night, with no radar, no guns capable of stopping vessels twice their size, and fighting two to six. The lesson learnt from the depth charge attacks was that one needed to drop the charge a paint-scraping-ten-feet ahead of an oncoming vessel to be sure of the explosion coming under her with lethal effect, not the fifty yards they had tried. But expecting decisive results when your only heavy weapon is a canister of explosive, to be dropped only yards ahead of the enemy, was expecting a great deal of the aggressive spirit of Coastal Forces captains. Only a courageous few attempted it.

Hitch and George Duncan both received a Mention in Dispatches for this action.

The action demonstrates as clearly as any the spirit with which Coastal Forces attacked the enemy when they found them. The two boats between them made six attacks. Only their speed and agility and the small target they presented saved them from disaster which would have come had the enemy hit them even once with a heavy calibre weapon. It is clear that the Germans were doing their best to escape in spite of their overwhelming superiority in weapons, a feature of warfare in the Narrow Seas all too common during the Second World War, and reflecting the clear orders that the E-boats worked within, that their job was to sink enemy merchant ships and not to fight it out with motor gunboats. No one who knows the history of the Germans at war can suppose that it was lack of courage that caused this tactical doctrine to develop. Yet it left the Royal Navy with a growing sense of psychological dominance in the Narrow Seas after a period in which the E-boats had had it mostly their own way.

It was in the autumn of 1941 that a Major Strickland, commanding a squadron of tanks in the Royal Armoured Corps, met Hitch. He had been asked by his brigadier to find ways of providing the officers and men of his brigade with 'some form of adventurous action'. Strickland met Hitch at Felixstowe and suggested an outing with tank wireless experts to see whether tank wireless communications could possibly be of use to motor gunboats at sea. They spent a day fitting three MGBs with tank W/T sets and then gathered at the boats in the evening. Let me quote Strickland:

I should have noticed the purposeful action going on but still thought I was going for a harbour trip. I was in service dress. One of my sergeants was ensconced beside a naval W/T operator in one of the MGBs. Each of the boats was fitted with a big ungainly W/T set which took up a lot of space and beside which our small efficient sets looked childish.

I stood in the small bridge behind Hichens and soon six MGBs were moving slowly out of harbour behind us, together with three MTBs. Once we got beyond the harbour defences these nine boats formed into wing groups of three MGBs, with three MTBs in the rear. It was a calm evening but there was a heavy swell in which the boats wallowed. One needed a strong stomach. At some signal, all boats increased speed and the wallowing stopped. Then all guns were manned and a furious gun testing commenced. The din was terrific.

Apart from the roar of the powerful engines, the firing of some twenty machine guns and nine Oerlikons created a shattering noise.

I went down to the small cabin below, took off my tunic and donned a naval jersey. In the W/T cabin I checked that one tank set was in good contact with the base and with all the boats of the flotilla. Hichens joined me and was delighted with the obvious success of our W/T sets.

Going up to the bridge, Hichens told me that we were on an operational trip, the purpose of which was to cover two Motor Launches from E-boats, out from Dover to lay mines in the approaches and exits to and from the port of Zeebrugge, the home of many E-boats. Every fifteen minutes or so, at some signal all the boats stopped, engines were switched off and a rigid silence was maintained in order that all hands might listen for the beat of E-boat engines. It was all very eerie and exciting. At times, despite straining ears, one could hear nothing but the lap of water against the boat sides. At other times, one did hear distant thrumming and with keen relish the flotilla would speed off to investigate. This was done a number of times. I imagined that the E-boats were also playing cat and mouse. It was cold and the hot mugs of sweetened cocoa were most welcome.

Sometimes a distant noise would be identified as a large vessel and we would move away from it. Making a huge arc we moved southwards and ran into mist. We stopped and listened. Now there seemed to be all sorts of sounds. One noise to the westward was said to be our two MLs. The other noises were from the shore. I was most intrigued to find myself, as it were, listening once again to German noises. We moved on slowly and as quietly as we could in the thick sea mist. We stopped again to listen and the engines of the MLs became louder and clearer. I was told we were drifting shoreward. Suddenly, I heard voices and the sound of machinery. Imagine my surprise when the mist drifted away for a moment and I could see the Zeebrugge mole with German sentries passing along it. Then the mist covered us again, thankfully. After some time at this waiting game, Hichens whispered to me that he thought all had gone well and that the MLs must have laid their mines. It was nearing dawn now and I understood that our little flotilla must leave soon or be caught in daylight by enemy shore batteries, aircraft or a German destroyer.

Staring through the mist at the Zeebrugge mole, I could hear all sorts of noises made by vehicles and machinery. The sound of voices came clearly as German sentries spoke to each other. Very eerie. Suddenly, Hichens was given some message from his base and on an order the flotilla set off. The roar of the engines drowned out all other sounds but searchlights began to probe the mist for us. We were off on our way home. It was very cold and more hot cocoa was welcome. There was some gunfire from the shore but the shells landed far from us. We must have been going at thirty knots. First light, or the first lighting of dawn, enabled us to just make out the other boats. When we must have been some fifteen miles off shore and the light was clearer, a shout caused me to look behind and up. A silvery shape in the air was following us. It was a German light seaplane. Hichens was quite unconcerned. When the watching gunners saw that the seaplane was lining up to strafe us the boats just jinked to the right or left in very rapid turns and the pilot had no hope of getting us in his sights. This game went on for about fifteen minutes and then the 'plane flew away.

After a couple of hours or so, and when I was feeling pretty hungry, we spotted our home shoreline. Sometime later, there was a sort of 'stand down' and the gun crews started cleaning up their guns and covering them. When we arrived home we were met by Commander Kerr and taken up to the wardroom for a very welcome and enormous breakfast.

1941 closed for Coastal Forces in general and MGBs in particular with a sense that they were at last beginning to make a difference. Len Reynolds, in his book *Home Waters MTBs and MGBs at War 1939-1945*, the classic history of Coastal Forces in British waters, who himself served in Dog Boats[1] in the Mediterranean in the second half of the war, believes that the quality of leadership in the boats had by then begun to bolster the steadfastness of the crews, who found in the fellowship of their small boats a great team spirit that was much to their liking. From being a part of the service where young officers with an aggressive spirit started to look

1. Fairmile D boats, always known as Dog Boats, were a larger, slower class of Coastal Forces craft, carrying torpedoes and with heavier guns than 'short' MGBs. They started to come into service later in 1942.

around them to see whether there was not somewhere else where they could be more usefully employed, Coastal Forces was starting to become the place to be if you wanted to make your mark quickly.

From January 1942 until the middle of March not a single action is recorded for the MTB and MGB flotillas on the east coast. There was considerable action in Dover Command to the south which had the advantage of radar covering the whole width of the Channel to help make contact with the enemy. The continuing lack of radar in MGBs and MTBs themselves, the winter weather, and perhaps a decreased willingness on the part of the E-boats to attack east coast convoys resulted in this prolonged lull.

Hitch says little about the period from January to March 1942 in his book, but this record does contain one vital clue to the success of the Sixth Flotilla, the great attention that they paid to the good order of such weapons as they had.

We settled down to our patrols again. To the never-ending guard over the convoy route, occasionally involving operations far afield; to its hardships and delights, its hard work and pleasures, its humours and disappointments.

The weather was much of it rough. Training rather than operating therefore loomed large. We had had two actions in November and December respectively and they had taught us many things. Chiefly that automatic guns will jam unless they are in perfect shape and their ammunition likewise. The type and amount of grease and oil applied could make all the difference between a perfectly working gun and a hopeless jam. This could be the difference between life and death for us.

I called my flotilla together and pointed this out. There was no easy way out for gunboats. If we were to have success we must fight for it. We could not do our duty by laying mines or discharging a torpedo, preferably unobserved, and then getting away as quickly as might be. It was possible to be successful in a minelaying ML or an MTB if the officers were skilful and lucky, regardless of the efficiency of the whole crew, but this could never be so in a gunboat. I told them plainly that we intended to seek out and engage the enemy; that unless their guns continued to fire and fire straight it would be they who would be killed and not the enemy. The alternatives were success or death. They must be efficient.

That talk, I believe, had a profound effect. Certainly thereafter we had no difficulty in keeping all the guns and ammunition in the flotilla in excellent condition and the keenness for target practice and improving the gunnery was manifest.

I am convinced that the steady hard work of patrols, apart from the engagements, trip after trip without making contact, often in appalling weather, was not without its value. The E-boats became aware that they were being hunted by small fast boats, that might pounce on them at any time and any place, and they did not like it. It made them cautious and ultimately caused them to cut down their operations considerably. This was basically the value of gunboats, rather than the extent of destruction wrought on the E-boats. There was considerable misconception in higher quarters, at times, on this point. The E-boats were too numerous and too elusive for us to hope to destroy them to any crippling extent, but if we could scare them and cut down their operating, we were achieving our object. Our Jutland for mastery of the Narrow Seas could not be fought in one great battle, flotillas of gunboats versus flotillas of E-boats, the winners to have complete mastery. It could be, and was, only achieved by continuous patrol and search and numerous small fights. Whatever else may be said on the subject, the grind of patrols was essential. It was our war and without it we would not have made contact on the occasions that we did. It made seamen of us, so that we could handle our boats and fight them when the occasion arose.

E-boat successes in the winter of 1941-2 had been much less than in the previous winter and we liked to think that the gunboats had played their part in bringing about this reduction. We were soon to have further concrete evidence of the value of our little craft, of the weapon that we had forged and were slowly perfecting. That evidence was supplied on the 21st/22nd April 1942, twenty miles due north of Ostend.

Just before the end of this period one event did occur which linked, for the first time, Hitch and his motor gunboats with another famous name from Coastal Forces, Lieutenant Peter Dickens, RN of MTBs. The two men first met in unpropitious circumstances, described by Dickens in his book *Night Action*. Dickens was then the First Lieutenant of HMS *Cotswold*, a small Hunt-class destroyer.

Returning from patrol in a calm and beautiful spring dawn, I said to the signalman on the bridge by way of conversation, 'This must be about where those E-boats were last night; I wonder if they laid any mines?'

The lights went out…, the compass binnacle rose up and struck me sharply under the chin, and all the *Cotswolds* became eligible for a change of appointment. Despite a forty foot hole in the bottom and round both sides we remained in one piece by virtue of the upper deck, but you could feel the two halves moving differently if you stood with a foot each side of the hinge. Mercifully our casualties were few, though some of them most were pitifully burnt when a fuel tank ignited. We asked for help to take them ashore and three motor gunboats speedily arrived under their already renowned leader Robert Hichens.

That was my first intimate contact with Coastal Forces and I fear I did not welcome them too graciously. Preoccupied with organizing a team to bail out the fore part of the ship with buckets, fighting a fire in the after boiler-room, trying to extract a man trapped in fetid air among the blistering serpentine pipes of the flooded forward boiler-room – failing – and being deservedly humiliated by seeing him brought out by Chief Stoker Wigfall five minutes later, I told Hitch to switch off his thundering, ear-blasting engines so that we could all hear ourselves think. I never dared to speak to him like that again, though neither did I ever want to. Two nights later he went over to Ostend and repaid those E-boats in kind.

The date was the 20 April 1942.

Throughout this period, in spite of increasing evidence that MGBs could, at last, find the enemy and hit them hard, sometimes very hard, Hitch was haunted by the fear that the Admiralty would lose patience and relegate fast short MGBs, his MGBs, to a support role and he with them, replaced by the more substantial but slower Dog boats. Even the second generation of short boats starting to come off the stocks in early 1942 might not change the official mind. Although the more heavily armed Dog boat was a valuable addition to the armoury of Coastal Forces, Hitch remained of the view that success in bringing E-boats to action would ultimately depend to a significant degree on speed equal to or greater than anything that the E-boat could achieve.

Due to the early failures of the short boats and their lack of striking success, it had been decided in high quarters that they should be, to all intents and purposes, discontinued. Their place was to be taken by the D class motor gunboat. This boat was to be much like an ML in appearance, one hundred and fifteen feet in length, with a high silhouette, an armament of two Oerlikons, 0.5s and a pom-pom, a two-pounder or 40 mm gun, and a speed of thirty-six knots. The reason for this decision was that the fast Power Boats would not stand up to the weather in war conditions; that stronger boats with better sea-keeping qualities were imperative. There was much to be said for this argument, but three mistakes were made by the authorities in weighing up the situation. Firstly, they were wrong in discarding the idea of building a boat that could outpace the E-boat. The high-speed, forty-to-forty-five knot boat was, in the view of the men fighting the E-boats, essential. It was difficult enough to catch E-boats with this speed; it would be still worse with only thirty-six knots. Secondly, it transpired that they had miscalculated the speed of the D class MGB. These boats achieved a maximum speed of thirty knots only. Thirdly, they totally failed to appreciate the merits of the redesigned and improved Power Boats hull, the seventy-one-foot-six-inch MGB.

The seventy-one-foot-six boat was very similar to the old one, except that, having studied their failings, the designer, Mr George Selman, had corrected most of the faults. Moreover they were faster, having a cruising speed of thirty-seven to thirty-eight knots and a maximum in fighting trim of forty-three to forty-four, and had much heavier armament, mounting a twin Oerlikon powered turret aft, a pom-pom[2] in a powered turret forward, and twin Lewis guns on either side of the bridge. This was something like a gunboat. When we first heard of it in December 1941 we could hardly believe that it could be true. Evidently the authorities thought likewise, because they only ordered one flotilla of eight boats[3] and were not at all concerned to try them out effectively, thinking that the D was the boat of the future.

2. A pom-pom was a two-pounder quick firing gun, approximately twice the calibre of an Oerlikon.
3. Originally three flotillas were ordered but in March 1941 this order was cut back to eight boats only. After Hitch's success on 19/20 November 1941 the original order was reconfirmed.

Having heard of the seventy-one-foot-six boat through Lieutenant Perry,[4] later to become our engineer officer, at that time working in the office of Rear-Admiral Coastal Forces, and realising at once that this was exactly what we wanted, I decided to agitate for the first flotilla. After our indecisive action with R-boats in December it was obvious that we must carry a pom-pom if we were to be really effective. Perry, who had worked for Power Boats before the war, and therefore knew what he was talking about, assured me that the new boats were good, that they had a triple-skinned bottom and really would stand up to their guns and the weather; moreover he doubted if the D-boats would do anything like thirty-six knots and pointed out that they carried no more guns.

I went to London to see what I could get. The general attitude at the top was that the seventy-one-foot-six boat had hardly been heard of, that it was unimportant, that the forward gun could not be used because of the bumping in the fore part of the ship, and that, anyway, the Ds were the things to have.

I asked when the first of the Ds might be expected to operate and was told 'by May or June'. Mentally I added four months to this and took stock of the situation. I knew that the first seventy-one-foot-six was just ready and that they were wrong about the gun forward being useless; it was the best and driest place in the ship in operating conditions; we had often explained this, but nobody listened. I believed Perry knew what he was talking about when he said that the boat was really well built. I decided in favour of the small, fast boat. Such a boat with forty-three knots was tempting compared with a high silhouette and a doubtful thirty-six. I never regretted my decision.

I pulled all the strings I could to get those first eight boats. The situation was difficult because the COs of the first two boats had already been appointed. Naturally I wanted to arrange a transfer of my flotilla personnel to the new boats as they became ready. My flotilla had had far more experience of fighting E-boats, five actions, than any other gunboats, in fact up to that time the only experience.[5] It would, therefore, have seemed the natural and obvious thing to do to try out the new and vastly improved boats in the hands of the men who had made the old boats work. This did not seem to be the

4. The same Lieutenant 'Pop' Perry Hitch had first met at St Christopher.
5. This must have been before Lieutenant Horne RN of the Seventh MGB Flotilla first captured, then sank, an E-boat off Ijmuiden in March 1942 in a very gallant action.

211

official outlook at all; already two boats, the first two precious craft that we would have given anything for in our recent scraps, had been given to comparatively inexperienced men, the next on the waiting list so to speak. I sought all my possible contacts, used all my persuasive powers. I doubt if I should have achieved success but for a lucky circumstance. At just about this time, C-in-C Nore[6] called a conference to discuss the use and development of coastal craft in his command, a most useful move which was several times repeated with valuable results. His Chief of Staff, at that time Vice-Admiral Rawlings, and the Staff Officer Operations for Coastal Forces, Commander Younghusband, had a complete grasp of the situation, understood fully our difficulties and limitations, and were also well aware of our potential value. They therefore agreed with us that the fast boat was vital for E-boat hunting and that we must have more and bigger guns. How familiar that cry was to become! At this conference I was able to give them details of the new fast boat, which was just what they wanted, and convince them that, in my opinion at least, it was a good boat and should work. Thus I obtained C-in-C Nore's backing to my agitation for the new boat and his influence carried the day. We were to transfer all the officers from the Sixth to the new boats of the Eighth as they became available, except for one which was already commissioned under Lieutenant Ladner, RCNVR,[7] who was to retain his boat and thus join my new flotilla. George Bailey brought the first boat to Beehive in April 1942,[8] we got the rest quickly in May, June and July of that year. They were to come fully up to our expectations.

Before Hitch formed the Eighth Flotilla with its new seventy-one-foot-six fast MGBs, he was to have one last major engagement with E-boats in his old seventy-foot boats. The events leading up to the night of the 21/22 April are fully described in Hitch's book and I leave it to him to set the scene, including his own account of his

6. Admiral Sir George H. D'Orly Lyon, KCB from April 1941 - July 1943 covering all Hitch's time in Nore command. Admiral Lyon constantly supported Hitch in his battle for better weapons in short MGBs.
7. Thomas Ladner, a solicitor from Vancouver, was happy amongst friends in Dover. Being sent to Felixstowe under Hitch's command did not, at first, suit him at all but the two men subsequently became good friends.
8. This was *MGB 74*. Bailey subsequently became Senior Officer of the Sixth Flotilla in July 1942. Rodney Sykes took over as CO of *MGB 74* when the seventy-one-foot-six boats formed the new Eighth Flotilla under Hitch.

first meeting with Peter Dickens, mentioned before, and then describe the bloody little conflict which followed.

The story of the Ostend action starts four days before the actual clash. The setting was somewhat dramatic. Early in April our intelligence had reason to suppose that a flotilla of minelaying E-boats had moved to Ostend with a view to operating from there. The reason was obvious. With the rapidly shortening nights it was no longer possible for them to work far north on the convoy route from Ijmuiden or the Hook of Holland. The distance from Ostend to the southern area, off Harwich, was less by almost half. Being conveniently stationed at *Beehive*, we were given the job of looking out for the attack from Ostend. Our plan was to place ourselves as close off Ostend as we dared at dusk and lie in wait for the enemy as they came out. We did this several times in the early part of the month but nothing happened. Then there was a period of rough weather, at least a week during which nothing could happen.

The first day that the weather moderated was, I remember, a Saturday, the 18th April. We were required for an N.I.D.(Naval Intelligence Division) job, landing spies on the Dutch coast north of Ijmuiden, and there still being a considerable sea running it was thought that the E-boats would not be out yet. In this we were right. We carried out our job without incident, though not without excitement. It is always thrilling to creep quietly in to the enemy shore, not knowing whether searchlights will spring to life at any moment and batteries shatter the stillness. On this occasion we lay within two cables of the beach for at least half an hour, but returned unmolested.

The weather was now perfect after the long spell of wind and we creamed home over a glassy surface undulating smoothly to the slowly dying northerly swell. We had only three boats working at the time, though a fourth was only temporarily in trouble, so the Nore decided not to send us out that night, Sunday, the 19th. We had had a tiring trip, about thirteen hours, but I remember asking urgently to be allowed to operate off Ostend that night. It seemed to me certain that the E-boats would come; they nearly always did on the first really suitable night after a blow and it didn't matter if we were tired. The critical time would be in the early hours of the night. If nothing happened we could relax and get some rest.

But they wouldn't let us go. We had our night in and the E-boats came. The first thing we knew about it was that all gunboats were called to immediate notice at ten o'clock the next morning, Monday. We were told to proceed forthwith to a position on the convoy route, about twelve miles direct from the entrance to Harwich, to assist the destroyer *Cotswold* that had been mined there.

We sped away, four of us, and soon found the stricken destroyer despite low visibility. She had been mined amidships and was wallowing low in the water. Towing assistance was on its way; all we could do was to take off the badly wounded men and bring them swiftly to hospital.

I remember vividly the scene on board. The ship stopped, rolling gently but heavily owing to the weight of water forward, the little groups of sailors on the deck, the dark shambles below decks, the badly wounded men being brought up from below, covered in fuel oil, many seriously burnt. One petty officer, taken aboard 64, was a livid purple wherever his flesh was exposed, his face and bald head a horrible sight. A bearded man appeared, clad in indescribable clothes and black with oil; I could tell at once by his voice and air of authority that he was an officer. I asked him if there were more to take and he briefly described the position. This was my first meeting with Lieutenant P.G.C. Dickens, RN, great-grandson of the famous author, at that time First Lieutenant of the *Cotswold*. Later he was to be Senior Officer MTBs at Beehive when I was Senior Officer MGBs and we were to work much together. His bearing on that occasion foreshadowed clearly the cool efficiency which was to make him the most successful MTB officer on the East Coast.

We roared back across the Shipwash with our load of burnt and lacerated flesh. We knew then more certainly than ever that our hunt for E-boats was worthwhile. If only we had been off Ostend the night before we might have saved this. Through the boom at thirty-eight knots, no little pleasure in this as the boom trawlers always delighted in waving us down even when we were doing our usual ten knots past them, and on to Shotley where we landed our cargo. There was nothing more we could do to help. The *Cotswold* was got in and beached on Shotley Spit. Before the day was out another destroyer, the *Quorn*, was mined and two merchant ships, all on the same minefield laid the night before by those E-boats. The *Quorn* was also saved, but the merchantmen sank.

We were off Ostend that night in a very vengeful mood, but the E-

214

boats were celebrating their success and we waited in vain.

Tuesday the 21st April dawned fine and clear. We returned in the early morning to fuel and wait for the night. The weather remained flat calm, perfect for our purpose. That night we mustered four boats. There seemed every chance of an action. The E-boats had been rested, the weather was right, they would want to repeat their success.

We sailed at seven thirty in the evening. I had decided to split my unit into two and place them five miles apart opposite Ostend, twenty miles off the port. We had timed it to arrive in our waiting position at dusk. We had to rely on hearing the enemy as it would be a dark night. By placing two groups it greatly increased our chances of making contact, though it correspondingly reduced our hitting power if we succeeded, but it was all important to catch them and stop them getting to the convoy route. We knew that they worked in sixes. I believed that two boats, fighting determinedly, could scatter and turn them. At all costs we must intercept.

MGBs 64 and 60 formed one group, 65 and 58 the other. Bussy Carr commanded 60, George Duncan 65 and Cowley 58. Bussy had not had much experience as a C.O. at this time and had only been in action as a First Lieutenant. Of an artistic nature and by inclination decidedly lazy, he yet managed in some effortless way to keep his boat in perfect order and do all that was asked of him; the secret probably being that his crew adored him. Fearless and Resolute George (Duncan) was the exact opposite, yet produced the same results. Intensely energetic and distinctly addicted to the parade ground manner, his boat was run in true gunnery style, whistles blowing and alarm bells sounding continually. He had taken part in one previous battle in command of 65 and before that another as a First Lieutenant. If ever a man was anxious to get at the enemy it was Fearless and Resolute George. Cowley, Kelly to his friends, the most junior C.O. in the flotilla, had only been in action as Howes' First Lieutenant. Small and slight, with an enormous nose, generally referred to as the Dreaded Beak, and a fearsome pipe, the smell from which was calculated to turn all stomachs but its owner's, he was always being twitted for being behind station and losing contact. This, needless to say, was unjustified after a short time, but it clung to him and in later days a boat returning one evening met a unit of the Eighth Flotilla going to sea and made the classic remark that 'he had met the Eighth and Kelly'.

215

The unit swept south in the gathering gloom, the rumbling roar of the twenty-four exhausts spreading away in gradually diminishing waves to a distance of fifteen to twenty miles on all sides over the still water. Low, dull clouds formed to the west and south, bringing the darkness down rapidly.

Swinging along through the gathering darkness, the mind's activity seems suspended, hypnotised by the sameness of the ever-changing particles of water thrown steadily from the hull, and the never varying wall of darkness ahead with its floor of unbroken, smooth sea. The thoughts wander, though the mind is ready and alert to the slightest hint of change, change which implies danger or the necessity for instant exertion.

On this occasion I had the presentiment of action to come, brought about no doubt by the extreme probability of E-boat attack that night. Thus overshadowed, my mind lingered over the recent parting with my family. My wife and younger son, Antony, were at Felixstowe, my older boy, Bobby, having recently returned to his preparatory school. My wife mercifully was able to school herself into a stoic absence of alarm at my doings, the only possible outlook; consequently our goodbyes were strictly unemotional and informal. But I always found the goodnight kiss to my youngest son a little trying when I knew I was set upon some specially likely venture. He was so very happy, so very unaware of what was going on. It was not easy.

In his fifth year he was at a particularly attractive age. My thoughts dwelt delightedly on his last bon mot. His mother had been reading to him and having finished a chapter had stopped, saying that it was time for his bath. Antony had not wanted to go to bed yet and, intrigued with the book, had urged more reading:

'Please go on, Mummy', he had said in his most winning voice, 'it's so very inquisitive'.

I thought absently of the fun it would be giving him an empty Oerlikon shell case if we had an action that night and I got home intact. I could see so clearly his upturned, excited little face and hear his pleased exclamation: 'Oo! Thanks, Dad.' Oh well, there was no harm in thinking about it, but no use getting down in the mouth. It was for such as Antony that we, and myself in particular, were fighting this war. All the more reason for getting at the enemy.

A voice broke into my reverie, Head's:

216

'Two more minutes to go before the second division split off, sir.'

The box lamp winked from 64 and the second division turned away to starboard.

The sparking wake flying back from the chine seemed to gather momentum with the closing in of darkness, the shortening range of focus increasing the appearance of speed. A few minutes later throttles were eased, engines cut. In the ensuing comparative quiet the throb of the other unit's engines could be heard clearly now five miles to the south-west. Then absolute silence. Such stillness as a windless night at sea alone can give.

We listened. Surely they would come tonight? Cocky with their success, the bastards; two destroyers and two merchantmen! Those poor burnt limbs and faces! If only we could prevent that and kill some of them too! If only? We were a tiny force. It would almost certainly mean two Oerlikons against twelve of theirs. But that devastated flesh like peeled pomegranates was vivid and searing to the mind.

We had stopped at ten o'clock. At ten thirty-five I suggested having some sandwiches and coffee as we waited in the 'dustbin'.

'We may not have much time later on,' I added. And I was right.

George Bailey, who was with me as a passenger, held the cups and I unscrewed the thermos top. As I did so the faintest steady whispering beat fell upon our ears like the rhythmic rustle of a flowing ball dress; the sound came from the south'ard. We stayed motionless, intent, the coffee and cups held poised, forgotten. Thus we must have remained for a minute or more. No longer was needed. The sound and its portent had become unmistakeable.

'Put away the coffee,' I said quietly, 'we shan't want it yet awhile.'

Curiously, that little remark, indicating that the fight was on, was to spring to mind whenever we recalled this action.

Noiselessly and swiftly the men went to their action stations and donned tin hats. The noise was a mixture of the throb of silenced engines and the splash of fast thrown washes; the E-boats were not far off. The bearing of the sound was altering fast. They were evidently going to pass quite close to the eastward of us, that is on the side away from our other unit. As I raked the darkness with my glasses I gave the necessary orders.

To 60: 'E-boats coming up from the south, passing to the eastward of us. I shall wait till they are level. Stand by to start up.'

217

To Head: 'Warn the engine room to stand by. Action stations. Pass a position to the tel.'

To Roberts, the tel: 'Call 65 on the R/T and say 'E-boats to the eastward. Join us. Course North 60 degrees East.' Then make an enemy report: 'Am engaging E-boats in position …'.'

They were almost level with us now, the sibilant murmur and muffled throb very close. I could not see them though it seemed I must; still I was sure of catching them. I lowered the glasses:

'Well. Here we go. Course North 75 degrees East, Coxswain. Start up.' This last shouted for the benefit of 60.

The six engines burst into life in quick succession, the boats swung round to port and steadied. The throttles were lifted swiftly; the roar of the engines reverberated as we settled to thirty knots. I for one had a queer feeling in the pit of the stomach, but what man, determined upon performing an unpleasant duty, has not? The more determined the man the deeper the sinking sensation, to vanish like a mirage as action is joined, and vital concentration required. I am willing to wager that Nelson, the embodiment of determination, with his sustained and impassioned urge to make contact with the enemy however disadvantageous the odds, felt these qualms as his seventy-four-gun ship of the line slowly closed the enemy squadron, maybe in sight of each other for many hours before battle would be joined.

I was standing on the canopy now by the mast, straining into the darkness with the glasses. It was not more than three or four minutes before I saw them. They were in line ahead, one, two, three, four; I could see no more but knew there were some as the white wash stretched out ahead in the gloom. Big fellows they looked too at that distance, about four cables. I jumped down:

'There they are right ahead. Steer 70, Coxswain,' I said as I increased speed. I did not want to open fire until we had got in close, where the surprise we hoped to effect would yield greater results; but, almost as the words left my mouth, the enemy's guns spoke, a single brilliant stream of light tearing towards us, then another and another. Someone had been keeping a damned good lookout aft.

A tornado of fire was blasting at us now as we tore into the enemy line, the sky seemed alight with hurtling meteors and comets, but we were a low, difficult target, half covered by our great white pressure wave thrown high round the boat, throbbing at thirty-eight knots. The whine of the enemy shells passing low over the canopy could be heard clearly above the bellow of our engines and the intermittent crash of our own guns. We had closed to within a cable or less now of the rear boat of the line, Edwards and Barnes were doing good execution. The bursts of our shells on the E-boat's hull were plainly visible. We were flying along still closing, heading him off. The E-boat next in the line loomed up dead ahead, seemingly vast and menacing with her guns flashing.

'Port Wheel!'

'Steady!'

We levelled out on her course and turned all our attention to her, leaving the one we had just passed to Bussy.

'Starboard a little.'

We swung towards, closing again fast. The E-boat broke away to starboard; again we were confronted with a third E-boat ahead. Bussy, engaging the rearmost E-boat, which turned away, lost contact with us; this was inevitable in his first action in command, at the tremendous pace of the fight and subject to the intense volume of fire, making visibility well-nigh impossible with the blinding tracer.

By this time we had been hit severely. The starboard turret, having got off one thousand rounds, was hit hard while the crew were reloading. Two hands had fallen wounded and the turret was out of action. Repeatedly the thud of enemy shells hitting the hull could be heard and felt above the general uproar. Bailey, who was standing beside me, received a splinter below his right eye, harmless except for a profusion of blood, and stung by this proceeded to wreak vengeance on the Hun with a stripped Lewis gun.

The third E-boat broke off also, and again we found ourselves charging yet a fourth. So I went on up the line until we had engaged and headed off the whole formation of six enemy vessels. As we swept round to starboard with the sixth boat at last we found the way clear and no enemy vessel across our bow. They had fled away to the eastward in confusion, making smoke. Almost immediately we lost them in the smoke and darkness, now that they were no longer on a steady course. Would they run for home, or reform and try to carry on towards our convoy route?

The answer to that question would indicate the measure of the fright we had given them. We knew we had hit them pretty hard, but apart from the first boat which had been engaged by 60 as well as 64, the remaining five had only suffered what we could deliver from our single Oerlikon and the starboard 0.5 turret before it was shattered, with occasional effective bursts from the port 0.5 turret as we approached the enemy head on. Edwards had been wonderfully cool with his Oerlikon, firing in short bursts and only when he knew he could hit. He realised it was essential to keep that gun going at all costs. The only way to find out what the enemy was doing was to cut and listen. This we did, but at once realised it was hopeless until we had collected our own boats, since they were bumbling around making a terrific noise in an endeavour to come up with the action. After much flashing of recognition lights we all made contact and engines were cut. We listened expectantly. Yes, there it was. A distant murmur away to the eastward, almost due east. That was indecisive information. It meant they were probably reforming and it was impossible to tell whether they would then make another bid to get through to the convoy route, or whether they would run for home.

The essential thing was to stop them getting on to the convoy route. If we went north-east at top speed for six miles or so and then cut we should be certain of being fairly near to them if they were attempting to go on. If they had turned for home we should hear them only in the distance to the south and probably fail to catch them again. But the essential need was to stop them getting through. Therefore the run to the north-east was the correct manoeuvre.

We formed up and sped away at thirty-six knots. The excitement was intense. Would they come on again? If so they would find a much stronger force this time, with three almost fresh boats and one damaged but still able to fight. I had ascertained from Bussy that 60 was all right, hardly hit at all and no casualties. She had been lucky. There was time now to take stock of my own boat. She was a shambles. Five of the crew were casualties, half the ship's company, several of them serious and one obviously dying. The starboard turret was shattered, there were gaping holes in the canopy, the hull was holed in thirteen places, some large gaping gashes, others no bigger than your fist where a shell had penetrated and burst inside. The decks were slippery with blood and oil. Luckily, because we had been heading towards our enemies almost throughout the action, nearly all the shell holes were forward and had burst in the empty living quarters, mercifully none below the water line.

Head reported the state of the ship below decks and the condition of the wounded men, asking for morphia. This I produced from my pocket, where I always kept plenty when at sea, a wise precaution as I found on more than one occasion. Head and Barnes looked after the wounded manfully.

Meanwhile I sent a signal:

'E-boats driven off to the eastward. Have lost contact. Endeavouring to intercept again.'

We reached our selected position and stopped the engines, slumping to silence instantly before the way was off the boats, as the flotilla had been trained to do when hunting E-boats where seconds might count. A moment's tense expectancy: then a slow spreading relaxation. There was no nearby clear sound, only a very distant faint murmur to the south. The enemy had had enough. They were going home.

'They're going back to Ostend,' I shouted to 65. 'We'll chase them in. We might pick up a straggler. Start up.'

We were off again pressing south at thirty-six knots. We might catch some of them and beat them up again, but they had a good lead.

Roberts despatched another signal:

'E-boats retiring to Ostend. Am following.'

The Coxswain took the opportunity of serving out a tot of rum. I remember drinking a little of the strong black liquid out of a cup as I stood in the dustbin, peering ahead into the increasing darkness; I did not like it, though it gave out a glowing warmth.

The visibility was coming down rapidly. With the dark clouds that had been gathering to the south-west had come a gentle southerly breeze, bringing with it a steadily increasing mist. Presently we could not see each other more than fifty yards off and had to decrease speed. This was bad luck as it gave the E-boats every chance to escape. When we had run down to an estimated position three miles off Ostend we stopped. I dared not carry on further in that visibility; we had no echo sounders and after an action it was impossible to be sure of one's dead-reckoning position to within a few miles. As we stopped we heard a low mutter to the south in the direction in which we estimated Ostend to be and after a few minutes this ceased rather abruptly. It seemed certain that the E-boats had got into harbour.

I remembered some remarks of the first captain I had served under in the war, an RN Commander of active mind and unusually wide outlook. He had interesting theories about the German as a fighting

221

man and a seaman. He had wonderful ships and equipment, he knew how to work his gear, he was efficient, and as a nation he was undoubtedly brave. Yet somehow he failed in open battle at sea. His immediate reaction, whatever the odds in his favour, was to turn away and run for his well-defended harbours. In view of the undoubted bravery displayed by the Germans on land, my captain's conclusion was that there was something about fighting at sea that affected him adversely. Being primarily a central European, the average German had not the sea in his blood. To fight effectively at sea you must first be happy and feel natural at sea. The call of the sea must be in your veins. England has this heritage. Even the soldiers felt secure when they reached the beaches at Dunkirk. If they could get to the sea they were all right, whereas the Germans showed their outlook by dropping leaflets giving a sketch of the B.E.F hemmed in at Dunkirk and calling on them to surrender as 'they were in a hopeless position, surrounded and with their backs to the sea.'

As I reviewed the events of the night I reflected that there seemed much truth in these theories. When I considered the cool and unflinching bearing of my men in the recent bitter encounter, many of them removed by but a few months from peaceful occupations ashore in garages, factories, fields, or machine shops, the full import of our sea heritage was brought home to me. These men had a thousand years of naval tradition behind them and the sea in their blood.

My boat was no longer much of a fighting unit, riddled with holes, few guns working and only half the crew left; it was important to try to get the wounded back quickly for treatment. I decided to transfer to 65 and let Bailey take my boat back to harbour. It was just after midnight. I called 65 alongside and, taking Roberts with me, went aboard. Bailey turned north and roared away into the night. With her stern towards us and her straight unsilenced exhausts, we heard her for fifteen miles.

I sent the last signal of the night:

'Visibility one hundred yards. E-boats entered Ostend. Am remaining in vicinity. 64 returning to harbour with casualties.'

Roberts was on top of his form. He had the air to himself, as there were no other E-boats out and the Nore were interested in us alone for the time being. We had driven off and put to flight a vastly superior enemy force and done our duty as gunboats. Sitting impudently off his harbour entrance daring him to come out again, we felt rather like Rikkitikkitavi[9] must have done after he had performed his function as a mongoose in fighting and killing the great cobra Nag and was waiting and watching for his still more dangerous spouse Nogaina.

The E-boats did not renew the assault that night or for many days. In fact, they did not work from Ostend again but moved to fresh fields and pastures new.

I have two other memories of this action. I had occasion to attend a conference at the Nore not very long after. The Chief of Staff discussed the engagement and ended up by saying: 'Since then we have had reports of several German bodies washed up in the Command. They are definitely E-boat personnel as they all have the distinctive uniform of the E-boat crews.'

We had exacted some revenge for the men blown to bits by the E-boat mines.

The other memory is the reverse side of the picture. A funeral party at Shotley cemetery, where we buried our dead in the port of Harwich. A clear, cold, windy April day. The rivers Stour and Orwell both visible from the raised promontory on which the church is placed, appearing as grey-brown serpents twisting between the low-lying green fields and woods. The flag-covered coffins, the red, white and blue bright in the clear sunlight, the puffs of smoke blown swiftly from the rifle muzzles of the firing party, the age-old words of the funeral service: 'Ashes to ashes, dust to dust.' A sobering memory with which to close the account. We were left to fight on, but our comrades were at peace.

It is hard to work out at this distance in time when it was that Hitch's reputation as the leading MGB Senior Officer in Coastal Forces was first established. Tommy Kerr had referred to him as 'an inspiration to his flotilla and all at HMS *Beehive*' when forwarding the Report of Proceedings after Hitch's action on the 19/20 December 1941, but it seems likely that the Ostend action in April 1942 put the seal on his reputation. He was awarded his first Distinguished Service Order (DSO), given to commanding officers for successful actions, and this award may well have added

9. A reference to Rudyard Kipling's story of a mongoose defending the dwelling he lived under in India against a pair of snakes who had come to live in its garden. I can remember my father reading me this story.

strength to his application for the seventy-one-foot-six MGBs, then building, to be assigned to his flotilla. It can have done no harm when it came to the next round of his battle with the staff of the Director of Naval Construction over the weapons that MGBs were permitted to carry. From the spring of 1942, until his death a year later, Hitch was a force to be reckoned with in Coastal Forces. He was at the height of his powers as an MGB Flotilla Senior Officer.

Chapter Eleven

Summer Patrols
May – July 1942

Inevitably it is the excitement and glamour of hard fought actions that tend to fill all naval histories and the memories of those who served in time of war. Important though they were in establishing the ascendancy of one side or the other, it was the routine patrols, night after night, that gradually denied German light forces their primary role in disrupting British coastal convoys, and took the war in the Narrow Seas to the Germans' own convoy routes up and down the coasts of the Low Countries and France. These convoy routes were less vital to the Germans than the east coast and Channel convoy routes were to the British, but they were important enough. Peter Dickens, in his book *Night Action*, summarises the strategic purpose behind offensive patrols at night off the coasts of Holland, Belgium and France.

The Germans found our attacks irritating and sometimes a downright nuisance. That is no justification for our existence by itself, for the true balance can only be struck by weighing the total effort devoted to MTBs against the results achieved, an involved and difficult calculation. I believe our force to have been inevitable as is borne out, partly by its very existence when few in high places liked or wanted it, and by Admiral Lucht, *Befehlshaber der Sicherung der Nordsee*, who wrote with feeling, 'We must not leave the enemy free use of the area off our coast at night.'

Why not? Because the convoys had to pass and were in danger both from direct attack and from mines laid in their paths; because if they

225

were safe at night they could avoid the greater threat of air attack by day; because we, the enemy, could not be allowed to reconnoitre the coast for invasion purposes, or pass secret agents across it, and because of the unknown – if we could operate as we would we might do anything and the Germans would only find out when it was too late. Every iron ore ship sunk meant fewer tanks; but every trawler sunk meant one less anti-aircraft escort, patrol vessel or minesweeper, and a growing shortage of either meant an increased risk to the ore-carriers or imposed delay on their sailings which was significant in itself, as well as making it impossible to send any escorts to the Baltic where they were desperately needed to support the vast military campaign in Russia.

So the arguments in support of our small-scale activities ranged far and wide and I suggest that an aggressive Allied presence off the occupied coast was as necessary to our strategy as its neutralization was to the Germans; and since only small craft could operate in those mined and shallow waters, and join with the Air Force in completing the diurnal cycle of pressure, MTBs had to be invented. That however was not enough to make them fully effective which I frankly admit they were not, and I believe the underlying cause to have been the ingrained dislike of flashy little boats by the RN Establishment. There were thus scarcely any boats to begin with, and then only bad ones until four years after the outbreak of war; but worse even than that, many RN officers appointed to Coastal Forces in the early days lacked inspiration, one or two being downright bad, and it was left to a forceful few, RN and RNVR both, to get the business moving at all.

What Dickens said of MTBs was just as true of MGBs, the two types of boat now working closely together, the MGBs providing protection to the vulnerable MTBs if attacked by E-boats with far heavier gun armament. It was already becoming obvious that what the Royal Navy really needed was what the Germans had built before the war, a combined motor gunboat and motor torpedo boat, with the speed, the guns and the hitting power of torpedoes, all within one hull. Awaiting that development, and indeed the delivery of the new more heavily armed MGBs, the Sixth MGB Flotilla went about its workaday tasks in the summer of 1942. Hitch told the story of this period and I will only occasionally add to or comment on his text.

Although the E-boats gave up Ostend we were not to know this for some time and we continued to operate there for a while. We had a narrow escape from disaster on one occasion. We had been acting as support to the Fifty-first ML Flotilla minelaying close off Ostend. At that time the plan was for us to lie off somewhere near so that we could come to their aid if they were attacked. That night our position had been the Kwinte buoy ten miles north of the harbour mouth.

We had run our D.R. down and about four miles short of our estimated position off the Kwinte buoy we had picked up a light dead ahead, flashing three every twenty seconds. It was never certain whether the buoy was going to be lit or not, and its characteristics were not known for sure. We assumed that this was our buoy. We ran on the additional four miles by which time the light seemed quite close, four or five cables off if it were a pretty bright buoy, and stopped.

There we lay for the rest of the night, undisturbed. The tide and wind drift according to our reckoning had set us several miles to the north-west, to seaward of the buoy, which we could see throughout the night, flashing steadily but getting gradually less bright. When the MLs had finished their lay and had got well clear, and before we returned, I decided to have a run in towards Ostend to see if we could flush any patrol vessels and beat them up.

Off we set at thirty knots. It was still pitch dark and there were four of us. We thundered steadily towards the coast. I intended to run up until the Kwinte buoy light was on the beam and then carry on for eight miles. That would bring us to within two miles of the entrance to Ostend. If we had sighted nothing, we would swing round and get out of it.

We went on and on. I watched the light, at first carelessly, and then more closely. I supposed it was drawing on the beam, but devilish slowly. I checked the rev counters. Yes, we were doing thirty knots. I asked how many minutes we had been going. Already eleven minutes. Five and a half miles and that blessed light was not yet abeam, didn't seem to have shifted bearing a great deal. We certainly must have drifted much farther than I thought.

How many minutes now? Fifteen. Seven and half miles and still we hadn't reached that light. Besides, surely it was getting very bright? Thus, starting with a false premise, I fooled myself; as the Fourth MTB Flotilla when they mistook their buoy, we very nearly caught up with our 'snowstorm', and much worse it would have been, since all four boats of the Sixth Flotilla would have landed up on the enemy coast at thirty knots.

Luckily my sense of anxiety overcame my blindness just in time. After we had been travelling for twenty-three minutes towards the land and had still not got the light on our beam, but very nearly, I realised that something must be wrong. Our D.R and estimate of drift could not be that much out. We turned and in doing so our exhausts faced landwards and, being heard above the offshore wind, the light went out.

Then I realised what had happened and how narrow had been our escape. The light that we had mistaken for the comparatively dim light of the Kwinte buoy was a powerful lighthouse on the end of Ostend pier, visible fourteen to seventeen miles. It was an easy mistake to make at first. The Ostend light had never been on before and we could not expect such a distant, bright beacon. But the distance run towards it and the greatly brightening light should have warned me in plenty of time. As it was I had gone in fatuous deter-mination to put the light on the beam, lulled into a false sense of security by the original incorrect estimate of the light. I nearly succeeded: had I done so we should have all been prisoners of war.

There is, however, much truth in the saying that, at sea, it is more important to be lucky than to be clever. I certainly went out of my way to prove it on this occasion.

Stranding on the enemy held coast has been the fate of quite a few British naval officers over the centuries, given their determination to keep the Narrow Seas under British control and hence close blockade of the enemy coastline. Hitch was lucky that it didn't happen to him. Navigation in those small, fast moving, noisy little vessels must have been a nightmare. The Sixth Flotilla still did not have RDF. Very junior officers, with extremely short experience of the sea, bent over small tables in their often madly bucking boats, attempting to keep a dead reckoning at night usually without any shore based navigational aids or buoys to help them, had a daunting task.

There was another incident connected with our Ostend period, which was discreditable so far as I was concerned. We had lain off the port all night, hoping for some convoy or patrol to put in an appearance. Towards dawn, utterly bored with the inaction, I had decided to carry out an offensive sweep close along the coast, despite the terrific noise we should put up at speed, making any form of surprise quite impossible.

We carried out our run without finding anything, the only result being multitudes of searchlights and flares from the shore. I had left it until late. Just as dawn was breaking and we were about to speed away from the coast to avoid air attack, David James' boat carried away a pendulastic. This meant a delay and then a maximum speed of eighteen knots. We just got out of sight of land as broad daylight was on us and then 61 had to stop again for some minor adjustment. These delays are rather exasperating for an S.O. The safety of the boats are his responsibility. I had been caught out taking a chance and had been put in an awkward position by the breakdowns. To make matters worse, the weather was blowing up rapidly; in a rough sea we were at a disadvantage against aircraft and we had stirred them up properly with our recent close in sweep.

In addition to this, you cannot know what is going on aboard the delaying boat, you cannot see for yourself the trouble and all you can do is to persuade yourself that they are doing all that is possible and endeavour to stifle one's restlessness. I was doing the best I could in this line, but the night had been a considerable strain and, to an impatient nature such as mine, it was difficult to restrain a growing feeling of irritability towards the erring boat, however much I may have realised at heart that they were doing all in their power.

At last David flashed OK and off we set at our eighteen knots. As soon as I had settled the throttles, I looked back as I always do to see that all were in place. There was not a sign of David. I immediately flashed an Aldis lamp astern, which should have been visible in the gathering light at a considerable distance. There was no response. Utterly exasperated, I stopped the unit again and flashed continually on the bearing where I supposed 61 must be. After several minutes there was an answering light and soon after *61* appeared. I flashed her:

'What is the matter?'

The answer came back:

'Nothing.'

So I stopped her and I regret to say poured out the vials of my wrath upon the unfortunate David's head. We went on and immediately I felt very ashamed of myself. It transpired later that David's coxswain had, in some extraordinary way, turned the boat one hundred and eighty degrees while David was raising his throttles and not looking out. Consequently when he looked out again, he could see no one and it took him a little time to realise that he was hastening in the wrong direction. It was an inept piece of work, but the sort of thing that may happen to anyone and I felt very badly about my loss of temper and slating David in front of everyone.

I am firmly of the opinion that the essence of being a good officer and leader of men is never to give an unfair, hasty answer or decision, and never to lose your temper and indulge in extravagant abuse, particularly with anyone who is doing his best. If an officer or rating is deliberately neglecting his duty or insubordinate, he may have to be dealt with harshly. But such was not the case here. I had offended against my own cardinal rules and let myself down badly.

There is nothing like learning from mistakes; I never forgot this incident and it often helped to restrain me in later days, when my natural impatience at delay or stupidity was tending to get the better of me.

One of the most surprising discoveries that I made in the research for this book was Hitch's reputation as a calm, imperturbable leader who seldom, if ever, behaved other than in a thoroughly gentlemanly way with his officers and, indeed, with his crew. It is not that I have ever doubted that he would always have wished to behave in that manner, but knowing from family history the shortness of his fuse and his great impatience with anything done less than perfectly, I had expected to hear many stories of right royal bollockings handed out by Hitch to those he led when they didn't come up to his exacting standards. Perhaps the self control that he generally exhibited, though not on this occasion, was one of his most remarkable wartime achievements.

After a time it became obvious that the E-boats had deserted Ostend. This and certain other considerations moved the scope of our operations farther north to the area between the Hook of Holland and Ijmuiden. We were continually ploughing over there with the minelaying MLs, or as cover for the MTBs, or on NID jobs.

Lieutenant H.L. (Harpy) Lloyd, RN, was by this time S.O. of the MTBs at 'Beehive' and we did many trips together. On one occasion

I remember going off to Flushing[1] in the first of the improved seventy-one-foot-six MGBs, *74*, with several of the old Sixth Flotilla and a party of MTBs under Lloyd. It was, as so often, a flat calm night and the thunder of our approach, reverberating across the still smooth water, could be heard up to twenty miles on all sides. This was not my idea of a surprise attack by an MTB, the invariable object of the MTB officer; but for some reason best known to themselves, the Admiralty had decided that silenced main engines were unnecessary, and that six knots on auxiliaries was all that was required – the official reason given, I believe, being that at more than six knots the wash could be heard before the auxiliaries. It seems to have been overlooked that the wash could not be heard more than a few hundred yards, but that main engines could be heard up to twenty miles.

We got to our position and the gunboats stopped. They were to wait there as support for the MTBs against E-boat attack. The MTBs split into two parties and bumbled off. They only had seven or ten miles to go from where we were lying, but they could not afford to waste the time in getting there at five or six knots in silence; so we heard them clearly until they cut their engines a mile or so from their objective.

Almost immediately a great uproar started from the direction of the shore. The heavy cracking thud of large guns, four-inch at least, and the yellow-green bursts of star-shell. At first, we thought it was an air attack, as the sound of aircraft had preceded it, and that it was shore batteries firing; but presently we heard a deep underwater thud, followed immediately by the criss-cross of distant low-level tracer. Then we knew that Harpy had run into something; we started up and sped towards the scene of activity, almost immediately getting an enemy report. But the firing was short-lived, lasting only about three minutes. By the time we arrived some fifteen minutes later we found nothing and so swept away to the eastward, in which direction we thought the enemy most likely to move.

What had happened was this. Two German torpedo boats, six hundred ton vessels like small destroyers, mounting four-inch guns, and several E-boats had been on patrol on the convoy route. They had been able to plot the MTBs' course and exact approach by the

1. In Dutch, Vlissingen.

engine noise. Harpy ran steadily on towards them and cut his main engines when only a short distance off. The Germans, realising that they were not going to get any further help as to the position of the enemy from the sound, and knowing the MTBs to be close, at once put up star-shell and endeavoured to engage.

The MTBs, in spite of being themselves surprised instead of the other way about, were fortunate in being very well placed for attack. Tom Neil in *MTB 70* found a torpedo boat right opposite him in the light of the star-shells. He promptly fired and secured a direct hit, probably sinking the German vessel out of hand. But he didn't wait to see, as the situation was distinctly hot and he could do no more good. Lloyd also fired at the other torpedo-boat, but probably missed. Then under the increasing hail of enemy shells the MTBs disengaged at forty knots to the north-west. They were fortunate in getting away with only minor damage, one officer killed and two hands wounded. A very successful exchange in the circumstances. The whole thing was over in little more than five minutes.

Harpy Lloyd had been a CO in the MTB group at Felixstowe from its earliest days, arriving in January 1940, and eventually became Senior Officer of the Fourth MTB Flotilla. He and Hitch started the practice of joint MGB and MTB patrols which was to be continued so successfully between Hitch and Peter Dickens. Peter remained a friend of my family after the war, and I saw him on a good many occasions and knew very well how important a role he had played in my father's naval service. I was to meet Harpy Lloyd only once and then, sadly, only a few months before his death. We were both guests of Vice Admiral Sir Fitzroy Talbot, by then a neighbour of mine in Dorset, who had spent a short and not terribly happy time in command of the Third MASB Flotilla. I could so much more profitably have spent that evening in his company had I by then already immersed myself in the details of my father's war service.

We drew a blank that night and for some time to come. There seemed to be practically no enemy shipping about, and in the quiet weather of early summer we roamed all round the Dutch coast and could find no target. Often we roused the enemy searchlights, shore batteries fired on us, but they would not send out the E-boats to give battle. Once we thought they were ready to give us a stand-up fight, but it ended in disappointment. It happened this way.

Boffin went over alone to a little place called Katwijk, to the south west of Ijmuiden, on an NID job. When closing the land he ran into a sleepy patrol of E-boats, who only just saw him at the last moment and chased him away. It seemed possible that something had leaked out from the shore end of the job. One could imagine the Gestapo descending swiftly on their victim; skilfully extracting the story. That patrol just off our objective was suspicious in view of the astonishing lack of coastal patrols in general. We were determined to attempt the job again and verify our suspicions. We devised another plan. The NID required two jobs to be done, one at Katwyck and another at Nordwyck, three miles away down the coast.

We decided to take two boats, *64* and *67*, go in together so that we could tackle a patrol if we had to fight, and then split when we had found our objective, each carry out our allotted task, and return independently.

We went on a perfect night, loaded up with our spies, desperate types we thought them. It was too perfect a night. The wind had gone right away. That meant that we should have to run in for a greater distance on our closed down S pipes at slow speed, making the chances of finding our objective in time less likely, and risking gassing our engine-room crews. There was always a grave danger of this with the pipes closed, as the back pressure in the exhaust pipes was greatly increased by the gases being discharged under water, and thereby all the little leaks in the long exhaust system were found out, resulting in a quantity of carbon monoxide finding its way into the engine room. We had many quite severe cases of poisoning in the early days of these pipes, and the way the engine room crews stuck it, disregarding the danger, was greatly to their credit.

The night being dead quiet was bad enough, but worse was to come. As we swept over the one hundred miles to the Dutch coast our wash became brighter and brighter until it was a great splash of white-green luminosity. We were in for as bad a night of phosphorescence as I can remember. On such a clear dark night as this our hulls would normally be visible about three cables at the most, without glasses. With the creaming phosphorescent wakes we could be seen, like giant fireflies, at a distance of a mile or more.

Fifteen miles from the coast we shut down our pipes and closed the shore slowly. Even at the reduced speed the phosphorus was shocking, lighting up the hull so brilliantly that I could read 67's

233

number on her bow at more than a cable. We found two small wreck buoys with their winking green lights three or four miles from the shore, and thereby we were able to tell that we were too far to the north. As it turned out later this was fortunate. We closed the shore and when we could see it clearly, about three or four cables off, we ran south along the coast in an endeavour to locate Nordwyck.

The noise from our roughly silenced engines seemed tremendous in that absolute stillness, the bright light from the phosphorus showering from the broken water at our bows, like a beacon reflected in the glossy smooth surface. We reduced to one engine. Staggering along at our slowest speed, about seven knots, it was still possible to read 67's number at more than two hundred yards. It seemed certain that we must be seen or heard and we were momentarily expecting a blast from the shore. Incredible as it was, nothing happened. It was two o'clock in the morning; the Germans were very fast asleep ashore.

Presently we found Nordwyck. You could see the lighthouse standing grey and unlit in the centre of the cluster of houses forming the little fishing village. We stopped. Our job was here; with a single pre-arranged spark of light to seaward we sent 67 off to her destination three miles south along the coast at Katwyck. Quietly we launched the dinghy. The NID men embarked. One was to be landed, another picked up. It was exciting and a trifle theatrical. The quiet movements, the hushed voices, the motionless boat on the unmarked shiny surface of the water, the black low line of the shore, the cluster of houses silhouetted against the skyline, the rigid finger of the light-house in the centre, the last handshake to the parting men, the whispered 'Good luck'; no sound, no light, no movement, only the gentle thud and splash of the muffled oars fading shoreward. But this was no theatre. At any moment the darkness might be pierced by a brilliant finger of light, the silence shattered by the roar of real guns.

Slowly the minutes passed. Presently we became aware of the stealthy approach of the little boat. She saw us and rounded up beneath our counter. In her were the same men as had left twenty-five minutes before. There was a whispered colloquy. I was told that we had better get out of it, as nothing more could be done. I gathered that the man who should have met them was not there; that this and other circumstances had aroused their suspicions. They feared a trap and were glad to be back aboard.

We began to steal softly to seaward. Suddenly the throb of high-powered engines reverberated across the still water from the southward, followed almost at once by bright streaks of red and green tracer. Red and green: that meant British and German. *67* must be in trouble. The beans were, so to speak, spilt. The noise of engines and battle had already broken out. We might as well open up.

'Open pipes. Start centre.'

'Steer south 55 west.'

We were off. Flying through a cloud of luminous wash in the general direction of the fight to the south-west. Suddenly two bright searchlights broke out close on the port quarter, streams of tracer sped from a spot on our starboard beam, near but not near enough. Behind us the shore was now thoroughly roused. Searchlights, shore batteries and their curious bobbing flares were all let loose without stint.

The firing to the southward had ceased as suddenly as it had begun. The brilliant nearby searchlights on the port quarter meant a patrol close to the south, the gunfire to starboard meant another a few cables to the north. I gave her the gun, and with her 3,500 h.p. at full stretch *64* fairly stepped along; running away for the first time; our orders were explicit, we must avoid action if possible, we had valuable lives aboard. Little as we liked the idea of getting out instead of attacking, this was a moment of great exhilaration. The bellowing throb of the engines, for once filling their great brazen lungs to the maximum of their capacity, only to clear them in a deafening, ear-splitting din; the vibrating thrusting surge of power beneath our feet; the rush of wind in the face as we bored into the encircling darkness at forty-five miles an hour; the dangerous game of 'Blind Man's Buff' as we made violent alterations of course to avoid on one side the groping fingers of dazzling blue-white light and on the other the nearby bursts of green and yellow tracer

We were lucky. The searchlights failed to follow us far enough to the north; the gunfire, directed by sound, passed harmlessly astern, since the exhaust gases, leaving the transom at over two hundred miles an hour, formed an area of maximum noise well behind the fast-driven hull.

It was clear that our passengers' suspicions had been correct; the agent ashore must have 'talked'. There were no less than three in-shore patrols, just off our objectives, an impossibility in normal circumstances. If we had not made our landfall to the no'thard and come down the coast close along the shore we should never have got in.

As soon as we got clear of our immediate personal troubles we called up *67* and asked how she was. She replied presently that she was all right, but being closely pursued by five E-boats.

We made to her:

'Indicate course, speed and position'

We got her reply as dawn was breaking:

'Course South 75 degrees West, speed thirty-six knots, position 52 degrees 25 North, 3 degrees 52 East.'

This was admirable. I had been afraid that she might have lost speed and been in grave danger. The course was the same as ours. Her position lay right in our line of advance, she was doing thirty-six knots as opposed to the thirty to which we had reduced. We were in the best possible position to give her assistance if needed; there seemed every chance of us falling in with her pursuing E-boats when they turned back. We went to action stations and licked our lips in anticipation. We would give the E-boats a run for their money anyway; the passengers would have to take their chance. We missed them, however, and both boats got back without further incident. *67* had had a close shave. We considered that we had been challenged by the enemy.

It seemed probable that they might continue their patrols next night; we determined to seek them out and give battle. We mustered a force of six gunboats and two MTBs. We had never before handled a unit of eight at night off the enemy coast; we determined to try.

The speedy armada roared its way across the North Sea. Just before dusk we spotted a Jim Crow, a German reconnaissance plane. He did not come near; there was no doubt that he had seen us. On we rumbled. We made no attempt to dissemble or hide our approach. We swept into position off the Hook of Holland and turned north-east up the coast. We churned our way up to Ijmuiden, trailing our coat, sighted the wreck buoys and, swinging around one hundred and eighty degrees, charged back again close in shore, to make certain we had missed no patrol.

By this time the coast was in a state of uproar. Flares, searchlights, star-shells and shore batteries opening up at us all down the line. Sometimes when we were only two miles off the coast it was unpleasantly accurate; they even scored one or two unimportant hits. We could find no trace of our quarry; Jim Crow had delivered his warning; if patrols had been out they had been withdrawn. They would not give fight. Probably just as well as the chaos that would have ensued with our unit of eight in action is terrifying to contemplate!

Our only satisfaction lay in the insolent challenge we had thrown down. We had swept the sea on the very threshold of their lairs. They had not come out. We liked to compare the turmoil there would have been at 'Beehive' to get out and at them if E-boats had been heard and sighted patrolling off the Cork light vessel!

These summer patrols were against a contented background in the home base of HMS *Beehive* at Felixstowe. It had not always been thus, but ever since Tommy Kerr took over in the late summer of 1941 *Beehive* had become a steadily more efficient and a happier base for the small fighting craft that went out night after night on patrol. To add to their contentment, the new seventy-one-foot-six boats began to arrive.

We began to get the new boats in a steady stream in April, May and June of 1942. During the nine months that *Beehive* had been under the new Captain, the scene had changed greatly. Many of the early MTB officers had gone, others had been eliminated. The gunboats had taken their proper position in the scheme of things, that is as full equals of the MTBs. Actually on account of the ubiquitous nature of their work, and because they operated considerably more often than the MTBs, they rather tended to monopolise attention for a change.

The base was now a very happy one. The boats worked hard and were keen; there was no sense of frustration. Most important of all the Captain helped and backed us to the limit in the development of our boats and equipment. This was most important to us, because ours was a new and developing form of warfare. We who were enacting it were the only people who really understood the problems. Certain it is that the Admiralty did not. Moreover it was no small thing, because we found that the only way to get what we wanted was to make it ourselves and show that it worked; then we had a chance of getting it taken up officially. Thus we had to make the S-pipe silencing locally and prove that it would work. Later we had to fit and try out the Bombard, construct the dual Oerlikon cradle, manufacture the light Oerlikon mounting, alter the power supply to the RDF, all important developments; all had to be put into effect and proved before there was any chance of obtaining official sanction and interest.

In every case the Captain had to stand the repercussions of such over-zealous and revolutionary behaviour. Without his willing attitude of aiding, abetting and standing by us, we could have done nothing. He knew we were only trying to get on with the war and make our boats efficient fighting weapons in the face of considerable official inertia; he was willing to take the chance. Like us, he did not really care what happened to him. Like us he had his bowler hat round the corner, his conscience was clear, they could give it to him if they wished; thus clearly demonstrating Wyndham Lewis's famous dictum that 'a bowler hat is not so much an article of wear as an indication of a state of mind'.

At about this time we achieved two important developments in the proper equipment of our boats. The first was the light type Coastal Forces hydrophone.

I have already shown how we had discovered that our only scientific chance of chasing and catching E-boats was by hearing them and intercepting on sound. Two recent actions had proved that things were going to be more difficult for us soon, unless we improved our technique. In March, when the Seventh Flotilla had captured their E-boat, they had ascertained that there were no external exhaust pipes. This confirmed an idea that had already been suggested to me, that it was possible to lead the exhausts of high powered engines under water and so silence them. The action off Ostend had added corroborative evidence. When we had heard them on this occasion, though they had passed quite close to us, the sound had been utterly different to the night of the 19th/20th November 1941. Then they had been vibrant, growling, full-throated beasts; off Ostend they had been sibilant, whispering, swishing sea-monsters, audible only because they were close and the sea wholly still and silent. Unquestionably the E-boats had been silenced by leading their exhaust pipes under water.

Listening for them at any range or in any appreciable breeze, we should have no chance of hearing them. I had another trouble in my mind, too. Often we had to close enemy ports, lie off them for hours on end, in conditions of extreme darkness and low visibility. Lying cut in this manner we were extremely vulnerable. We could not expect to start up and get under way in under three minutes; until we did so we were like a log on the water, unable to fire most of our guns which were power operated. A German destroyer or torpedo boat seeking us out with RDF, coming up wind on a dark night, would be upon us before we had a chance of doing anything and could smash us to pieces with their main armament at point blank range. This was a very real worry, as mine was the responsibility for the safety of the boats when we kept these dangerous vigils.

By chance I had heard of an idea, which, if it worked, could solve these difficulties. Lieutenant Perry, whom I have already referred to, always a fountain of bright ideas, having almost complete knowledge of our boats, their hulls, engines and operational problems, having built and demonstrated them before the war, and having been in command of an operating boat during the war, at that time working in RACF's office in London, mentioned that experiments had been made with a light type hydrophone, which could be dropped over the side when the boats stopped and brought aboard again instantly when required.

This seemed a most promising line of approach. If it worked it would solve both our difficulties. We should be able to hear the E-boats under water in spite of wind and their silencing; we should have ample warning of the approach of any hostile ship when lying off enemy harbours, whatever the wind conditions and visibility. I made enquiries and found that the idea had been dropped as there was no requirement! I discussed the matter with the Captain. He took the idea up most enthusiastically, having been a submariner in the last war and therefore well versed in the potentialities of the hydrophone.

The Captain took the problem to the Flag Officer in Charge, Harwich. The new F.O.I.C. was Rear Admiral H.H. Rogers,[2] a Cornishman, utterly determined to back any worthwhile development, however unofficial. He took up the light hydrophone idea in a big way. He got his A/S[3] officers on to the job. In a short time we had the first experimental set. Apart from the standard amplifier, the main part of the hydrophone appeared to consist of a long piece of light gas piping and the cut-off bottom of an enormous kettle! But it worked; it worked magnificently and beyond all expectation. After a short period of experimenting we began to get very satisfactory

2. Hugh Hext Rogers was also a cousin, being related to both Robert and Catherine.
3. Anti-submarine.

ranges. In addition, the equipment was almost foolproof, and so light, twenty-five pounds in all, that it could be rigged and shipped in a matter of thirty seconds.

Admiral Rogers' tenacity had resulted in a most important step forward in our tactical development. In a short time the equipment was to become general throughout Coastal Forces on the East Coast. It was to be the basis of our anti-E-boat tactics during the ensuing winter.

For the modern yachtsman, accustomed to built in electronics of considerable sophistication such as GPS and echo-sounders to gauge depth, it may come as a surprise to hear that the hydrophone at that time was a lightweight instrument hung over the side of a boat with its engines cut, whose operator put on earphones and sat, often with his legs dangling over the side, listening for propeller noises. Sydney Dobson, who operated a hydrophone as one of his special duties in *MGB 111*, described to me this primitive method.

The other important improvement that we managed to get under way at this time was the silencing of our boats. I have told how we were satisfied that the E-boats were being under-water silenced. I discussed the feasibility of doing the same to our boats with all the engineer officers I could. Perry thought it would work if we fitted underwater scoops, to provide suction and so help the gases away. Others thought that, as the speed of the exhaust gases was in the region of two hundred m.p.h. in the pipes, there would necessarily be tremendous back pressure, making the scheme impossible. I kept an open but hopeful mind. I heard in imagination those soft-voiced E-boats off Ostend and thought that, if they could do it, so could we.

Luckily about this time, late May or June 1942, Rear Admiral Coastal Forces came out with us in the old boats for an operation off the Dutch coast. In bright moonlight on a quiet night we swept up from the Hook to Ijmuiden. We encountered no enemy, but R.A.C.F. was able to see at first hand how handicapped we were by having no better silencing than that provided by our S-pipes.

Discussing the matter the next morning, I was able to propound my theories about under-water silencing. He saw the importance of the development, if it were possible, and at once arranged a conference with British Power Boats to see if experiments could be started immediately. At the meeting Colonel Searle, the managing director of the company, and Mr Selman, the designer, could not have been more helpful. The latter got out designs forthwith. Within three weeks the first boat[4] was tearing up Southampton Water at forty knots in almost complete silence before our admiring eyes. Best of all it was demonstrated that it in no way adversely[5] affected the engine boost or the back pressure.

We had achieved the most important requirement of all. It was a tremendous stride forward in our search for operating efficiency. Alas, my new flotilla by this time having been completed, I was to see all the new boats benefit from our discoveries, without being able to induce the authorities to fit the boats already built and about to operate.

My only consolation was the somewhat vicarious satisfaction of seeing that the success which had attended Power Boats' under-water experiments had stirred Vosper's and the authorities sufficiently to arrange a general conference and trial to see how best to silence all boats, including the MTBs which needed it even more than we did.[6] They had been operating now for three years of war and for a long period beforehand without making any attempt to silence their main engines.

Whether connected with experiments on the silencing of engines or not, engine room crews were always in danger of being gassed. This came from little leaks in the exhaust system resulting in a quantity of carbon monoxide finding its way into the engine room.

We had many quite severe cases of poisoning in the early days and the way engine room crews stuck it, disregarding the danger, was greatly to their credit. Without their willing co-operation in the face of this risk, we could never have used and developed the boats as we did. Only the night before, an elderly stoker named Gibbs, Captain Gibbs his messmates used to call him, the owner of much property in peacetime, had been found lying on his face passed clean out, severely gassed. The fastening of one of the exhaust pipes had

4. This was *MGB 79*. The earlier deliveries to the Eighth Flotilla were thus not silenced at high speeds.
5. Silencing added perhaps two knots to the speed of the seventy-one-foot-six boats. MGB 'silent' speed was still only fifteen knots but they were quieter than they used to be at higher speeds.
6. MTBs received Dumbflow silencers in 1943.

broken, resulting in the pipe lifting and causing noise. Gibbs had lain flat on his stomach holding down the flap by hand. He had hung on until the fumes, coming up from the pipes, had knocked him flat. It was only the noise recurring from the released pipe that saved him, as it called attention to his condition. It is men like Gibbs who, in the last resort, save the British Empire from defeat by her enemies, and, by their quiet acceptance of any duty that may befall, enable the country to hang on to victory. Here was a man of over forty years, used to a quiet and prosperous business life in peacetime, unquestioningly lying flat on his face in a little cockleshell of a boat, at two o'clock in the morning, a few miles off the coast of Holland, hanging on to a hot exhaust pipe, until he passed clean out from carbon monoxide poisoning. And he did not consider that he was doing anything unusual or even surprising. Could keeping faith with your country go further?

By July 1942 five of the new seventy-one-foot-six MGBs had been delivered to form the new Eighth Flotilla and at the end of that month Hitch was to lead them down to Dartmouth, leaving the older seventy-foot boats in the Sixth to continue under George Bailey. However, Hitch records the last actions of the Sixth Flotilla while still nominally under his command, although he was away commissioning *MGB 77* at the time.

The new Flotilla, the Eighth, was forming up. I was to have the fourth boat, *77*, and in June Head and I went away to take her over. While I was away at Southampton getting my new boat, Boffin was in charge of the Flotilla. One night he came across some enemy patrols on their coast and was fortunate in being able to engage a small minesweeper on her own. He was in his new boat, *76*, followed by *64*, and Bussy Carr in *60*. It was the first time that our new armament, a two pounder and twin Oerlikon turret, had been in action. Ably supported by Bussy with his single Oerlikon and 0.5's, Boffin, without damage to his unit, savaged that minesweeper until large pieces of her upper works fell off and she was a battered and smoking wreck.

Another interesting shaft of light on this moment of change in the Sixth Flotilla's command comes from Able Seaman Roland Clarke, who joined the Flotilla on the 16 June 1942 as a gunner in *MGB 67* under George Bailey. At the time of the action, described below, Hitch had just left for Dartmouth.

I had not long to wait for my baptism of fire. Our patrol had begun on the night of July 29th as it usually did, about 9pm. All crews on board by 8.30. *67, 61* and *60* slipped from the harbour in line ahead out past the boom defence and then into V formation with nine engines at three quarter throttle, the roar vibrating for miles around and past the Cork and then the Sunk light vessels, wrecks in sight. Here the order for action stations and a practise shoot at the sunken masts. Then the order would be to keep an extra sharp look out as soon as we were well over our own shipping lane. Darkness falls about eleven o'clock leaving us with roughly ninety miles to go to the Dutch coast at Ijmuiden. With thirty miles to go, on silencers. No smoking is the order. Even this small light would be noticed miles away. We are closing in now to the enemy coast and gradually turning to starboard to start a patrol down to Ostend, past the mouth of the Scheldt. Nothing to report. Down the coast we go, still on silencers. We have not even been spotted as yet. At Zeebrugge we stop engines and lower the hydrophones over the side. All is still and quiet except for the occasional wave as it laps the side of the boat. A report! Engines can be heard on the hydrophones. All is tense. 'Disengage silencers! Start up engines. Full speed ahead.'

We make our way past Ostend and at 2.15 we spot a faint blue light, 'Action Stations' are given. Speed is the thing, and surprise, but evidently we were not the only ones looking for trouble. We were challenged and apparently had met two of our own MTBs under Lieutenant 'Harpy' Lloyd, RN, also intent on destroying the convoy, which could now be seen silhouetted in the darkness. Lloyd goes in from seaward and fires both fish, hitting the first merchant ship. Both *61* and *60* had gone between shore and convoy to distract their attention. As we turned to attack the second merchant vessel, three flak trawlers which had not before been spotted were on the point of turning about to engage us. But *67* was not dismayed. In we went until not a gun on the merchantman could bear on us. As soon as we were under her bows a depth charge was dropped. This finished the second vessel. Now for the flak trawlers. At this time they were in line ahead and we were going straight for them, with *61* and *60* attacking from

243

their rear. What the remaining crew did not know was that the Coxswain, Commanding Officer and First Lieutenant were out and the boat was careering along on its own with the port 0.5 turret on fire and fire in the engine room and a hole in the bows at waterline level a yard across. Several of our crew were killed but the Coxswain, CO and First Lieutenant were not too serious, but were however out of action. Bunts Newton from Catford and myself were able to deal with the fire on deck and the engine room personnel with the one below and the Skipper gave us our course for home before we gave him morphia. It was 2.35 when we started back, Bunts and myself taking turns at the wheel and the mess deck pumps, the mess deck being half full of water up to our waists. The CO must have been spot on with the course. We hit the Sunk light vessel at 5.30 and entered harbour with a crash stop with wire hawsers, fire tenders, pumps and ambulances standing by.

Roland Clarke's description gives the reader a fine sense of the chaos and excitement of close action between small warships at night.

By July 1942 Hitch had five new boats forming the nucleus of the Eighth Flotilla, *74* to *78* with *79, 80* and *81* hard on their heels. As battle casualties mounted, other boats joined the flotilla, *111, 112* and *115* in the winter of 1942/43. Hitch has already outlined how he assessed the quality of the new seventy-one-foot-six motor gunboats coming off the production line at British Power Boats through his connection with George Selman and the advice of the Engineer Officer at *Beehive*, his old friend Pop Perry. It is worth now looking in some detail at what British Power Boats had achieved.

First of all the new boats were bigger than the old seventy-foot boats. An extra foot and a half doesn't sound very much, but if you design in a broader beam, the result in terms of cubic capacity is a worthwhile increase. The old boats had displaced thirty-one tons laden and the new were forty-six tons. They were still midgets but they were larger midgets, capable of carrying a heavier armament.

They were initially no faster. They had been designed to do a maximum of forty knots, the same as the old boats, but when underwater exhausts were fitted this increased their speed by two to three knots, which gave them the edge over the old boats. More importantly, they were more reliable. The old boats had particularly suffered from trouble with the drive mechanism, the often cursed pendulastic, and with their propellers. The new boats had direct drive on the centre engine, and although they still did not achieve the levels of reliability claimed for E-boats, they were a great deal better than their predecessors.

Of the greatest possible importance they had the potential to be quieter. Flat out the three Packards were still awesome close up but they now had silencers on their two wing engines permitting twelve knots of relatively quiet running and, due to Hitch's exasperated insistence on the potential for underwater exhausts reducing noise dramatically, the later boats of the class had all three engines giving much reduced noise at their cruising speed of thirty-five knots and silent running up to fifteen knots. When coupled with the extra two knots of speed it can be seen what a dramatic difference that made to the MGB's capacity to stalk the enemy and achieve tactical surprise.

Partly because they were bigger and partly because those who operated them were at last being listened to, for the first time they carried guns capable of doing real damage to E-boats. The new boats had a two-pounder quick firing pom-pom forward of the bridge, where Bath had always said it was too wet to have a gun, not understanding that in the conditions in which MGBs could operate, force four or less, the foredeck was the driest place in the boat. If MGBs were to be aggressive and their role was to attack the enemy, it hardly made sense to have their main armament aft so that it could not be brought to bear until they had nearly drawn parallel with an E-boat. In addition to the pom-pom, there was now a twin Oerlikon aft with a powered mounting, doubling that weight of fire. They had twin Lewis guns firing 0.303 bullets from abaft the whaleback, of little effect upon a hull but quite capable of killing deck personnel at close range. Right aft they carried a Holman Projector for firing flares. One addition to the armament that may surprise the reader was a mortar, a Blacker Bombard. If you consider the way a mortar works, lobbing a relatively heavy projectile in a high arc so that it falls on its target, it will be seen that the chances of success when aiming a mortar from a fast moving, bouncing MGB at even a slow enemy vessel, in darkness, were not terribly good. It is hard to find records of where these mortars had much success other than the night Hitch was killed. Nevertheless it was there on the foredeck, backing up the guns and appears to have been the result of Hitch's search for heavier weapons to deal with larger targets than the E-boats.

Finally, there were still two depth charges, the heavy weapon of last resort when faced with a ship too large to suffer much damage from the two-pounder pom-pom. The hazardous nature of a depth charge attack on a surface warship was to continue to test the resolve and skill of MGB officers and men until finally the Admiralty accepted the need for the torpedo to replace the depth charge as the weapon capable of dealing with larger ships.

There were other important changes. For the first time radar was fitted in MGBs. It was not that radar's advantages had not been recognized before, but simply that production limitations and the priority given to MGBs had resulted in them remaining unavailable. The type 286 radar was fitted in the Eighth Flotilla, which was not trainable, so that the boat had to be manoeuvred to port and starboard to sweep ahead. Nevertheless it did give a capacity to pick up the presence of enemy vessels at night before they came in sight and Hitch was quick to make use of his new detection system. He must also have been glad at long last to have echo sounders to help with navigation and the hazards of the shallow east coast, and the same radio navigation system that the MLs had had for their precise minelaying.

Last but not least, for the very first time MGBs had a very small amount of armour plate, half an inch thick, surrounding the bridge, protecting coxswain and officers when at action stations. Up till then there was nothing between anybody and the enemy other than wood. At least psychologically that provided some reassurance. For those standing totally exposed behind their guns on the deck even that fig leaf was absent. The new boats had armoured shields for the forward pom-pom and the Oerlikon aft, but the two Lewis gunners remained totally exposed. The Lewis guns were eventually replaced by the 800 rounds per minute 0.303 Vickers machine gun.

The one adverse change in the new boats was the degree to which they became dependent upon power training of the guns. It had been obvious from the earliest days of MGBs that in action the hydraulic lines which provided the power for training guns were vulnerable to shellfire. The experience of being unable to train guns when in close action was as frustrating and dangerous as anything could be. Hitch's lecture to his crews about the absolute necessity of keeping weapons in first class condition if they were to be reliable in action was of little avail if incoming fire rapidly made guns un-manoeuvrable. In the new boats both the two-pounder pom-pom and the twin Oerlikon were powered. With the pom-pom this was unavoidable due to its weight, but Hitch, in his everlasting search for better and more reliable weapons, was soon to conclude that a hand-trained twin Oerlikon was a more reliable weapon, and a much lighter one, than its powered equivalent.

Although in no way related to the arrival of the new seventy-one-foot-six boats, it is worth reflecting for a moment on how the experience of Coastal Forces in general and MGBs in particular had affected sea-going clothing. A small ship navy was never a dressy place and from the earliest days officers shrugged out of their reefer jackets and into sweaters and oilskins when they went to sea. What rapidly became apparent was that the tendency to get extremely wet for prolonged periods, as well as the number of deck personnel who were completely exposed to the elements without even the shelter provided by an open bridge, needed some very much better designed clothing than the traditional souwester, oil skins and rubber sea boots. A one-piece waterproof suit was developed, under which padded underclothing could be worn. Leather boots were sometimes bought by the more experienced, following the example of fishermen, because they kept drier and warmer. These garments were bulky but essential for deck personnel unsheltered from the elements.

Charles Mercer, who served in both *MGB 21* and *MGB 122*, remembers vividly the discomfort of life on board an MGB on patrol in the winter.

> Once you left harbour, you never left your post, until you got back the next morning. There was only a three foot walkway either side of the bridge and canopy. There were no guard rails. The clothes we wore at sea would include a singlet and pants, a thick white submarine jersey, a thick kapok boiler suit, and then on top an oilskin boiler suit. It used to be so cold in the North Sea that we couldn't undo our trousers to do a 'wee' so sometimes I just used to wet my underwear. We were often out for sixteen to twenty hours and all we had to eat or drink was a gallon of soup in a safari flask between fifteen of us.

Hitch himself had acquired something which looked rather like the siren suit that Churchill made famous and that was what he would wear on the bridge, or indeed in his favourite position when going into action, standing on the whaleback behind the bridge, holding on to the stumpy little mast, a position from which he had the best possible view of what was going on around him, communicating to the coxswain through a fixed speaking tube. If the Lewis gunners felt exposed standing behind their weapons on the open deck, they could not easily complain if their Captain and Senior Officer chose to expose himself even more in such a position.

This then was the new weapon which had been forged from the experience gained in the early motor gunboats, which Hitch had continuously sought to modify and improve. The consequence of the fitting of silencers and radar was a marked increase in the number of contacts with the enemy compared with earlier experience. The Sixth MGB Flotilla had been in five actions with E-boats between April 1941 and June 1942. The Eighth was to see considerably more action between July 1942 and April 1943.

When they did go into action their chances of decisive success were hugely increased by the two-pounder pom-pom forward and the twin Oerlikons aft. The frustration of so many of the previous engagements had been that, in spite of surprise, greater speed and, arguably, far greater determination to bring the enemy to action, the results, with rare exceptions, had been indecisive. The enemy might have been turned back from their purposes, taken a good many casualties, and needed repairs before they went to sea again, but the chances of sinking them were not high. That was now to change.

Chapter Twelve

Dartmouth
July – September 1942

'Here's something that will interest you, sir.'

I was passing through the S.D.O[1]. and the teleprinter operator was bending over the tapping, tinging mechanical marvel, deciphering an 'immediate' secret signal. I stopped and looked over his shoulder.

'All MGBs of the Eighth Flotilla are allocated temporarily to Plymouth command and will proceed .....'

The machine tapped swiftly on, but not fast enough for me. This was news indeed. Where were we going and why?

'... forthwith to Dartmouth.'

So it was Dartmouth, the West Country. To my Cornish eyes, tired of the low East Coast shoreline and the grey muddy North Sea, there came visions of high granite cliffs, steep hills, magnificent headlands, clear blue deep water. My first impulse was pleasure and excitement, followed quickly by a natural reaction. We had a happy ship in *Beehive*, good messmates, comfortable quarters and efficient equipment, understanding and exceedingly helpful senior officers. We might not be so lucky at Dartmouth and anyway we did not want to leave all that *Beehive* meant to us for good. Still the signal included the word temporarily. As long as we came back a change would do us good. Besides, I wanted specially to work on the French coast and round the Channel Islands. I had lived for six years in Guernsey and sailed my little boat from St Peter Port in the difficult and dangerous waters off Sark, Herm and Jethou. It would be fine to see them again.

Ruminating thus, I walked off in search of Boffin and Bailey. We

1. Signal Distribution Office.

249

should have to get busy. The signal said forthwith. When an operating signal says that it means it. What were we to do about the old Sixth Flotilla? No Senior Officer had been appointed. I was running it as well as the five boats of the Eighth that had so far arrived. Bailey had been offered the flotilla. He was by far the most suitable man. Though he realised he must take the job, and that it was best for him to do so, he was loath to give up his new boat, 74. Now matters must come to a head.

I met Boffin in the passage, showed him the signal and watched the effect.

'I wonder what the reason is?' He said. His reaction had been more practical than mine.

'Can't imagine. Start the boats fuelling at once, will you Boffin?' I said, as I recaptured the signal and hurried on to the S.O.O's[2] office. Lieutenant Leigh, RNVR, our new S.O.O., received the signal with the comment:

'Another of those ultra secret ones, I suppose, to be burnt before reading!' But when he had read it he showed considerably more interest. 'I think I see a connection here,' he said, flicking over the leaves of an official-looking pink file.

'Take a look at that.' He was holding out the Natal, the secret daily intelligence sheet on naval happenings for the previous day. I ran my eye down the sheet until my attention was riveted suddenly: 'Strong force of E-boats attacked eastbound convoy off Start Point. Seven merchant vessels and three escorts sunk.'

There had been a long lull in E-boat activity in the North Sea during the short nights. No attacks or excitements since the Ostend affray. Now it appeared that our friends had sought a new field and had caught the authorities napping. We were to try conclusions with them in the chops of the Channel. It was an interesting prospect and somewhat flattering. Evidently E-boats and the old Sixth, now rapidly turning into the Eighth, were firmly connected in the official mind. We were particularly anxious to get our new boats in close contact with the enemy.

We sailed at first light the next day, the five of us that had up to then commissioned and worked up. Bailey, abruptly thrust into command of the Sixth, was relieved in 74 by Rodney Sykes, who had

2. Staff Officer Operations.

joined us in command of *67* when Boffin went off to commission *76*. Rodney was a young sub-lieutenant, RNVR. He was tall and dark and handsome and at this time much concerned with the prospects of his approaching wedding. He was a welcome addition to our circle.

75 was commanded by Lieutenant Tommy Ladner, a barrister in civil life but now of the Royal Canadian VR. He was the only new member of the flotilla. Before I met him I had done my best to get one of my old officers into his boat, but he had fought back and won and very glad I was too when we had got to know him. With his slow, sardonic manner, his glimpses of unexpected hilarity, his forthright outbursts and his deep humanity beneath a sceptical exterior, he became a great favourite in the flotilla. His crew doted on him.

Boffin had *76*. Head and I had *77*. Fearless and Resolute George had *78*. David James and Bussy Carr were at Weymouth working up *79* and *80* respectively, and Kelly had just left for Power Boats to take over *81*.Thus was the new flotilla formed, later to be dubbed 'the Estimable Eighth' by Commander Swinley, the training commander at the working-up base at Weymouth.[3]

It was a Sunday morning, the 12th July 1942, and at this early hour of six it was as bright and fresh a day as man could desire. There was a northerly wind that almost made the turgid waters of Felixstowe dock sparkle. The boats looked very trim, their paint new, the brass work of their two-pounders, the apples of our eyes, shining, the black, slim, evil-looking twin Oerlikons lined up fore and aft, the battle-cruiser flag[4] fluttering bravely at *77*'s yard arm, the red streak of the answering pendant eight fluttering from the other four, the fifteen 1,350 h.p. Packard engines throbbing, the crews standing expectantly at their stations.

I shook hands with the Captain and stepped aboard. We had been at *Beehive* a year and four months and the Captain did not think we should return. I had a feeling we should.

The battle-cruiser flag was hauled down; the boats slid from the dock, headed seaward and gathered speed. To any eyes the sight was beautiful, with the spray flying from the bows, the pennants fluttering; to our eyes accustomed to the usual unit of two or three gunboats with single Oerlikons and 0.5s, that line of five boats was

---

3. HMS *Bee*.
4. The use of a large white ensign by 77 as a flag signalling the Senior Officer's intention to proceed to sea must have been a personal habit of Hitch's.

not only a lovely but a formidable one. Five pom-poms and ten Oerlikons, beside the Lewis guns! The E-boats had better beware!

I could not help feeling proud of my command; early days for that. We had to prove ourselves yet. The experts ashore did not think our boats would work. We were being given our opportunity without delay. We must make these graceful North Sea greyhounds not only work but fight.

All through the long summer day we sped south and west. The high white cliffs of Dover and Beachy Head gave way to the still higher West Country granite walls. At lunch time Boffin, twenty-five yards on my port quarter as though tied by string, held up in triumph a large plate of hot stew when he saw me eating sandwiches. Across West Bay at thirty-five knots, the whole unit still perfect, bright sun and a dying breeze. The E-boats had attacked two nights before, had had a rest, and moreover was it not a Sunday! They would be out for certain.

I sent a signal:

'ETA (expected time of arrival) Dartmouth 2000. Five boats ready operate tonight if 3,000 gallons 100 octane available.'

Needless to say this was altogether too sudden for the operational authorities at Plymouth. We arrived. The E-boats came, but of course we had not been sent out. We were getting to know the habits of these gentry, sometimes to their cost!

The ensuing days were a chaotic whirl for me. Settling the flotilla in, dashing to Plymouth to discuss the method of operation, finding equipment, workshops, offices. Fortunately the day after our arrival was rough. It gave us a chance to look round. I found myself carried off to Plymouth by our local operating officer, Lieutenant Commander Daintry, RN, Chief of Staff to NOIC, Dartmouth, whose offices were at the college. Daintry was the greatest possible help to us. By nature of the fraternity who want to cut red tape whenever they see it and get on with the war, he was entirely on our side.

We arrived at the Moat, the underground operations rooms for Plymouth command. I was taken to the S.O.O., a commander, and we at once discussed the best method of coping with the E-boats. In this case there seemed an obvious solution. Unlike the East Coast, where they operated from Ijmuiden and the Hook indiscriminately, and often from Ostend and Den Helder in the Texel, here they had only one port from which they worked, Cherbourg. The Ostend tactics seemed clearly indicated. If we could place two units twenty miles off the port at dusk, we should have every chance of catching them wherever bound. S.O.O. agreed; the only trouble was air reconnaissance – it was pretty hot down here, he said; Focke-Wulf 190s. I told him that we were generally spotted on our way over in the North Sea. One of the chief advantages of the proposal was that, if we succeeded, it would prevent them carrying out their plans.

At that moment the great man himself, the C-in-C,[5] came in. There was considerable deferential scraping and shuffling; I was introduced. At that time I had never seen so many rings except on the King; I was not a little overawed. My proposal was explained to him.

'That won't do,' he said. 'You'll be seen on your way over.'

'But will that matter, sir,' I said somewhat hesitantly, 'We generally are.'

'The aircraft will report you and the E-boats won't come out,' was the reply.

There was a silence. I did not care for an argument with so many stripes. But I was nonplussed. I had to say what was in my mind and, I fancy, in the minds of us all.

'Shall we not be achieving our object in that case, sir?'

'No. You are here to destroy the E-boats. You will not sail before dusk.'

That was all. I could say no more. Did he realise that E-boats were powerful, well-armed boats, one hundred and fifteen feet in length, with diesel engines, and that we were seventy-one-feet-six petrol-driven boats, admittedly with superior armament at last? Did he know that there were eighteen of the enemy boats operating out of Cherbourg and that there were only five of us? Did he know that there were twice that number of E-boats to take their place if necessary? Did he understand the great difficulty inherent in any search for these elusive fast craft at night?

He might as well suggest that the circling fighter protection for the convoy was there for the purpose of destroying enemy bombers! Its sole effect is to prevent them attacking and the object is achieved. However, there it was. We were not to sail till dark. We were to let the E-boats get over unmolested and have our only chance of engaging

5. Admiral of the Fleet Sir Ian Forbes. Hence the reference to an abnormal number of rings of gold braid, four thin and one thick.

them when returning, after effecting their nefarious purposes.

The next night, Tuesday, the 14th July, we sailed at dusk. It was a clear moonless night, with a gusty westerly wind. Looking back, the high cliffs enfolding the river Dart showed black and stark against the afterglow in the western sky. As we swept out from the lee of the Start at thirty-two knots, the very feel of the water was different. We were no longer treading on the short crisp waves of the North Sea with a springy, chattering step; we felt the uneven heave and lop, the almost imperceptible slow undulation of the entrance to the Channel; the boats tumbled and slid, surged and thumped fitfully. My mind flew back to that first operation of all. Much had happened since. Now we really had a quarry and a chance of getting him; a still better chance of dealing faithfully with him when we did. I compared the C.O., who rather desperately endeavoured to cling on to his leader on that dark and rainy night in February 1941, with the Senior Officer who now led his well-found unit of four boats, selected to oppose and harry the eighteen E-boats working out of Cherbourg. There had been hard work, yes, but luck too; how much luck only the seaman can realise. I had much to be thankful for. Had I changed with my changing fortunes? I supposed so. More confident. Less afraid, not so much of the enemy as of senior officers. Sure of my control over men.

'Boat astern flashing Harry, sir.'

My signalman roused me from my somewhat complacent reflections. *78* was in trouble, a minor defect, but she must return. The box lamp flicked; leaving 78 limping home, the unit sped away south-east, *75, 76* and *77* in a tight arrowhead.

It was dark now, the sky frosty with stars, the sea an unending sequence of shapeless black lumps. Time passed.

'Light bearing green twenty-five, sir.'

I lowered my glasses.

'Yes, flashing four every twenty seconds, Head.' this into the wheel-house; 'I think that's Alderney.'

'That's right, sir. We must be a good fifteen miles off, though.'

'It looks a long way,' I replied. I was gratified at remembering the navigational haunts of my youth. It was surprising, though, finding the light on full power. Just like peacetime. Very different to the North Sea, I thought. It looked as though no one had been chivvying them much of late.

Presently Cap de La Hague[6] light loomed up ahead. We got a fix and stopped in our position, twelve miles north of Alderney, in a line from Cherbourg to the Start. This was something like it, deep water, no mines, bloody great lights visible seventeen to twenty miles, no sandbanks, and high, steep cliffs to mark our landfall in the morning. Why had we been wasting our time on the East Coast?

I sniffed the freshening westerly wind. A good three to four now and gusting to five. Always an uncomfortable place near Alderney, the lop had become a confused lump and surge. Turrets were beginning to swing and bang.

'No good for E-boats tonight,' I yelled across to Boffin. 'The bastards won't like this.'

'No,' came the reply. 'I wonder why they take the trouble to give us all this illumination?'

'Maybe aircraft,' I shouted back.

Silence reigned, save for the gentle breaking, splashing, thudding cacophony of a boat lifting and dipping in a confused sea. We kept watch, mesmerised by the ceaseless uniform flashing of the two powerful lighthouses, so familiar of old; this was the Channel I knew; I might have been in my little boat, lying off waiting for daylight before attempting the passage through the Race of Alderney; it was hard to realise it was war.

If nothing happened by two o'clock our orders allowed us to close the French coast or the Channel Islands and seek out any enemy patrols or convoys. As the second hour of the middle watch drew to a close I debated the point mentally. The wind was freshening, there would be a most unpleasant tide rip off the Race; no proper weather for fast gunboats; and very little likelihood of anything being about. Better to wait here until near dawn, then return to harbour. Yet there were the lights winking an invitation. Cliffs I knew; islands I had clambered over. I wanted to see them again, just their bare stark outlines, their familiar grouping. Something impelled me towards adventure that night. I entered the wheelhouse and plotted a course for the entrance to the Race.

'Start up.'

'Course South 15 degrees East, Coxswain.'

'South 15 degrees East, sir.'

6. The north-west headland of the Cherbourg peninsula.

Muttering engines rose to a growl, steadied to a roar. The unit lurched and thudded southward. The light, fine on the starboard bow, increased in brilliance. The bare outlines of Alderney could be seen now through glasses. Speed was reduced, centre engines stopped, thereby cutting the unit's noise to a minimum. We were about to enter the Race. How familiar the scene was; the cloudless, windy sky, the broken black chunky sea, the barely seen steep rising cliffs against the skyline. Of a sudden a small white light showed clear and steady in the surrounding darkness of the horizon.

'Light bearing green sixty-five, sir,' came the cry.

'Yes, yes, but the bearing?' I was craning round the compass.

'Starboard wheel. Steer South 50 degrees West.'

The unit steadied into the head sea, much less in here close under the north shore of Alderney. Action stations were sounded, tin hats donned. Staring through the glasses, standing on the canopy by the mast, I could just discern two dim hulls.[7] At our twelve knots we were overhauling slowly.

'Make Nuts with a red light'; this to Patterson.

The little lamp, carefully shaded from ahead, flicked out the thrilling signal: long short, 'Enemy in sight.' Silently, signlessly, the unit fell into line ahead; the fighting formation. The wind was in our teeth, we could not be heard; we should not be seen until right upon them; we had effected surprise, the most important factor of all in this warfare of speed and wood and petrol, against size and steel and steam.

They were large trawlers, clearly visible now, heading west at about eight knots. I hung debating that inevitable question, when to make the signal for pulling in centre engines. The danger of being heard, against the danger of being caught without one's speed. With a fresh head wind the former was the lesser evil. The light flicked twice; the unit burst into an ominous growl; the spray parted wide with the speed increased to twenty knots. We were level now with the offshore and rearmost vessel. She had seen us at last. She was challenging, two longs and a short. I dared not wait longer, the next move might be a well aimed four-inch brick and she could not miss at that range, less than a cable. Neither could we!

I pressed the fire buzzer.

7. Although Hitch makes no reference to it, as the new seventy-one-foot-six boats had radar, the ships they then sighted had already been picked up.

The next few minutes provided a welter of impressions for me, beginning with a crescendo of noise and light, passing through tense anxiety and ending with stark fear such as I had never known before.

Three pom-poms, six Oerlikons and six Lewis guns burst into life almost simultaneously from the gunboats. With the gun muzzles a few feet from one's ear, the noise was terrific, the light from the muzzle flashes, the tracer and the bursting shells, dazzling and bewildering, the effect most gratifying. That trawler, hard hit and surprised, scarcely returned the fire at all.

We were accelerating now, tending to turn in across her bows towards the other trawler, when I saw a small tanker ahead. In a flash the position was clear. The two trawlers were the stern escort of the tanker; there were almost certainly more escort vessels ahead. But here was our chance, the near escort subdued; the way into the tanker open and exposed.

I turned and made a long red flash to the fiercely firing boat astern; the signal to disregard the Senior Officer's movements.

'We'll depth charge this bastard,' I shouted to Curtis.

It was all he needed. He knew what was required of him. I lifted the throttles high as he headed in across her bows. The little boat leaped forward quivering with unleashed power, her guns projecting streams of brilliant light into the rapidly nearing hull.

Head was by me now.

'Stand by to let go port depth charge,' I yelled.

The stream of shells hitting the enemy vessel, some penetrating, some bursting on the outside, lit up the outline of the ship, as though she was one of Brock's famous firework images on the last night of Henley. In the vivid, scintillating glare her bow wave, pressed outward and upward at what must have been her maximum speed, caught my eye and held me transfixed.

I had been conning the coxswain on, at least so I thought; but in the uproar and confusion I doubt if he had heard or understood. Would we clear that upthrown white bow wave, that sharp straight bow? I thought not, but I could do no more. It was out of my control. Curtis had the wheel and I must leave it to him. I remembered anxiously how we had practised this very attack on a trawler off the entrance to Harwich. How control on that occasion too had slipped from me at the end. How Curtis had flipped the stern of old 64 right in under the overhanging bows. How the trawler's crew had run in astonishment to the side to watch and had received our wash right over them and high up on the wheelhouse. How we had missed them by a bare two feet. How I went back to apologise and how stuffy they had been. Well there would be no going back to apologise this time!

In the event I think we cleared the enemy's bow by less than ten feet, after one of the most magnificent pieces of steering by Curtis that I ever witnessed. But not before we had received a withering blast from the disengaged escort vessel, just astern and to port of the tanker, and from the latter herself now almost overhanging us. You could feel the boat shudder at the shower of blows; shrapnel flew whining in all directions; a dazzling blaze of fire burst forth at my very feet in the wheelhouse.

We had got there. Head had pulled the depth charge release at the exact moment and a few seconds later the boat shook to the under-water explosion. It had been a model attack. Just one of those rare occasions when everything goes right. And rare indeed they are!

It was at that moment that I knew real fear. The wheelhouse was a blaze of brilliant light. It seemed that we must be irretrievably afire. It was obvious that the entire upper deck crew had been knocked out by that infernal blast. Something had to be done about it at once. My sensations at that moment are still vivid. I was stricken with fear, real fear. I remember thinking desperately 'I shall never get back, I shall never see Catherine or the children again.' I fancy I was near to panic; but fortunately the fear of panic had a stimulating effect. I was literally galvanised into activity, the activity that was required.

I stepped down into the wheelhouse and set about me. Head quickly followed. Stamping and striking we subdued the flames, made more vivid by flares lit from the exploding ammunition. When darkness reigned again in the wheelhouse, fire could be seen down the passage in the after magazine. The power pipes to the pom-pom had been severed, the oil had run aft on to the floor of the magazine and was there burning fiercely, licking ominously round the loaded Oerlikon pans.

We crammed down the passage way and jumped on the flaming pool. Barnes, though wounded, dropped down from the Oerlikon turret above and helped. We worked in silence amidst the deep throated bellow of the engines, opened wide. In a few desperate minutes we had the situation in hand.

258

I struggled back into the dustbin to regain control after a five-minute interlude. The sight was dramatic enough. The throttles were hard up; with the boat light of fuel and the engines giving 2,800 revolutions, she was travelling at about forty-five knots, or just over fifty miles an hour. The cascading plume, which normally hangs ten or twelve feet astern, was gone; at this speed she was right up, leaving a clean straight wake, hard as a board. The attack had taken place less than two miles to the North of Alderney. Curtis, cool as ever in action, after slamming the throttles hard up, had swept her away to seaward in a large curve ahead of the astonished forward escort; we were now tearing north from the scene of action. To the south the Alderney light, already several miles astern, had been turned out; a dull red glow was visible, shrouded but unmistakable. Through glasses the position was clear. The tanker was stopped and on fire. She was covered in a cloud of smoke, some from the fire no doubt but certainly most of it laid to hide her. Occasionally bright star-shells burst to the northward and in their light I could pick out some fast small craft, moving round the stationery glow, leaving a high flung trail of smoke.

We were many miles clear now. We stopped, called up the others and asked if they were all right. On getting satisfactory replies a rendezvous to the north was proposed, and we did meet up with *75*, but *76* went back alone.

77 was badly knocked about. Almost the only part of her that had escaped was the engine-room. Power gone from the turrets, no guns to fire, the ever-recurring story. But what intrigued me most was a large shell hole, a two-pounder, in the canopy just opposite the dustbin. We had had no armour in the old boats. These had a half-inch of hard steel all round the dustbin. The two-pounder shell had burst on impact with the canopy and exploded in the passage way. Like a mouse nibbling chunks out of cheese, the flying splinters had gouged out cavities a quarter of an inch deep in the armour on the opposite side of which we had been standing. Without that plate all in the dustbin would have been killed and it was the first time we had fought with any armour! Upon such little chances do our destinies depend.

But others had not been so fortunate. Once again half the crew were casualties, one dead and two of them very bad. I had lost the equivalent of my whole crew in two successive actions within three

259

months. Yet such is the British sailor, the more you grapple with the enemy, the more he likes you. It was truly spoken by Sir John Jervis[8] when he said:

'The men are not yet created who can stand against the British seaman when properly disciplined and led.'

How should this be otherwise when the more they fight, the more they want to fight. Their appetite grows with what it feeds on.

At reduced speed, in a bumpy sea, we plodded home. Again the morphia was produced from my pocket and made to perform its merciful service. Again the decks were slippery with blood and cluttered with shell cases. Edwards was among the wounded. He was lying in the wheelhouse now, smoking a cigarette. For once he was not sucking his teeth, either humorously or with a grievance; he was obviously cheerful. Too obviously. I realised it must be serious. I fear he will never handle his gun at sea again. A steadier and more accurate shot has not come my way.

The Lewis gunner, a quiet effective worker, greatly liked in the crew, was terribly wounded in the head, throat and stomach; obviously dying. As I knelt by him, seeing if there was anything more we could do, I realised he was conscious. I thought of my first introduction to motor racing. The fierce glare and heat of a Continental day in June; the dry dusty sun-baked tarmac; the rise and fall, the whine and snarl of the highly tuned supercharged engines; four cars tight-bunched dicing for a lead. The blue one in front touching a bank, slamming madly across the road, hurtling into the hedge at over one hundred m.p.h., leaving the driver unhurt, lying across the track. The second car, low and white, driven by an Englishman, turned deliberately aside to avoid that body, disappearing through the hedge into a field. The third, also low and white, driven by a Frenchman, screaming across the prostrate form. The fourth, a red car, mine, flagged just in time to stop short of the red shambles. The rapid clearance, glimpses of the slow-moving ambulance as the cars raced past. That was all.

The Englishman, who had driven off the road in a vain attempt to save the leader, had shot out of his car removing the lower part of his stomach and testicles in the process. He had got up, walked round the car remarking how little it was damaged, apparently in no discomfort. Suddenly the pain began to come. He collapsed in a dead

8. Sir John Jervis, later Lord St Vincent, the victor of the battle of Cape St Vincent, was First Sea Lord for a significant part of the Napoleonic Wars.

faint and died soon after. Thus is nature merciful to her badly injured sons. It was a comfort to remember in circumstances such as these.

Dawn found us fifteen miles off shore, heading for the Start. Steadily the massive cliffs loomed nearer; instead of stark magnificent outline only, detail could be seen. Deep black gashes like wounds, green turf clinging low over the brow where the slope was easier; the brown of the plough clear cut to the very edge of some precipitous height, gulls wheeling high overhead; the stunted thickset form of the Start lighthouse, the tall spare shape of the day mark above the entrance to Dartmouth. All so familiar. Had I dreamed the events of the past few hours?

Suddenly I was back to my childhood. I was a small leggy boy of seven, in a little sailing boat, barely capable of making to windward against a one-knot tide. I was off the towering cliffs to seaward of St Anthony,[9] sailing daringly, though I did not know it, to the eastward with a soldier's wind; running up the Cornish coast filled with the spirit of adventure, the blood of my ancestors, like enough wreckers on occasion as so many were in that outlying county, throbbing with this taste of freedom and responsibility; that curious combination of emotions apparently so opposed yet inevitably inseparable for he who goes down to the sea in ships.

It was the day I took possession of my first sailing boat, a little twelve foot open boat with a lug sail and no centre board. Her name was *Arethusa*. He who understands these things will realise that she was not the boat to beat back against a head wind and sea. But the gods who decide these matters were evidently of the opinion that this was not the moment to settle the fate of this ignorant and youthful mariner. He was to be reserved for further execution upon their turbulent domain. The wind backed fast and, freshening from the south-east, gave me a soldier's wind back again.

Here I was, still in essentials the same leggy boy, still in a small boat off those uncompromising grey west country cliffs: truly the boy is father of the man. I was still revelling in it, my blood had not lost its zest for the sea. No matter that it was thirty knots now and seventy feet of boat, instead of four knots and twelve feet. Was I not nearly six feet instead of four and a half? It was all in proportion; you cannot escape your fate.

9. St Anthony's Head is the eastern boundary of the Carrick Roads, Falmouth's great anchorage. Just inside it lies St Mawes where Hitch lived from 1915 - 1919.

We slid up the river, the town still sleeping on either bank, and made fast to the pontoon to land our dead and wounded. All was still and peaceful, the ships reflected in the tranquil water, smoke rising straight in the quiet air. With the coming of day the wind had dropped. The Dart looked exactly as I have seen it so often on a fine summer's morning, soft toned delicate greys and blues, before the sun has lifted above the high eastern ridge; only the bodies, wrapped in blankets, lifted on stretchers, seemed incongruous. It was evident that Dartmouth was hardly used to this, though the medical arrangements could not have been better. A rather harassed looking elderly commander presided. I explained patiently that we had had a fight; had five casualties; no, I was not one of them. I put my hand up to my face and understood why he was looking at me somewhat askance, it was covered in blood from a shrapnel scratch. No doubt I looked a trifle piratical.

After the action off Alderney on the 14 July, Hitch received a bar to his DSO. When he went to Buckingham Palace on the 22 September 1942 he received both his original DSO and the bar on the same occasion, uniquely in the view of Rear Admiral John Myres, writing in the journal of the Orders and Medals Research Society. Other awards made in relation to Alderney included a very well earned Conspicuous Gallantry Medal for Able Seaman John Barnes, the wounded Oerlikon gunner who had helped put out the fire on board 77, together with a Mention in Dispatches for Chief Motor Mechanic Vic Stay and Ordinary Seaman Albert Parkin. Able Seaman Reginald Baker, who died after the action, received a posthumous Mention in Dispatches. Tom Ladner in 75 was also awarded a Mention in Dispatches.

Of these awards the one that stands out is the Conspicuous Gallantry Medal for John Barnes. Wounded as he was, he had had no need to drop down into the inferno below him and help his two officers put the fire out and he quite rightly received an award that is not often given.

This fierce little action, coming as it did at the very outset of our stay in the West Country, had a galvanising effect and drew attention to our arrival. Circumstances were such that throughout the six weeks we were to remain something was continually happening to us. This had a refreshing and stimulating effect upon the keener spirits of the locality, though I fancy some of the tireder types were glad to see us go.

Prominent amongst the former was the Coastal Forces base doctor, Bob Swan, a Canadian, who thus early was called upon to show his worth. And what a showing he made! He was tireless in his efforts on our behalf. He concerned himself not only with the wounded, but with the active sea-going personnel. He studied our problems and produced valuable suggestions. Nothing was too much trouble for him. He noticed that we came in with red, sore eyes after a rough night, and he produced eye shields and eye lotions. He saw that several of the men and one officer were beginning to suffer from a bout of hay fever and he produced the necessary preventative before they were fully aware of their trouble. He saw that we were working night after night, and he produced Benzedrine and vitamin pills. At one time I went out on ten successive nights and, at another, eight nights running. There were occasions when I was considerably exhausted, but I was determined to deal faithfully with the E-boats and I knew that opportunities for rest would come when the weather broke. Swan's concern on my behalf, however, was often quite embarrassing. He would shake his head over me and utter the direst warnings if I continued. I was not used to such attention.

In the meanwhile things were happening at sea. *77* went to Power Boats to be renewed. She needed it, poor dear; *79* and *80* arrived. We began to feel ourselves a flotilla. Being away from our normal base and on our own tended to throw us together and foster the flotilla spirit. We made a good start at Dartmouth and, which is more unusual, we were able to keep it up. But we had to work for our success; night after night; only a pause if the weather broke. And for the first few weeks there were not many boats. We did nineteen operations in under six weeks. Tiring maybe, but worth it. In the end we achieved our object and had some nights of unforgettable beauty as well.

On three occasions during the moonlight period we were called out suddenly and despatched to Cherbourg on suspected E-boat reports. Nothing resulted. Possibly the reports were erroneous; possibly the elusive enemy, now well aware that he was being pursued, retired to the Channel Islands, knowing from coastal reports that we were lying in wait for him off Cherbourg.

Though uneventful, those passages will live in our memory. The loud rap on the door breaking through the heavy first sleep of physical exhaustion. The huddle of dressing, strange garments caricaturing the human shape. The mental effort to throw off the film of sleep, achieved only with the first deep breaths of the clear, cool night air.

The still beauty of the enfolding hills, sharply contrasting in the bright moonlight; the western slope showing pale and clear, house windows throwing back the toneless light with sinister glint and sparkle; the eastern bank silhouetted sheer and stark, a stygian blank wall of darkness surmounted by the silhouettes of trees clearly limned against the pale luminosity of the sky. Between, the twisting glassy streak of the tidal estuary, itself sharply divided, half in deep impenetrable shadow, half a brightly reflecting mirror for the moon, like a great shark with back glistening black and white underbelly.

The stealthy tumult aboard. Engine-room crews running aft, hatches slamming, gun covers ripping off, orders shouted, muttered curses, all instantly drowned by the full-throated bellow of the first started engine. Thereafter concentrated noise, broken only by the momentarily louder coughing bang of yet another set of cylinders bursting into brazen-lunged life. The whole swelling into a cacophony of sound reverberating between the towering heights on either bank.

The comparative quiet as the boats slipped into line ahead, creeping for the boom gate, a signal lamp blinking, the engine revolutions dropped and steadied by the load, only to give place again shortly to a still more thunderous cadence, tempered by the roar of wind past the ears, as the boats lifted to their speed and settled to a steady thirty-seven knots.

Those were the nights for beauty. The brilliant disc of a full moon high in the heavens, the gently heaving surface of the Channel throwing back its light in innumerable glinting facets, the palely reflecting mass of high land dwindling to the north-west, to be matched in less than two hours by the first glimpse of Cap de La Hague, huge and sinister, outlined in black bulk against the moonpath. Few of us will forget these swift night passages and few, I fancy, were totally unaffected by the splendour of the scene.

The boats themselves seemed to show at their best in such a setting, like a beautiful woman knowing that she wears a becoming dress. The scars of battle, the imperfections of paintwork, the smudges of oil, all the little blemishes inseparable from a fighting ship engaged in her never-ending struggle, were lost in the all-embracing half tones. Only the grace and exhilarating strength of the swift moving hulls was apparent. The eager up-thrust of the bows, the sweeping run lost to sight aft behind the sharp rising pressure wave, the far flung arc of spray flying back from beneath the forefoot, the steady rising plume up-driven from the thrusting pro-pellers gleaming white and transparent in the moonlight, like some enormous fountain in a fairy story of a giant land, the impermeable yet never ending tracery of the interlacing wash, the sharp points and glints of light from the black gun barrels.

We spoke little at such times. The scene was all absorbing.

I remember on one occasion stopping off Cap de La Hague. It was flat calm, full moon, clear, a strong tide running south-west through the Race of Alderney. We swirled round the rocks off the north-west corner of land, the lighthouse, unlit, a gaunt finger pointed heaven-wards; into the Race at a good six knots borne on the swift running ebb. Steadily we moved across the narrow stretch of water, the boats pointing now one way, now another, pirouetting individually in the strong eddies. Down past Alderney, so near and so clear in that July moon that we could see each house nestling against the west-ward rising slope of the little island. It seemed incredible that the enemy should be unaware of our presence, that they should not see us sitting quietly on the moving stream of water like giant sea birds, wings folded, heads tucked at rest.

As if voicing my thoughts, a scrap of conversation from the engine-room hatch floated forward:

'Can't think why they don't see us,' the voice was deep and quiet.

'Probably thinks we're f*****g great seagulls, if they thinks anything at all,' came the response in broad Cockney.

'They'd go for us hammer and f*****g tongs if they was to know who it was.'

The voices drifted away. We were off the south-eastern extremity of Alderney now. The boat, caught in a strong eddy, swung rapidly through north and west towards south. I found myself staring intently ahead, hoping to pick up the outline of Guernsey. Guernsey! What memories the name evoked. Carefree days, school and univer-sity holidays, my motor bike and little boat. How I had delighted in her. Choosing the very limit of weather, exhilarated by the danger and struggle, until the fishermen shook their heads and said that I was not long for this world. But here I was; what would they think now, if they knew? They would be pleased, I fancied, and wish us well.

My reverie deepened. Searching back into those early days, I wondered why I had needlessly sought discomfort and danger in that little boat. It was clear to me that I had been groping unknowingly towards a philosophy that was not yet deeply imbedded. Security, life without risk; it was all wrong. In seeking for these humanity was following a false God. Life was inherently insecure. Why fight the inevitable? Why not out-face it and dare the worst? That was at bottom the philosophy that I had developed, through lonely days in small boats and later at the wheel of a racing car. The advantages had soon become apparent. Living an ordinary secure life ashore in peacetime I had found that small things often loomed large, out of proportion. Little annoyances assumed the aspect of real grievances, fleeting unworthy pleasures ranked high with the real treasures of life. True values were getting mixed. I may have been specially prone to this; certain it is that I often found myself in a rage over a minor inconvenience, or unduly cast down because I had been deprived of some trifling amusement. I had found that the most decisive way to clear the head, to regain proper values and humility, was to experience a real whiff of danger. Some may use religion, some music, others drink; for me, danger. It is unforgettably effective. To feel real instant fear of death; to contemplate the infinite, not from the security of a comfortable armchair, but as something imminent, pressing, that may engulf you now or before tomorrow's sun has set. That gives you cause to think. Values sort themselves as if by magic. Petty anger, pride, worthless ambitions take a nasty knock. Instead of returning home and finding fault you realise how wonderful it is to have a home at all.

That this point of view, the necessity for living dangerously, is fairly generally appreciated, is shown by the popularity of dangerous sports. Sailing, hunting, big game shooting, motor-racing, all bear witness to this philosophy. Each can be made dangerous, and in my opinion the value of a sport can be measured in direct ratio to the danger involved.

A sudden swing of the boat brought my mind back to the present. Alderney bore nearly north now, receding. It was easy to practice my philosophy these days. I recalled how Gotelee, borrowing my old brakeless bike, had delivered himself of the remark:

'I presume it is part of your policy of living dangerously that your bike has no brakes. I just now nearly killed myself.'

Good old Goaters! Life was never dull with him around. But it wasn't often dull anyway! Under the stresses imposed by leading a gunboat flotilla I found myself more and more often soothing my irritability and ignoring my discomforts with the remark:

'Why worry? It's a bloody sight better than being face downward in the North Sea!'

There is much truth in that seeming truism.

Alderney was growing smaller. A faint light was perceptible in the east. We started up and returned to Dartmouth.

The E-boats were hanging off. Though we had not yet been able to make contact, they had grown wary with the knowledge that they were being pursued. They took evading action. Instead of working out of Cherbourg only, they took to using St Peter Port as well. It was impossible to know where best to lie in wait for them. Our chance came suddenly and unexpectedly.

On the night of the 1st/2nd August we were on our way to a patrol position to the north-west of Guernsey. There were four of us. *80* [10] leading, *76, 78* and *75*. As was our custom we left Dartmouth at dusk, had a practise shoot, and headed away to the south-east. As dark closed down we ran into a thick belt of fog. Speed was reduced, shaded stern lights switched on, but still it was difficult enough, impossible to see a boat farther than fifty to sixty yards. Altogether it was an unpromising start; I seriously contemplated returning on account of the weather. Finally deciding to give it a bit longer, I was suddenly electrified to receive an RDF[11] report of E-boats to the north of Cherbourg proceeding towards the English coast.

We altered course at once, midnight, for Cherbourg. The strategy clearly indicated was to close their port, lie off awaiting their return, and pounce upon them at the last moment; the chances of missing them elsewhere being so great as to make this the obvious plan.

We were some sixty-five miles from Cherbourg. From the reports

10. *MGB 80* was Bussy Carr's boat. Yet Hitch refers to Francis Head as first lieutenant in her that night. Perhaps Hitch, as Senior Officer, brought Head as an extra officer. Carr was certainly out that night.
11. A radar report from either another ship or from a shore based set monitoring the Channel.

that now started to arrive in a stream it appeared that there were two groups of E-boats out and that they were heading north. Clearly their intention was to lay mines or patrol on the convoy route; they would not be returning for hours; we had plenty of time. So we maintained our reduced speed in the prevailing fog and soldiered on towards Cherbourg.

The reports continued to pour in:

'E-boats one hundred and fifty degrees Portland Bill thirty-four miles'

'E-boats one hundred and forty-eight degrees Portland Bill thirty-two miles'

'E-boats one hundred and forty-six degrees Portland Bill thirty-three miles'

What was that? A sudden doubt assailed me. I looked at the plot. There had been a steady run of reports giving reducing distances. But what about the last one? Probably only an inaccurate range, I thought. Nevertheless I was anxious for the next signal:

'E-boats one hundred and forty-six degrees Portland Bill thirty-five miles'

My God, they had turned back. Met the fog, I supposed, and given up their project. There was only one thing to do. Go like hell. The box lamp flicked twice

'I'm going to do a high twenty hundred, Head.' This to the First Lieutenant.

The thunder of the engines redoubled; the boat trembled and lifted, the pressure wave and plume aft first rose then sank as the hull, thrust forward at thirty-eight knots, raised by the upward drive of the propellers, touched the water on the surface only and left a flat, clean planing wake.

I looked anxiously astern. This would prove a testing time! The fog was still thick, though with occasional patches of light mist giving promise of better conditions to come. This would show whether the flotilla training had sunk in. Thirty-eight knots in these conditions was asking a lot. I thanked the Lord for the composition of the unit. Boffin and George Duncan were the best I had, always thirty yards on the quarter as though tied together by string. Ladner was more problematical. He had not been with us long and had occasionally been in difficulties. He did magnificently. All four boats fled to the eastward in a snarling, thundering wedge, uplifting to the spirit. Here

268

was justification for the efforts made to keep our band of officers together. Only by continuous practice as a flotilla and with full confidence in each other could we manage such a speed in such conditions. The flotilla spirit, the feeling of comradeship in difficult and dangerous achievement, was never more keenly felt.

I looked at the chart. The E-boats had little more than twenty-six miles to go before they were in harbour, we had sixty-five. Here also was justification for the decision to adhere to the fast boat. At all events on this occasion speed was the essence of the situation. Could we do it? There was just a chance. The E-boats would not be hurrying. They would do the last few miles as they closed the harbour entrance at quite slow speed. With a little luck we might make it. It was worth trying.

I looked up from my anxious scrutiny of the rev. counters and boost gauges and peered into the all pervading fog. It was still bad, but definitely tending to thin. At that pace, forty-three miles per hour, and in those conditions of very low visibility, the boats gave an incredible impression of surging speed. With the particles of fog skimming past the eyes at short focus, nothing visible beyond the fast flying spray thrown alongside, the impression of speed was irresistible.

Looking astern I saw one of the stokers appear from below and gaze out from the after magazine hatch. After a moment's contemplation he turned to the reload number and yelled:

'The old man's in a f*****g awful hurry tonight.'

He had estimated my sentiments precisely!

Time passed, the E-boat reports ceased, the fog dispersed, the night became clear and still. Only the thrust of the propellers, the roar of the engines, the rush of cool air past the face continued steadily, remorselessly. There were the lights. The Casquets, Alderney, Cap de La Hague. Like peacetime! Navigation for the E-boats was evidently to be no chancy affair. By the same token it was admirable for us. I recollect scrambling and sprawling over the wheelhouse roofing in a prolonged effort to get precise fixes as the line of lights literally swept past, the bearing of one altering radically in the time taken to sight another.

Would we get there in time? I was reminded irresistibly of that first chase at eighteen knots. The same insistent query. But this time the flotilla was revelling in its full power and speed. Coursing past Cap de

La Hague, excitement crystallised. Tin hats were substituted for the normal miscellaneous headgear of the tea-cosy variety, the men were at their action stations, rigid and tense mentally, but swaying and giving physically to the peculiar dancing motion of the hulls as they stepped lightly from one gentle acclivity to another on the seemingly smooth yet eternally restless surface of the sea.

As the roar of our engines subsided, a subdued rumble, like the residue of a long drawn out and slowly dying thunder clap, became audible from the direction of the harbour. They had beaten us to it. They were just entering. After all that effort we were too late. Missed them by five minutes. How we cursed!

That was no good, though relieving to pent up exasperation; the elusive bastards! I studied the plot. There definitely had been two distinct groups out according to the reports. Perhaps only one had got back so far. The last signals showed the later group returning further to the westward, going south to pick up Alderney light. If they had not got in yet, and from the times of the reports there was just a chance that this might be so, had they returned slowly they would be coming along the coast on a south-easterly or east south-easterly course and must arrive at any moment. Unless, of course, they had gone to St Peter Port.

We listened intently, eagerly, with a growing sense of frustration as the seconds slipped by. A few minutes passed thus. I was beginning to despair.

'Do you hear anything to the south-west?'

This from Boffin across the narrow space of smooth water that separated us.

There seemed to be just the faintest rhythmical murmur. Dead silence, all attention strained in the same direction. The murmur became a regular thud, thud, muffled but recognisable:

'Start up.'

'Course South fifteen East.'

There was no time to lose. Swift action must follow instant decision if we were to get them before they were in. They could not be more than two miles at the most from the breakwater, but they would be going very slowly now.

Never has the unit got off and formed into line ahead more swiftly and eagerly. We were about to give the E-boats the surprise of their young but far from innocent lives. Most of the gunboats' personnel realised this and there was anticipation and relish in their every movement as they went to action stations again, this time with the sure knowledge of a fight.

As we closed rapidly the dark line of the breakwater showed black and menacing, now less than a mile away. A half-mile to the southeast the hull of a motionless ship became apparent, lying stopped, or at anchor, just off the breakwater. Drawing nearer her outline could be recognised. She was a German torpedo boat, about six hundred tons, like a small destroyer. What an opportunity if only we carried a torpedo! Stopped, unsuspecting, had she seen us she would merely have waved a friendly hand knowing that numerous E-boats were entering harbour. How I longed to detach the last of my line of four boats, ordering her to torpedo that ship and then rejoin!

But we had nothing with which to hurt her seriously; the E-boats were our quarry. We held on, disregarding that silent shape. Nevertheless the incident was not without importance. The missed opportunity was so obvious, so disappointing. The iron entered into my soul. From that moment I realised that to be really offensive to the enemy, on all occasions, in every way, we must carry torpedoes, and I never ceased from then on to agitate and pester the authorities until I achieved my aim. That it took nearly a year, a year of war, before the first move was taken, that I incurred bitter antagonism in the process, and that I had to lose three of my precious eight boats, the last in circumstances of awe-inspiring peril, endangering to an unwarranted degree the rest of the unit of four boats, before my request was acceded to and the first experiment made, you shall hear.[12] But the seed was sown at this precise moment, in the early hours of the morning of the 2nd of August, within a mile of Cherbourg breakwater.

There they were at last. The low unrelieved silhouette! Four of them in line ahead, barely moving. Awaiting permission to enter as like as not. I felt a great surge of triumph at that moment. We had got them at last. It had been hard work, night after night, difficult, trying work. But they were momentarily at our mercy now; we had effected the best possible form of surprise; we licked our lips,

---

12. Hitch was killed on 12/13 April 1943 and the third action he refers to took place on 28 February/1 March. Thus this part and the rest of his book must have been written in March or early April 1943.

mentally reversing the old blasphemous use of the grace in the days of close fought broadsides.

'For what they are about to receive .....'

Altering course slightly to starboard, we moved under the stern of the last in the line. We opened fire. Four pom-poms, eight Oerlikons, and eight Lewis guns poured a hail of death into that aftermost boat at a range of one hundred yards. She lit up aft with a bright flash. Each one received the same treatment as we turned slowly up the line. I heard an excited shout from the port Lewis gunner: 'Cor. Look at them jumping over the side.'

Indeed, the consternation in that unit of E-boats[13] must have been well-nigh complete. At all events the fire they succeeded in returning was negligible. The gun crews were probably mostly killed trying to close up and very likely many of the guns were already unloaded. For was not the breakwater entrance a bare mile away? We continued to circle the now motionless E-boats, raking them with fire. Their consternation was probably equalled by the amazement ashore and in the neighbouring torpedo boats. They could not think what was going on. It must have seemed to them that the E-boats had suddenly gone mad. The torpedo boats began to approach, the shore batteries to put up tentative star-shell, but still after eight minutes of slaughter we held the field almost unmolested.

Then they realised what was happening and one of the finest displays of pyrotechnics that I have ever seen was unloosed. Shore batteries put up innumerable star-shells, four-inch shells from the torpedo boats and other batteries began to sing by, bursting with brilliant effect. The sight was unforgettable. Pale yellow green luminosity from the slowly dropping shower of star-shells, fierce red, green and yellow streaks of tracer, interlacing in fantastic patterns, vivid splodges of light where the big shells were bursting; roar of engines, crash and stutter of guns, the almost silent, motionless line of E-boats, glittering white in the artificial radiance, seemingly strangely helpless in their immobility; the dark line of the breakwater spitting bright flashes of flame irregularly, viciously, up and down the line, like a crazed xylophonist striking his keys wantonly and at

13. Peter Scott interviewed *Kapitän Leutnant* Charlie Muller, a captured E-boat commander, in late 1944 who claimed that the E-boats based in Cherbourg at that time had not suffered any losses from enemy action in August 1942. Possibly the vessels attacked were R boats or Muller did not tell the truth.

random; the cautiously approaching towering hulls of two torpedo boats lit brightly by the occasional bursts of our two-pounder shells on their sides, still obviously puzzled, but the flashes from their guns gaining in momentum as they closed; the line of gunboats, weaving and storming round their quarry, still magnificently together in tight line ahead formation, the spray thrown back at twenty-four knots reflecting the green effulgence of the star-shells in a luminous halo round the hulls.

It was no time for losing oneself in the wild beauty of the scene. Though the fire from the enemy's big guns was mercifully inaccurate, there was so much of it by this time that the gunboats were beginning to be hit. It would only be necessary to stop one properly in such a situation to lose the boat. We had had twelve minutes of concentrated fire, we had wrought our destruction, more and more of our guns were falling silent with stoppages as the pace of the action began to tell. It was time to get out.

Passing swiftly between the line of E-boats and the now adjacent but still startled torpedo boats, delivering the latter a final burst of two-pounder at point-blank range, 80 led away into the welcoming darkness to seaward. Throttles were lifted. We were gone as suddenly as we had come. It was a full ten minutes before the enemy appreciated our absence. To our unbounded delight the battle still raged behind us; the unfortunate E-boats, unmercifully pounded from the shore, stung to a belated and mistaken retaliation, aided by the torpedo boats, fired back at the breakwater. Thus the ball was kept rolling.

Four miles to seaward, well clear of the star-shell, we stopped to count the cost and enjoy the fun. The cost was surprisingly light, almost always the case when complete tactical surprise is effected. Two minor casualties, a few holes in the boats, *75* and *80* leaking forward; nothing serious.

The battle died down, the light died out of the sky; as darkness settled in, Boffin shouted:

'What's that glow?'

Glasses were raised long and searchingly. Then, as the distant glow broke out and brightened, it was obvious. A cheer went up. There were two of them alight. You could see the separate blazes, about a cable apart, bright pillars of fire. Nothing could control them. Two done for and the other two badly spoilt – no doubt about that!

Speeding home to the welcoming granite cliffs in the slow spreading light, thoughts wandered happily over the events of the night, happily because this time there were no limp, sagging, disfigured bodies aboard the gunboats; happily because we had done our duty in seeking out and engaging the enemy closely under the very shadow of his shore batteries, secure in the knowledge that this would anger him greatly.

I reviewed the swift chase, the stealthy approach, the sudden onslaught. How different to the days of old. I recalled how Nelson had described the start of a fight with a Spanish frigate. He had hailed the Spaniard:

'This is an English frigate.'

And demanded her surrender or he would fire. And the 'noble' reply, Nelson's own word, that delighted him so:

'This is a Spanish frigate and you may begin as soon as you please.'

How different this exchange to our recent gangster tactics! Certainly the amenities of war had deteriorated!

We had anticipated correctly; the enemy were very angry. That night the German wireless announced 'Nine British boats attacked off Cherbourg; five had been destroyed.' The greater the lie, the more the vexation!

After the Cherbourg action on the 1/2 August, George Duncan received the DSC, Petty Officer Alfred Hartland of 76, the DSM along with Leading Seaman Laurie Nichol in 75. Mentions in Dispatches went to Able Seaman Ralph Hubbard of 78, Telegraphist Julian Barnes, Sub-Lieutenant Ronald Carr and Ordinary Seaman Isaiah Hale of 80, and Hitch himself received his second Mention. The ways of Honours and Awards Committees are sometimes obscure. For good reasons, records of how decisions are taken are not kept. However, one cannot help wondering, in spite of no doubt being accused of partiality, why after so stunningly successful an action as the attack on the E-boats or R-boats off Cherbourg Hitch only received a Mention in Dispatches. Award fatigue?

Perhaps the greatest importance of the Cherbourg action was the stark demonstration of how inadequately MGBs were still armed to tackle anything much bigger than an E-boat, even after they received their two-pounder pom-poms. To pass a stationary torpedo boat in the dark and be able to do nothing about it must have caused Hitch an unprecedented degree of frustration. A German torpedo boat, really a small destroyer, would have represented an extraordinary prize for the midget MGBs had they had even one small torpedo each. Hitch makes clear in his book that this was the moment when he determined to fight for MGBs to carry torpedoes, having experienced the frustration of working with MTBs with the differences in silencing, speed and indeed tactical doctrine. The job of an MTB was to approach unobserved to within torpedo range, fire and then retreat. An MGB's job was to approach as close as they could get before attacking with guns and then they had to be at almost point blank range to be effective. Thus the tracks of MGBs and MTBs, even when operating as a single unit, could seldom be the same so that the MGB's targets of opportunity were not often there for the MTB to sink with its torpedoes. The only answer was to combine the two types of weapon in a single hull, without the loss of speed and the high silhouette that was inherent in the solution of the Dog Boat. Hitch was to spend much of the last six months of his life fighting for the installation of eighteen-inch torpedoes, the size carried by Fleet Air Arm Swordfish biplanes of pre-war design, against an Admiralty convinced that it knew best and that the MGB would lose its essential edge of speed if encumbered with the additional weight of torpedoes. They found it hard to accept that those who took the boats into action and knew how they behaved could be right in judging that the weight of two small torpedoes added could be balanced by removing less essential weight, such as heavy powered turrets, and reserves of ammunition rarely called upon in the short, sharp, point blank fights that MGBs sought.

The fine weather continued. My recollections of this period are of night after night at sea, the slowly losing battle in the effort to make up sleep by day, of bathes in the turgid waters of the Dart with my children, of lessening friction in the base, greater freedom and understanding as the original inhabitants got used to the young, lively, and somewhat unruly visitors.

In the midst of our night patrols we were suddenly called upon to do a job by day. I remember that we were all sitting in 81's wardroom. It was midday, gin time, and Kelly[14] had just performed prodigies

14. Lieutenant J.A. Cowley, RNVR, always known as Kelly because he came from the Isle of Man.

with the bottles. We were all dead tired, I had slumped into a half recumbent posture on the wardroom settee and shut my eyes. Conversation became general when the drinks had got round. Suddenly a somewhat dishevelled matelot shoved his head into the wardroom, removing his cap, and said:

'Lootenant-Commander 'Ichens wanted on the telephone.'

Regretfully I drained my drink and climbed wearily and laboriously to the upper deck on the base ship,[15] where the instruments were situated.

The voice came through distinct and impersonal:

'There's an airman in the water in position 49 degrees 03' North 03 degrees 15' West. That's about sixty-five miles south of the Start. All available gunboats to search the area forthwith.'.

I found myself saying: 'But we've just come in from sea,' and swallowed the remark as unworthy and irrelevant.

'I'll take all the boats that are fuelled. Will you give me that position again?'

As I wrote down the latitude and longitude, my mind dwelt on the air factor. It would take us to within twenty miles of the French coast and all of sixty or seventy from ours; the day was brilliant, clear and cloudless; the gentle northerly wind would be wafting the roar of our engines towards the enemy coast; Brittany had an unpleasant reputation for fast, efficient striking forces, especially the recent Focke-Wulf 190.

'Will there be air cover, sir?' I asked.

'Yes, full cover will be laid on. I'll see to that,' came the reply.

Thus reassured I returned to the boats. Within seven minutes of the news breaking, they were letting go and dropping down the river, past the boom, between the close-gathered towering hills, frowned on by the lifeless, staring apertures of the old castle to starboard, beamed on to port by the rugged wave-worn hump of the Mewstone, basking in the hot sunshine like a friendly leviathan. Thrashing to sea, gathering speed in a tight wedge, the three boats, *75, 78* and *81*, sped past the Start and steadied on their southerly course at thirty-three knots.

15. *Aberdonian*, where the first lieutenants were accommodated. Eric Archer, who joined the Eighth Flotilla as Bussy Carr's Number One, when he returned in command of 115 remembers *Aberdonian* as having cold baths. These could, however, be brought to an acceptable temperature by adding live steam from a pipe which happened to pass through the officers' ablutions.

The grey embattled mass of Prawle Point was still towering high on the starboard quarter when the Spitfires arrived, zooming, circling, diving, weaving like friendly seagulls following a trawler cleaning her catch. We were not used to such assiduous attention. Generally we had to fend for ourselves. Still this was entirely an air force affair and we took it as our due, nevertheless highly gratified.

The two hours' run to the position passed quickly enough, beguiled for me by the highly diverting and persistent efforts of George Duncan to get one of his Lewis guns to fire properly, whistles blowing, the whip crack of the 0.303, silence, more whistles and orders, until the wretched little brute finally saw reason and fired in an unrelenting stream.

Boats were spread four miles apart for the search. We scanned the smiling sunny, wind caressed face of the sea, seemingly so benevolent to our eyes, accustomed to her darkened countenance of dusk, night and grey dawn, finding it hard to realise that a fellow human was near at hand in dire distress.

Suddenly 75 altered course slightly to port and began to slow. We raced over to her as she lay stopped, strong arms helping a man from a yellow rubber dinghy alongside. The aircraft circled twice, dipped low in salute, and sped away to the north. The blue vault of the sky was totally empty. Sky met sea all round in varying shades of blue, nothing to be seen save the three little boats in a cluster, small dark specks in that dazzling void of sun-drenched, gently heaving water.

The airman was a Czech. He was slightly hurt and could speak little enough English. We gathered that he thought there might be another airman down in the vicinity, the man he had been looking for. There had been another position given, a little to the east and north. I decided to search through it and then return home.

As the minutes went by in our solitude, eyes began to turn apprehensively to the south where the French coast lay little more than fifteen miles away. In such glorious summer weather it seemed absurd to do anything but lie on the decks sunbathing; yet the gunners sat rigid in their turrets, scanning the sky for the tiny death-dealing dots that would hurl themselves down sun at over two hundred miles an hour.

Nothing happened until nearly two hours later. As we lifted the land on the northern skyline, a snarling, swerving batch of fighters tore down on us and resumed their assiduous and now totally unnecessary attentions. Either because it was tea-time, or for some more subtle reason, we had been without escort throughout the most dangerous period of our trip. Still we had not been attacked and it had been a lovely day!

Though we did not know it, our time at Dartmouth was drawing to an end. *77* came back renewed in body and soul by her creators. Power Boats personnel had swarmed aboard almost the moment she arrived and after a few weeks' intensive work she was as good as new, better in some ways, as various modifications had been possible.

The day after her return, we sailed to the south and in the early hours of the morning looked for trouble between Guernsey and Jersey. We found it in the shape of four patrol trawlers. We surprised them and shot one up severely. Then tackled the others. Fully roused, their fire became more accurate. Hits on our boats would be fatal; engines damaged or petrol tanks ignited and the ship was lost; our fire could have little more than severe nuisance value on a trawler, inflicting some damage, killing personnel, necessitating patches in plates; nothing more, unless we were exceptionally lucky and set one on fire, a very unlikely occurrence.

We were not to throw our valuable and specialised boats away on trawlers. We disengaged, but not before Bussy Carr had received an all-but-fatal wound. A 0.303 bullet passed right through him, puncturing his lungs. We sped home. Knowing that his life hung on a matter of minutes, our anger can be imagined when we ran into thick fog thirty miles from the English coast. Speed was maintained, RDF switched on, a new gadget so far as we were concerned. The high land ahead gave magnificent echoes. Fixing on the Start and Berry Heads, we altered course for Dartmouth. Visibility two hundred yards, speed still thirty-three knots, the range coming down.

'One thousand yards.'

'Five hundred yards.'

The situation was tense.

'Three hundred yards.'

I began to ease.

'Two hundred yards.'

As we slowed to a crawl the black cliffs appeared through the fog towering high. We had missed the entrance. But not by much. I recognised some outlying rocks. We were two miles to the eastward of the opening. Creeping along the shore, soon getting echoes on the

Mewstone, we felt our way in and Bussy was in hospital little more than thirty minutes late on normal conditions. He received expert attention at once, was operated on and nursed back from the very threshold of death. Time, I understand, had been the crucial factor. He was lucky that the new boats had, for the first time in the history of fast motorboats, been fitted with RDF.

Our last promising trip was also a sweep off Jersey, this time with a torpedo boat, *241* of the Twenty-First Flotilla,[16] alas quite unsilenced at any speed above six knots! And what a noise that boat made! There seemed to be a specially vibrant quality in her deep-throated roar. Certain it is we could pick her out above and distinct from other boats at great distances. 'The Hammers of Hell' we called her. She lived fully up to her reputation this time.

We swept round the south and west of Guernsey at a respectful ten miles, in the hopes of avoiding detection. Not a bit of it. The night was quiet. With the 'Hammers of Hell' going full bore, star-shell and flares were going up all along the thoroughly alarmed enemy coast. Thus as the end of three years of war, with many years of peacetime experiment and experience beforehand, the British Admiralty effected the universally desired surprise attack by MTBs!

Having disclosed to the entire neighbourhood that fast offensive craft had arrived just south of St Martin's Point, we reduced to our silent six knots for the sweep towards Jersey. At that speed we could only just complete it before the approach of dawn would force us to retire, our position and course again obligingly revealed by the appalling uproar.

Halfway through our sweep we were startled by reports of E-boats. They were moving south. Plotting the reports eagerly, it soon became apparent that they were headed for Pleinmont Point, evidently intending to approach St Peter Port by the southerly route. They had thirty miles to go by the plot. They would be there in under the hour at their present speed. We were about eighteen miles from the vital promontory, round which they must come and where we must catch them. We could not make it at *241*'s silent speed of six knots. We could not leave her alone off the enemy coast. We had to take a chance.

16. Her CO was Sub-Lieutenant Jim McDonald RNZNVR who was to become Senior Officer of the Twenty-First Flotilla and win a DSO, DSC and two bars, and be twice Mentioned in Dispatches.

We sped back to Pleinmont and cut three-quarters of a mile south of the lighthouse. The sea was windless, undulating gently. The night was clear and dark. They must have heard us, but the E-boats would be here in half an hour. Maybe they thought we were E-boats! So we encouraged our hopes as we donned our tin hats. It was the ideal place for a scrap. Smooth water, plenty of sea room, no shore batteries to protect them this time. Only one thing worried us. David James was aboard my boat, 77, and David had a hoodoo. He had been with us from the first, had done as many operations of every type as anyone, yet he had never made contact with the enemy. Always something happened to avert action if David was there, however likely the set-up. The next day, with David's boat laid off, a fierce fight would result from the most unpromising situation. It was quite uncanny and it was beginning to get him down.

He thought the spell was to be broken this time. Les Hanois light came on, illuminating the rocks scattered in horrid profusion to the west of the high point of land. That would be to fix the E-boats in their landfall as they skirted the south of the island. They would be on us in less than fifteen minutes now. Tension increased. I walked round the silent ship, admonishing the gunners to hold their fire until the range was closed to the minimum. Final touches, the last preparations for battle, were made. Time passed. No sound, no distant mutter or soft swish. They must have slowed. Something was wrong. Why were they not here yet?

My suspicions deepened. We started up and roared along the south coast of Guernsey until clear of St Martin's point. Just what I had begun to fear. The harbour lights were on; the E-boats must have been entering or already in. The shore had heard us bear down on Pleinmont and stop. Quickly they had warned the E-boats by W/T, put on Les Hanois to lull our suspicions and give the E-boats a bearing, and got them in north about, while we waited hopefully at the southern entrance. The 'Hammers of Hell' had done their stuff and David's hoodoo had triumphed again.

The night produced nothing more memorable than David's remark about Benzedrine. The doctor had been keen to try the effect of two tablets of Benzedrine on us. It was reputed to keep away sleep and pep you up. David was a great and notorious 'zizzer'. A 'zizz' is naval slang for a sleep. On this occasion he had tried two tablets. Returning home in the morning, he remarked:

'I don't think much of Benzedrine. I felt just as cowardly as ever and went 'hard-a-zizz' by midnight.'

That was the end of our single-handed contest with the E-boats in the west. They moved and almost exactly six weeks after our arrival we received our sailing orders. We were to return to Felixstowe to renew the North Sea battle. We considered that we had had the best of it. We felt rather proud of ourselves and tremendously flotilla conscious because we had been working on our own. Pride, as usual, was to come before a fall!

We were to leave the inhabitants of the Dartmouth base sharply divided. Half wanted to come with us, the other half thanked the Lord that we were going.

In the first pearly light of a September day, we slipped, I should like to say silently, but it would be a singular untruth, for the last time between the crowding hills, turned our backs on those well loved rough faced cliffs, and directed our lifted bows to the eastward. The whole flotilla, all eight of us! We like to think this a unique feat; certainly it was unusual to have all eight boats of a flotilla in running order. Thirteen hours later seven of us crowded into Felixstowe Dock, *78* only having fallen by the wayside, shedding a propeller off the Isle of Wight.

Looking back at the long line, incredibly long to one used to three or sometimes two boats only, revelling in the spectacle of grace and power, bows up, spray bursting on the hulls, pennants flying, I recalled my feelings as we had sailed to the west six weeks before, new and untried. I had loved and trusted my boats then, but with a half timid expectant love, the least bit apologetic. The same feeling that I had felt for my Aston-Martin as, overhauled, tuned, personally and completely reassembled, burnished, polished, I drove her tenderly along the straight impersonal, sun-baked French roads to her first race.

Now my feelings for the boats were similar to the familiar trusting affection for my car, with which I had returned from that gruelling twenty-four hours at Le Mans; true she was running on three cylinders only, her brakes were a thing of the past, she was no longer burnished and polished, but every touch of the steering wheel was a caress, every pressure of the throttle pedal an intimate contact.

Now the boats and I understood one another and with under-standing comes true affection, not to replace but to supplement

281

proper pride. I knew what they could do for us. I realised when I was calling for special efforts, efforts that might strain and hurt; I recognised when I was asking too much.

As we rounded Landguard Point I patted the smooth apparently insensate metal fingers of *77*'s throttles; she understood.

We were royally welcomed. It was exciting seeing old friends, gratifying to be amid familiar and comfortable surroundings. But we could not help regretting the late scene of operations. The North Sea, cold, foggy, mine ridden, could produce nothing to touch the deep water of the chops of the Channel and the beauty of the high Channel Islands' cliffs.

Chapter Thirteen

Short Run to a Swift Death
September – October 1942

In the course of our purely anti-E-boat activities at Dartmouth we had had three engagements in quick succession, only one of which had involved our true quarry. On each occasion we had required torpedoes; against the convoy off Alderney, to sink the stationary German torpedo boat at the entrance to Cherbourg and to deal effectively with the patrol of four trawlers north of Jersey.

I have described how forcibly this need had been brought home to me. The more we thought about it and discussed it the more obvious the requirement became. Half our value as offensive craft was wasted through inability to deal with any target larger than an E-boat, except for the rare and excessively risky chances of delivering a successful depth-charge attack. If even one torpedo could be carried we would have a good chance of tackling bigger game when the opportunity occurred. The ultimate ideal for the small fast boat was obviously for the gunboats to carry torpedoes and the torpedo boats sufficient guns to enable them to tackle E-boats. If this could be achieved there would be a vast saving of boats and personnel. Both types could tackle either job. When the weather was unsuitable for the small MTBs to operate on the enemy coast, there was danger of the larger E-boats attacking and the torpedo boats could assist the gunboats in their continuous watch and ward to seaward of the convoy route. When operational requirements took the gunboats over to the enemy coast, they could ship their torpedoes and be prepared for any target that might be encountered.

The difficulties confronting us were twofold. The inability to carry much extra weight in our light craft, and the extraordinarily intractable attitude taken up by the authorities immediately responsible for the development of our boats who turned their faces deliberately and steadfastly against our pleadings. The intense struggle that ensued, a struggle that lasted over many months and waxed bitter as more and more evidence in support of our contention piled in from seaward in the shape of burnt and battered boats staggering back from the enemy coast, was exclusively concerned with the human element. The weight problem was easy of solution had the authorities concerned not been possessed of an archaic outlook against which we battered our wits and tongues with as much effect as seabirds against the hard exterior of a lighthouse!

For another requirement of ours, by one of those fortunate twists of circumstance which rarely occur, dovetailed in with this necessity for reducing weight. The new seventy-one-foot-six gunboat was entirely armed with power-worked turrets driven by oil pressure from pumps in the engine room. These turrets were excellent, and where they were essential, as in the case of our two-pounder, which could not be controlled from the shoulder, nothing could have been better; but they were heavy, they were extremely vulnerable, and they could not be used when the boat was stopped, since the gun pumps were driven off the wing propeller shafts. Action experience showed that the pipes were almost invariably punctured by splinters if the boat was hit at all severely; this would certainly put the turret in question out of action and possibly bleed the whole system and disable both turrets. True, after our early action off Alderney when 77's two-pounder was knocked out, we got the pipes laid along the keel in future, instead of under the deck, where they were much more vulnerable, but even so the defect of vulnerability was a serious disadvantage.

No less serious was the inability to fire when lying stopped, unless the ten horse power Ford auxiliary was started and the pipe lines switched over to another pump, when one turret could be used. When lying out and listening, the running of the auxiliary made audible warning of the enemy impossible. The problem was insuperable; we had to accept the disability.

For these reasons, where guns could be carried without involving the use of a powered turret, we were most anxious to do so. The Oerlikon could be controlled just as well, or almost so, from the shoulder, as had been the custom in the old boats. *Beehive*'s Gunnery Officer, Lieutenant Woods, RNVR, had had the simple but brilliant idea of constructing a dual cradle on the lines of the twin cradle in the powered turret and putting it on the existing single hand-worked mounting. Bailey had seen the importance of the idea and had pushed matters on and soon after our return from Dartmouth the first dual cradle was completed and proved satisfactory in trials on our boats.

Meanwhile we had been calling out loudly for a lightly constructed, hand-worked Oerlikon mounting. The mounting given us weighed one thousand five hundred and thirty pounds. We considered that we could have one built for three hundred or four hundred pounds if only the naval constructors would get away from their mediaeval ideas of mass, weight and strength and had repeatedly asked for it. As soon as we got the new boats, on the 2nd June 1942 to be precise, we had put up a requirement for a light mounting to carry an Oerlikon in the position of the Holman projector aft of the powered turret, the latter being moved elsewhere where it could function equally well.

It was suggested that the total weight of the gun and mounting need not exceed seven hundred pounds, that no extra ammunition need be carried, and that we had taken equivalent weight out of the boat in the shape of excess water and other unnecessary equipment. The suggestion was approved by the operating authorities and sent to the Admiralty where it immediately got bogged, or at any rate slowed and ensnared, in the hands of the appropriate authorities and civil servants.

The whole thing fitted like a jigsaw puzzle. If we could be given our light mounting carrying two guns we could replace the powered twin Oerlikon mounting aft. This would give us hand-working guns and save weight, thereby enabling us to ship torpedoes.

The Captain saw the point and backed us to the full. Indeed, he led us in the campaign. Our Flag Officer in Charge was magnificent, likewise and the Nore lent its aid. But would the shore authorities, who had the power to say yea or nay, listen to the sea-going officers or operating authorities? Not a bit of it. At first our ideas were treated as childish, our suggestions scarcely considered. As we persisted and became more obstreperous and some notice had to be taken, we incurred increasing odium and were treated as definite nuisances. The only thing that strengthened our arm was fighting.

They had to take notice of action reports. It had always been the same. Our ideas and requests had only received attention if backed by recent and decisive engagements. For months we had been pressing for some form of rapid R/T communication direct from captain to captain. We required it as much as fighter pilots. Our actions, in the dark, at high speed, with the tremendous noise, gun flashes and tracer, made signalling between boats as necessary and difficult as between fighter aircraft. Yet no one listened to us until, as a result of our series of actions at Dartmouth, we pressed and pressed for it, forcibly comparing our position to that of aircraft. Then at last the principle was adopted and four months later my flotilla, the first to be fitted, received a number of experimental sets.

Thus it was that we had to become involved in much more fighting and take considerable punishment before our gun and torpedo ideas received any serious consideration; even then the issue was only joined and the result remained in doubt for many months.

We returned to *Beehive* to find a somewhat depleted Sixth Flotilla. Bailey had had a fierce engagement not long before in which the torpedo boats had assisted. A merchant ship had been torpedoed and Bailey had wound up the show by going bald-headed for a flak trawler and depth charging her. It was an extremely gallant affair. The trawler had been well and truly dealt with, but not before she had wreaked bitter vengeance on *67*, Bailey's boat, during her close-in attack. Several of the crew were killed, nearly all on the upper deck wounded, including Bailey himself in the bottom. This, though it inconvenienced him considerably, mercifully did not incapacitate him, and he succeeded in subduing a fire in the port 0.5 turret, while the boat careered madly along, unsteered, weaving her way drunkenly. In the end, he just got her back to harbour half-full of water forward. A merciful Providence had decreed that the engines should be undamaged and reliable to the end.[1]

We immediately resumed our work of escorting the MLs on their mine laying ventures. Formerly we had had to lie off because our silencing had been inadequate. In the new boats slow speed and silence were improved. We reckoned that if we were to protect them

---

1. David James, in the 1956 edition of *We Fought Them in Gunboats*, footnoted: 'For this gallant action he was awarded a richly deserved DSO.' This action is the one described by Roland Clarke in Chapter 11. Bailey was subsequently killed in a Coastal Forces Control Frigate, HMS *Trollope*, shortly after D-Day.

effectively we must be with them during the trickiest part, the run in over the last few miles. If a patrol was met we would tackle it and allow the MLs to by-pass the trouble and get the mines to the right place. This soon led to our next fight.

We went with Tubby Cambridge and his henchmen to lay mines two and a half miles to seaward of the entrance of the Hook of Holland.[2] Necessarily it was a dark night, quiet and windless. Creeping stealthily in, when a bare mile from the laying position, a bright light flashed ahead, seemingly challenging. We stopped, endeavoured to detect what it might be, consulted together and decided to carry on, the gunboats straight for the position of the light, the MLs slightly to port for the laying position.

All went well, the MLs did their stuff and retired. Nothing happened. We cut and waited. We were looking for trouble. The particular form of trouble that we expected was a patrol of four flak trawlers that we knew to be stationed in that vicinity. Presently we picked up a hydrophone contact, unmistakably slow reciprocating engines. It is hard to convey the thrill of such a moment. To know that the enemy is near, that you can intercept, that he is unaware of the surprise in store for him. The stealthy tracking down, the gunboats stealing along, subdued, held in leash, in close line ahead. The first glimpse of black shapes, blacker than the surrounding darkness:

'Enemy Red 45,' the tensely awaited signal. There were two hulls visible at first, out ahead of anything else, heading for the Hook, now less than two miles distant. We closed, gathering speed. A blue light flashed, challenging us with 'W's'. We replied with 'C's'. I thought the long short long short, unevenly made, might worry them. It did; they challenged again and yet a third time. That was all we wanted. We were right in close by now, about two hundred yards, where we could not miss these slow-moving solid hulls. Then the guns spoke.

In the event it turned out to be a small convoy entering the Hook. Due to the fact that we intercepted it so close to the harbour mouth the merchant vessels were ahead of the escort trawlers and we were able to wreak much havoc before they came up and the action became less one-sided. We disengaged fifteen minutes later with a number of holes in our boats, a few minor casualties and three guns

2. This action took place on the 14/15 September 1942.

still working, but cheerful and well pleased with ourselves. The enemy had been considerably damaged and remarkably scared.

77 had been hit several times and I fancied some had been in the engine room. I sent for Stay. A face appeared, covered in blood and oil, unrecognisable until the familiar words came:

'Top line, sir. One of the oil tanks is stuffed up with rag and I had to plug one of the exhaust pipe jackets. But she'll be all right.'

Some motor mechanics could be worth their weight in gold. A shell had exploded in the engine room, slightly wounding Stay in the face, puncturing one of the oil tanks and putting a hole in an exhaust pipe jacket. With jets of intensely hot oil and sea water pouring over him, Stay had promptly plugged both holes and kept the engines running without a falter.

The action had again demonstrated our requirements. Had we carried torpedoes, those two unsuspecting and unprotected merchantmen would have graced the sandy bottom at the entrance to the Hook. In the later action with the escort, two of our powered turrets had been put out of action.

For this action Hitch was awarded a second bar to his DSC. Again one wonders why a bar to a DSC was thought appropriate for an attack on a merchant ship which did not result in its sinking, whereas the destruction of at least two E-boats off Cherbourg six weeks earlier had merited a Mention in Dispatches. Perhaps the authorities at the Nore thought that he had been short-changed for the action off Cherbourg and were making up for it with a measure of generosity.

Boffin Campbell got a DSC for his work commanding 76, and Tommy Ladner in 75 a second Mention in Dispatches. Petty Officer Motor Mechanic Frederick Innis in 76 and Chief Motor Mechanic Vic Stay in 77 received the DSM. Being instrumental in the award to Vic Stay of a DSM probably gave Hitch more pleasure than anything else. It had been Vic's robust optimism on the night of the 12/13 November 1941 that had decided Hitch to continue the patrol at the reduced speed of eighteen knots after 64's pendulastic started to give trouble for the umpteenth time. Engine room crews were not often in the limelight, yet they toiled in the most unpleasant conditions and their attention to duty made the difference between whether or not these small, delicate boats got into action.

In less than a month we were to have another engagement and suffer our first serious loss. Meanwhile the weather was rough. It was the time of the equinoctial gales, and operations were few. Nevertheless I went through a most alarming period. I received warning, a hint only, that the authorities were looking for an officer to teach gunboat tactics at the working-up base and that my name was being seriously considered. I investigated matters and found that it was all too true.

I was only too willing to help in developing and teaching tactics, but my view was that I could best do that by remaining at sea and passing on ideas, experiments and lessons learnt to a whole-time shore authority. I felt that if I went ashore I should soon be out of date. Tactics developed so fast that after a short time I should lack confidence in my ability to teach sea-going Senior Officers. I should feel that they knew more than I did. My experience in fast gunboats was of value at sea, where I could try out new ideas and continue development. Besides, from the personal point of view, I had just got a flotilla fully worked up of which I was very proud. It would be bitter to have to leave it.

At first it seemed that the authorities would not see my point of view. I went through a nerve-racking ten days. To be on the beach. To see my boats put to sea knowing that perhaps never again would I lead them. Never again to feel the lift and dance of the hulls as we headed for the enemy coast. Never again to feel a unit wheel at a word of command. With the war continuing, never again to feel the exhilarating anxiety of real responsibility at sea, the power of life and death, your brains against the enemy's, with wounds and death as the stakes. It was unbearable. I wrote a letter explaining succinctly my views and my unsuitability for a teaching job. It worked. To my intense relief the appointment went elsewhere.[3]

On the evening of the 2nd October we set out, as so often before, to accompany the MLs. The old moon would rise at 1.30 in the morning. The lay, to take place on the enemy convoy route near the Middle Bank, was scheduled for 1.15. Thereafter we were at liberty to search where we would and good luck to us.

All went according to plan except that we were a little late. A hump-

3. Hitch was offered promotion to Commander, and the command of HMS *Bee* at Weymouth where MGBs worked up. The authorities probably felt he had had more than his fair share of danger and stress and needed a rest. They may well have been right. Peter Dickens noted in *Night Action* that, had Hitch been RN, he would have had to do as he was bloody well told, but that senior RNVR officers were granted more latitude.

backed moon was riding low in the heavens by the time the mines were laid. It was a fascinating scene to watch. The white grey hulls glimmering dully in the faint moonlight, their straight stems throwing up a feather spray of water at their creeping gait. The sharp orders intoned at exact intervals. The clank and clatter as each long, black, cylindrical object fell at the word of command. The glint and flutter of spray thrown high on board from the splash. The sluggish roll of the boat, released thus sharply of a heavy load on her gunwale

Their work done, the MLs headed for home. Clear of the Dutch coast we bid them good night, stopped and considered how best to seek out the enemy.

We knew there was probably a trawler patrol a short distance away to the north-east. I slipped into the wheelhouse to study the chart. The tiny confined space, dimly lit by the red tachometer lamp and the plotting lights, seemed tight-packed with instruments and equipment. the echo sounding machine, white and lumpy, a compass, the new Hallicrafter R/T set, headphones, the first to be issued, hanging on the bulkhead, our experimental gyro repeater, the instrument panel, and RDF repeater, dotted with varied brightly coloured knobs, a CB safe, navigating instruments, polished and shining under the shaded light, lashed to the curving canopy a fireman's axe, the blade gleaming sullenly, the white sheet of the chart covering the little table on the starboard side. If the dustbin was the head of the ship, containing her eyes and brains, the wheelhouse was her heart, the source of life and energy. Some oilskins, hanging against the side, swayed gently to the quiet movement of the boat. Her heart was beating; there was life here, apparent in every rustle and creak. A ship is only dead, really dead, in dry dock or hoisted ashore. Then her gear hangs still and listless, even the softest slap and ripple of the sea is absent, animation seems suspended, her heart stopped, until life returns upon renewed contact with the water.

I put my elbows on the edge of the chart table, head in hands, and contemplated the position. We were opposite the outlet of the East Scheldt; the patrol was said to be in the Buiten Deep to seaward of the mouth of the River Maas. My eye, as it travelled up the Dutch coast, caught the black lettering and uncompromising confirmation of the word Roompot. Roompot! This name had greatly pleased us, written as it was across our charts opposite one of our most fruitful hunting grounds. In search of a collective call-sign for the new

290

flotilla, the Eighth, we had lighted upon it, altered the spelling to Rumpots, and adopted it as descriptive of our social activities. Listening Germans, intercepting the oft repeated cry of 'Hitch calling Rumpots', doubtless considered it as yet one more confirmation of the inveterate madness of all Englishmen.[4]

Following up the coastline there was the Buiten Bank and Buiten Deep. It was no more than twelve miles. We should be going northeast, the moon would be on our starboard bow, the distance being short we could afford to proceed at low speed in silence. If the enemy were there we should have every chance of surprising them.

The decision was taken. We had had a run of successes without serious loss. Though this may have tended to over-confidence, I had enough sense to see that surprise had been the decisive factor throughout. On every occasion, except the Ostend battle where we had not decisively damaged the E-boats, but had turned them from their purpose by sheer hard fighting, the object had been obtained as a result of complete tactical surprise. It must always be so in our type of warfare. Fighting at night, generally against vastly superior and more powerfully armed vessels, extremely vulnerable in our unprotected bulk of high octane petrol, the lightning thrust was our chance. Catch the enemy on his heels, go for him bald-headed, hit him hard and quickly, then get out. That was how to make war with our little ships. Stab him again and again with rapier thrusts. To increase the effective weight of those thrusts was our continual concern. By the summer of 1942 we had a boat, still only seventy-one-foot-six inches long, that had a sting which would have seemed incredible to our eager eyes in the early days when, a bare two years

4. After the 2005 Coastal Forces Remembrance Service at *Hornet* I was entertained to lunch by Eric Archer and James Shadbolt, sometime Eighth Flotilla commanding officers. After lunch had run its liquid course, the two distinguished elderly gentlemen joined in singing a chorus they had learnt as first lieutenants in the Eighth under Hitch. It went:

Oh, we are bold bad types
We're in the Coastal Forces
Dicing with death
Out on those great white horses
We drink our gins & whisky
Just like Alley Sloper's sauces
And everywhere we go
We take our rum pots.

before, we swept the seas with nothing but our 0.303 automatic guns.

They say that pride goes before a fall. Maybe I was over-confident with our recent success. Certain it is that I was about to have it brought home to me in forceful manner that good luck, the supreme importance of which I had always maintained, was at least as vital an element as surprise in the attainment of victory at sea. We were heading for our first serious loss.

The boats got under way on their wing engines, bumbling off quickly at twelve knots. *77* was leading with *78, 81* and one of the old Sixth Flotilla boats, *60*. We swept up the coast, the moon, riding high now, fine on our starboard bow. Visibility was good. It would be possible to see our quarry quite a mile away, possibly farther.

Boffin was with me in *77*. I was standing on the canopy top scanning ahead steadily through glasses. We had always sought out the enemy and attacked and so far all had gone well. But there was an uneasiness lurking in the back of my mind. Surprise was essential with bigger ships, such as trawlers. Could we effect it in this bright moonlight and good visibility? If not, an attack would be wrong. The risk would be too high for the possible benefit. But the Eighth Flotilla always attacked! Commonsense and experience were at variance with inclination.

Nevertheless I decided that unless I could surprise them and cause a diversion I would not allow an attack to be pressed home close. The men might even have to see the enemy pass by unmolested. A bitter experience, but in this form of warfare conditions must be selected in order to achieve success. Thinking thus, suddenly I saw them. First one small black blob in the moon path, then another. I held my peace and watched. There was another and yet a fourth. Thirty seconds more and I was sure that was all. I slipped down from the canopy.

'There they are, bearing Green 20, four of them,' I said quietly to Boffin. 'We'll stop the unit and settle a plan of attack.'

Vigorous use of the lungs brought the unit to a halt. Engines were cut. So far so good. We were in a perfect position. The enemy approaching slowly, on a course to pass us a few cables to starboard. They were in line abreast doing about four knots. I was up again on the canopy, watching intently, thinking furiously. Down moon; well camouflaged as we were they would not see us until they were a few cables away. We could give them a good dose of two pounder and Oerlikon, but that would not be decisive. We could not get one separated in that close formation and good visibility. Should we try out our much discussed and practised 'Attack Single'? This was our method of executing a thought-out and pre-arranged depth-charge attack, where we had tactical surprise, as on this occasion. Briefly the plan was for one boat to be detached. While the rest of the unit attacked the enemy with gunfire at moderate range, thereby causing a diversion, attracting all attention in their direction, the detailed boat would dash in from the opposite side at maximum speed, drop her depth charges close in front of the selected target and disappear as rapidly as she had come, afterwards rendezvousing with the rest of the unit in a pre-arranged position to seaward of the scene of the attack.

The depth charge was an exceptionally clumsy and dangerous weapon; to be effective it meant closing to within a few yards of the enemy; but we had no other, nothing that could sink a trawler. Here was a chance to try out our oft-discussed plans. The trouble was the moonlight and good visibility. Such an attack needed conditions of darkness and low visibility if possible; then the single attacking boat could not be seen until very close. Tonight, if unlucky, she might be sighted at several cables and have to run the gauntlet going in.

I looked down moon. It was surprisingly difficult to see our little boats in the toneless obscurity. With a well sustained diversion there should be every chance of the attacking boat getting right in unob-served. We should never get a better chance of pre-arranging such an attack. Had we not always attacked before? With a bit of luck we should get one of them. Luck! The fickle jade had been on our side too long. How was I to know that she was absent tonight?

'We'll do an 'Attack Single'.'

It was settled.

The enemy were drawing steadily nearer. Time was short. Who should make the attack? Thoughts raced through my mind. My first reaction was to do it myself. A bare two months before 77 had carried out a successful depth charge attack. She had been smitten, but then there had been no diversion. We were the most suitable, the most experienced. But the limelight had consequently fallen all too brightly upon us and me in particular. The depth charge attack off Alderney, the battle off Ostend, both had been solo affairs; the resultant accla-mations embarrassing so far as I was concerned. I desperately wanted my other officers to share to the full in the Flotilla's success. George

Duncan I knew to be pining for an opportunity. He had kicked himself for days after the action off Jersey. He had been last in the line, the best position for breaking off and delivering a depth charge attack at the Commanding Officer's own initiative. The first trawler attacked had been well subdued. George considered that he could have seized the opportunity and finished her off with a depth-charge. I knew that had been on his mind, that he was dead keen for his chance to make up for the opportunity he considered he had missed.

Thus swiftly I reasoned, as the black shapes of the enemy loomed larger and clearer. After the event I taxed myself bitterly. Why had I not undertaken the attack myself? Had not fear, personal fear, fear for my own wretched body played its part in the decision? With George gone and myself unhurt and in comfort at home, such reaction was inevitable. The great advantage of naval warfare, especially our small ship fighting, was that as leader one shared to the full the risks and hardships of every member of the flotilla. Mercifully absent was the terrible responsibility, so often inherent in military command, of ordering others to the attack whilst remaining oneself in comparative security. Had I funked it on this occasion? Had I sent another man in because, even subconsciously, I had feared for my own life? Later the thought tortured me. I have tried to analyse precisely my feelings at the time. Confident as I was then, possibly over-confident, I do not think that anxiety for the result, either for *78* or *77*, consciously affected my decision.

'Would you like to carry out the attack, George?' I shouted. I knew the question to be superfluous. Nothing would hold George back.

'Yes I would,' came the unhesitating reply. A very brave man was started on the short run to swift death.

Details were settled. We were to attack on the beam, work round up moon, slowly extending the range, leaving the down moon side clear for *78*'s attack, which was to be delivered as soon as possible after we had got the fight well under way.

We were on the trawlers' beam now, about four cables distant. Their course was south-west, the moon bore east. *77, 81* and *60* crept away, moving through west to south and south-east, closing and turning slowly on opposite courses to the enemy. They were less than three cables away now, large as life, the moon path just astern. Still they did not see us. Two cables off, they challenged us; it was time to start. A stream of tracer swept from the gunboats into the nearest trawler. Slowly at first, rather hesitantly, the answering fire gathered momentum, each trawler in turn becoming alive to the situation. We increased speed to twenty knots, circled round the stern of the enemy, slowly opening range as we became silhouetted against the moon and their fire improved, maintaining a steady barrage of tracer.

Minutes went by, still no sign of *78*. She was slow. I had expected her attack soon after we had become fully engaged. We had hit that first trawler hard, the others in varying degree; we were being hit ourselves from time to time, but most was passing over, the tracer seeming to flare out and up at you like a projected flame, the near bullets whistling shrilly.

It was not until we had worked round to the south-east of the enemy that a sudden eruption of tracer from the trawler in a south-westerly direction indicated that *78* had gone in. Up till then all their fire had been directed towards us. This burst of tracer was at right-angles to the general direction of their shooting. Short, sustained, it was immediately followed by a violent criss-cross of tracer; evidently *78* was firing back and being fired on more heavily. This again was only momentary, lasting at the most for a minute or two. Then silence.

We had ceased fire at the sign of *78*'s attack. We drew away down moon, passing across the trawlers' line of advance. Suddenly I noticed a patch of mist. I remembered then that a peculiar obscurity had been developing round the moon during the engagement. Was there a fog coming up? This was the first real indication of it.

Using glasses, I could watch the enemy about half a mile away, without fear of them seeing us. They were stopped now, huddled together in a bunch, a cloud of black smoke hanging over them. George's attack had been a success by the look of it. It seemed that they were standing by one of their number. If only we had torpedoes, what an opportunity! Stopped in a close group!

At that moment the fog came down in real earnest, blotting them out. I turned my attention to *78*. All seemed to have gone well. She had evidently got in unobserved. This was evident from the momentary nature of the engagement. By the same token she had got out again quickly. Had she suffered severely and been slowed up, the cross-fire would have been prolonged. At the worst she would have been stopped or set on fire; either eventuality would have been obvious. It seemed that all was well. Good old George! Of one thing

I was sure, the attack had been pressed home to the limit. To within a few feet of the enemy's sharp rising bows.

We called him up by R/T and W/T. No answer. That was nothing. It was rare that one of our boats, delivering a determined attack and suffering some damage, was able to use her wireless again. More often than not the aerial was shot away, the set itself damaged or the power supply cut off.

'Tracer in the air, sir,' an excited shout from Head.

'What bearing?' I replied.

'Over there,' said Boffin pointing to the north-east.

That was different. Tracer shot in the air was our flotilla signal of distress. It was an extremely efficient method of calling attention to oneself, the tracer leaping skywards being visible for a great distance in good visibility. Later it came to be very generally adopted in Coastal Forces flotillas.

'Starboard wheel.'

'Steer North forty-five degrees East, Coxswain.'

'North forty-five degrees East, sir.'

We sped shorewards in the direction of the tracer. There had been but one short burst. Few had seen it; I had not. Whether or not this was a signal of distress from 78 will perhaps never be known. At the time of writing it is still mere speculation. It might have been fired from the shore, a bare three miles away. Certain it is that no other shots were seen, though we raced to the estimated position of the firing. If it was *78*, continued firing in the air would have been expected. Possibly more were fired, but the tracer may have been enveloped in the thick mist.

Viewed in the light of later knowledge this was a disaster. At the time we were comparatively unconcerned. We had no reason to suppose that *78* was in dire distress. We thought her W/T was out of action, that if she had fired in the air it was with a view to rendezvousing, especially as she had apparently not repeated the signal.

We stopped and in the ensuing silence listened. There was nothing to be heard except the faintest bumble to the north and north-east. If that was George, he was going strong and a good way off. If he were in trouble we would hear his engines near by, or his guns. So we thought. There was nothing. We listened with the hydrophone. The trawlers could be heard intermittently to the south, stopping and starting, maintaining the same bearing. Evidently they were moving

296

around slowly in the same position, further evidence of their discomfiture.

A signal came through. It was from Harpy Lloyd, who was investigating the Hook of Holland, ten miles to the north of us, with a unit of MTBs.

'Two E-boats stopped in position …'

A quick look at the chart showed them to be just north of the Hook. Exactly what we had been praying for. Blast this fog! I sent a signal in reply:

'Am proceeding from position … to find and attack E-boats.'

We bumbled north as fast as the fog would allow. It got worse. Off the Hook it was an impenetrable blanket. It was hopeless. We could find nothing in this. We stopped in the hope that we might hear something by ear or hydrophone. Nothing! The silence of the grave! Soon it would begin to dawn. We began to creep out, to head for home. A few miles clear of the land the fog vanished as if by magic. With little to go on I was, nevertheless, worrying about *78*. Something intuitive, unreasoning, hammered at the back of my brain. Anxiety, unwelcome, unbidden, was there. Here was an opportunity to continue the search.

'We'll nip back to the scene of the action and fire a lot of tracer in the air,' I said to Boffin. 'It's only twelve miles; we can just do it before dawn. If by any chance he went gash[5] around there, he'll see it and answer.'

This we did. Burst after burst of red tracer roared heavenwards from our twin Oerlikons. There was no reply. Just before first light we finally turned for home, mentally satisfied. If they were in trouble there, they must have seen us. It was clear now, as clear as it had been thick before. We roared home across the North Sea in the slowly gathering light of a grey dawn.

'I expect we'll meet *78* at the Sunk Light,' said Boffin.

'Just about,' I replied. But still there was that gnawing anxiety at the back of my head. We tied up in the dock. No, George had not got in yet. We gave details of the fight. We had breakfast, baths. Shaved and dressed. I met Boffin again.

'I expect he went gash in one engine,' I said; 'he wouldn't be in for another two hours in that case.'

'That's about it,' Boffin replied.

5. Went gash meant broken down.

Two hours later there was still no news. We went to SOO's office to see if the Cork Light vessel had rung up with anything to report. Nothing.

'He may have had two engines knocked out,' said Boffin. 'If so he wouldn't be here for three or four hours yet.'

'Maybe that's it,' I said. 'Or maybe his remaining plums packed up on the way over.'

But we could not conceal from each other the anxiety in our eyes.

'Could he have hit a mine on his way home, do you think?' I said.

'There's always a chance,' said Boffin.

The minor casualties and damage in the other boats were forgotten, unimportant in the increasing anxiety.

An aircraft search was instituted without result. Our gloom deepened. In the afternoon we laid plans for our own search. They might have hit a mine or be near the Buiten Bank still, though the chances of finding them were low. The Sixth Flotilla searched the western half of the return journey. We swept the eastern half, ending up quartering the scene of the action firing tracer in the air repeatedly. No reply except star-shell, flares and tracer from the nearby Dutch coast. In the early morning we headed sadly home. There was nothing more we could do.

Bitterly I taxed myself for not having delivered the depth-charge attack myself. In the increasing westerly wind, keeping watch alone in the dustbin, I communed with myself. Forlorn and self-tormenting was my mood. Though I could not reconstruct what had happened, something impelled me to bid 'good-bye' to George. In my mood of self-abasement, it seemed unforgivable that it was he and not I. It seemed that by not being killed or captured with him I had let my friend down.

George had been straight and simple and brave. So full of life, so keen on his job. Of all the people that I knew Conrad's praise of the Anglo-Saxon male seemed most applicable to him. A man of courage, initiative and hardihood, yet so little stained by the excesses of many virtues.

We could not construct an adequate theory as to the loss of *78*. The short outburst of firing, the fact that the boat appeared to have disengaged satisfactorily, the almost negligible attempt, if any, to attract our attention; how to reconcile these observations with her non-appearance? Had she hit the trawler, or a sweep perhaps? If so we must have seen something of it at the time. Had she been hit in the engine room and stopped? If so surely she would have been able to attract our attention.

We still do not know at the time of writing what happened. We only have scraps of guarded information to go on. They are as follows:

The German wireless reported that they had picked up the crew of a speed boat off the Dutch coast hanging on to the wreckage of their craft. The First Lieutenant got word home that he had been badly wounded with the Coxswain in the dustbin, and that George Duncan had been killed beside him. From another prisoner we had the mysterious message that *78* had done what the Fourth had done at Dover, a reference to the grounding of the whole unit.

It would seem therefore that *78* received a most unlucky blast of fire in the dustbin, killing the Captain, wounding and knocking out the First Lieutenant and the Coxswain. With the 'brains' of the ship out of action she had careered on at over forty knots, no one had recovered sufficiently, or with sufficient intelligence to stop her or guide her away from the enemy shore, before she had struck the sandbanks less than five miles away, a matter of under eight minutes. It seems to be the only theory that even approximately fits the facts. Later the First Lieutenant recovered sufficiently to destroy the boat. They were picked out of the water from amidst the wreckage next morning. Some day we may know the truth. The only thing that I am quite certain of is that George pressed home his attack to the limit and with success. No man could have engaged the enemy more closely, the Navy's time-honoured endeavour. Thus he died.

George Duncan's sad death ends my father's book. The last words must have been written in the first two weeks of April 1943 before he himself was killed in action on the night of the 13/14 April.

The loss of *MGB 78* and his friend and long serving brother-in-arms George Duncan weighed heavily upon Hitch's conscience. Given the uncertainty about what had happened to *78* a Board of Enquiry was ordered. The two issues in front of the Board were what had happened to *78* and whether the depth charge attack ordered by the Senior Officer was justified in the circumstances.

The Court heard the evidence of Hitch himself, Sub-Lieutenant Rodney Sykes, commanding *81*, Lieutenant K.H. Perry, who was out as a guest in *81* with Sykes, Boffin Campbell who had been a passenger in *77* with Hitch and Sub-Lieutenant J.D. Dixon, the

Commanding Officer of *60*. They had all read Hitch's Report of Proceedings on the action and declared themselves in complete agreement with it as a fair description of what had happened.

The questioning surrounded the issues of whether *78* had successfully delivered its depth charge attack and why it had then disappeared, whether it had been *78* firing tracer into the air as a distress signal that had been spotted by some boats, and whether breaking off the search to pursue the E-boat report had been justified. After hearing the evidence the Board's conclusion was brief:

> The President and members of the Board were satisfied that under the circumstances adequate steps were taken at all stages to search for *MGB 78* and the loss is regarded as one of the misfortunes of war.

That was not quite the end of the matter. Rear Admiral Hext Rogers forwarded the findings of the Board of Enquiry to the Commander-in-Chief Nore and he in turn forwarded them to the Secretary of the Admiralty with the following covering memorandum:

> It is conjectured that *MGB 78* sustained some damage as a result of collision with one of the enemy's vessels or some other cause unknown, the extent of which was not realised until no call for help could be made owing to the W/T being out of action and low visibility preventing the use of visual signalling.
>
> Nore Operational Memorandum 113 purposely leaves a wide discretion to the officer on the spot as to the degree of risk which may justifiably be accepted. In this case the object of the operation was to cover mine laying by MLs, and would have been sufficiently served by engaging the patrol trawlers with gunfire. Lieutenant-Commander Hichens, however, would have been fully justified in seeking to destroy one of them if the conditions favoured a surprise attack, eg if one of the trawlers was isolated from her consorts. Available evidence does not indicate that *MGB 78* was overwhelmed by gunfire, but a depth charge attack on a formed body of ships in line abreast is necessarily a risky one, and requires more favourable conditions than were present on this occasion. It is proposed to inform Lieutenant-Commander Hichens accordingly.

This politely phrased criticism of Hitch's decision to order a depth charge attack was rejected by the Admiralty. Captain D.M. Lees,[6] then DDO(C), in a covering memorandum dated 29 October 1942, wrote:

I do not concur with C-in-C Nore's covering remarks and the sentence gives a fair indication of the lack of offensive spirit in the C-in-C's office. MGBs cannot destroy trawlers by gunfire. They can do so with depth charges. Accordingly Lieutenant-Commander Hichens planned his operation so that three of his MGBs created a diversion from up moon whilst his fourth boat carried out a surprise depth charge attack from down moon. All Coastal Forces actions are risky and it is considered:

(a) That the risk taken by Lieutenant-Commander Hichens was justifiable.

(b) That it would be a great mistake to damp the ardour of the gallant officers serving afloat in Coastal Forces by administering a reprimand for what was, in fact, a well planned operation.

It must be realised that Coastal Forces actions cannot be fought without occasional losses and one would have expected Commanders-in-Chief to back up their Senior Officers when such losses occur instead of reprimanding them.

Below this forthright dissent from a senior staff officer in the Admiralty is written by hand:

Approved. I would like to see a draft which makes clear that their Lordships do not hold Lieutenant-Commander Hichens to blame.

On the 18 November a letter was sent to the Commander-in-Chief, Nore by the Secretary of the Admiralty.

Their Lordships are not disposed to blame Lieutenant-Commander Hichens for the loss of *MGB 78* and it appears to them that the risks taken in this case were justifiable. They consider that anything in the nature of a reprimand in these circumstances would tend to discourage

---

6. DDO(C) stood for Deputy Director Operations (Coastal). One of his sons, Sir David Lees, by the long arm of chance is a long standing business acquaintance of mine and colleague on the Takeover Panel.

the excellent offensive spirit which has so often been shown by the Coastal Forces under your command, a result which, their Lordships appreciate, you would deprecate strongly.

By the command of their Lordships. S.H. Phillips.

There was a sequel to this judgement. David James, who was taken prisoner after his own boat was lost in February 1943, met Sub-Lieutenant Eggleston, George Duncan's first lieutenant in *78*, in a prisoner of war camp. Eggleston confirmed that they had dropped their depth charge but that George had been killed outright on the run in. They had fired tracer into the air vertically but shortly after-wards the ship's company had had to leave their sinking craft after hitting a sand bank. Hence no further firing. After several hours in the sea, all bar George had been picked up by the Germans.

It was also clarified after the war that the depth charge had been dropped right under a trawler's stem and she had sunk. Thus, in spite of the tragic loss of Duncan and his boat, the depth charge attack had achieved its objective.

Hitch had been in action on the night of the 2/3 October and had gone out again on the afternoon of the 3rd in his search for *78*, to return in the small hours of the 4th. Yet he was called upon again to take a unit to sea on the afternoon of the 5 October when a signal from the Admiralty was received at *Beehive* to say that a large merchant vessel with an escort had left Boulogne and was pro-ceeding north-east. Presumably *77* was not in a fit state to go to sea again because Hitch went out in Boffin Campbell's *76*, accompa-nied by Tom Ladner's *75* and no less than five MTBs, *30, 69, 70, 241* and *29*. This joint patrol was aimed at giving the MGBs the chance to create a diversion while the MTBs could stalk the larger prey. It didn't quite work out that way on this occasion.

The unit arrived at the designated position off the Dutch coast at 2345, cut their engines and set hydrophone watch. Almost imme-diately they heard the sound of propellers from the south-west. They didn't think that this could be the convoy they were waiting for which was not due to pass through their position until 0130. They had orders to avoid contacting patrols until the arrival of the main target, so Hitch ordered the unit to withdraw on silent engines to a rendezvous about three or four miles to the north-west of the original position. As they were doing so, with their main engines still cut to keep silence, they were attacked by two German torpedo boats, approximately 600 tons each, and a number of E-boats. It seems likely that the Germans either had intelligence of their coming or had observed them and laid an ambush. Hitch thought afterwards that possibly they had been spotted when they had briefly turned on recognition lights at the rendezvous point. However as it was, both MGBs and MTBs were at a severe disadvantage because their powered gun turrets would not function until their main engines were started and it took time to gather speed, their best defence against enemy gunfire. In the confusion, *MTBs 29* and *30* collided with sufficiently severe damage to *29* that, although she started on her way home, she disappeared. One of the other MTBs put a torpedo into one of the E-boats and sank it, an unusual event because E-boats normally had too shallow a draught to be successfully attacked by torpedoes and, indeed, were not regarded as sufficiently important enemy craft to expend a torpedo on.

MGBs 76 and *75* suffered considerable shellfire damage while they were disengaging from the scene of the action. They became separated. *75* was so badly damaged that Tom Ladner took her behind a buoy they came across where she was out of sight of the pursuing E-boats, laid low until they had gone and then limped back to Felixstowe on one engine. *76* received hits from a number of incendiary shells which started a fire. This was successfully put out and she also made for the English coast, waiting short of the convoy route at 0400 for fear of running into further E-boat patrols, and then starting again at 0600 when the coast was likely to be clear. At 0635 there was a sudden explosion and the entire canopy around the cockpit blew out and the deck above the petrol tanks burst open. An incendiary shell may have lain dormant in one of the petrol tanks, exploding more than two hours after it had been fired.

The entire boat was ablaze within thirty seconds, apart from a small section forward where the crew gathered. It was realized that the boat would have to be abandoned. The whole of the crew, with the exception of the motor mechanic who was killed by an exploding shell, took to the float and were rescued an hour later by *MGBs 61* and *64* who, returning from a quite separate patrol, found them, having seen the fire at a great distance.

That is the bare outline of what must have been Hitch's most unsuccessful action during his time in MGBs. Two eyewitness accounts survive which are worth repeating.

Although his account confuses the events of the 2/3 October, when George Duncan was killed, with the events of the 5th/6th, it is interesting to record Tom Ladner's description of what happened to *MGB 75* this night, contained in a letter he wrote me:

> Along the coast were large navigational buoys which could be mistaken for small vessels. They marked the shoreline, which was a sand bar. I myself was under very heavy fire and I headed close to the next buoy and stopped. The convoy moved on and I could see in the dark that Hitch was attacking it from the other side of the convoy with torpedoes and all attention was directed to his boats. When the convoy had moved off and quiet was restored I hung by the buoy and tried to assess what had happened to my boat. We had three gunners who were wounded, two engines out of action and one engine reasonably operational as far as I could tell.
>
> I waited around for some time to see if someone would come to check up on us. ... When I concluded that no one was coming, on one engine I started to return to base. It is hard to recollect how much time passed but when daylight came and as we approached the English coast we met some offshore patrol vessels who communicated with our base and finally someone came out to tow us back in.
>
> I could never understand why Hitch did not send somebody out from the base or otherwise to pick us up or help but then I did not know what his problems were.

Hitch's problems made it impossible for him to send succour to Tom Ladner.

The best account of what happened to *76* came to me from John Motherwell, another Canadian, who joined the Eighth Flotilla as a spare officer the very day that the unit had put to sea, the 5 October.

> It was my understanding that we were to be off Blankenberg at midnight and the tanker was expected in half an hour to an hour after that. We got to our intercept point and all the engines were shut down so that the primitive hydrophones could be used. This involved putting a receiver on a long pipe over the side in a bucket. The first report said that the operator could hear many propellers close by and

just then the enemy shooting started. They were obviously there first, expecting us. I am unable to tell you any of what happened on the surface around us because I was confined to the wheelhouse to help keep track of the navigation and there were a lot of alterations of course. We were hit before we got moving and a fire was extinguished in the tank space. We withdrew and then tried to go back but were again hit and I hit the deck and saw the flash of a tracer passing through our hull just below the wardroom hatch about a foot below my nose. I was then briefly on the bridge and saw multicoloured tracers going back and forth, the German ones passed above us and our own red were going towards what I think was a trawler. There was also a parachute flare burning, an eerie and dangerous sight.

Lieutenant-Commander Hichens was standing on top of the canopy holding on to the mast. Our fire broke out again and once more methyl bromide extinguishers were used to put it out. We withdrew shortly after this and went to a rendezvous point but no one else showed up. I did first aid in the wardroom for two of the crew who had received minor flesh wounds on their arms. The sickly smell of one hundred octane petrol was very strong and we smelled smoke again and started out through the mess deck when there was an explosion and we climbed out of the forward hatch to find the rest of the crew all gathering there on the foredeck. The whole mid-section of the boat was on fire and our ammunition in ready use started exploding.

Lieutenant-Commander Hichens was very composed and ordered the Carley float over the side and the crew were then ordered to go over the side. One poor lad panicked because he couldn't swim and ran back towards the stern and I think he was blown over by exploding ammunition. The rest of us who could swim took turns hanging on to the side of the Carley float, which was nearly submerged by those who couldn't swim. Lieutenant-Commander Hichens showed great leadership and courage and kept everyone from panicking. Shortly after we left the boat there was a great explosion that blew it in half and I remember seeing the two pounder pom-pom on its turret mounting dropping off the bow section shortly after this. The fire was covering what was left of the stern section and I believe that the engines got blown out of the bottom. The wisdom of telling us to go over the windward side was very apparent then. Another thing was glaringly apparent as everyone, excepting Lieutenant-Commander Hichens, had taken off their goon suits and were without flotation. They were just too heavy and too hot so no one even had time to get back into them.

I really don't know how long we were in the water but it became light and shortly after we could hear engines in the distance. Lieutenant-Commander Hichens thought they would be friendly but I recall him reminding everyone to give only rate and number if they weren't. We were now worried as to whether they would see us as the wind had blown the still slightly burning and floating bow section of 76 some distance away, I think close to a mile. Lieutenant-Commander Hichens soon recognised the sound as friendly and it turned out that they were two of his old Sixth Flotilla boats. They went to the bow and then shortly after saw us and came over to us. It turned out that they had seen the reflection of the fire from their patrol area some distance away and decided to come and see what it was. I remember that I was too weak to climb the scrambling net and had to be helped up but was soon wrapped in a warm blanket with a large tot of rum for medicinal purposes. We were soon back at *Beehive*.

It was an ugly introduction to Coastal Forces work for Motherwell and few young officers can have been thrown, quite literally, in at the deep end as he was on their very first night. He survived this awful experience to write to me from his home town, Calgary, Alberta.

Hitch must have been mortified to lose a second gunboat within three days, even though the casualties were surprisingly light. Unfortunately we have no record of what he thought about this disaster. His Report of Proceedings has not been traced and he had not reached this point in his book when he was killed.

Chapter Fourteen

Final Winter
October 1942 – March 1943

From mid-October onwards the chances of good operational weather steadily reduced and the Eighth Flotilla, although putting to sea for the grind of regular patrols, were not again in action until the end of February 1943. That makes it a good moment to pause and consider what life at *Beehive* was like in that fourth winter of the war and the third winter for Hitch in Coastal Forces.

By all accounts *Beehive* was a happy place in spite of the shadow that must have been cast across the Eighth Flotilla by its two losses. Peter Dickens had arrived in September to replace Harpy Lloyd as Senior Officer of the Twenty-First MTB Flotilla. Hitch and Peter Dickens were the two dominant Senior Officers in the base, setting the tone for the officers and crews of the Coastal Forces boats based there, though it would be quite wrong to exclude Tubby Cambridge from a leading role. With his great girth and remarkably small cap, he was both a genial and a commanding figure and he led the MLs with skill. No one who understands what Coastal Forces achieved during the war would denigrate the role of MLs, principally dedicated to mine laying, but they were not the sharp end of Coastal Forces and, rightly or wrongly, it was the MGBs and MTBs whose exploits *Beehive* personnel were particularly proud of. Thus it was to Hitch and Peter that they looked as role models.

Of course the man who ultimately had responsibility for the proper working of *Beehive* as a Coastal Forces base was Tommy Kerr, the retired commander called back for the war. Everyone liked Tommy Kerr and it was clear that he had exactly the right touch for dealing with the disparate components of his command.

To the very young men who went out night after night to patrol and fight he was an avuncular figure who looked after their best interests, fought their battles for them with authority and who was there to take the salute for each and every boat as it exited the dock. They knew he would also be there at whatever hour of the night or morning they returned.

Beehive had a range of specialist staff officers reporting to Kerr, including the Staff Officer Operations (SOO) responsible for transmitting C-and-C Nore's orders, briefing captains, and ensuring that they had all the available intelligence about what they faced each night. Most of the rest of the staff officers were involved in the maintenance of the boats. In Hitch's view the most important of these was 'Pop' Perry, his old friend from *St Christopher*. Perry was a co-conspirator with Hitch in the modification of MGBs in the teeth of Admiralty indifference, backed to the hilt by Tommy Kerr. Another conspirator was Lieutenant John Woods, the base Gunnery Officer, who modified the single Oerlikon mounting to carry two guns. A key player in the base staff was Lieutenant Commander H.R. Lillicrap. The delightfully named Lillicrap, inventor of the Lillicrap Patent Razor, as one brother officer discovered to his great delight, was in charge of the shipwrights. Since HMS *Warrior* was commissioned in 1860, the Royal Navy had steadily lost its wooden warships, so that by the time of the Second World War shipwrights accustomed to working in wood must have been rather rare. Lillicrap was clearly an exception. Peter Dickens in *Night Action* remembers him well.

Old Lillicrap reigned over the Shipwrights in the great hanger along the hard and in him past and present met. Our boats could hardly be more uptodate, yet they were built of wood as Nelson's had been and strangely satisfying were the sounds of plane, saw and mallet on chisel, the feel of ankle deep shavings and sawdust, and the sweet smell of newly worked 'onduras me'ogany'. Lillicrap's standards were so high that it was hard to prise a job away from him until it had reached perfection, whatever the urgency, and his decision on what should or should not be done was adamantine.

His weakness was the Battle of Jutland as Henry Franklin, having frequent occasion to be in his office, discovered. 'What's that you were telling us about the *Queen Mary* blowing up, Mr Lillicrap?' Ten minutes later the master carpenter would shake himself back into the present and ask ' Was there something you wanted?' 'Well, I just thought it might improve our fighting efficiency if we had a shelf in the ward room with holes shaped for Gordon's gin bottles.'

Tommy Kerr had another very large group of base personnel whose memories did not go back to Jutland. These were the Wrens. By this stage of the war almost every job in the Navy onshore that could be done by a woman was so done. They didn't just serve in wardroom and galley and type reports. All vehicles were driven by Wrens and boats' crews for shore bases were also Wren manned. Tractor drivers who hauled MGBs and MTBs up the slips for maintenance work had Wren drivers, and plotting rooms working on German wireless intercepts and radar monitoring were dominantly Wren manned.

Cameron Gough, another young sub-lieutenant joining the Eighth Flotilla at *Beehive* in the autumn of 1942, commented:

> There were a great many Wrens round about the place and very many attractive ones. There was some kind of semi-secret establishment where the Wrens had been chosen for their brains. Most of them had university degrees and, strangely, most, if not all, were very attractive. Perhaps I have got this wrong and they were chosen for their looks and happened to have brains and university degrees.

Wrens, of course, threw up disciplinary issues of which most naval officers, particularly those as old as Tommy Kerr, had little previous experience. The extra-marital relationships which inevitably arose in those wartime conditions were dealt with by Wren officers. However, there were many other rules to break and Tommy Kerr had to enforce base discipline. Another young officer remembers him at Captain's Table, the routine where by minor disciplinary offences are dealt with by the Captain without much more formality than that induced by the presence of a very senior rating, normally the Master at Arms, responsible for the ship's discipline, bringing each offender forward to stand rigidly to attention in front of the Captain seated at his table. On this occasion the delinquent Wren resorted to the oldest defence known to woman and dissolved in tears. 'Don't you cry at me, young woman' said Commander Kerr and gave her ten days stoppage of leave.

The first lieutenants and spare officers of the boats, living at the Cliff Hotel well outside the confines of the base, had a good social life at *Beehive* when they weren't preparing their boats for sea or out on patrol. There were games of rugby and hockey; the hockey sometimes mixed. Scottish dancing also exercised the young men and women. David James remembers duck shooting in the salt marshes of Suffolk, and I can remember going with my father to shoot pheasant on somebody's broad acres, travelling there in that wonderful Aston Martin with its rich oily odours. Few birds were shot that day, no doubt because birds were not 'put down' during the war so that only the occasional wild bird would have been flushed over the guns. I have a clear recollection of Hitch only shooting one bird and that it fell inconveniently into an enormous patch of brambles from which even the most intrepid spaniels were unable to retrieve it.

Hitch's own life must have been divided between his duties as Flotilla Senior Officer who, after going to sea, had reports to write, operations to prepare for and the development of MGBs, the subject of an extended paper engagement with the Admiralty. Somehow he also found time to write *We Fought Them in Gunboats* which he started in October 1942, and to then go home to his wife and children in the little villa we rented overlooking the sea. I don't know how often he got home. Bad weather would have meant the cancellation of operations and an evening with his family. My mother and I were always there, for I was a attending a local school a short walk from our little house. My brother was at his preparatory school and home only for the holidays.

We did occasionally go to London but I think it was always because there was something that my father had to do there, a visit to the Admiralty, or of course those awe inspiring moments when we went to Buckingham Palace for an investiture. I remember sitting with my mother in the Investiture Room while, somewhat above us, the King stood on a dais pinning medals on officers queuing up to reach him, taking the decorations from a cushion held by a deferential equerry. We caught sight of my father taking his turn up the sloping ramp and were then reunited with him in a great crowd of Army, Navy and Air Force officers, all standing around looking cheerful with their new awards pinned on their chests. Family legend recalls King George as saying to Hitch on one of these occasions: 'What! You again!'

310

I was always aware of the arrival of another decoration for my father, even at the tender age of five or six. This was because my teddy bear, a favourite toy and close companion, put up ribbons and rosettes whenever my father did. Teddy remained a much decorated bear in my toy box for many years and still has a place of repose in my daughter's room in my Dorset home.

It must have been a strange life for men like Hitch, out at sea night after night, all too frequently in action, returning to their families and the normal humdrum life of wartime England, with its shortages and inconveniences.

In his book *The Little Ships*, Gordon Holman, a fellow Cornishman, gave an interesting contemporaneous account of life in Coastal Forces, and it is worth quoting his description of how he met Hitch in October 1942.

My first meeting with Hitch was at a Coastal Forces base on the East Coast. I had heard much of him, not only in official communiqués but from senior RN officers closely associated with Coastal Forces. I had been impressed by the way they acknowledge his pre-eminence in all directions where small fighting craft were concerned. Many times I had heard them say, 'Well, Hitch says ...' and they obviously regarded that as the last word on the subject.

I was directed to a large, old fashioned building where I was told I should find the Senior Officer. It was a typical naval establishment, with well polished floors and a generally shiny and bare appearance.

When I entered I found, standing in the middle of a large room, one naval officer – an RNVR Lieutenant Commander. He received me very civilly but with no warmth. The Commanding Officer was away and he was acting for him in his absence. Unfortunately he knew nothing about my visit but if there was anything he could do for me he would be happy to do it.

From a smaller room, the door of which was partly open, I could hear other voices, obviously in earnest discussion. I suspected that I had interrupted a conference and began to feel that I was in for an altogether unfortunate day. Then, as the Lieutenant Commander half turned, I caught sight of his medal ribbons and had an even bigger shock. There could be no mistaking the DSO and bar and the DSC, also with something added. Some extremely rapid thinking convinced me that I had met Hitch.

311

I said that I hoped I would not prove a nuisance and, if it was convenient, I would like to meet some of the officers and ratings.

'Certainly,' said the Lieutenant Commander, without enthusiasm.

Then a curious thing happened. Hitch said, 'I suppose you would like to see some of the boats?' adding, 'Have you ever been in any of them?' I said I had and he, as a matter of polite conversation, asked, 'Who did you go with?'

'Dunstan Curtis,' I said.

It was an answer that had a remarkable effect on the Lieutenant Commander. For the first time he looked very keenly at me and said, 'When did you go with Dunstan Curtis?'

'When we went to St. Nazaire,' I told him.

Hitch looked at me silently for a moment — almost as if he did not believe me — then he turned on his heel and crossing to the half open door said, in a way that embarrassed me yet made me feel very proud, 'Here, you fellows, come and meet a bloody fool who went to St Nazaire in Dunstan Curtis's boat!'

It was not the introduction that I had planned or intended but Hitch's words admitted me to the brotherhood of that eager, cheerful company of young officers and began a day that I shall remember as long as I live.

Holman's presence at one of Coastal Forces' most gallant and bloody operations, clearly opened a door at *Beehive*.

Several of his contemporaries remember one aspect of Hitch's frame of mind at that time. Perhaps it is best summarized by Peter Dickens in *Night Action* where he recalls a conversation about what they would do after the war.

I took the 'flu and Robert Hichens came to cheer me up. I asked him what were his plans for after the war and he replied, so casually that I could not at first put a meaning to his words, 'I shan't survive the war'.

I said something banal like 'Oh, go on' but he was not fooling and slightly amplified his point though without particular emphasis or philosophical analysis. 'I'm quite certain of it; but not to worry', and he smiled.

I stared rudely, trying to understand but failing. If I knew anything in that line it was that I should survive, not through logic but merely that I could not comprehend not doing so; and as I stared a conviction that had been growing on me during our months together in *Beehive*, that Robert not only stood head and shoulders above the crowd but possessed the elements of greatness, became fixed in my mind permanently. Despite our being nominally equal as Senior Officers of MGBs and MTBs respectively, I acknowledged his superiority with uncharacteristic disinterest, and still hated to be thought that he and I were in any way comparable.

Over this period, there were, of course, a number of changes in the senior personnel of the Eighth Flotilla and, indeed, changes in boats. Tommy Ladner had gone on long leave to Canada after 75 was so badly beaten up on the night of the 5/6 October 1942. Some months later he was to return and take command of one of the new Dog Boats, heading for the Mediterranean and very considerable personal success as a commanding officer. Boffin Campbell took over 75 when she returned from her substantial refit, his own boat 76 having been sunk on the morning of the 6 October. Cameron Gough joined him as first lieutenant. He was later to command 81, by then renumbered as *MTB 416*.

In November 1942, *MGB 111*, under the command of John Mathias, came to replace George Duncan's 78 lost in October, and a few months later he was to have as his very young first lieutenant, Midshipman James Shadbolt, of whom more later. *MGB 112* joined at the end of November, replacing 76, under the command of Derek Sidebottom, always know as 'Flatters' possibly because he often spoke of going 'flat out', but more plausibly a shortening of Flatarse, a play on his surname. Finally, in January 1943, Bussy Carr rejoined Hitch in command of *MGB 115*, with Eric Archer as his first lieutenant.

There was one other significant change in personnel. George Curtis, who had been Hitch's coxswain since they commissioned *MGB 64* in February 1941, finally succumbed to the appalling stress of life at the sharp end of MGB warfare. With considerable moral bravery he told Hitch one evening in January 1943 that he didn't think he could face further duty in *MGB 77* and asked to be given a change of posting. Hitch, who may well have seen some signs of impending trouble, immediately agreed and George went ashore, followed by a brief period of nervous breakdown, from which he recovered to join destroyers later in the war and to continue his long service, ending as a chief petty officer. He had been with Hitch in every action in which *64* and *77* fought and it had been his skill and judgement that pulled off the depth charge attack on a tanker off Alderney in the summer of 1942, and indeed his sharp ears that had picked up the sound of E-boat engines in November 1941, resulting in the capture of *S.41*. Hitch must have been very sad to see him go. His replacement as senior coxswain was Tom 'Dollar' Hartland. Another coxswain remembered him:

> Smashing man but his crew wasn't smart like ours. They were always in action and getting hit and, funny thing, wherever they were hit there was the rum bottle and it had to be written off 'lost by enemy action'. I said 'What a pity the rum bottle got broken Tom', and he said 'Yes, but I just managed to save that little bit out of the bottom'.

Hartland sounds like a man after my father's own heart. No doubt he was hand picked.

What was life at sea like during that winter of 1942/43 for the men in the MTBs and MGBs based at Felixstowe? Nasty, brutish and short? Perhaps a closer description would have been boring, freezing and wet. E-boats were less frequently operating on the British coastal convoy routes and convoys had much strengthened escorts by that winter. The coming of improved radar to the destroyers made it impossible for the E-boats to lay ambush as they had before by lying silent, waiting for the convoy to pass before they pounced.

There were broadly speaking three types of patrol that engaged most of the MGBs time. One was to accompany minelaying MLs and stand guard over them while they laid their dangerous cargoes along the Dutch, Belgian and French coasts, before being released to go looking for trouble, while the MLs headed for home. Then there were the Z patrols, the Z line being seven or eight miles further offshore than the coastal convoy routes on the British side. Along this line, given improved intelligence gathered about E-boat movements, MGBs would either lie in wait or move slowly on their silenced engines to position themselves for the interception of any E-boats picked up either by shore radar, destroyer borne radar on the convoy routes, or through wireless interceptions. The latter grew steadily more sophisticated through the growth of Y stations manned by Wren personnel, intercepting German R/T from E-boats on very high frequencies. The E-boats from the beginning talked freely amongst themselves about their courses, speeds, intentions, and sometimes even their damage. Until January 1942 the system suffered from the disadvantage that the only clues Y stations had to the actual whereabouts of E-boats was the VHF range of the station or the hearing of the E-boat talk. After that date, VHF/D/F towers were set up at the Y stations and it became possible to obtain not only bearings but also fixes on individual E-boats. All of this would be fed through to the waiting MGBs, giving them chances of interception undreamt of in the early years. Aerial reconnaissance also played a major role in tracking E-boats attempting to penetrate the Z line through to the convoy routes. If an E-boat patrol left before dusk there was a fair chance that it would be picked up by air reconnaissance and liaison with the RAF steadily improved.

It was the joint patrols with MTBs that perhaps gave MGBs their greatest chance of seeing action. By 1942/43 the Germans were moving little freight by sea, but what they did move they moved at night and under heavy escort. A typical night convoy would consist of only one or two merchant ships, mainly iron ore carriers from Sweden, or return cargoes of coal, escorted by as many as six to eight warships. Thus attacks on such convoys were bloody affairs, unless they could be stalked by the torpedo carrying MTBs and sunk at a distance which permitted the MTBs to retire safely at speed.

When MGBs and MTBs worked together the standard tactics were for the MGBs to carry out a diversionary attack, circling the convoy and its escorts at high speed, firing into them, not with the hope of doing much serious damage but with every chance of distracting enemy eyes while the MTBs came close enough to launch their torpedoes. Such diversionary tactics, though seldom degenerating into the close actions at which MGBs could hope to destroy the enemy, where nevertheless likely to produce their crop of casualties, and occasionally the vulnerable little wooden boats received damage from which they were either slowed or caught fire.

Such an action was fought by Hitch on the 27/28 February 1943. Hitch, as Senior Officer, took a large mixed unit over to the Dutch coast, consisting of MGBs accompanied by MTBs and escorting MLs. He was in his own boat, 77, with by David James in 79, Kelly Cowley in 81 and John Mathias in 111. There were four boats of the

Fourth MTB Flotilla, *70, 32, 69* and *72* under their own Senior Officer, John Weedon, and three minelaying MLs of the Fifty-First Flotilla. The MGBs were to escort the minelaying MLs until they had finished their lay and were then free to look for trouble. The MTBs were to look for an enemy convoy of which Nore evidently had intelligence. Hitch was not in overall command but there is little doubt that it was understood that the Senior Officers of the MTBs and MLs would fall in with any request for cooperation that Hitch made.

In the story of this complex operation it is best to start with what happened first to the MTBs. Having left Felixstowe at 1615, approximately dusk, the MTBs, on reaching their assigned position off the Dutch coast at 2315, had switched to auxiliary engines to achieve silence, stopping from time to time to listen on hydrophones. Twenty minutes later, *MTB 70* noticed a large mine bumping down the side of the boat. It was floating very low in the water with four of its horns visible. It was of an old Dutch seven-horn type. It must have been an extraordinarily frightening moment to watch this black, sinister cylinder tapping its way down the side of the hull before disappearing into the darkness astern. The MTBs crept away at four knots, sighting no less than fourteen other mines in the process. They had by chance rendezvoused in a mine field and it must have shaken them.

Meanwhile the MLs proceeded to lay their own mine field, completing the operation at 0100 on the 28 February and then set course for home. The escorting MGBs parted company to join the search for the convoy and set hydrophone watch. Sydney Dobson, the Oerlikon loader in *111*, remembers sitting on the foredeck with his hydrophone over the side, listening for the convoy. Only seven minutes later Sydney heard noises on the hydrophone which he thought sounded like a large group of vessels. Hitch waited until direction and speed were clear and at 0136 proceeded south-east at twelve knots on silenced engines on an intercepting course. MGBs were well ahead of MTBs in the speed they could make on silenced engines in the winter of 1943. At 0145 they saw lights ahead, strung out from north to south, including what looked like some green navigation lights indicating that the enemy vessels were proceeding from north to south approaching the Dutch coast, because the MGBs could see their starboard navigation lights. Why an enemy convoy in the middle of the war should have had its navigation lights on remains a mystery. Presumably they were so close to their base that they thought it safe. They appeared to be moving at about six knots. Even more oddly, the escorting warships were all on the shoreward side of the convoy, rather than with some to seaward as one would have expected.

Hitch sent a W/T signal to the MTBs giving the enemy's position, course and speed, in the expectation that the MTBs would close and make a torpedo attack on this substantial target. Unfortunately the W/T was defective and the signal did not get through at once. It was not passed on by other boats until 0230. Hitch, unaware of this, believed that the job of the MGBs was to shadow the convoy rather than to attack it and to await the coming of the MTBs, which he believed to be close by. He was, of course, unaware that they had found themselves in the middle of a minefield and had moved well to the north to get clear of it. When the MGBs found themselves within three cables, 600 yards, of the oncoming merchantmen that the convoy was formed around, he decided to stop the MGB unit because it would have been difficult to move at so slow a speed shadowing from seaward. The alternative of turning away from the merchant ships would have meant presenting the boats' exhausts to the enemy and probably being heard. By that time, MGBs had a ship-to-ship radio system called a Hallicrafter, but one boat's Hallicrafter was defective that night so that 77 had to make a shaded lamp signal to her to warn her of the impending stop. Unfortunately the light must have reflected off some part of 77 because very shortly afterwards the escort to the eastward of the convoy challenged and then began to fire star shell and open up with heavier guns. The attempt to shadow unobserved had failed. There seemed little point in remaining under fire illuminated by star shell so the MGBs withdrew to the edge of the star shell area and then again proceeded south on a course parallel to the convoy.

Meanwhile the MTBs, having finally received the delayed enemy report from the MGBs, divided into two groups. *MTBs 32 and 72* proceeded across the line of the enemy convoy on its southward advance in order to wait in a suitable position and then attack from the shoreward side. *70 and 69* remained to seaward. The Senior Officer of the MTBs was still of the opinion that there was plenty of time to close the enemy and carry out a silent attack.

The MGB unit had by then lost sight of the convoy in poor visibility. *MGB 77*'s RDF set was defective. The convoy had switched off its lights. The hydrophone produced no contact. So at 0240 the unit proceeded further south at twelve knots to the entrance of the Hook of Holland. Here they lay in wait. At 0311 a red light was seen on the starboard bow which Hitch assumed to be one of the convoy switching on its navigation lights momentarily. This told him that the MGBs had got to the shoreward side of the convoy as he was now seeing a port navigation light and this was confirmed two minutes later when a star shell was fired from the westward. Hitch signalled the enemy position to the MTBs and suggested that he make a diversion, since it seemed likely that the convoy would shortly turn into the entrance to the Hook of Holland now less than a mile away. The MGBs cut their engines and lay in the path of the oncoming convoy, between it and the harbour. However, almost at once an escort vessel was sighted approaching from the northward which turned towards the unit, followed by two other escorts. These were apparently three trawlers or two trawlers and a minesweeper; substantial vessels. As it was apparent that the MGBs were in the line of advance, although as yet unsighted, Hitch got under way to engage. There was a sharp exchange of fire at the close range of a cable or less, with the enemy apparently hard hit as after some minutes his fire slackened considerably.

As the four boats roared into the attack, *MGB 79*, although not the junior boat, was TAC (Tail Arse Charlie) as the boat in the rear of any formation was known. Hitch had placed her there because she had on her stern the first experimental shoulder trained twin Oerlikon. The base staff at *Beehive* had developed this version of the gun in the teeth of Admiralty indifference or downright opposition to the suggestion that you could have a twin Oerlikon without the whole weight of a powered mounting. *79* apparently saw another target as the MGBs engaged. It was standard fighting instructions that, although the normal assumption was that when going into action you stayed in line ahead behind your Senior Officer and conformed to his movements, it was always open to an individual commanding officer who saw an opportunity he thought he ought to take to act upon it, regardless of the fact that his Senior Officer was unaware of this. The last boat in line was normally regarded as the most appropriate boat to detach itself in these circumstances. Whatever David James had seen which justified detaching himself from the unit, he ended up in desperate trouble. *MGB 79* was hit severely by gunfire from one of the escorts and her petrol tanks exploded. With her engines out of action and all power gone from the gun mountings, fire blazing from the wheelhouse, MGB 79 was helpless, except for the experimental hand worked twin Oerlikon and her two Lewis guns. The Oerlikon gunner was wounded and David, having little else to do with the boat dead in the water, ran aft and himself fought the twin Oerlikon until the flames from the engine room made the Oerlikon position on the stern untenable. He then ordered his Lewis gunners to fire tracer into the air – the Eighth Flotilla's distress signal – went round the depth-charges removing their primers, jettisoned the confidential books and ordered his crew, who had mustered on the bows, the only part of the boat not yet in flames, to jump. The W/T office was on fire and no signal could be sent. David had little expectation that his tracer fire would be observed in the heat of the battle that was going on visibly to the west. He ordered his crew to swim some forty yards away from the blazing boat and stay together, with the one life raft that had survived.

Meanwhile the other three MGBs had completed their turn round the stern of the enemy escorts and then, as star shell was being put up from all directions, including from the shore, with enemy fire increasing heavily, disengaged to the north-west. It shortly became apparent that MGB 79 was not in company and Hitch was about to signal her on the W/T when tracer was seen being fired vertically from the south-east, that is towards the enemy. He turned the unit round and almost at once saw a fierce blaze from the same position which he closed at high speed. Let me now quote his own words from his Report of Proceedings:

MGB 77 stopped thirty yards from the vessel and began to try to take the crew aboard, ordering MGB 81 to make smoke. The position was extremely unenviable since the MGBs were clearly illuminated by the ring of light caused by the fire and it was obvious that numerous enemy vessels were close by but could not be seen outside the ring of light, except that two of them, approximately a cable away, were showing single white lights which made their position clear. MGB 81 made smoke and circled again to make another burst of smoke but this was not of much avail as there was a moderate breeze from the side on which the enemy were clustered and the smoke immediately cleared.

The difficult task of getting the men on board in their heavy clothes was proceeded with. Fortunately *MGB 77* was able to get six and *MGB 111* one before the enemy's fire became so severe as to make it essential to move. It was impossible for the MGBs to retaliate as their propellers were stopped and therefore there was no power on their turrets, and also the enemy could not be seen except by their gun flashes, whereas the gunboats were clearly illuminated. The MGBs were able to remain close to the burning wreck for a matter of ten to fifteen minutes only because the enemy did not fire appreciably for the first nine or ten minutes. The only reason for this would appear to be that they thought it was E-boats performing the rescue work and not British boats. Later, however, more enemy vessels came in from the south-west and saw the gunboats clearly silhouetted and opened intensive fire.

The gunboats were hit at once and *MGB 77* set on fire and it was essential therefore to move off. Three or four men had to be left, including the two officers, but they were observed by the last boat in the line clambering on to a Carley float and in the bright light thrown from the fire there is little doubt they would have been picked up subsequently by the enemy vessels.

The MGBs proceeded at 0354 to the north-west, engaging enemy vessels on either side until out of range, illuminated by star shell throughout, and when they got beyond the limit of the star shell stopped with a view to extinguishing the fire in *MGB 77*. This was located in the W/T office which had been hit. It produced volumes of smoke but very little flame. It was finally extinguished, after using up all the fire extinguishers, by hacking a hole in the canopy top and continually pouring buckets of water down.

At 0415 the unit proceeded to return to harbour and at 0430 sighted two vessels moving slowly or stopped, which on investigation proved to be two MTBs, *70* and *69*. These joined up and the entire unit returned to harbour, arriving at 0630.

MGBs 77, 81 and *111* had eight wounded and had picked up seven of the personnel of *MGB 79*, two of whom were wounded, and another, the motor mechanic, was immediately killed by an Oerlikon shell on board *77*. All three boats were damaged in the hull and superficially on deck, *MGB 111* having her RDF aerial shot away. *MGB 111* also lost the use of both her turrets due to a hit in the engine room which bled the power pipes and received ten or twelve hits elsewhere, one of which damaged the pom-pom. *MGB 81* was hit in the engine room which put the Oerlikon turret out of action and received three other hits. *MGB 77* was hit in the engine room putting her telegraph out of action and in the tank space and several places on deck, including the W/T cabin which caught fire. The Oerlikon shell in the tank space made a very small hole and burst inside, which is somewhat unusual with German Oerlikon shells, making numerous holes in the port tank. Fortunately the tanks did not explode.

Thus the bare story of the rescue of most of the crew of *79* in the face of overwhelming enemy force. Fortunately Hitch's report of proceedings is not the only record we have of what happened that night. David James, in the delightful book he wrote after the war about his time in German prisoner-of-war camps and his two escapes, *A Prisoner's Progress*, in its first chapter describes how he came to be captured.

At 3am, having already seen the MLs off home, we ran into a small German convoy just off the Hook of Holland. In the course of the ensuing battle my boat was badly crippled and ultimately set on fire. Soon she was blazing from stem to stern, so we abandoned ship and swam about forty yards away, so that we and our rescuers, if any, should not be implicated if the tanks or depth-charges were to explode.

Almost at once, having seen our distress signals, Hitch and two other boats returned. It was an extraordinary scene. The burning boat shed a vivid light over the whole area, while shadowy flak trawlers circled around in the wings. On this brilliantly illuminated stage, surrounded by the enemy, Hitch calmly stopped engines and started to pick up survivors. By the grace of God the enemy must have taken our rescuers for E-boats, for it was some minutes before they opened fire.

Treading water in the background awaiting my turn, I began to have high hopes of being saved, but it seemed to be a maddeningly slow business hauling chaps aboard in their thick, water-logged clothes. Suddenly realising who we were, the trawlers opened up again and Hitch had to move off. He had picked up six men in circumstances of some peril; it had been a wondrous effort. I can see him still, calmly standing on the canopy directing operations. Six weeks later, at the height of his powers and fame, he was killed.

The moment our boats left was one I had long been anticipating, but it was nevertheless heart-rending. Then, seeing a Carley float with three men on it, I swam over and clung on. Almost at once, the boat commanded by Lieutenant John Matthias, RNVR, gallantly returned for another attempt. He stopped rather far off, then swung on main engines to come alongside. When he was pointing in our direction the trawlers opened up again – he had to forge ahead in a hurry – the Carley float was swept aside. His bow hit my shoulder ... bump, bump, bump, down the bottom ... this was clearly IT, the three screws couldn't possibly miss me ... still, better to be killed outright than to drown slowly ... hope I don't break his props or he'll have a job getting clear ... a roar overhead ... a double somersault like some bit of driftwood tossed by a mountain torrent, and the boat had passed me unscathed. I couldn't break surface in the confused water ... took deep breaths to hurry things up. Shouldn't all the past incidents of life flash past a drowning man? I began to summon them up – home, family, windjammer, ballet, Hitch, my boat ... odd the way even in death one has the urge to play the right part ... growing dimmer now, how easy it is to go ... a pale watery moon appeared and I found myself on the surface. Thirty yards away a familiar voice was saying, 'Look, Jack, there's the f*****g skipper.' I turned, saw the Carley float, and with a final effort reached it.

There are two men still alive today who served in *MGB 111* that night and have told me their story. James Shadbolt, as the very young first lieutenant of *MGB 111*, still a midshipman, was in his first action:

Although brightly lit by the blaze, there was a lot of smoke about to obscure what was going on. Both *111* and *77* stood by the burning MGB, pulling the crew out of the water, until the enemy came to life and started firing, at which point both Hitch and Mathias thought they had to pull out. I had run aft when I saw two men in the water on the side away from the fire who turned out to be David James and his coxswain. I threw them a heaving line and started to pull them in when Mathias ordered the boat to turn away. I hitched the line around a depth-charge, ran up to the bridge and tried to persuade Mathias to stop for a moment while we got the two men in, but Mathias felt that

322

his duty lay in withdrawing due to the heavy fire and the extreme like-lihood of taking casualties. At some point James and the coxswain must have let go.

Sydney Dobson also pulled a man out of the water with the huge difficulty involved of getting men in sodden clothes up the side of a motor gunboat in the absence of any scrambling nets or ladder. The man made some comment such as 'Thank you, mate' and went below to get out of his wet clothes. When they returned to harbour Sydney found that the man he had rescued was dead, killed by enemy fire which had passed through the hull of *111*.

While all this was happening the MTBs were at last attempting to attack the convoy. At 0330 they saw the star shell which triggered the MGBs attack, somewhere to the south. They realized they had lost the necessary bearing for their attack and tried to work into another position but were handicapped by the confusion of guns and star shell which were being fired from the shore. The unit had no RDF. Similarly *32* and *72*, inshore of the convoy, were blinded by the star shell, but after spells of high speed on main engines and intervals lying still using hydrophones, a ship was sighted ahead of them at 0425, the range being about 600 yards. She was then seen to be a trawler, which was not a torpedo target for *32*'s Mark VIII torpedoes, a new and expensive variety, so that *MTB 72* was about to be ordered to attack when a star shell was put up and heavy fire opened from the target. Both MTBs at that moment were lying with their engines cut. *32* crash started and disengaged to starboard but the commanding officer of *72* was killed and the coxswain wounded. *32* came round in a full circle to assist. However *72* got underway as *32* came abeam and both boats disengaged, losing touch as they did so. *MTB 32* subsequently sought to regain contact with the enemy but, not having done so by 0455, abandoned the attack and set course for the waiting position.

Hitch was not slow to draw to the attention of the authorities yet another example of the shortcomings that even the second genera-tion of MGBs still suffered in their armament. His report of operations continues.

It is considered that this action bears out very forcibly the require-ments put forward recently by the small MGBs, namely the fitting of one, or if possible two, eighteen inch torpedoes, and the fitting of light Oerlikon mountings. As it was, three turrets were rendered useless through damage to the power system and on all occasions when the boats were stopped, as was necessarily the case with one damaged severely, no main armament could be fired. The light mounting, which was being tried out experimentally on *MGB 79*, proved most effective and, since it weighs only seven hundred and thirty pounds with the two guns on it, it is hoped that the rest of the Flotilla can be fitted as soon as possible.

It is considered that the personnel of the MGBs behaved admirably under the extremely trying conditions necessitated by the attempt to save the crew of the burning boat. Although subjected to severe fire without being able to retaliate, they worked unceasingly and with complete disregard to their personal safety in an endeavour to save their comrades.

Hitch's report of proceedings, written on the 2 March, went in under cover of a note from Tommy Kerr. This is turn was forwarded to Commander-in-Chief Nore under cover of a summary by the Flag Officer in Charge, Harwich dated 8 March.

1.   I consider Lieutenant Commander Hichens was right not to attack the large merchant ship with guns, which would probably only damage her, when there seemed (and in fact, there was) a good chance of the MTBs being able to sink the ship. The MTBs were unlucky not to sight her. In spite of having once been seen, the shadowing by the MGBs almost to the mouth of the Hook was a very fine bit of work.

2.   Great gallantry, to the verge of rashness, was shown by Lieutenant Commander Hichens and his band of brothers in trying so hard to rescue the crew of *MGB 79*. Had the crew remained on board, the rescue would have been easy.

3.   A perfect torpedo target was again presented to the MGBs. The demand for torpedo tubes in the seventy-one-foot-six inch MGBs on this coast was first forwarded on the 8th October and appears still to be under discussion.

Ever since the conference called in March 1942 at which Hitch had made the case for continuing in service short, fast MGBs, Piers Kekewich, as Rear Admiral Coastal Forces, had been a supporter. On his staff he now had Captain H.T. Armstrong, DSO, DSC and bar, RN, a First World War CMB veteran and now Captain Coastal

Forces, Nore. 'Beaky' Armstrong, a fighting officer, had no time for the Admiralty's bureaucracy. He entirely agreed with Hitch that, if changes were to be made on the timescale that made a difference in war, then it might well be necessary simply to make the changes and present a fait accompli to the Admiralty. Armstrong was aware of what *Beehive* was doing to develop a shoulder trained twin Oerlikon in place of the heavy powered mounting that had been imposed upon the new seventy-one-foot-six boats. Just looking at a model or photograph of those boats with their intricate mounting for these quite small weapons poses a question mark in the mind. The solution that *Beehive* came up with, essentially the old Oerlikon shoulder trained mounting modified to carry two barrels, was a simple, practical solution.

On 25 February 1943 Admiralty officials had joined Selman and Hitch at Hythe to inspect *MGB 123* which had been set aside and mocked up with twin Oerlikon mountings, both as designed by *Beehive* and by the Admiralty, and then proceeded to reject the *Beehive* lightweight model in spite of the views of Hitch and Selman as to its superiority. At that point Selman, in exasperation, handed Hitch the wooden mock-up of the *Beehive* gun saying 'Here, take this and give it to your young boys.' Hitch did, and I can remember the black wooden guns being presented to us to our enormous joy. But MGBs did get lightweight twin Oerlikons shortly afterwards.

The issue of torpedoes was harder fought and more intractable. The Admiralty's view was quite simply that MGBs were there to fight E-boats and should get on with it. You didn't fight an E-boat with a torpedo. Additionally, if you shipped a torpedo, it would slow you down so that you would never catch your E-boat. When Hitch repeatedly pointed out that, in looking for E-boats, they often found bigger targets, and that he knew perfectly well how to take enough weight out of his boats to compensate for the additional weight of the torpedoes without loss of speed, he was simply told that this was contrary to Admiralty policy. When a bureaucrat says that what you want to do is contrary to policy it means that he can't think of any other better reason and doesn't want to discuss the matter further.

Again, with the support of both Rear Admiral Coastal Forces and Commander-in-Chief Nore, Hitch and Armstrong simply got on with experimenting with shipping torpedoes, making room for them in weight terms by reducing the fuel load, stripping out some of the accommodation non-essentials, reducing the amount of ammunition carried and, of course, reducing the weight of the twin Oerlikons. A Coastal Forces Periodical Review article in the edition for January to February 1943, issued in March 1943, contains an article on *MGB 77* being experimentally fitted with two eighteen inch torpedoes. The Operations Division (Coastal) of the Naval Staff of the Admiralty in April 1943 wrote a short editorial referring to the most important steps currently being taken to concentrate on a combined MTB/MGB in both large and small boats. The Admiralty had never had a problem with the larger Fairmile D boats being hybrid but, in spite of earlier optimism, these boats could barely do thirty knots and thus were not suitable for hunting E-boats, by then doing between thirty-eight and forty knots, even though they gave a good account of themselves when they happened to clash with E-boats.

The fight over the shipping of torpedoes came to a head about the time of Hitch's death. Perhaps it was one more example of MGBs suffering loss when attempting to sink larger vessels using that bizarre weapon, the depth charge dropped under the oncoming bows, that finally produced a Damascene conversion amongst the Admiralty officials responsible for MGB armament. Or was it that Lyon and Kekewich simply ignored the Admiralty and continued trials by fitting torpedoes they had to hand, the lightweight eighteen inch type, which had been taken out of the old First MTB Flotilla when it was disbanded and stored at Felixstowe? However it was, by the summer of 1943 the battle was over and it was recognized that the seventy-one-foot-six MGBs were to carry eighteen inch torpedoes. *MGB 77* was sent to Weymouth in May 1943 for torpedo trials, subsequently continued at *Hornet*. By September *MGB 75* had undergone satisfactory torpedo equipment trials, the old Eighth Flotilla was renamed the First MTB Flotilla and *MGB 77* changed its number to *MTB 414*. In spite of the change of name there appear to have been lengthy delays in fitting the flotilla with tubes and some boats never got them.

Looking back at this distance in time it seems extraordinary that so much heat was generated over an issue where the outcome must have seemed stunningly obvious to those at the sharp end. One of the small sadnesses of the timing of Hitch's death is that he may never have heard that his call for torpedoes in short MGBs had been accepted.

Chapter Fifteen

A Misfortune of War
April 1943

On the night of the 12/13 April 1943 Hitch, as Senior Officer, took a unit of four motor gunboats to sea as close escort to motor launches of the Fifty-First Flotilla who were minelaying off the Dutch coast. Hitch was in *MGB 112*, whose Commanding Officer was Derek Sidebottom. In company were *MGB 75* under Boffin Campbell, *111* under John Mathias, and *74* under Rodney Sykes. The lay was to be off Noordwijk and the MGBs and MLs reached their position at 0237 on the morning of the 13th. While the MLs were laying mines, a green light was observed to the north-east. As soon as the lay was completed the MGBs parted company, leaving the MLs to return home.

The Eighth Flotilla unit moved quietly at eight knots, well within the speed at which their engines were silenced, and they used their RDF to search for the origin of the light they had seen. At 0311 they picked up a contact at 2,000 yards, ten cables, and when they were within three cables they could see two trawlers on their port beam, signalling to one another with a blue light. At this point RDF contact was lost but with a modest increase of speed to ten knots, followed by stopping to use the hydrophone, they picked the vessels up again bearing south-west, detecting reciprocating engines. At 0346 they started up for the attack, increasing speed to twelve knots, still just within the silent range for those boats not yet converted to underwater exhausts. The RDF picked up the contacts again at five cables and they were sighted at three cables, steering to the south doing about eight knots. Hitch could now see that the contact was in fact one trawler and another smaller vessel, probably a gun coaster. He slowly closed the range to half a cable, the enemy still being unaware of the motor gunboats' presence. This was achieved by manoeuvring the boats until they were in a position to approach up wind, thus effecting complete surprise. Hitch then ordered an increase in speed to twenty knots and all the gunboats opened fire, including *112*'s Blacker Bombard, a spigot mortar firing a heavy projectile capable of severely damaging a ship the size of a steel trawler, carried on the bows of the boats but seldom used. They had never previously hit an enemy vessel with one, but on this occasion it was seen to register a hit. Hitch ordered a turn away so that the effect of both the gunfire and the mortar strike could be observed. At this time the trawler was seen to be on fire and there was an internal explosion, but observation of the target was difficult owing to the quantity of star shell put up by the engaged enemy and by enemy patrols to the south of it. Another boat reported firing two-pounder pom-pom shells into the trawler after the first red glow of fire was observed within her and seeing flames spouting high as the projectiles struck home. No doubt had Hitch not been killed, the MGBs would have gone into the attack again to finish her off.

Both Hitch and Derek Sidebottom saw the engine room hatch of the trawler lift off as the result of some internal blast, emitting a vivid flash of light and an audible explosion. Hitch said in excited tones 'My God! She's in flames all over. We've pulled it off ...' At that moment a twenty millimetre Oerlikon shell hit the bridge of *MGB 112*, killing Hitch and seriously wounding Derek Sidebottom, his first lieutenant, one Midshipman Okey, and Wing Commander Theodore Edwards, RAFVR, a friend of Hitch who was out that night to observe how MGBs operated.

There are different views as to precisely how this carnage was achieved by so small a shell. Sydney Dobson, who was in *111* that night, thought that Hitch must have stepped down from the canopy where he normally stood when going into action, holding on to the mast. How else could the shell have killed him and wounded three others down in the dustbin? Boffin Campbell also held that view. However, Jimmy Shadbolt, also in *111*, thinks that the shell may have hit the mast and exploded, sending a shower of splinters into the dustbin but killing Hitch who was still standing on the canopy right beside the mast.

Derek Sidebottom lay fainting the dustbin with his arm,

shattered at the elbow, almost hanging off. However he was able to give general directions to Theodore Edwards, who remained on his feet in spite of the shell splinters he had also suffered and it was Edwards who took *112* out of action towards the rendezvous point where *MGBs 111* and *75* could come alongside. *74* appears to have failed to find the rendezvous. There was a fourth naval officer on board, a Fleet Air Arm pilot being given a rest from flying, also confusingly called Edwards, who had been operating the Blacker Bombard. Sandy Edwards took command once he realized what had happened on the bridge.

At the rendezvous Boffin Campbell in *75* picked up his megaphone and shouted 'Hitch, can you hear me?' Sandy Edwards replied 'I'm afraid Hitch has been killed'. Boffin remembered a stunned silence and then the noise, picked up by the intercom which was still on, of his telegraphist blubbing into the microphone.

John Mathias sent Jimmy Shadbolt across to *112* to see what he could do to help. Shadbolt found Hitch laid out in the narrow corridor leading aft from the dustbin, covered by a blanket. At first sight he thought he was merely unconscious and felt his pulse before he was sure that he was dead. Although killed cleanly and immediately by a shell splinter in his chest, he was evidently not deeply disfigured. He then gave morphine to Derek Sidebottom, who was sitting on an ammunition chest. Shadbolt asked Mathias whether he could take *112* back to Felixstowe but was told to return and navigate *MGB 111*. Boffin Campbell, now Senior Officer, subsequently recorded that he sent *112* back to *Beehive* at top speed under Sandy Edwards' command to get Sidebottom to hospital as rapidly as possible. However Sydney Dobson has a clear memory of Sidebottom being helped over to *111* where he made him as comfortable as his shattered arm allowed.

In *MGB 75* Boffin seemed to be in a trance. Cameron Gough, his first lieutenant, remembers him standing in the corner of the dustbin aloof and apparently unaware of what was going on around him until well into the return passage. *75* made a slower passage than *112* because *75*'s centre engine would not start, it having been unused for the last hour as it was unsilenced. Cameron was navigating and in the thick weather quite uncertain of his starting point after all the manoeuvring involved in stalking the trawler. He had to pray that he would find a buoy he recognized when they approached the east coast. In the event they found a merchant ship at anchor just beyond the convoy route and got directions from her.

As *112* came into the old Felixstowe harbour where the MTBs and MGBs berthed, they were amazed to see every man and woman on the base lining the dockside and surrounding the steps where they came alongside. Most of the Wrens were in floods of tears. Peter Dickens remembers that moment when Hitch's body was brought ashore.

> I cannot define what I felt as I saluted his body carried up the steps at the dock entrance; there was no shock because I knew what had happened to be inevitable, but sadness at the loss of someone so outstanding was poignant and very deep, so deep that I quite forgot the selfish picture I had at first formed of my own corpse being carried up those same steps. Remember Hichens. A perfect, gentle, indomitable knight in very truth.

The news of Hitch's death had been broadcast as an uncoded message during the return passage of the MGBs and it was soon percolating throughout Coastal Forces. In some cases there was disbelief. Hitch was invulnerable. Len Reynolds, sitting in the wardroom of his brand new Fairmile D Boat, *658*, in Milford Haven, waiting to make a passage to the Mediterranean and his own gallant participation in Coastal Forces' battle for the control of that sea, remembers the stunned silence when they heard the news. His Commanding Officer, Tommy Ladner, had of course been in the Eighth Flotilla and had just returned from long leave in Canada.

> At one of these parties someone switched on the radio. The war in Africa was holding our attention closely, and there was a pause in the conversation as the news began. The hubbub rose again as interest fell away, until Tommy Ladner suddenly snarled "Quiet!" The voice of the announcer seemed to be personally addressing us rather than a vast unseen audience, and there was that sort of breathless tense silence in the wardroom which was rare — and the more memorable for being so.
> 'The following communiqué was issued by the Admiralty today:
> On each of the last two nights Coastal Forces have had short sharp engagements with enemy patrol craft close to the Dutch coast. As a

result of these engagements considerable damage has been caused to the enemy and many casualties must have been inflicted on their personnel.

During the course of last night's engagement it is regretted that Lieutenant Commander Robert Peverell Hichens, DSO, DSC, RNVR was killed. The other casualties sustained during these two nights were two officers and two ratings wounded. Next of kin have been informed.

All our ships returned safely to harbour.

Tommy sat looking at his glass, his mind back in the summer of 1942 when he had followed Hichens night after night as a CO in the famous Eighth MGB Flotilla. I myself had never met him, but I knew well his amazing story of leadership and determination which had done more to give Coastal Forces their reputation as the Navy's most constant striking force at this time than any other single factor.

Peter Scott, halfway back across the Channel, also listened to the news on the BBC:

... when the shattering announcement came over the air that Hitch had been killed in action off the Dutch coast, Robert Hichens, my old friend of fourteen-foot dinghy days, the family solicitor, who had won more decorations than anyone else in Coastal Forces, had been struck and killed instantly by a stray shell right at the end of a successful battle, I remember that we stopped, as was our wont, to compare positions at the entrance to the swept channel through the minefield and at the same time pass the news to the other boats. There was a shocked incredulity in their tone as they answered. Surely there must be some mistake they seemed to say. Others can be killed in action but not Hitch.

I remember how he had taken me to sea on my first visit to HMS Beehive, the Coastal Forces base at Felixstowe, a year before; how we had met only a week or two before in London to plan a new assault on the Admiralty in order to get our policies on heavier armament through; how I had heard that he would very shortly be asked to take on a training job at HMS Bee at Weymouth as a rest from operations, and how I had greatly doubted if he would accept it. For me it was a cheerless, empty night.

331

I did not attend my father's funeral. My brother and I were taken on a picnic by Nancy Campbell, Boffin's wife. My Aunt Loveday came up from Devon and she and my mother endured a church packed both with senior naval officers, from the Commander-in-Chief Nore downwards, together with as many boats' crews as could be spared. He was buried in Felixstowe churchyard, one of a long line of young men brought back from those fierce clashes at night on the far side of the North Sea.

Nore Command, in its report to the Admiralty dated 25 April ended with a final paragraph:

> The loss of Lieutenant-Commander Hichens is deeply regretted by all in the Nore Command and especially by the officers and men of Coastal Forces, whom he had inspired by his gallantry, skill and devotion to duty. It was at his express wish that he had not been withdrawn from the Command of the Flotilla which he had led in so many gallant actions. It was indeed a misfortune of war that he was killed by what appeared to be a stray shell.

At the end of April Peter Scott was asked to make a broadcast on the BBC about Coastal Forces. I have the original script which he sent to my mother on the 21 April, asking for her permission. He summarized Hitch's career in Coastal Forces and indeed their competition in International Fourteens before the war. It ended:

> The officers and men who fight these battles will not forget Robert Hichens. He left a rich legacy, the fruits of his energy in the development of the boats, and the fruits of his experience in the way that they should be handled and fought, and then that other thing, that example of courage that makes people think as they go into action: 'This would have been a mere nothing to Hitch.'

For the action on the 12/13 April Derek Sidebottom was awarded a bar to his DSC and Hitch received his third Mention in Dispatches. Behind this slightly odd final award lies a strange story.

David James, after returning from the prisoner-of-war camp from which he had escaped within a year of being taken prisoner, met Tommy Kerr again who told him that he had put up Hitch for the Victoria Cross after the action on the 27/28 February 1943 when David had been captured. Before sending in the recommendation, he had told Hitch of his intention. Hitch had demurred, saying that he felt on reflection that he had endangered both his boats and their crews in trying to save comrades and friends in the water, and that on balance it had not been the right decision and therefore he did not think it was appropriate that a recommendation for the VC should go in. Respecting his strongly held view, Kerr took no further action until after Hitch's death. In David James's words:

> Six weeks later, after his death, Commander Kerr did make the recommendation, which the Admiralty rejected on the grounds that Hitch himself had given. One may perhaps be surprised at the attitude of mind which refused to give the highest award posthumously to one who had fought so bravely and brilliantly, but surely there could be no [better] proof of Hitch's remarkable character than that he himself should have tried to stop the recommendation on conscientious grounds.

It has not proved possible to follow all of the paper trail from Tommy Kerr to the Admiralty's Honours and Awards Committee. However, one document has been retrieved, a letter from Commander-in-Chief Nore, Admiral Lyon, to the Secretary of the Admiralty Honours and Awards Branch.

10th May 1943

> The attached recommendations for immediate awards are forwarded for favourable consideration.
>
> The Flag Officer in Charge Harwich has stated in respect of the late Temporary Lieutenant-Commander Hichens: 'I consider that his rescue attempt on the 27th/28th February 1943 was one of the bravest actions of his career. He risked the safety of several valuable ships and men in order to pick up a few of his friends from the water. In his Commanding Officer's opinion, and incidentally in his own opinion, he was wrong to do this, and he did not expect his name to be forwarded.
>
> In view of these facts and the subsequent action in which he lost his life, I consider he is entitled to a high posthumous award.'
>
> And I fully concur in this opinion.

Behind the slightly convoluted language is the statement that both

Rear Admiral Rogers and Admiral Lyon thought that the VC should be awarded, in spite of the charge that Hitch had been rash in stopping two MGBs to pick men out of the water in the presence of the enemy, thus hazarding both ships and crews. Evidently someone more senior in the Admiralty took a different view. It should not be the policy of any navy to hold out the prospect of the most coveted of awards to those who hazard their ships without weighing the odds of success and the importance of that success. Yet, prejudiced though I may be, I believe that David James's judgement is correct and that the Honours and Awards Committee should have accepted the recommendation of Kerr, Rogers and Lyon to award the VC. The only award which can be made posthumously other than the VC is the Mention in Dispatches. Its award in this case, I believe, confirms that it was indeed the VC that was under consideration.

A final quotation from David James is appropriate. In his epilogue to the uncensored version of *We Fought Them in Gunboats*, his final paragraph reads:

> He went as he would have wanted – cleanly and without fuss, at the very zenith of his powers and fame. Who can doubt that his life's work had been completed and that in intensity and quality his brief life of thirty-four years had seen more achievement and had been of more eternal value than those of most of us who lived twice as long. The blood of an earlier generation of Cornishmen ran in his veins; like Drake at Cadiz he had singed the enemy's beard in the mouth of their own harbours and played his part in defending England's shores.

Perhaps Hitch, had he lived, would have taken a grim satisfaction in a letter, written from the Admiralty on the 3 July 1943, referring to the Flag-Officer-in-Charge Harwich's submission:

> Seventy-one-foot-six MGBs are to be fitted with two eighteen inch torpedo tubes and the *Beehive* designed twin Oerlikon mounting will replace the power twin Oerlikon. Retrospective fitting will be carried out as and when possible.

Did it take Hitch's death finally to stir the technical departments of the Admiralty into accepting the repeated recommendations of those who fought at sea?

Chapter Sixteen

Aftermath

After Hitch's death, the Eighth Flotilla was sent west to Dartmouth again. It was inevitably much changed. Not only Hitch but David James and Derek Sidebottom had gone, Boffin Campbell asked for a new posting and the changes that had taken place in the autumn of 1942, including the loss of George Duncan and Tom Ladner, going on long leave to Canada, meant that the Flotilla was essentially led by a new group of men. John Mathias initially took over the position of Senior Officer but was shortly superseded by Lieutenant F.N. Stephenson, RN. Mathias was back in command as Senior Officer by January 1944. Francis Head, Hitch's sometime first lieutenant, became CO of *MGB 75* and then *77*. Sadly he did not survive the war, being killed in a motorcycle accident. David James returned to England a year later, having escaped twice from prisoner-of-war camp, once in full naval uniform as Lieutenant Ivan Bugerov of the Royal Bulgarian Navy, but he did not rejoin the Eighth Flotilla.

In late September 1943 the boats of the Eighth MGB Flotilla were re-designated as MTBs and became the First MTB Flotilla. All the boats took MTB numbers starting with a four. Despite being designated MTBs it would appear that only two received their eighteen-inch torpedo tubes, *414* and *415*. Those who had not already made their own shoulder trained twin Oerlikon mountings received an official one at long last, reducing their dependence on powered gun training with all its vulnerabilities in action.

The Flotilla had further actions ahead of it. Based in Dartmouth, it operated around the Channel Islands again and had a number of successful encounters with the enemy. Very sadly, in late July 1944 off Cap d'Antifer, it was involved in a fierce battle with a larger force of E-boats. *MTBs 430* and *412* were lost, with eleven officers and men missing, in exchange for one E-boat. John Mathias, the Senior Officer, was himself badly wounded.

The First MTB Flotilla soldiered on to the end of the war in Europe. *414*, once *MGB 77*, was at Felixstowe when a token unit of E-boats were met in the North Sea and escorted into harbour on Sunday, 13 May 1945. *S.205* and *S.204* were carrying Admiral Brauning who brought charts of the German minefields to be handed over to C-in-C Nore.

Within three weeks of VE Day, the Eighth Flotilla had been disbanded and the boats paid off preparatory to sale out of the service. There is a particularly fine photograph of *MTB 414*, flying her paying off pennant, against a background of Channel chalk cliffs, taken on the 21 May 1945 when she was en route from Felixstowe to Poole where the boats were laid up. A range of fates awaited them. Most ultimately ended up as house-boats on the mud of various south-coast and east-coast creeks. One at least survived that indignity and is still at sea today. *MGB 81* was rescued from its houseboat grave and put back into its original condition by Robin and Phil Clabburn, father and son. It was re-launched in 2004 and can still do forty-four knots, albeit at a high cost per mile. She went over to Caen on the sixtieth anniversary of D-Day, in which operation she had participated, carrying her last Commanding Officer, Cameron Gough, seated in a comfortable chair on the fore deck. There can be few old warriors who return to the scene of their youthful glory in the self same boat, plane or military fighting vehicle sixty years after the event. Today she lies at Buckler's Hard and faces an uncertain future in the absence of any maritime museum willing to lay her up.

The Navy has no Coastal Forces boats any longer. A decision was taken in 1956 to pay off the First and Second Fast Patrol Boat Squadrons. The Navy was faced with the requirement to reduce its cost to one compatible with the requirements of the Cold War and to be able to fight a limited war, but no longer a global war. Given the consequential reduction in the number of ships the Navy faced, sacrificing the residual coastal forces flotillas seemed less damaging than cost-cutting alternatives. The last class of MTBs, the Brave class, went out of commission in 1970. Fast Patrol Boats within NATO became the domain of the growing West German

Navy who took over responsibility for the Baltic, with boats evolved from war time E-boat designs.

Many other navies disagreed with the Royal Navy's judgement in this matter. The Israeli Navy, for instance, have a number of heavily armed Fast Attack Craft, as do a number of its potential enemies. It is possible to pack a very considerable punch in a very small and expendable hull. But every navy has its own priorities and the Royal Navy has opted to concentrate on submarine and anti-submarine warfare and the capacity to deliver aircraft and invasion forces to distant parts of the world. The threat of an enemy-held coast of Europe is no longer a scenario under active consideration. But then nor was it in the 1930s.

The fate of *MGB 64* is also worth recording as it was Hitch's own boat. In August 1943 she had been on patrol and was caught out in extremely bad weather under the command of a temporary CO. She was, by then, an old boat, still suffering from failures of the pendulastic couplings to the prop drive. The Sixth Flotilla was no longer used for offensive operations but it patrolled the Z line; the imaginary line beyond the British convoy routes where coastal forces, particularly the older MGBs, undertook defensive E-boat patrols.

On a night when unforecast bad weather blew up, *64* began to make water and, when her stern was practically submerged, it was decided to take the crew off, with *58* coming alongside to do that. A witness remembers the coxswain jumping across to *58* still clasping a rum jar firmly to his chest in the best tradition of all good coxswains. *MGB 58* stood by expecting *64* to sink but she did not and more valuable stores were retrieved. In the end they had to leave her wallowing, but a reconnaissance aircraft sent out to look for her could find no trace a few hours later. She must have foundered.

There was a fair amount of press coverage and comment on Hitch's death. It came out in dribs and drabs, with Peter Scott's broadcast at the end of April 1943 receiving particularly wide coverage. There was a short obituary in *The Times* on the 14 April, and comment in a wide range of popular papers. A much wider coverage appeared in the *Sunday Express* in September 1943 when they serialized his, as yet, unpublished book *We Fought Them in Gunboats*. It came out in successive editions and encapsulated what he had to say rather well, though leaving out most of the criticism of the Admiralty's policy of under-arming MGBs, at the censor's insistence. When the book itself was published in February 1944 there was further acclaim, with a particularly good article written in the *Illustrated London News. We Fought Them in Gunboats* was reprinted free of censorship in 1956 but made little impact. Occasional press articles appeared on anniversaries. *The Guinness Book of Records* in 1966 noted that Hitch had been the most highly decorated RNVR officer. His RN equivalent pipped him on points with a DSO and two bars and a DSC and bar, but won in two world wars.

After my father's funeral my mother returned to Cornwall, initially to stay with my grandmother who, at that stage of the war, was living in a house in Perranarworthal. Enys had been commandeered for use as the Dutch Naval College which had been evacuated from The Hague in 1940. Shortly afterwards we moved back into the house in Falmouth that my father had bought at the beginning of the war to provide my mother with a bolthole from Treworval, recognizing that with petrol rationing she was uncomfortably cut off in the depths of the country, and perhaps also detecting my mother's distaste for the rural squalor that surrounded the farm. We lived in Falmouth until the end of the war when we were able to repossess Bodrennick from the family who had leased it for the duration. In the summer of 1946 we thankfully returned there to live and my brother and I grew up there. My mother never moved again.

My brother and I were sent to school at Stowe. For some reason my mother had never taken to Marlborough and there was an obscure row over being asked to contribute to the cost of the Second World War memorial to old Marlburians. However it came about, it was to Stowe that we went. From there we both went on to Magdalen, my brother to get a first in chemistry and I a mere second in law, but where we both had a wonderful time. Most of Magdalen's sons would regard their years there as the best they had and would not have exchanged it for any other college at Oxford.

Between school and Oxford we both joined the Royal Navy for our National Service. My brother was in destroyers and an aircraft carrier. I went to the Mediterranean Fleet, learnt to become a shallow water diver, and spent nine extremely happy months in an anti submarine frigate, HMS *Ursa*, some of the time doing anti-gun

338

running patrol around Cyprus. Both of us acquired a lasting affection for the Senior Service. After Oxford my brother and I both joined large natural resource companies, in his case Shell and in mine Rio Tinto, a mining giant. We have spent our lives in these and similar companies. My brother retired some years ago to live at Bodrennick again, my mother having died in 1990.

My mother lived at Bodrennick happily enough, watching us grow up, gently settling in to county life surrounded by friends she had known since her youth. However she maintained her links with the Navy and particularly Coastal Forces. In 1947 she was asked to unveil a portrait of my father painted by Peter Scott and presented to the RNVR Club at 38 Hill Street, London, W.1, paid for by a subscription raised amongst Hitch's brother officers. The fund was organized by David James. The portrait still hangs there and is a fine likeness of my father on the bridge of his little warship. I have a good copy of it in my home in Dorset.

In September 1954 she was also asked to unveil the memorial to Coastal Forces at HMS *Hornet* in Gosport. It was a grand occasion with a line of Fast Patrol Boats moored behind the memorial, a Royal Marine band playing, a great crowd of ex-Coastal Forces' officers and men, and senior officers of the post-war Navy. I can remember a message arriving for me in HMS *Theseus*, where I had just commenced naval training, asking me to attend but which I begged off on the grounds that I didn't want to be considered singular by my new mess mates, and in any case would look mildly ridiculous in a round cap and bell bottoms at the easily embarrassed age of eighteen on such an occasion. In retrospect I am sorry that I didn't attend. My mother kept up with many of her late husband's naval friends, especially David James, Peter Dickens, Boffin Campbell and Bussy Carr.

My brother married and had a family of three and in turn now has four grandchildren. I have also been very happily married for over forty years and our one daughter has given us three fine grandchildren who will in time, I hope, want to know something of their gallant great grandfather.

Inevitably I was brought up to revere my father's memory. The strongest condemnation of my many shortcomings was to be told that my father would not have approved of my conduct, which apparently had a particularly sobering affect in my early years.

Later, perhaps naturally, a modest sense of rebellion set in. I was inclined to argue either that I had to make my own judgements in these matters or alternatively that he would indeed have approved of any conduct showing a mutinous spirit.

In the Navy of the mid-fifties his name was well remembered. I certainly found from time to time that my own extremely modest attainments were compared unfavourably with his reputation and it made life, if anything, slightly more difficult in the Service. However it did occasionally open important doors, not least the gates of Magdalen whose dons might otherwise have looked askance at my none too scholarly progress through Stowe. I can remember moments throughout my life when I either came across individuals who had known him or had heard of him and thus showed a friendly interest in me which they might not otherwise have taken.

I read his diary of the years 1939 to 1941 when I was in my thirties during a fortnight's naval reserve training in Mounts Bay near my old home in Cornwall. It caused me to go back and reread *We Fought Them in Gunboats*. Nevertheless it was more a background memory than a guiding light as far as my own world and career were concerned. Occasional meetings with men like Peter Dickens and Bussy Carr were convivial but did not lead to a much better understanding of what they had all been facing in the early 1940s in the Narrow Seas.

This filial neglect ended abruptly in the early 1990s when Admiral Bill Pillar, Chairman of the RNVR Officers Association and what was, by then, called The Naval Club at 38 Hill Street, asked me to join a fund-raising committee for a new charity called Wave Heritage. It had been formed to help preserve 38 Hill Street as an historic building and as a memorial to the RNVR. Admiral Pillar had started his naval career in the RNVR and knew all about Hitch. The project gradually developed, from one designed purely to preserve 38 Hill Street, into gathering all the information necessary to produce a complete Roll of Honour of all those killed in the RNVR in the Second World War. The dead were dominantly officers because those who had joined the Navy after the outbreak of war on the lower deck were classified as Hostilities Only ratings and did not join the RNVR unless they were commissioned, so that the only lower deck members of the RNVR were ratings who joined before the war and never became officers; a relatively small group.

In the end we collected over 6,000 names of those killed, a number which astonished all of us, no matter how well versed we were in the naval history of the Second World War. The book was unveiled by the Duke of Edinburgh and is on display today beneath Hitch's portrait in The Naval Club.

In the course of fund raising, the chairmanship of which I took over on the untimely death of the original incumbent, I had cause to write to a large number of surviving ex-RNVR officers, and some of them naturally wrote back, generally with much appreciated financial contributions, but adding that they had known Hitch during the war and perhaps recalling some episode which had involved him. I both corresponded with and met a surprising number of ex-Coastal Forces veterans, and indeed some ex-Wrens who had known my father. Perhaps the most gratifying discovery was that retired Chief Petty Officer George Curtis, DSM, lived in Weymouth, half an hour from my Dorset home, and still treasured a battle damaged clear view screen from the wheelhouse of *MGB 64*. We are now good friends.

As a result of these contacts I was asked to address the annual meeting of the Coastal Forces Veterans' Association in 2002, with Hitch as the theme. This meant a good deal of work to put together something worth saying, so that his diaries and his book were reread. My notes for the speech were the best summary I could make of what Hitch had achieved during the war. That, in turn, led directly to the feeling that his was a story worth retelling and here it is.

At the very least I hope this book will cause him to be remembered by his great grandchildren with some of the admiration and affection felt by his two sons. He didn't only tell Peter Dickens that he didn't expect to survive the war. He also told his wife but added: 'but I shall live on in my sons'. I hope in some way that he has.

Index

346